The Dinner Party

SINCE1970
Histories of Contemporary America

The Dinner Party

Judy Chicago and the Power of Popular Feminism, 1970–2007

JANE F. GERHARD

The University of Georgia Press *Athens and London*

Athens, Georgia 30602
www.ugapress.org

Set in Minion Pro and Myriad Pro by Graphic Composition, Inc.

Printed digitally

Library of Congress Cataloging-in-Publication Data

Gerhard, Jane F.
The Dinner Party : Judy Chicago and the Power of Popular Feminism, 1970–2007 / Jane F. Gerhard.
pages cm. — (Since 1970: Histories of contemporary America)
Includes bibliographical references and index.
ISBN 978-0-8203-3675-6 (hardcover : alk. paper) — ISBN 0-8203-3675-0 (hardcover : alk. paper) — ISBN 978-0-8203-4457-7 (pbk. : alk. paper) — ISBN 0-8203-4457-5 (pbk. : alk. paper)
1. Chicago, Judy, 1939- Dinner party. 2. Chicago, Judy, 1939- —Criticism and interpretation. 3. Feminism—United States. I. Title.
NK4605.5.U63C482 2013
709.2—dc23

2012043503

British Library Cataloging-in-Publication Data available

Contents

Acknowledgments *vii*

INTRODUCTION Toward a Cultural History of *The Dinner Party* *1*

ONE Making Feminist Artists: The Feminist Art Programs of Fresno and CalArts, 1970–1972 *21*

TWO Making Feminist Art: *Womanhouse* and the Feminist Art Movement, 1972–1974 *48*

THREE The Studio as a Feminist Space: Practicing Feminism at *The Dinner Party*, 1975–1979 *76*

FOUR Joining Forces: Making Art and History at *The Dinner Party*, 1975–1979 *109*

FIVE Going Public: *The Dinner Party* in San Francisco, 1979 *149*

SIX The Tour That Very Nearly Wasn't: *The Dinner Party*'s Alternative Showings, 1980–1983 *180*

SEVEN Debating Feminist Art: *The Dinner Party* in Published and Unpublished Commentary, 1979–1989 *211*

EIGHT From Controversy to Canonization: *The Dinner Party* in the Culture Wars, 1990–2007 *246*

EPILOGUE A Prehistory of Postfeminism *283*

Notes *291*

Index *333*

Acknowledgments

I CAN'T SAY THAT *The Dinner Party* taught me that my vagina had a history, a politics, or even a collective to join. That honor falls to Anne Koedt, author of the 1970 "The Myth of the Vaginal Orgasm" and muse of my first book, *Desiring Revolution*. But studying the art and writings of Judy Chicago and then meeting her did teach me many things and for that reason, my first acknowledgment goes to her. I met the artist in 2009 at her home in Belen, New Mexico, where she opened her memories and archives to me with characteristic generosity. I interviewed her four times in a two-year period and regularly corresponded to double-check facts. After our first meeting, Judy grinned at me and said in a low voice, "It got you. *The Dinner Party* got you." She had seen it happen before and she was right. With that credential clearly established, Chicago sent me materials she had not yet chosen to archive with her papers at the Schlesinger Library, particularly the financial side of *The Dinner Party*'s history. She has been an avid supporter of this book, and for this and for all her help, and the help of her husband, photographer Donald Woodman, I offer a heartfelt thank-you. But my gratitude to Judy stretches beyond my vested interest in my own book. I take inspiration from the way she has lived her life, both as an artist and a person of integrity. Although she faced tremendous obstacles, she never let them stop her, and so has become a role model for me as I face new challenges in my life. I also want to thank her for being that ballsy (so to speak) radical feminist in 1970 who demanded that women reclaim their bodies, their destinies, and a right to a different kind of history. This book is a tribute to that big bang of radicalism we historians call second-wave feminism. Thank you, Judy Chicago, for being a feminist.

I also want to thank the women of *The Dinner Party* who took time out of their busy lives to remember, once again, those heady days of working at the studio against crazy deadlines and seemingly insurmountable odds. In the course of writing this book I met with Susan Hill and Diane Gelon numerous times; Susan sent detailed comments on the section of the manuscript that involved the loft and the technical details of embroidery, and Diane helped me understand the crazy finances of the studio; these conversations proved extremely useful and I am very grateful for their willingness to talk to me and their insistence that I get the details right. A warm thanks to Kate Armand, Ruth Askey, Jan Marie DuBois, Audrey Cowan, Johanna Demetrakas, Ken Gilliam, Shannon Hogan, Ann Isolde, and Juliet Meyers, who individually and collectively (what a night that was!) cast light on the transformative experience of working on *The Dinner Party*. A special shout-out to Ann Isolde, who sent me excerpts from her personal diary and shared her recollections of researching the Heritage Floor and to Juliet Meyers for her honesty and willingness to say what others would not. Mary Ross Taylor talked with me on the phone, regaling me with Through the Flower stories and her razor-sharp interpretations and then sent me envelopes stuffed with information from the Houston exhibit and the 1990 congressional debates over arts funding. Cleveland organizers Mickey Stern and Marcia Levine spoke to me over the phone to tell me about their journeys to, through and away from *The Dinner Party*. Ann T. Mackin sent me "Values in Voices: Judy Chicago's *The Dinner Party*, Cleveland Exhibit, May 10–August 9, 1981, The Audiences Speak" (2006), her master's thesis at Ursuline College, and her "raw data" on the Cleveland comment book. I emailed with April Harkins about the Boston show, Ellen Strong and Jeanne Van Atta about the Cleveland show, and met with Meri Jenkins, wife of Peter Bunzick, about the trials of traveling with *The Dinner Party* in the 1980s. I also corresponded with Debra Hirshberg, Jill Fields, Suzanne Lacy, Mira Schor, Faith Wilding, Amelia Jones, Di Robson, and Gretchen Mieszkowski. Many thanks to you all for your good help and for helping to set me straight. Any mistakes that remain are mine and mine alone.

This book was written with two readers in mind. The first, Mari Jo Buhle, trained me in the art of history writing and gave me a taste for the complexity of the past. She brought a feminist-inspired culture to her work with graduate students, teaching us to work hard, plot our own courses, and to never base our successes on tearing one another down. She was the reluctant pack leader to generations of ambitious and competitive offspring, ever calm and assertive (on the surface, at least), presciently suggesting that in some distant future we would see one another as dear friends, not as irritating seminar competition. She was absolutely right. In addition, and even more importantly, she gave me a feel for the 1970s with her careful reading of my work over the years. She once called me her BFF, and if it's true, it's definitely one of my most awesome accomplishments ever.

The second person I kept in my mind as I wrote is Maia Brumberg-Kraus. She is whip-smart and unschooled in feminist historiography and so a perfect imagined audience for me. When, to quote a *Dinner Party* studio volunteer, I would "get lost in the abyss of *The Dinner Party*," I would mutter to myself: "what of all this would Maia care about?" I'm sure I missed the mark regularly, but a heartfelt thanks to Maia for her friendship, wit, and numerous dinner parties over the years. Others from my A Team include Deirdre Fay, who helped me loosen the grip of the past from my present; Ruth Feldstein, who makes me feel smart even when I'm convinced that this reflects badly on her; Zeb and May Stern, now teenagers, who suffered my obsession with vaginas with stalwart good humor; and David Stern, who makes my planets orbit.

This project started with a paper I submitted to the Schlesinger Library Summer Research Seminar in 2008. There I was lucky enough to meet Claire Potter who, along with Robert Self and others, workshopped my Judy Chicago paper. "Follow the money," was her sage advice. A year or so later, Claire acquired the book for a new series at the University of Georgia Press, "Since 1970: Histories of Contemporary America," which she coedits with Renee Romano. Their support, and particularly Claire's friendship, has been invaluable. I want to thank Derek Krissoff, Beth Snead, and John Joerschke at the press and Deborah Oliver for their help in getting this project into the book you hold now.

I want to thank the Radcliffe Institute for Advanced Study for their support of my work at the archive, as well as a scholarship to "women's history boot camp" in 2008. A big shout-out to the amazing reference and librarian staff at the Arthur and Elizabeth Schlesinger Library on the History of Women in America, Radcliffe Institute for Advanced Study, Harvard University, who felt like the only people I saw during certain researching months. I am also extremely grateful to the National Endowment for the Humanities for the yearlong fellowship I received in 2010–11 that enabled me to have my first-ever sabbatical in fifteen years of teaching.

I have many people to thank for treating me so well at Mount Holyoke College: Kavita Datla, Joe Ellis, Penny Gill, Lowell Gundmundson, Holly

Hanson, Jeremy King, Jon Lipman, Elizabeth Markovits, Fred McGinnis, Lynn Morgan, Mary Renda, Nadya Sbaiti, Robert Schwartz, and Holly Sharac. Special thanks to Lynda Morgan, who fed and watered me over the years, who helped me carry the ups and downs at MCH with a savory gallows humor, and who regularly reminded me that the center isn't always what it's cracked up to be. I owe Dan Czitrom much for his loyal friendship, his efforts to keep "the human in the humanities" in this age of corporatization of higher education, and for regularly donning a white hat to do battle with the deans over funding for adjuncts like me. I want to thank Don O'Shea, who helped fund this project. To my former Mount Holyoke students: You have cheered me, inspired me, challenged me, and restored my faith in the joys of learning each and every week without fail.

The Dinner Party

INTRODUCTION

Toward a Cultural History of *The Dinner Party*

JUDY CHICAGO'S INSTALLATION *The Dinner Party*, the most monumental work of the 1970s feminist art movement, has been praised, damned, celebrated, and denounced since its debut in 1979. In fact, it delineated the need for women's history, but strangely until now it has had no history of its own. This is particularly surprising because contemporary accounts are plentiful. *Mademoiselle* and *Ms.* discussed *The Dinner Party*, as did *Newsweek*, *Mother Jones*, the *CBS Nightly News*, the *Cleveland Plain Dealer*, the *New York Times*, *Art in America*, and *Artforum*. People stood in line for hours to see it wherever it opened, while art critics pondered the reason for the public's enthusiasm. Even the United States House of Representatives debated the significance of *The Dinner Party*.

A visitor to the Brooklyn Museum today can see *The Dinner Party* in all its grandeur. Six large woven banners introduce the religious and feminist themes of what comes next. Three large tables (each forty-eight feet long) are arranged in a triangle; thirty-nine places are set for a grand dinner party for women, thirteen along each table, or wing. The first wing seats in chronological order notable women "From Prehistory to Rome"; the second, "From Christianity to the Reformation"; and the third, "From the American Revolution to the Women's Revolution," reaching to the mid-twentieth century. Each place setting commemorates a woman of historical significance, and each features an oversized china plate carved and glazed in the shape of a vulva or butterfly, designed to represent the woman commemorated. Each plate, along with its chalice and utensils, sits on a richly designed 30-inch-wide and 51-inch-long runner embroidered in stitching appropriate to the guest's historical era. Millennium runners, elaborate altar clothes that combine ecclesiastical and domestic white-work needle techniques, cover each of the three corners of the table and mark the transitions as sacred. The porcelain-tile floor under the tables radiates light, illuminating the names of 999 "women of merit" painted in glossy gold script. These names comprise streams of influence moving across time, connecting outstanding women to an overarching female network and genealogy. Between 1979 and 1989, Acknowledgement panels—listing the names of every person who worked on the piece over the five years of its production—traveled with it but are no longer on permanent display. The exhibit as a whole creates the feeling of being in a religious sanctuary where specialized lighting illuminates a series of secular altars. Viewers move around the installation, looking at the details in front of them and across the large triangle at the backs of runners that they can see only from afar. At the end of the exhibit, they can read Heritage Panels that detail the histories of every woman named at *The Dinner Party*. Today's visitors to the Brooklyn Museum can hear Judy Chicago's tour of *The Dinner Party*, originally recorded in 1980, on the museum's cell-phone gallery guide.

The Dinner Party emerged from unique feminist production conditions and circulated in unique market conditions under which its version of feminism could be sold to a mass audience. It completed its journey to "the museum" and achieved its status as canonical art under unconventional circumstances, to say the least. With origins in the West Coast feminist art movement of the early 1970s, *The Dinner Party* embodied a kind of art that few Americans outside of activist or bohemian circles had seen before. It brought to the mainstream a feminist representation of women as constituting a "sex class" and as a group sharing not only female body parts. but also a history of oppression and a culture of resilience over time and place.

Furthermore, Judy Chicago challenged the idea of art as the product of a single auteur. While *The Dinner Party* was a frank monument to Chicago's aesthetic and political views, media coverage—including from feminists and antifeminists, supporters and critics—coupled the feminist messages of the art with the feminist story of the making of *The Dinner Party*. Accounts of the art and the unique production of *The Dinner Party* circulated together, blurring the line between the art and the practice of Chicago's style of feminism for those who read about or viewed the installation. The studio's publicity campaign, designed by Diane Gelon, frequently referred to the impressive number of four hundred: four hundred women and men freely gave their time to the project over five years. Although four hundred individuals indeed worked at the studio at one point or another, only twenty-three people did the bulk of the work and labored along with Chicago each week for three years, making it possible for the artist to complete her ambitious masterwork.[1]

Indeed, much as it runs counter to the artist's ethic and vision of the project itself, it is difficult not to put Judy Chicago at the center of this history. The making of *The Dinner Party* involved epic struggles for money, help, and recognition. The circulation of *The Dinner Party* became its own parable about the feminist artist, casting her as an avenging David going toe-to-toe with the Goliath of a male-dominated art establishment. When museums refused to show the installation, groups of women in five US cities organized to bring feminist art to alternative settings in their communities. They mobilized local media, churches, art, and reading groups; they recruited friends, families, and banks to build venues and a national audience for *The Dinner Party*. Unexpectedly, each nonmuseum show not only succeeded but made money for its organizers.

But the enthusiasm for Chicago's style of cultural feminism also met new political challenges during the Reagan years, challenges that threatened the preservation of the installation and the mobilization of feminist art itself. After ten years of exhibitions, in 1990 Chicago tried to donate the piece to the University of the District of Columbia for its newly proposed multicultural arts center. Soon, she found herself in the middle of the congressional sex wars, in which "taxpayer-subsidized obscenity" became a front for conservatives to fight freedom of expression within government funding for the arts.

Despite these dramatic reversals of fate, *The Dinner Party* found a home in art history textbooks and finally in the formal museum world as the new millennium began. In the Brooklyn Museum, where it is on permanent display for the near future, a visitor can almost hear one of *The Dinner Party*'s goddesses (Ishtar, perhaps) or activists (maybe Susan B. Anthony) ask, "How did I get here?" That story of origins and struggle, of art and feminism, is at the heart of this book.

The path that *The Dinner Party* traveled—from inception (1973) to completion (1979) to tour (1979–89) to the Brooklyn Museum (2007)—sheds light on the history of US feminism since 1970 and on the ways popular feminism in particular can illuminate important trends and transformations in the broader culture. After all, US feminism has never functioned only as a political movement. The challenges it posed, the excitement it generated, even the fear it inspired, came from its confrontation with well-established and well-worn habits that played out in homes, schools, houses of worship, offices, bedrooms, movie theaters, and museums. Most importantly, feminism changed the narratives of what mattered and, by doing so, changed history itself. The second-wave feminist revolution that occurred after the 1960s, like its predecessors, took hold in and on culture.

This makes the history of monuments to that movement imperative. *The Dinner Party* offers a unique case study of US feminism as a cultural force, one that challenged the definition of art and history—the distinction between fine art and craft, women's "questionable" status as art makers, and the terms by which museum directors and boards of directors established value. It raised questions about what constituted "greatness"—how narratives of the past neglected entire groups, how history shaped ideas of womanhood as well as how actual women lived their lives.

The Dinner Party also offers a case study of how feminist ideas radiated out through cultural pathways to nonactivists, becoming relevant to those lives that cannot necessarily be documented in histories of those devoted to feminism's political causes: the Equal Rights Amendment (ERA), abortion rights, or the antipornography movement. Many women and men who did not participate in feminist activism found a way to express their belief in women's equality by working on *The Dinner Party*, organizing a community showing of *The Dinner Party*, or by buying a ticket to see *The Dinner Party* on exhibit. The ideas of women's equality, women's history, and women's culture, translated into art by *The Dinner Party*, spoke to many viewers and made seeing the controversial work an event worth traveling to and lining up for.

Few works of US art have ever inspired such an outpouring of reaction and sustained attention from the media and audiences as did *The Dinner Party*. This book brings three frameworks to bear on this crucial cultural feminist moment: *The Dinner Party*'s roots in the feminist art movement; its place in both fine art and popular culture; and its shifting status within US feminist thought. Together these frameworks illuminate how and why this piece of controversial feminist art became an unexpected blockbuster and eventual icon. A focus on the installation itself precludes a full history of Judy Chicago, as well as her impressive artistic output before and after *The Dinner Party*, a book that is long overdue.[2] We first meet the artist in the early 1970s as she absorbs and articulates the promise of radical feminism. For Chicago, this meant a focus on women and making art out of female "content," which she defined as the messy and contraband stuff of a female life led in a female body. "I wanted to express what it was like to be organized around a central core, my vagina, that which made me a woman," she wrote in her 1975 memoir, *Through the Flower*.[3]

These terms—*women*, *female*, and *female body*—were for her and her cohort powerfully enabling in their simplicity (and are a good reminder that feminist theory in 1971 did not resemble what has come to be known a generation later as gender theory). Women as vagina-bearing people faced discrimination externally (legally, economically, socially, sexually) and diminishment internally or psychologically by patriarchy, not only or not just by individual men. Chicago, a heterosexual radical feminist, embraced separatism as a strategy, not a solution, and always harnessed her feminism to a larger humanism.

Decades after the project of women's history was initiated, we still know too little about feminism's impact outside the East Coast: *The Dinner Party* opens questions about how this radical vision played out nationally. Chicago's style of feminism, born in artistic circles on the West Coast in the 1960s and 1970s, became the basis for representations of feminism displayed in *The Dinner Party* and practiced in Chicago's studio that depart significantly from those embraced by radical women elsewhere. The history of *The Dinner Party*, then, rests on a detailed look at how Chicago practiced feminism in her classrooms and in the feminist art programs she helped launch in the early 1970s.

Once Chicago and her group of workers completed *The Dinner Party* in 1979, the story must shift away from Chicago and her artistic vision to the reception and dissemination of the ideas that framed the exhibit. I follow *The Dinner Party* on its unconventional tour, its published and unpublished reviews, and through to its struggles to find a permanent home for women's art.

Similarly, my treatment of the feminist art movement begins with its origins as an expression of West Coast cultural politics but does not follow or detail the vastness of that enterprise. Instead, our attention moves to the diverse and dispersed feminist debates about *The Dinner Party* as art and as feminism that had their origins in that movement. Finally, my treatment of radical feminism, also complex and multifaceted in 1970, moves into an account of the fractious and competing understandings after 1980, and the final defeat of the ERA in 1982, of what ought to matter to feminism. This book does not do a full accounting of the "end" of the movement phase of seventies feminism, but it does make a case for reevaluating the sustaining role that popular culture played for select feminist insights in the 1990s and beyond, or what I call here postfeminism. By considering *The Dinner Party* over time, we bring the elements of these overlapping histories into focus.

This history of *The Dinner Party* is based primarily on archival research, most importantly, on the Judy Chicago Papers housed at the Arthur and Elizabeth Schlesinger Library on the History of Women in America at the Radcliffe Institute for Advanced Study, Harvard University. It also draws from archives and clipping files held in Houston, Cleveland, and Belen, New Mexico, that have not yet been added to the Judy Chicago archive. Interviews with crucial participants ensured that the archival and paper trail squared with actual studio practice. Close readings of published accounts by Chicago about her feminism and the making of *The Dinner Party*, as well as the published account of *The Dinner Party* in magazines, newspapers, art criticism, and feminist journals, helped to shape this story. A full reckoning of Chicago's place in art history is absent from this book. This is primarily an account of the intersection of *The Dinner Party* with that amorphous thing we call American feminism.

Who Is Judy Chicago?

The artist Judy Chicago began her life as Judy Cohen, born in 1939 and raised in the city of Chicago. In this first version of herself, she was the daughter of a Jewish leftist organizer father and a working mother, Arthur and May Cohen. Like many radical feminists, she grew up listening to the stories of social justice and community activism her father told in their living room crowded with union folks and, from an early age, had a keen sense that she had great things to offer the world. The second version of this woman's biography, which we might call the story of Judy Chicago, is quite different. In this story, told in her memoir, *Through the Flower*, she is a feminist artist who came of age battling modernist and machismo cool on the one hand and the tokenism of the exceptional female artists on the other; who changed her name to wipe away any vestiges of dependence, applied the radical notion of women's equality to her studio art classes and later at the new Woman's Building in Los Angeles in the early 1970s; who made *The Dinner Party* and became the controversial face of the feminist art movement for a generation.

Interestingly, the point of intersection in these two origin stories is Chicago's father, who believed in his daughter and who, in turn, the artist deeply admired. Perhaps because of this, Chicago's feminism always involved and embraced men. Men as lovers, peers, allies, and friends populated her inner circle even as she developed her critique of patriarchy and gender-based discrimination for *The Dinner Party*. She married three times, losing one husband to death, another to divorce, and finding in the third a partner for life. Yet even with loving men (or men to love) around her, the fuel driving the artist's evolution from Judy Cohen to Judy Chicago rested squarely on the age-old dilemma faced by female artists: how to be an artist of ambition in a cultural world where all the men were artists and the women were wives, girlfriends, and amateurs.

As she was beginning her career, Cohen/Chicago desired above all else to be an artist in her own right and chose a place where generations of Americans have gone for personal reinvention. She moved from Chicago to Southern California to study art at the University of California in Los Angeles in 1957. She entered a cultural environment that was politically innovative: in a matter of years, it had become a thriving place of student, worker, race-based, feminist, left, and liberal activisms. Los Angeles also contained a bifurcated art scene. The region's behemoth entertainment industry overshadowed the formal institutional art world. This, in turn, inadvertently fostered an informal, community-oriented alternative art scene.[4] Cohen/Chicago dated an African American philosophy student and attended NAACP protests. She hung around the art circles thriving in Venice Beach, where she met her first husband, Jerry Gerowitz, who had been court-martialed in 1954 for refusing to sign the McCarthy-inspired anti-Communist loyalty oath then required of members of the armed services.

After a year in New York City in 1959, Cohen/Chicago returned to LA, married Gerowitz, and finished her undergraduate degree. When Gerowitz died in an automobile accident in 1962, the young widow struggled to regain her sense of herself and her life. Her art and her studio practice gave her solace and purpose. She completed a master's degree in painting and sculpture in 1964. Over the next six years, as Judy Gerowitz, she made a reputation for herself as an abstract painter, changed her name to Judy Chicago, and competed with her peers, both male and female, for recognition, resources, and exposure.[5] In 1970, Chicago took a job at Fresno State College, south of LA. There she could translate a reputation falling incrementally behind those of her male peers into a job, a studio, and a chance to rethink herself as an artist. In this climate, where the story of *The Dinner Party* begins, Chicago dreamed ambitiously of making a new kind of art that would imagine human liberation through the female form and that could speak directly to real people and not only to the art elite.

The Feminist Art Movement

This book places *The Dinner Party*, the idea of *The Dinner Party*, and Judy Chicago in the feminist art movement of the 1970s but can only gesture at what a rowdy and gloriously ill-mannered "movement" it was. *The Dinner Party* became one of that movement's icons only after many, many years of functioning more as a lightning rod of controversy than as a rallying point for sister artists. Importantly, *The Dinner Party* actualized mainstream elements of a white-hot feminist critique of art, museums, and art history. However, it never tried to nor could it ever "represent" the aspirations of feminist artists as an actual or imagined group. That said, charting *The Dinner Party*'s path from subcultural feminist art making to museum mainstay does cast light on the chronic problems women artists and feminist art have faced, and still face, and it chronicles the strategies that generations of feminist activists have employed to disrupt the conflation of "what is" with "what might be."

The feminist art movement that Chicago participated in during the 1970s emerged in response to both trends in art and styles of social protest. All postwar artists in the US worked under the heavy cloud of modernism. In the 1960s this burden was compounded by an abstract expressionism entailing a level of abstraction that made new art, as historian Michael Kammen has argued, "virtually inaccessible and meaningless to all but a relative modest number of insiders who had acquired the visual vocabulary and acuity" to appreciate it.[6] Abstract expressionism dominated art markets and modern art holdings alongside the era's much friendlier newcomer, pop art. This phenomenon drew its inspiration from mass culture and was most famously popularized in the work of Andy Warhol. If abstract expressionism seemed deliberately cryptic, pop art announced its references and "message" loudly and clearly. It embraced commercial culture, not casting it off as degraded or unworthy.

Abstract expressionism and pop art dominated the formal art scene in the 1960s, creating new rules of their own but leaving intact the gender rules about who an artist might be. Many aspiring artists in these years railed against both the narrow range of aesthetic options and about making art as a commercial product bound (if one was "successful") for corporate collections, galleries or private homes. In response, they turned toward ephemeral or "art-off-the-easel" works and "art-for-art's-sake" events, and women were prominent in this group. This new movement included new forms and formats, and newly accessible technologies, in installation, conceptual, performance, video, and body art.[7]

In her essay "Against Interpretation" (1966), Susan Sontag identified these forms as a protest against the "museum conception of art" and art made only for critics.[8] Chicago, for example, learned pyrotechnics in order to produce smoke sculptures that moved, dissolved, and faded away.[9] Other women and men incorporated overtly political themes in their artwork, including criticism of the Vietnam War and US race relations, and organized themselves into protest groups. The Art Workers Coalition, formed in 1969, brought together critiques of imperialism and the museum "system," targeting the Museum of Modern Art, the Metropolitan, and the Whitney for their dusty "art-historical mausoleum" orientation.[10] Black, brown, leftist, and feminist artists organized themselves to protest exclusions at the nation's major art museums.

As activist artists protested their exclusion from the institutional art world, they also questioned the role of art and its place in either supporting the status quo or, conversely, empowering communities through new forms of representation. Artists and writers inspired by the black power movement led the way by explicitly linking political revolutions to cultural revolutions. The black arts movement from the mid-1960s to the mid-1970s challenged not only representations of "blackness" in US culture but understandings of what "blackness" itself signified. The West Coast's black arts movement adopted a multimedia aesthetics, embracing the materiality of craft as a strategy for questioning the parameters of "art" and infusing ordinary objects (including quilts, advertising icons, and bodies) with aesthetic and cultural significance, something the 1970s feminist art movement adopted.[11] Such innovation, more possible in a West Coast arts scene that operated at a distance from eastern cultural institutions, translated into a range of new forms, most notably, performance art.[12] It also translated into making new spaces in which to show art made for communities historically absent from art museums.

Chicago also would have been aware of the prominent role women played in the black arts movement, and their intensive development of a feminism that included men in its vision. The nation's first Museum of African American Art opened in 1976 in a former Macy's in Los Angeles, embedding art in an easily accessible place. The Watts Art Festival began in 1966 and ran until the mid-1980s; Gallery 32 opened in 1968 and became one of the few places showing innovative work by black artists, including "Sapphire, You've Come a Long Way, Baby" in 1970, which was the city's first survey of African American women artists. For the three years of its existence it functioned as a gathering place for discussions about art and politics and offered tangible ways to connect community funds to Afrocentric causes through fund-raisers like those for the Black Arts Council, the Black Panthers, and the Watts Towers Children's Art programs.[13]

Women artists in the 1960s and 1970s participated in a broad coalition on the left that viewed art as central to consciousness and, thus, to social change. In a 1980 interview with Chicago, Faith Wilding, and Suzanne Lacy, all founders of the West Coast feminist art movement, each articulated her view of art's social relevance. For Lacy, the artist functioned "as visionary—model maker, structure creator, community organizer"; for Wilding, art created "a space in which for a moment there is freedom from the acceptance of daily coercion of violence and custom . . . [where] new images can be subversively leaked into the world."[14] Chicago argued that art should circulate broadly and not be limited to or by museums. "I believe that is what artists have to do if they really want their work to reach out and affect a wider audience—make images that are clearer about subjects that people care about, and find ways to make those images seen by more people than gallery-goers."[15] The imprint of left-leaning African American cultural practice on Chicago's generation was clear.[16]

The cultural nationalism that Judy Chicago and others in the feminist art movement invoked worked through the category "woman," identified the oppression as "patriarchy" and the solution as a revolution of consciousness aided by art made by, for, and about women. This style of cultural feminism did not represent the full range of views or art made by feminists on the West Coast but became one powerful theme of the movement and the moment.

Popular Feminism

The phenomena that comprise the history of *The Dinner Party* developed not only out of a converging of trends in art and social protest but also from the intersection of these trends with changing consumer tastes and markets.[17] Motivated by personal, regional, and generational experiences, Chicago felt a tremendous commitment to making art that could speak clearly to those outside of the elite art world, and she cultivated popular relevance within a fine-arts orientation. This, along with the sheer monumentality of *The Dinner Party*, connected the project to a mass audience from the beginning. Chicago's need for skilled help and the project's need for money in the form of personal donations, corporate gifts, and grants brought an unprecedented degree of attention to *The Dinner Party* during its production and subsequent tour. Such attention placed the work squarely in the realm of popular culture as well as an evolving gender politics that included women with significantly different agendas under the rubrics of feminism.

During the years of its production (1974–79) and its tour (1979–89), *The Dinner Party* took its place among a range of new feminist-themed cultural products created by the women's movement. US media culture—newspapers, magazines, television, news, bestselling books, and feature films—found in feminism a lively narrative and an engaging approach to favorite national topics like personal transformation, individualism, meritocracy, and the ability of US society to rid itself of social ills like discrimination.[18] For mass audiences, consuming feminism through popular media helped show the ways in which feminism could be harmonized to fit with current family arrangements, heterosexuality, and the workplace without too much strife or social change.

This dynamic also drew women who were not already activists to feminism. Susan Douglas has argued that the mass media helped make her a feminist and "it helped make millions of other women feminists too, whether they take on that label or not."[19] In part through the media, feminism ceased to be "only" a social protest movement and started to become a regular part of mainstream cultural thought, as with the most basic insights of a distilled and simplified feminism circulated in—and sometimes disappeared into—popular culture. By 1970 publishing houses began elevating feminist theory into best sellers and the national media regularly covered the feminist movement with a quirky, "what will they think of next!" kind of fascination. In television series that aired on one of only three national channels, and thus reaching huge numbers of viewers, feminist-inspired plot lines abounded: *The Mary Tyler Moore Show*, *All in the Family*, *Good Times*, *One Day at a Time*, and later, *Cagney and Lacey*, *Murphy Brown*, and *Dr. Quinn, Medicine Woman*.[20] One can make similar lists for popular novels, Hollywood films, and hit radio singles. After 1970, consumers could regularly come into contact with what historian Amy Farrell defines as "a feminism that is widespread, common to many, and one that emerges from the realm of popular culture."[21]

Thanks in part to the media, feminist gains, attitudes, and achievements moved into the mainstream of US life, driven there by cultural commodities, not only political reforms and actions. Yet the weaving of select feminist views into the mainstream of US culture should not be approached as a historic inevitability. As scholars like Farrell and Susan Ware have demonstrated, the process by which feminist views enter the mainstream at all requires a history. If others have traced it by following specific forms over time, for example, consciousness-raising novels, *Ms.* magazine, or television shows, I add to that project here by tracing one feminist-themed object—*The Dinner Party*—as it moved into the mainstream through exhibitions and media coverage.[22] When it is properly framed as both art and popular culture, it becomes clear that *The Dinner Party* drew from both the sensibility of social protest and the liberal mainstream, a combination that made its message versatile and provocative. An eager viewer could see in it the presence of women's desire for women throughout time or the value of women's domestic work, depending on what that viewer focused on and wanted from it.

The Dinner Party's popularity (and its eventual canonization) came and has come exactly from its ability to offer up a variety of messages and showcase potentially radical feminist views in unthreatening ways. This has been a winning strategy, to use the old suffrage phrase, carefully crafted over the process of making the art itself. With it, Chicago produced the first feminist art blockbuster to effectively straddle mainstream museums and alternative art spaces to reach hundreds of thousands of viewers.

Feminist Theory

The last context in which I situate *The Dinner Party* is US feminist theory, which by the 1970s had become an academic field: women's studies. One issue dominated the trajectory of *The Dinner Party* in a shifting and evolving feminist discourse: Chicago's essentialism, namely her use of the vulva as a symbol of universal womanhood. In the 1970s, one of the more potentially subversive aspects of *The Dinner Party* was Chicago's frank use of the female body as an artistic form. For example, facing criticism of *The Dinner Party*'s vulva-shaped plates, Chicago explained that she did not view this definitive aspect of women's bodies, or, as she called them, cunts, as a mark of shame to be hidden or denied. "I don't have cunt hatred," she explained. "My work starts with an assumption about feeling okay about being female and universalizing from there."[23] Chicago's use of the female body, when coupled with her message about women's culture and patriarchy, became deeply synchronized with the style of seventies feminism that salvaged women's uniqueness from a male-centric society and is commonly called cultural feminism.

Catharine MacKinnon's call for a feminism boldly unmodified holds an enduring appeal when we look at the sway that cultural feminism achieved in the popular landscape through phenomena like *The Dinner Party*.[24] Despite the dream of unity, second-wave feminist activists quickly parsed themselves and their writing into chosen and unchosen categories that have since had an enormous impact on how history is written: politico, socialist, liberal, radical and later, women of color, cultural, lesbian, prosex, and antisex, are but a few. Such distinctions carried weight among the converted but were almost meaningless to onlookers.

The label *cultural feminism*, refreshingly clear as a description of a feminist practice oriented around culture, has a complicated history, however. For critics, cultural feminism supported three indefensible positions, or in the words of scholars Leila Rupp and Verta Taylor, had three great "sins"—essentialism, separatism, and an emphasis on alternative women-centered culture. For supporters, it signified the productive cross-pollination between lesbian and feminist communities.[25] As a term, its meaning rested on its opposition to *politics*: for activists, the distinction worked off the assumption that politics targeted social change, whereas culture engaged individuals and thus represented a feel-good form of collective self-help. Perhaps for these reasons, Judy Chicago neither used the term nor identified herself as a cultural feminist. This did not stop others from putting her into that category. For this reason, cultural feminism, as a style of feminist engagement and as a label, factored into *The Dinner Party*'s relationship to the broader feminist movement and its subsequent history.

Cultural feminism fell into disrepute in the 1980s, a matter I historicize here with the hope of restoring complexity to its ossified reputation. The academic critique of cultural feminism began in earnest at the Scholar and the Feminist IX Conference, "Towards a Politics of Sexuality," held on April 24, 1982, at Barnard College in New York City. The conference gave voice to deeply felt conflicts within a feminist movement that was fragmenting quickly over the relationship between ideas and political practice, a debate subsequently referred to as "the feminist sex wars."[26] At the conference, the young activist-scholar, and soon to be important chronicler of radical feminism, Alice Echols criticized what she saw as the devolution of radical political critique into "cultural feminism." She defined cultural feminism as the tendency to equate "women's liberation with the nurturance of a female counter culture," a "polarization of male and female sexuality," and a "celebration of femaleness."[27] Echols added her voice to others who opposed the drift in orientation toward social and sexual regulation in feminist activism.[28] In the aftermath of the conference, the term *cultural feminism* came to stand for a feminism no longer sufficiently invested in activism. More precisely, this meant a feminism not devoted enough to the right kind of activism—activism waged collectively, focused on structural power, and committed to dismantling systematic expressions of gender and gender discrimination.

Echols was certainly not the first to identify a shift within the larger feminist movement. Redstockings member Brooke Williams had posited a binary between true "radical" feminism and what she called cultural feminism in 1975, which she identified as the death knell of radical feminism.[29] Feminist theorist and music critic Ellen Willis, writing in 1984, confirmed that this was the date when it all began to go wrong. By 1975, she wrote, "The women's liberation movement had become the women's movement, in which liberals were the dominant, not to say hegemonic force. . . . Feminism had become a reformist politics, a countercultural community, and a network of self-help projects (rape crisis centers, battered women's shelters, women's health clinics, etc.)."[30] For Willis, lodged in the male-dominated fields of music and journalism, the counterculture of women's alternative spaces represented feminist retreat or accommodation at best.

While Echols, Williams, and Willis had correctly identified a significant intellectual shift in feminism, their dismissal of culture as not political enough proved premature.[31] In the tradition of the New Left counterculture, groups of feminists in the 1970s had indeed turned their energies toward building alternative cultural institutions and intellectual traditions, music, bookstores, and iconographies that celebrated women's historical experiences and their femaleness.[32] In embracing women's difference from men, these feminists saw themselves as pushing their political analysis of patriarchy past the various ways men oppressed women over time and place and toward a new view of power that would better incorporate difference.

In these cultural locations, women's way of knowing, their ethics, their different voice, and their different sexual desires would be valued. Feminist critics of pornography, growing louder each year, ambitiously hoped not only to regulate where a consumer could buy sexual services or commodities, but also to rewrite the script of sexual desire itself, for both men and women.[33] For these feminists, all the ways that contemporary women might be unique under patriarchy could become qualities available to everyone once men and women enjoyed a more authentic and robust equality. Cultural feminists had strong allegiances to liberal, women of color, and lesbian feminisms, and many moved along networks of friends and allies into and out of activist groups while participating in alternative women-centered cultural groups. Separating women's countercultural sensibility from their feminist politics could not be done easily or, if done, was hard to sustain.

Yet the cleavage of 1970s feminism into radical and cultural, and into the misleading categories of prosex (those against censorship of images) and antisex (those against pornography), which occurred in the pressured atmosphere of the early 1980s when Reaganism began its transformation of US political culture more generally, had far-reaching implications. These implications were most evident in the ways that this struggle mapped onto subsequent historical accounts of second-wave feminism. The tendency to equate feminism with political activism rather than with cultural production is most graphic.[34] Focusing on gender-affirming content and its practice in art and culture, expressions of cultural feminism have tended to be minimized or dismissed in scholars' map of what counts as feminism, even though late twentieth-century practitioners of feminism saw it as a vital location for political struggle.

This simultaneous confirmation of gender difference and critique of gender discrimination, the mutual embrace of difference and equality, have long existed as generative tendencies in US feminism.[35] A closer look at the 1970s and 1980s, as well as at the recent history of feminism, demonstrates the inadequacies of old distinctions within our scholarship.[36] This book attempts to lift the grid of sectarian battles off one expression of "cultural feminism," *The Dinner Party*, to reengage with that movement's strengths and limits. I argue here that cultural feminism's celebration of women's difference as the basis for equality provided the traction for a long-lasting expression of feminism in popular culture. Embracing sexual difference—enjoying gender differences between men and women—has often (but not always) been harnessed effectively to feminism, and Judy Chicago tightened those connections in ways that have yet to be remarked upon. Eve Ensler's hugely popular play, *The Vagina Monologues*, first performed in 1996, with its intertwining celebration of the vagina and its critique of violence and discrimination that vagina-bearing people face, is only one of many examples of the force of a popular form of feminism that confirms women's differences from men even as it presses for the end of gender discrimination.[37]

The immense popularity of *The Dinner Party* underlines its roots in the feminist art movement but also in a set of popular values shaped by its culture feminism. To a mass audience alert to changing gender relations, it embodied the blend of radical and cultural feminism in the 1970s that helped nurture a lively and thriving women's movement. For all its lack of radical credentials, *The Dinner Party* performed a radical task. It reached a diverse audience as an ambassador for feminism and did so as an event, a space, a cultural product, and a set of interlocking insights about "women." The cultural space of *The Dinner Party* provided many viewers, activists and nonactivists alike, with a way to experience the exhibit as a member of "woman," a way into the subject position of seventies feminism, no matter one's biological sex or political leanings.

By creating—even if temporarily—identification with and between women, *The Dinner Party* also invites viewers to imagine what a history of Western civilization that equally valued women's contribution might look like. By doing so, it asks viewers to question what actions count as history, which actors count as significant, and why many of the women of *The Dinner Party* have been forgotten. It also, without doubt, raises troubling questions that it cannot adequately answer: where are women of the global south and east in this "history of women," why are all but two great women seated at the table white, and what do vaginas have to do with women's status? Above all, it raises today, as it did a generation ago, questions that spur debate about what a community of women can or should look like.

Such questions are clearly in evidence in the coverage of *The Dinner Party* in local and national newspapers and magazines, women's journals, feminist newsletters, letters to the editor, comment books that were part of the original exhibit, and letters to the artist. Yet in comparing published and unpublished responses to *The Dinner Party*, we can also see a piece of art that transcended its own controversy or eluded the terms of the conversation about it. There is a consistent enthusiasm for *The Dinner Party* by audiences that does not appear in published commentary, suggesting a gap between professional evaluations and popular taste that is occluded when histories of feminism focus on voices found in established (or radical) institutions and organizations. Critics from the left and the right might have denounced the essentialism of *The Dinner Party*, but what does it mean that so many individuals reported finding its imagery powerful and insightful?

Take for example this story, one of many found in the archive of letters sent to the artist. On April 26, 1982, Hilary McLeod, a young Canadian, wrote to Judy Chicago about going to Montreal with her infant daughter, mother, and sister to see *The Dinner Party*: "This weekend I experienced women's generosity in a most powerful way as a result of visiting your *Dinner Party* in Montreal." The group arrived at the museum and struck up a conversation with the women in line around them. They chatted about Chicago's memoir and their excitement at finally seeing the work. Yet, quickly it became clear to McLeod that the four-hour wait was simply too long for her as a nursing mother with a fussy baby. As she prepared to leave,

> Our companions in the line came to my rescue. One of them went to the front of the queue where a group from her town had been waiting . . . and explained my plight. "No problem," they said, "Tell them to saunter on up and join us." Their sisterly concern saved the day . . . I wanted to share this experience with you, as others shared with me. Such camaraderie is happening everywhere between women, but for so many to come together to help a nursing mother view a feminist art exhibition, which was itself deeply moving, seemed particularly appropriate.[38]

McLeod and many others who viewed *The Dinner Party* reported having experienced something valuable from the exhibit: the space of the museum transformed temporarily into a literal and metaphorical community of women. The art offered a new way of seeing and the supporting materials clearly articulated a narrative about women's history and resilience that many had never heard previously. The letter also captures a voice typically left out of our histories of second-wave feminism: a woman who encountered feminism through cultural consumption, that is, by paying money for a museum ticket, reading Chicago's memoir, and following media coverage on *The Dinner Party*.

While we might be unable to connect this woman's cultural consumption of feminism to activism, we can speculate that, through these encounters, select elements of feminism became familiar to her, her sister, and mother, and perhaps to others in line with them. It suggests that the cultural sea change that was the women's movement took place not only through protest but also through art and ideas that, together with political activism, helped forge a new consensus that women's liberation could be made to fit with existing institutions. The unique archive of *The Dinner Party* gives historians a coveted glimpse into reception, into how individual viewers understood what they saw. While we cannot know the ultimate uses to which individual viewers put their encounter with Chicago's style of feminism, we can hear (if we listen) what they took from viewing *The Dinner Party*.

Finally, *The Dinner Party*'s place in feminist history and memory has been marred by the accusation that Chicago exploited the women who worked at her *Dinner Party* studio. A close examination of the archival records and interviews with key players refutes this charge. Disgruntled workers left, as did people who hoped the studio would be an art program to help them make their own art. As the project administrator, Diane Gelon, put it, "no one put a gun to their heads and made them work at the studio. People who were there wanted to be there."[39] Memoirists and historians of 1970s feminism have made abundantly clear that accusations of a feminist as egotistical, opportunistic, or abrasive were pervasive and often crippling to feminist groups.[40]

The unfortunate practice of criticizing leaders for the traits that made them effective cannot slip unexamined into our histories of feminism or of *The Dinner Party*. This book looks at the ways Chicago practiced feminism in her classrooms and her *Dinner Party* studio and highlights its strengths and limits. It assumes that Chicago did not control or produce the feminist meaning that students and workers made of their experiences, but rather that the process she engaged in enacted feminist values and practices. As is explored in the following chapters, these included consciousness-raising and frank talk, group processes that enabled students and workers to participate fully and grow personally, and the expectation that women's creative work, chosen freely and done well, could make a difference in the art world.

What follows is an account of *The Dinner Party* as it intersects with the history of US feminism since 1970. Chapters 1 and 2 situate Chicago in the West Coast feminist art movement and Chicago's Feminist Art Program (FAP), where she practiced radical feminist techniques in her classrooms. She and the FAP students from the California Institute of the Arts built *Womanhouse* in 1972, the first environmental art installation that examined the home and domesticity through an overtly feminist lens. Chicago moved to an alternative feminist art program, the Feminist Studio Workshop, housed at the LA Woman's Building, in 1973 and from there, began work on what would become *The Dinner Party*. Chapters 3 and 4 examine the ways feminism infused both Chicago's studio and the aesthetic choices of *The Dinner Party* as she and a handful of workers literally constructed it, plate by plate, stitch by stitch, historical fact by historical fact. Chapter 3 examines the practice of feminism in Chicago's *Dinner Party* studio and reconstructs the ways that volunteers encountered her style of feminism. Chapter 4 takes each component of the art—the runners, the Heritage Floor, the place settings, and the opening banners—and reads them as bringing the art and practice of feminism together.

Chapter 5 connects *The Dinner Party* to networks of supporters through the overlapping efforts to fund and promote the work. The financial history of *The Dinner Party* is a record of its ability to garner support—financial and otherwise—from a wide array of women. This chapter also walks the reader through what he or she might have seen at the San Francisco Museum of Modern Art in March 1979 where *The Dinner Party* opened for the first time. Chapter 6 examines the unlikely success of *The Dinner Party* as a blockbuster despite the collapse of its anticipated museum tour. Community groups in five cities organized to bring the work to alternative art spaces, and this chapter examines this second wave of volunteerism associated with *The Dinner Party*. Chapter 7 turns the lens away from people and volunteers and on to the published and unpublished response to *The Dinner Party* between 1979 and 1989. Critics and commentators writing in the art press, national magazines, local and regional newspapers, women's magazines, and feminist journals debated the meaning of the piece, whether it inspired or offended, whether it was art or politics. Published responses are contrasted with unpublished reviews from audiences and fans by way of comment books from two community shows—Cleveland and Boston—and letters to the artist. These show a public familiar with the controversies surrounding the piece and document what viewers appreciated—or rejected—about *The Dinner Party*.

Whether the artists wanted it to or not, *The Dinner Party* also ultimately met the challenge of the public political sphere on the way to its final home in Brooklyn, New York. Chapter 8 situates *The Dinner Party* in the 1990s as it entered the fray over government funding for the arts and confronted shifting trends in feminism. Denounced as obscene on the floor of the US

House of Representatives and criticized as essentialist and insufficiently multicultural by postmodern feminists, *The Dinner Party* appeared headed to the dustbin of history. Yet, with resurgent interest in the feminist art movement of the 1970s and the growth of postfeminist culture, at the start of the new millennium Chicago found herself welcomed into the museum world that had long scorned *The Dinner Party*.

This is the story of how she got there.

CHAPTER ONE

Making Feminist Artists

The Feminist Art Programs of Fresno and CalArts, 1970–1972

IN 1970, ARTIST JUDY CHICAGO took a position at Fresno State College (FSC, now the California State University, Fresno). She arrived on the innovative campus for the spring semester, not sure of what to expect.[1] Professionally, she brought with her a reputation as an up-and-coming artist with a recognizable name, a quality that enabled her to push the FSC Art Department in new directions. Personally, she arrived with the feeling that she needed a way to reconnect to original content for her art.[2] Worn down by the pursuit of recognition in the modern art scene for over ten years, Chicago wanted to move toward a "female-centered" art. Part of this involved, in her words, "moving away from the male-dominated art scene and being in an all-female environment where we could study *our* history separate from men's and see ourselves in terms of our own needs and desires, not in terms of male stereotypes of women."[3] Relatively soon upon her arrival, Chicago launched the nation's first feminist art program and began to *practice* feminism in often uncomfortable but always exciting new ways.

Fresno, a college town in the center of the San Joaquin Valley far from the more vibrant urban art centers of Los Angeles and San Francisco, was not such a far-fetched answer to the artist's question of where to reinvent herself. The college had reinvented itself in the wake of the civil rights, antiwar, and student protest movements of the 1960s.[4] In 1966 FSC opened the Experimental College in direct response to faculty and student calls for a more relevant and engaged curriculum. Fresno launched a range of programs that offered classes in the new fields of Chicano, black, ethnic, and women's studies.[5] With such a forward-thinking faculty and an administration begrudgingly responsive to the changing cultural climate, Chicago hoped she had placed herself in an environment with enough support to allow her to experiment and enough farmland between herself and LA to allow her to grow in new directions in relative obscurity.[6] "I felt that I had built my identity and my art-making as a person—as an artist—on the framework of reality that I had been brought up in, and now that framework had changed, so I wanted some time out, to look around and find out what was appropriate now," she told an interviewer in 1971.[7]

Progressive politics and sexism remained tightly in step, in Fresno and elsewhere. In her first semester, Chicago taught a coed class where she found her male students gave her "a lot of resistance" and in short order had "taken over."[8] Dismayed at the passivity of the female students and the unfounded confidence of the male students, Chicago announced during class one day that the "men aren't to talk at all." An excruciating twenty minutes passed until a courageous female student raised her hand.[9] At that moment Chicago determined that she would address the unique problems facing women artists, or women who wanted to be artists. Some of Chicago's male students booed her, finding her style abrasive and her politics absurd. Attrition rates in her classes were high. Yet, while some students dropped out, others pledged undying support, finding Chicago inspiring.

No matter what students felt about their professor, a buzz surrounded her, only amplified when one of the nation's foremost art journals, *Artforum*, ran a full-page ad, placed by the Jack Glenn Gallery, for her show at the small and relatively new California State College at Fullerton, Orange County, in LA in 1971. The ad featured a headshot of Chicago wearing a headband and dark glasses and announced, "Judy Gerowitz hereby divests herself of all names imposed upon her through male social dominance and freely chooses her own name: Judy Chicago."[10] A second full-page ad, in the *Artforum* December issue, showed Chicago in a boxing ring, an image that evoked the machismo that characterized the art world and against which the artist railed.[11] The set of images, and Chicago's linkage of art and feminist politics, secured her place as one of the leading figures of the emergent feminist art movement.[12] The catalog for the Fullerton show, written by gallery director Dextra Frankel, confirmed her buzz-worthiness, and the *LA Times* critic confirmed it, describing Chicago as a "leader in the vanguard West Coast art scene."[13]

Even with these hard-won accolades, the environment for female artists was not good as Chicago began her teaching career. Work by women artists was not widely available to the public through the museum world. For example, in 1969, women comprised 8 out of the 143 artists represented in the Whitney Museum annual exhibit.[14] College art schools were no better. Very few programs could boast of a single female artist on their faculties. While art schools admitted a majority of women into their programs, they graduated very few artists who later became recognized or whose work showed. Neither did the work of women artists in the past find a place in art historical works or art publications. In 1970, 88 percent of the reviews in *Artforum* discussed men's work, as did 92 percent of *Art in America* reviews.[15] From these accounts, one could conclude that few women artists of merit existed either in the past or present. In 1972, 100 percent of arts grants sponsored by the National Endowment for the Arts went to men.[16] This translated to women artists earning a third of what their male peers earned, a mere $3,400 to men's $9,500 in 1970.[17] On the West Coast, the art infrastructure was less foreboding yet still statistically closed to women. On a typical day in 1971 at the Los Angeles County Museum of Art, art made by women comprised a mere 1 percent of what was on display.[18] In the major locations that gave structure to the making, selling, and displaying of art—the nexus of art schools, galleries, museums, art history, and art critics—women were nearly completely absent in 1970. These facts, coupled with the untapped talent of a new generation of female artists and an ascendant women's movement, led groups of women on both coasts to organize.

The first woman-centered shot fired against the established art world came in 1969 in New York City, home to the nation's premier "taste-making" art institutions, particularly for modern art, such as the Museum of Modern Art and the Whitney Museum. Famous for its numerous museums, galleries, and art schools and for its reputation as the only worthy destination for an aspiring artist, New York was also the home of many young and radical artists. Informed by antiracist and antiwar protests, female artists organized to challenge the lack of diversity in the city's museums, both in terms of what they showed and whom they hired. Women Artists in Revolution (WAR), part of the Marxist-inspired Art Workers Coalition, protested the Whitney Annual 1969, the nation's major show of new modern art, where work by female artists made up less than 18 percent of the work displayed. The following year, when the Whitney Annual again opened a show comprised of works done almost exclusively by white men, African American feminist artist Faith Ringgold organized Women, Students, and Artists for Black Art Liberation (WSABAL).[19] She went further than the WAR feminists of the year before by demanding compensatory quotas at all city museums to correct for decades of underrepresentation for black, female, and student artists. Ringgold and others engaged in a strategic "politics of representation" that looked critically at the contexts and sociopolitical dynamics behind the process of evaluation.[20] Ringgold, along with her daughter, Michele Wallace, became founding members of the National Black Feminist Organization (NBFO) in 1973.[21] The work of Ringgold, along with West Coast artists Ntozake Shange and Betye Saar, represented the highly productive linkages between the black and feminist art movements in the early 1970s.[22]

To sustain the pressure on the museum world, activist groups organized themselves into the Ad Hoc Women Artists' Group, led by Ringgold, Lucy Lippard, Brenda Miller, and Poppy Johnson. In 1970 the Ad Hoc group issued a call for greater representation of women in Whitney's annual—a full 50 percent.[23] The group "zapped" the museum by staging a sit-in and picket at the museum.[24] The handout they distributed read "THE WHITNEY STAFF SUFFERS! GRAVELY! FROM ACUTE MYOPIA! This show is more about the artists they couldn't see than about the ones they have included." The group's top honor for the group most neglected went to "America's women artists, of all colors."[25] The Ad Hoc group met weekly in various studios, with no formal officers or structure, making it responsive to members' concerns but ultimately ineffective in identifying and enacting an agenda.

In 1971 a new group with a more professionally visible profile formed. Women in the Arts (WIA), organized by Elaine de Kooning, an influential abstract expressionist painter and wife of renowned painter Willem de Kooning, and Sylvia Sleigh, a realist painter married to the curator of the Guggenheim Museum, Lawrence Alloway, added their voices to the call for greater gender inclusivity in the city's art scene. WIA drafted an open letter to the major players of the New York art establishment—the Museum of Modern Art, the Brooklyn Museum, the Metropolitan, the Guggenheim, the Whitney, and the New York Cultural Center—demanding an exhibition of five hundred works by women artists.[26] *Art News* reported on the growing feminist agitation. A special issue devoted to women's art in January 1971 included Linda Nochlin's groundbreaking article, "Why Have There Been No Great Women Artists?" where she situated artistic genius as an outgrowth of social privilege, not mere "talent."[27] When, for the third straight year, feminists again picketed the Whitney Annual, a group of women extended their activism to print, launching *Feminist Art Journal* in 1972. It pledged in its opening issue to "encourage women artists of all persuasions to discuss and illustrate their work."[28] After years of protest, the agitation began to pay off. The "Women Choose Women" exhibition opened at the New York Cultural Center in January 1973, showcasing the work of 109 contemporary female artists, the first and largest woman-only art event of its kind.[29]

West Coast activism followed a similar pattern but had distinctive features. It began in 1971 when the Los Angeles County Museum of Art mounted a large and much-anticipated show on art and technology. The show acted as a call to arms to LA's many feminists and women artists since it did not include a single piece of work made by a woman.[30] Concerned women organized themselves into the Los Angeles Council of Women Artists. Founders included artists Joyce Kozloff and Channa Horwitz, designer Sheila de Bretteville, and artist-journalist Vicki Hodgetts.[31] Within months, it boasted a membership of 250. The council's immediate goal was to bring attention to the discrimination in the "Art and Technology" show, but it quickly expanded to address the broader pattern of discrimination in the museum's hiring practices, in its selection of artists to display and in its awarding of prizes. In coming together to protest the sexism of the LA museum, women from around the area met each other, many for the first time.[32]

From the beginning, West Coast feminists added a populist element to their art activism. Networks of West Coast women emphasized the role of art in feminist expression. They understood art, particularly community art, as a powerful vehicle for enlightenment, and as such, important to social transformation.[33] In this way, art in Southern California in the 1970s pioneered a kind of popular feminist sensibility, one committed to individual women's feminist awakenings as much as transforming the art establishment. The feminist art programs Chicago and others opened in the 1970s—in colleges, art schools, and community centers—contributed to the West Coast movement's distinctive sensibility.

Like others in her generation, Chicago was no stranger to a hostile art world. She, like them, confronted the nexus of institutional and personal sexism as she fought her way into the California art scene. But as she began her teaching, she was dismayed that gendered hurdles to success in the art world were all but invisible to her art students, both male and female. The female students imagined themselves as artists able to compete on equal terms; the male students had no inkling that their female peers faced a monumental institutional infrastructure that was hostile to them. Many male art faculty members assumed that women as a group did not produce great art and instead dallied in the arts as a hobby. The investment on all sides of the classroom—students, faculty, and administration—against seeing the disadvantages facing women art students impressed itself on Chicago. Her next move—to start a feminist art program—positioned Fresno as a staging ground in the larger struggle to win a place for women in the male-centered art world.

The Feminist Art Program at FSC

We all had "a special sense of risk and importance and a freedom from history."

Through trial and error, Chicago designed an application of radical feminist theory—or a practice of feminism—to her studio art classes and did so with the expressed goal of giving women tools to combat the hostility of the male-dominated art world. In May 1970 Chicago posted a flyer in the FSC art department announcing her interest in teaching a women-only class. She began the interviews with a simple question that she felt would help her identify students with a real commitment to the hard work of becoming an artist.[34] Nancy Youdelman explains that during her interview, "Judy asked me if I wanted to be a professional artist: I answered that I already was an artist. She quickly replied that I was not. I was stunned by her directness and, quite frankly, I had never met anyone like her before. Later I realized I had no conception of what being an artist really was, professional or not."[35]

Once admitted to the class, students joined Chicago in the interview process, "so the decisions became group decisions," explained Chicago in a 1971 interview. "The decisions [who to admit] were based on which girls had the most drive . . . which were prepared and strong enough to relinquish make-up, relinquish being sexual objects, relinquish the privileges that a male society bestows on women."[36] Chris Rush described the mix of confession and fear that drove her interview: "That day of the interview, we were having an anti-war strike with bomb scares and tear-gas filling the hallways. It was scary and exciting. Dori and I were in the hallway together waiting to be interviewed by Judy, Faith, and Cherie. I went in first and told them about how much I hated my father and about my horrible sex life. They really responded positively to that and asked a lot of questions—seeming kind of tough and intimidating. I told Dori to do the same thing. She was also accepted."[37]

The first meeting of admitted students devolved into a polite "tea party," with the students sitting quietly waiting for something to happen. Chicago watched with mounting frustration. Finally she decided to speak her mind: "You know, you are boring the hell out of me. You're supposed to be art students. Art students talk about books and movies and ideas. You are not talking about anything."[38]

The students sat in dead silence until one woman spoke, offering the artist a glimpse into the world her students occupied: "Well, maybe no one has ever asked us about those things before."[39] Chicago described the moment in her 1975 memoir *Through the Flower*: "They began to tell me about their lives and relationships, about how, when they went to parties, the men did most of the 'serious talking.' . . . They were always introduced as Sue or Carole or Nancy, just 'girls' who were expected to go along with the men. We discussed the idea of making demands upon each other, about learning to exchange ideas, feelings, and thoughts. Soon the room was filled with discussion and excitement."[40]

This encounter pushed Chicago further down the path toward rethinking art studio practice. She realized that to move these students—not some abstract category of "art students" but the people in front of her—into a position from which they could produce art they would first have to learn to take themselves seriously, value their own thoughts, read widely, think critically, and learn to trust themselves. Chicago called this nexus of traits—the women's hesitancy to be fully realized individuals—"personality structures" that blocked women from being effective artists. They needed a good dose of feminism to make them into artists.

Yet, not all students who enrolled in Chicago's class needed feminist enlightenment. Faith Wilding had arrived at the college in 1969 in a "battered VW bus," having driven from Wisconsin to Fresno so her husband could take a new job as an assistant professor of English. Wilding had a BA from the University of Iowa and was interested in doing postgraduate work in art history at FSC. While in Wisconsin, Wilding and her husband, Everett Frost, joined Students for a Democratic Society (SDS) and participated in the antiwar movement; later she described her feminist awakening coming in part from the contradictions of being a female political activist.[41] Once settled in Fresno, Wilding couldn't help but make connections between her reading of Simone de Beauvoir and her alienating life as a "faculty wife." One of the first friends she made was Suzanne Lacy, then a graduate student in the psychology department. Lacy shared Wilding's leftist sensibility, having witnessed the United Farm Workers movement in her native town of Wasco, California.[42] Lacy found her way into feminist groups while volunteering in the Great Society's inner-city program, VISTA, in Washington, DC, in 1968 and 1969.[43] Once Lacy and Wilding found each other, they determined to start the campus's first consciousness-raising group, following the guidelines set out in the underground feminist journal, *Notes from the Second Year*. The first meeting drew thirty-plus women. Lacy recalled that she and Faith sat dumbfounded, unsure of what to do. "We began talking about sex."[44] Within a few months, fifty women regularly attended the meetings, sharing their experiences of sexism in their relationships, extended families, their departments, and in the culture that surrounded them. Education became a primary and enduring element of practicing feminism in these years, underwritten by the belief that ideas and insight could change consciousness, which in turn would lead to social change, woman by woman.

Moved by the outpouring of stories and the interest in feminist ideas, Wilding proposed a course in the Experimental College for the spring of 1970 titled The Second Sex: On Women's Liberation. The administration deemed it too controversial for course credit with its frankly political list of topics (which included Marriage: The Couple as Cooperative Commune, and Abortion and Contraception: Does a Woman Have a Right over Her Own Body?) and so was retooled as a student activity in the Student Union on the eve of Chicago's arrival on the faculty.[45] The two met when the chair of the art department brought Chicago to Wilding's home. "Although Judy scared me a bit with her confrontational manner," Wilding jumped at the suggestion that she join Chicago as her teaching assistant for the new Feminist Art Program.

Gaining admission to Chicago's class was a bit harder for Lacy, despite her obvious feminism. During her interview, Lacy, a graduate student in psychology, "turned the tables on Judy and interrogated her about her psychological methods and expertise, causing Judy to become suspicious of her intentions and even wondering if she was possibly a spy from the FBI."[46] Wilding vouched for her friend and reassured Chicago that Lacy could be trusted. Lacy and Wilding became among the program's most illustrious alumnae.

At the beginning of the fall semester, Chicago set out the major features of the country's first feminist art class. With the support of the art department chair, Heinz Kusel, Chicago secured permission for her all-woman class to meet off-campus to allow them literal and metaphorical space.[47] Fifteen students enrolled, but by the spring many enrolled in the expanded Feminist Art Program (FAP), making it their top priority.[48] All but one biracial student were white, and all presented as heterosexual; most came from working-class families and in many cases were the first members of their families to attend college.[49] In this way, they reflected the racial and educational profile typical for early second-wave feminists: young, white, and relatively privileged.[50]

Chicago designed a demanding and interdisciplinary course of study for the students. During the week she expected them to put in long hours of work related directly and indirectly to the course. For Monday evening seminars, students read feminist theory by notables like Ti Grace Atkinson, Roxanne Dunbar, Simone de Beauvoir; literature by Collette and Anaïs Nin; histories and biographies of well-known female artists like Frida Kahlo and Mary Cassatt. They visited area libraries to research lesser-known women artists. Chicago assigned *Our Bodies, Ourselves*, by the Boston Women's Health Collective, as required reading in 1971, drawn to its ideologically trustworthy illustrations of the vulva and its positive account of female biology generally. In addition to a heavy reading load, the students were also expected to log between four to eight hours in the studio daily, either on their own work or on constructing and maintaining their collective space. On Wednesday nights, they had group dinners in the "rap room" of the studio, where the group scrutinized each other's work and behavior as women and as artists (a practice known as criticism-self-criticism). More difficult even than this grueling schedule was Chicago's requirement that students financially support the building of their studio at a rate of $25 a month, a large commitment for many students.[51]

At the start of the fall semester, the group searched for a studio space and remodeled it for their needs. This was a teaching exercise. Chicago tasked students with doing the nitty-gritty labor artists do: work with real-estate agents to see potential locations and negotiate the details of leases. Eventually the group settled on an old community theater, formerly an army barracks, across the street from an adult movie house at 1275 Maple Avenue.[52] The students next learned how to remake a space into a studio, including the nuts and bolts of building, remodeling, and repairing. They put up sheet-rock walls to display their work, refurbished the kitchen, plunked a big table (adorned with a wooden barrel of local red wine) into the dining area, and set up a meeting area for group discussions.

Chicago viewed the creation of a workable, serious studio as a way to both teach the students concrete building skills that most women never learn and to show them how to overcome their ingrained sense of dependency on men to solve their problems. "I wanted them to feel that they could 'take care of themselves'—something, it turned out, few of them felt," she wrote.[53] Nancy Youdelman recalls that most of the women had never done hard physical work before: "We worked very hard. And sometimes it was so difficult emotionally as well as physically that we thought we were just going to come apart. We got the studio ready by serious cleaning, building new walls, putting up sheetrock, and painting; we made a fantastic workable space for ourselves, and a safe work environment that was entirely ours and miles from the college."[54]

Chicago demanded total commitment from her students and held herself to the same exacting standard. She drove them to Los Angeles to meet gallery owners, collectors, and other artists, called them when they were sick, and devoted far more hours to interacting with her students than did most professors or art instructors.[55] Much of her willingness to extend herself in this way came from her identification with the students. Writing in her memoir about building a wall at the studio, Chicago explained that it symbolized for students that "they could accomplish anything they set out to do," but for her, "that wall taught me how deep a need I had to work with other women, to see my struggles reflected in theirs."[56]

Chicago and her students invented a new form of feminist education, cobbling together a strategy for combining radical feminism with studio art practice. Practicing modern feminism always started with consciousness-raising, one of the basic structures of the women's liberation movement. Feminist consciousness, established through education and insight, provided the identity that feminism as a movement required. Thus, the FAP, like other feminist groups, had to create "woman" as a political identity as part of its fundamental endeavor. The group also separated themselves from what they defined as male-controlled and male-dominated spaces like mixed classes and mixed studios. According to Wilding, the FAP gave female students "the opportunity to build a separate place which they controlled and in which they could evaluate themselves and their experiences without defensiveness and male interference."[57]

As in many other women's groups in the 1970s, separatism operated as a powerful strategy to enhance women's exploration of their weaknesses and their strengths.[58] The group also created their own women's studies curriculum by seeking out female role models from the past in dusty volumes of art history, mythology, and literature as well as reading contemporary feminist theory. Lastly and crucially, they gave each other "encouragement to make art out of their own experience as women." This combination, explained Wilding, opened up a whole new world of possibilities to the students and "paved the way for a new feminist art." Since the program was the first of its kind, everyone involved felt "a special sense of risk and importance and a freedom from history."[59]

Personal Politics

> I was totally bewildered. I knew something was going to be demanded of me besides good art, but I did not know what.

For the first two months of the program, Chicago devoted herself to working directly with the students' "personality structures," psychological and social habits she believed kept the women ornamental and shallow. "I understood that only if I found out about their particular personality structures would I be able to unravel the things that blocked them in developing themselves."[60] This made Chicago's classroom a complicated space to negotiate. To make art, they had to first make themselves into competent, confident, and assertive people, a process that relied on psychological insight and a confessional mode of talk to achieve. For Chicago, frank talk would show and tell the students how to stop being "the second sex," a focus that harnessed radical feminism to personal, if not always therapeutic, change.

Role-playing proved to be a powerful way to get the students to connect their daily life experiences of sexism to their social identities as women and eventually to their (feminist) art. Chicago directed students to dive deep into themselves and prepare to share what they learned. Student Cheryl Zurilgen described one assignment: "Think about walking down the street and try to contact those feelings you get when guys start 'coming on.' Put those feelings into some form, a poem, a script, a drawing, painting, sculpture, whatever expresses most accurately those feelings."[61]

This process of enacting emotions through role-play pulled participants into recognizing their own habitual daily gendered and racialized experiences as not just experienced by themselves privately but as socially produced and shared. Performances centered on personal experiences of the body and growing up female. "Several women did a piece about their feelings about the size of their breasts, which later became a full fledged photographic work."[62] Other exercises focused on the students' relationships to their mothers. Chicago's unpublished notes explain that "These [exercises] can be done in conjunction with the consciousness-raising session on mothers. The women stand in a circle. They each say mommy three times, trying each time to say it louder and more angrily. After several rounds, words are almost spit out in rage. This is a good exercise for getting to their anger."[63] Role-playing enabled students to tap into powerful feelings of anger, joy, and fear; not all of it came from the material alone. The group subjected each piece to rigorous and lengthy critiques. The FAP's use of role-playing became some of the first stirrings of feminist performance art.[64] They performed their work in December 1970 for a graduate art seminar at the University of California at Berkeley and in early 1971, at the Richmond Art Center in Oakland.[65]

Practicing feminism in 1970 involved critiquing more than just the relationship between men and women. Progressive education in the late 1960s and early 1970s called for a dismantling of the roles of teacher and student, criticizing such cold-war formality as inauthentic, bureaucratic, and marginalizing to the native authority of young people.[66] Many practices employed in Chicago's classroom reflected this spirit of equality, particularly those of consciousness-raising and rap sessions where everyone was allotted the same amount of time to share. At the same time, the realities of class requirements and evaluations reasserted the unequal distribution of power between teacher and student. This contradiction, the tension between equality and difference within the group, troubled the FAP throughout the year and resulted in Chicago and her students having very different experiences of feminist art education.

Chicago believed that feminist education rested on "non-authoritarian" relations between teacher and student where each can approach the other on "real terms": "Roles must break down. . . . Thus I can say to my students: 'I am exhausted. I need to be by myself for a week and work.' They can understand this and respond to my need by structuring the group for the week in such a way that it can sustain itself during my absence. Similarly, they can tell me when something is happening in the group that doesn't please them or meet their needs. Thus the teacher becomes more of a facilitator of growth than a 'teacher' playing the role of someone who knows something."[67] Chicago stressed that the authenticity of the contact between feminist teacher and student worked on both parties. "The class was as good for me as it was for the students. It was a wonderful experience to be able to share the struggles I had had."[68]

Such a pedagogy—practicing feminism through consciousness-raising and confrontation—required skillful negotiation, honesty, and trust, values that at times altogether disappeared under difficult group processing. After all, Chicago did not participate in consciousness-raising sessions but facilitated them, giving her the choice about what to share of her personal experience and when. Students did not have the same level of control. This left many describing the program as thrilling and traumatic, often in the same breath. One participant recalled the experience of group sharing and confrontation as "soul searching, gut wrenching, tumultuous, cleansing, exhausting, exhilarating" and the studio as "suffocating and uncomfortable one moment and nurturing and comforting just a short time later."[69]

Karen LeCocq recalled her sense of excitement and fear at the prospect of joining the FAP for the 1971 spring semester. At their first meeting, Chicago explained to LeCocq that the women in the program had established "a community, not a 'teacher/student thing.'" To outsiders, the community appeared clannish and unwelcoming. LeCocq visited the group's weekly Wednesday night dinner with trepidation. "That first night, I sat at the table attempting to size everyone up. Yet, it was very strange, I couldn't put them in any frame of reference I'd ever experienced." She described witnessing Chicago as a facilitator of student experience rather than an authority figure: "At the close of the dinner, one of the women who was upset about something, threw her plate against the wall and it shattered with a loud crash. Judy said, 'Go ahead, Vanalyne, break all the plates if it makes you feel better.' With that, Vanalyne started picking up plates off the table and hurtling them fast against the floor and walls. Each plate hit their mark with a loud crash and shattered into tiny pieces. I'd never seen anything like it."[70]

LeCocq later showed the group slides of her work and interviewed with Wilding, Lacy, Jan Lester, and the plate-hurling Vanalyne Green. Wilding drove LeCocq back to campus afterward and told her she was accepted. "I was totally bewildered. I knew something was going to be demanded of me besides good art, but I did not know what." Almost immediately, she balked at both the emotional and practical demands of the program. Getting to the studio was arduous, requiring either a thirty-minute bus ride or an hour-long bike ride. LeCocq also felt ambivalent about the art: "In the weeks that followed I was to experience much pain, self-doubt and anger. Everything I heard the women say, I thought was hostile, their artwork I thought was pure crap. I didn't want to be identified with such crap. . . . Yet I was afraid to tell the women their art was bad. I thought they would tell me I had a man's perception. I was very afraid. I didn't want to BE changed. This was very different from changing on your own."

The tension between being changed and "changing on your own" played out everywhere but most regularly in the rap room, the site of the most difficult and transformative group confrontations. Despite the attempts to make it cozy with a patchwork of carpet samples and oversized cushions, LeCocq confessed to always being "a little afraid as I entered this room. It meant that I was about to be confronted on something that was too uncomfortable to talk about or I would have to witness someone else's discomfort."[71] Green also felt ambivalently about the rap room, particularly at those times when the women would "gang up" to confront someone about their weakness or antifeminist behavior. "The program encouraged a Darwinian fight for life among the women students and we often abandoned each other to gain [Chicago's] approval . . . We all behaved very badly," she later recalled.[72]

Ambivalence about change—on what terms and under what conditions—shaped many students' experiences of the program. The lines between assertiveness and aggression, between words being hurtful or helpful, blurred depending on how the encounter felt to those who participated in the frank talk. For Chicago, consciousness-raising and confrontation were ways that feminism changed women. "One of the first steps in a Feminist Art Program is to help women feel comfortable about being aggressive, ambitious, and directed."[73] Students now describe the experience quite differently. Green recalls it as "brutal, revelatory, a nightmare, an awakening, a shattering, revolutionary, sadistic and an invitation to be a different kind of person."[74]

Personal transformation and frank talk were dangerous freight to trade, and Chicago was often ambivalent about the processes she had initiated. During one particularly fraught consciousness-raising group on personal appearance, Chicago suggested that Cheryl Zurilgen relied on her waist-length blond hair to get favors from men. Over the next two days, Zurilgen, Shawnee Wollenman, and Nancy Youdelman each cut their long hair short.[75] A shaken Chicago called her friend Miriam Schapiro, who told her not to worry, that it was only hair and it would grow back.[76] Writing about the incident in her journal, Chicago recalls her own upset when she stopped wearing make-up and cut her hair short. "I experienced the sheer terror of facing the world with my plain face. Oh, what they do to us with these notions of 'pretty' and 'ugly' and how hard it is to let go of all of that and just be human."[77] Even as the artist believed that a feminist classroom enabled the professor to drop some of the pretense of leadership in the spirit of collective sisterhood, the reality of their unequal positions in the classroom granted Chicago greater authority and greater responsibility over what happened. She confessed to feeling anxious, overwhelmed, and terrified at times.[78]

Taxed by the psychological demands of personality reconstruction, Chicago determined at the end of the first semester that the group was ready to devote itself to making art. "I told them that henceforth I was going to relate to them almost entirely on the basis of work." Chicago decided it was time to "transfer the dependency of the group upon me to dependency upon the structure of the group itself." The students met this announcement with anger, "crying jags, depressions, and self-deprecating remarks," the artist later recalled.[79]

Chicago's decision, made unilaterally, appeared to mark a serious change in the dynamic she herself had put into play. The emphasis on "personality structure" and challenging deeply held beliefs about femininity, sexuality, and identity had bonded the group through the sheer intensity of the feelings it drew out. This announcement, delivered midstream it seemed to many, revealed Chicago's belief that the process of personality reconstruction was about making the students into better artists, not just empowered women. It abruptly shifted the confessional mode of talk on to new terrain, making the personal necessary to the art, and the art a recasting of the personal. The transition was bumpy.

Making Feminist Art

Lo and behold, it turned out that cunt art was political.

The unique artistic environment, rife with conflict and ambivalence, nevertheless generated a sense of freedom in students as they approached their art. The student art produced at the program did, in fact, startle many who came to see it. The Fresno group's exploration of the female body, specifically the vulva, took place in tandem with other women artists on the West Coast making "cunt art" and with the women's health movement.[80] Wilding recalled that the depictions of the female body in *Our Bodies, Ourselves* and the instructions for how to achieve orgasm led the group to examine "our own and other women's vulvas, vaginas, and cervixes, with mirrors and flashlights," and then "to depict—realistically, metaphorically, and poetically—what we saw and felt."[81] The body, dressed and undressed, moved from a whispered contraband in the art world to the center of feminist artistic production.

For her final project, Karen LeCocq built a vaginal space into which viewers entered. It consisted of a small room from which she hung 120 nylon threads from the ceiling with round plastic discs at the ends. She covered the floor with four-inch-thick polyurethane foam and cut a slit down the center wall that the viewer had to "slip through" to enter. In the four corners of the room she installed crimson fifteen-watt bulbs under the foam to "cast a warm rich glow." A small fan blew the hanging discs. In a 1971 paper explaining her project, LeCocq wrote, "The concept behind the soft, spongy foam coving the floor, the liquid movement on the ceiling and the push-in, expanding contracting entrance, all deal with my experience as a woman. I am allowing the viewer, in a sense, to enter inside me."[82]

For Nancy Youdelman, the program's open approach led her to explore the performative aspects of femininity through costumes.[83] She stocked a studio room with fabrics, accessories, and dresses found at local thrift shops for the group's performances.[84] With Dori Atlantis behind the camera, and FAP students as models, Youdelman produced a series of photographs such as *Kewpie Doll, High Society, Bride,* and *Victorian Whore* in 1971.[85] A second series of photographs titled *I Tried Everything* (1971) documented Youdelman's fourteen-day effort to enhance her breast size.[86] Dori Atlantis explored menstruation in *Legmenstr* (1971), a black-and-white photograph of a thin line of paint snaking its way down a woman's leg.[87] LeCocq's *Feather Cunt* (1971), a black pillow that encased a dark red vulva that was surrounded by bright pink feathers, combined materials for a vivid three-dimensional piece.[88] Faith Wilding's 1971 watercolors, *Womb, Menstrual,* and *Peach Cunt,* used color and shadow to make the vulva into art and move the body away from a literal object toward a site of potentiality.[89]

Performance pieces explored the experiences of occupying a female body from multiple perspectives. *A Menstrual Life* explored the intersection of personal, medical, and popular rituals. In unpublished staging notes for the performance, the audience enters a white room, where each member is handed a brown bag with the words "My Menstrual Life" stamped on it and containing a single sanitary napkin, a sanitary belt, and two safety pins. They take seats on pillows on the floor, where a sixteen-millimeter color film of a woman's body from waist to knee plays. The woman on the film goes through a series of familiar activities: "taking a bloody Tampax out, putting another one in, taking off a bloody sanitary napkin, attaching another one . . . douching, washing the vaginal area, spraying it with feminine hygiene spray, etc." When the film ends, an audiotape begins with a voice reciting slang terms for menstruation: "the curse, flying the red flag, the streak, on the rag, falling off the roof, etc." When the tape ends, a woman comes out and gives a medical presentation on menstruation, ending with the rhetorical question posed to the audience, "Isn't it nice to grow up and be a woman?" A second woman enters and reads "accounts of various folk cultures and their dealings with menstruation." The piece ends with a new tape of women speaking about their experiences with menstruation and a third woman reciting poetry or lyrical prose on the same topic.[90]

In one of the better-known performances of the Fresno program, Dori Atlantis, Susan Boude, Vanalyne Green, and Cay Lang collaborated in *The Cunt Cheerleaders*. Documentary footage captured the squad wearing pink and red satin costumes with "C.U.N.T." appliquéd to their shirts as they greeted New York radical feminist Ti-Grace Atkinson at the Fresno airport in 1970:

> Split beaver, split beaver,
> Lovely gooey cunts
> Split beaver, split beaver . . .
> We come more than once!
>
> Ladies on the toilet
> Open that door!
> You don't have to
> Hide yourselves anymore.
>
> Your cunt is a beauty,
> We know you always knew it,
> So if you feel like pissing
> Just squat right down and do it![91]

Atkinson looked miserably uncomfortable at this welcome.[92] Wilding recalls her muttering something about the women being "pretty ballsy," particularly when a cheer went up as a group of red-costumed Shriners exited the same plane.[93]

The Cunt Cheerleaders, whether seen as ridiculous or bold, surely helped secure among East Coast women the West Coast movement's reputation for "cunt art." Divides between East and West Coast feminists around the status of the female body as a marker of women's difference opened in these years. New York feminist Shulamith Firestone's radical pronouncement that moving all reproduction to laboratories would be the only way to truly liberate women from the oppression of bodily difference appeared in her 1970 manifesto, *The Dialectic of Sex*.[94] *The Cunt Cheerleaders* clearly represented a different approach, one that embraced the female body precisely for its difference from men's. According to Wilding, cunt art stood in for "the whole (desiring) body. Our investigative art began to show that there was a lot more to 'cunt' than met the eye, for lo and behold, it turned out that cunt art was political."[95] This kind of radical feminist essentialism claimed bodily difference as fundamental without seeing the body as inherently limiting for women's liberation.

Whether or not feminists agreed that cunt art was political, the Fresno program gained notoriety for it. Two important events took place in the spring of 1971 that testified both to the growth of the West Coast women's art movement and to the Fresno program's place in it. The first involved the coming together of two ambitious feminist artists—Chicago and Miriam Schapiro—who pushed each other to reimagine the place of women and gender in the art world, and the second, a conference, held at Fresno, that marked the formal "birth" of the feminist art movement in Southern California.

Shortly after the studio had been completed in the fall of 1970, Miriam Schapiro, a painter sixteen years Chicago's senior who held a position at the Art School at the California Institute of the Arts (CalArts), paid a visit and left impressed: "When I left [the Fresno studio visit] I began to think about my own teaching and the agony I felt most of the time, because I couldn't reach my students. . . . I was caught in a system that wasn't functional, that system contains the fixed role-playing of the student/teacher relationship. Most of the time it doesn't work because the teacher is not free to make real human demands on the student. Nor is the student aware that she can make the same demands on the teacher."

Schapiro and Chicago began to visit each other's studios regularly and to share their feelings of alienation and embattlement in the art scene. Schapiro explains that viewing each other's work "was the first time for each one of us to truly trust another woman artist and discuss openly what our work was all about."[96] Chicago records the relief she experienced in finding a peer in the older, more professionally established Schapiro: "I needed an older woman, a mother figure, I guess, who could support *my* desire to be independent in the same way I was providing that kind of support for my students. I also needed a female peer, something I had never had."[97]

Chicago and Schapiro worked together to consolidate an emergent network of women artists in Southern California. In doing so they came to see the importance for feminist artists to rethink the meaning of spaces—work spaces like studios and display spaces like galleries. Their new mindfulness to the authority certain spaces commanded built on a new understanding of the feminist classroom as a space of personal and artistic transformation. In the spring of 1971, Chicago and Schapiro launched a visiting tour of women's studios to see their work, much of which never appeared in traditional venues. The two were shocked to learn that, of the forty women they visited, most had no formal studio. These women artists "worked in their bedrooms or went to work on the dining room table after the husband and the children had left in the morning and worked there interrupted by chores, until the family returned at night."

As the two artists toured, it gradually occurred to them that rather than being deficient, these home studios represented an alternative model of art making. These were "authentic creative atmosphere(s)" where "art was indistinguishable from life" and where the artist did not require "the male trappings of scale, space, whiteness, and loneliness" to work. "What these women showed us was that we had paid a tremendous price for our own minimal glory. We had given up intimacy and coziness and craziness and wild, wild imagery in order to play like the men and find visibility." Seeing these women make art outside of traditional studios helped Chicago and Schapiro articulate a critique of the entrenched "male" values of the art world. Since much of women's art remained outside of formal art settings, it existed for its own sake, to be seen by friends and family in private spaces. For most of the art world, this disqualified it as serious art. According to Chicago and Schapiro, this distinctively female reality disqualified the art worlds' narrow criterion for inclusion. Women's art, they argued, required new ways of seeing that could appreciate the circumstances of its production and its connections to communities as well as "the strength, the power, and the creative energy of our femaleness."[98]

Schapiro and Chicago felt the wind of history against their backs. The synergy between feminism and women's art seemed to be more manifest with each passing week. Schapiro, who thought more institutionally than Chicago, understood the potential of her position as a faculty member and wife of the dean of the art school to help women artists get a toehold in the highly competitive art world. She suggested that Chicago move the program. Chicago agreed, but only if she could bring her Fresno students with her. In an astounding letter to the admissions committee at CalArts, Chicago explained why they had to come as a group: "We all have to begin together . . . because we're all we have and we have a big job before us. We must unearth the buried and half-hidden treasures of our cunts and bring them into the light and let them shine and dazzle and become Art. We must recover our history, rebuild our humanity, and reconstruct our community."[99] For Chicago, the winds of history blew at a full-force gale. Women's bodies, women's art, women's history, women's communities—any term could stand in for the other—but together, they constituted the making of a new social reality. Such optimism, not unique to Chicago or the FAP but characteristic of the feminist moment, was intoxicating.

The second notable event in the unfolding of the West Coast feminist art movement took place in the late spring of 1971, when Chicago and her Fresno students took the unusual step of inviting women artists from the region to see their work and tour their studio. Approximately seventy-five women artists from Los Angeles and San Francisco came to see what had been going on. Paintings and prints tended toward images of vulvas and dark spaces, "cunt art," while performance pieces explored social roles and socialization. The students performed *The Rivalry Play*, where two women, one fat and one rich, meet at a bus stop and start a fight, "each trying to overcome the other in an age-old feud between women who fight each other because they cannot fight their real oppressor." A second piece involved a "(fe)male" butcher and a woman whom he connects to a milking machine that extracts blood from her, while an audiotape plays the sounds of a slaughterhouse, representing "women's brutalization." The group also screened student films such as *Steak Film* and *Bathtub Film*, which show women eating and bathing "apart from any relation with men."[100]

In her memoir, Chicago describes the event as consolidating what the Fresno group had accomplished: "The weekend was filed with identification, laughter, tears and warmth. I cried, feeling that the weekend had somehow changed the meaning of the year. Now what we were doing was out in the open. . . . It was like being at the moment of birth, the birth of a new kind of community of women, a new kind of art made by women."[101] Wilding also uses metaphors of birth to describe the experience, explaining that the gathering was the first time many of these artists had seen art that so "openly exposed the female experience." It was a moving and portentous event. "That weekend, in tears, laughter and night-long discussions, the west coast women's art movement was born. It was also the end of the Program as it had been, hidden and private in Fresno, away from the stress and pressures and male standards of the art world."[102]

CalArts

Urging young women artists to make extraordinary demands on themselves is hazardous.

Chicago and nine of her students moved to Los Angeles with high hopes. CalArts had much to offer all of them. Chicago would have feminist peers among the faculty with Sheila de Bretteville, who headed up the newly formed Feminist Design Program; Paula Harper, who taught women's art history; and Miriam "Mimi" Schapiro, who with Chicago would codirect the new Feminist Art Program.[103] Women's studies burst open at CalArts as Chicago and her students arrived, with courses being offered across the curriculum. Lacy recalled, "There was a massive amount of feminist consciousness and activity there."[104] CalArts put material resources into their new art and design programs, offering generous funds for equipment, studios, and materials.

Word of the new FAP program spread through feminist networks. Potential applicants wrote to Chicago throughout the late spring and summer, asking for information. Many of these queries testified to the sexism women faced in art schools. One wrote, "I am leaving undergraduate school filled with resentment. I resent the dishonesty, the fear, the inanity and the sexism my professors have laid on me. They have all spoken well of my work when forced to (to my face), but have never encouraged or helped me in any way." She wanted an environment that allowed her more leeway. "My art is the product of my experience and conditionings. Giant paintings of stripes and restful nude women have nothing to do with my life."[105] A freshman at Bard College explained that she had become "totally disillusioned with the educational system and its sexism; especially in the art department . . . I feel my identify as a woman should come through in my paintings. Studying under men at Bard does not allow for this."[106] Chicago and Schapiro enrolled twenty-three female students.

The FAP at CalArts re-created the elements of feminist art education set out in Fresno: a heavy reading load of feminist theory, time in area libraries to do research into the history of women artists, consciousness-raising and rap groups, critiques of student art, and a substantial studio requirement. This time around, the group of students did not start from the same level of unknowing: nine of the twenty-three students had already had a year of feminist art process under their belts, knew Chicago and her techniques, and had lived through the shifting dynamics of authority in the feminist classroom. As with Fresno, the group faced the prospect of not having an adequate space as the school year began in the fall of 1971. At the suggestion of Paula Harper, an art historian at CalArts, the group decided to combine their literal problem of where to house the program with an experimental group project designed to highlight the ideological and symbolic conflation of women and homes. The end result was *Womanhouse*, an art installation built by FAP students in an abandoned house just off campus on a residential street in Hollywood.

Schapiro explained the ideas behind *Womanhouse*, most centrally the importance of women's lived experiences to feminist art: "We asked ourselves what it would be like to work out one of our closest associative memories—the home. Our home, which we as a culture of women have been identified with for centuries, has always been the area where we nourished and were nourished. What would happen, we asked, if we created a home in which we pleased no one but ourselves?"[107] Chicago sounded a similar note. "Women had been embedded in houses for centuries and had quilted, sewed, baked, cooked, decorated, and nested their creative energies away." What would happen if, she asked, if "the same activities women had used in life be transformed into the means of making art?"[108] Ironically, as it turned out, before the students could explore the "female arts" of homemaking, they would have to engage the "male arts" of home repair and construction.

As in the Fresno program, practicing feminist transformation figured centrally in the experience. Wilding, who transferred to CalArts, explained that reconstructing the house would "force the students to begin pushing their role limitations as women and to test themselves as artists."[109] Right from the start, however, the students faced challenges far more daunting than those in Fresno. The house, miles from campus and far off city bus lines, was in poor shape. It had been unoccupied for twenty years and repeatedly vandalized.[110] It required a host of repairs, from glazing windows to sanding floors, rebuilding walls, and painting. The group had leased the house for a mere three months. The repairs had to be done in a matter of weeks. The space was cold, without working heating or plumbing and with many broken windows. The students took to eating all their meals at a nearby restaurant so they could use its bathroom. Fixing the space to a workable state required the students and their teachers to learn not only how to problem solve as a group but also how to enact their solutions. The house on 533 North Mariposa made the simple act of hanging a wall, as done in Fresno, seem like child's play.

Readying the house for use was a grueling job, requiring long days, blistered hands, and tough skins, literally and metaphorically. For the women transferring from Fresno, working on *Womanhouse* must have felt eerily familiar, a case of "déjà vu all over again" if ever there was one. New students to the FAP referred to the weeks of repair as "feminist art boot camp."[111] Many of the students grappled in painful ways with their sense of not knowing how to repair a window or fix a toilet, and their resentment and fear at the tasks became both a major feeder for conflict in the group as well as a personally transformative experience. For weeks, the group moved between confrontational consciousness-raising sessions and long hours with power tools. Many confronted the task before them with a mix of shock and dismay over what they had gotten themselves into. Chicago and Schapiro put a distinctly feminist pedagogical spin to the experience. Schapiro minimized the uncomfortable feelings of panic and resentment in an interview she gave to *Art Journal* in 1972. She dryly noted that "The art of (window) glazing was unknown to both Judy and myself." She also downplayed their dependence on men to help them: "Working out of our circular methods, it was discovered that one of the girls' fathers owned a hardware store and was willing to teach the women to install windows. So while a crew went out to buy paint in order to paint the entire house, . . . another crew traveled 40 miles to the hardware store to get the special instruction they needed. A plus out of this experience came when the father donated the glass."[112]

Whether glazing windows was an "art" or a cruel joke lay in the eye of the beholder. While FAP students repaired twenty-five broken windows and used fifty gallons of white paint, they listened to their instructors dismiss their anger and discomfort with a feminist narrative of personal growth. Chicago explained to them that as a group women neither had experience in pushing themselves hard nor the tolerance for the frustration and fatigue of doing demanding tasks. She wanted to instill in her students the value of laborious struggle, and the message that the amount of hard work invested in the piece was proof of one's passion.[113] At the same time, she believed female art students were at a genuine disadvantage to their male peers by the simple fact of women's ignorance about how to build things and how to approach large material problems.

Some students enjoyed the challenge of home repair. LeCocq found the manual labor on "the deconstruction crew" to be liberating and approached it as performance art. "Armed with crow bars and sledge hammers, we would attack walls and anything else that was in the way of the project. . . . Dressed in Levi's, a blue work shirt and work boots and carrying my tools, I felt all this power and freedom, what I imagined it must feel like to be a man."[114] Other students felt that doing manual work because men did it ought not be the point of a feminist art program. Some thought that the value put on manual work indicated that male values had infiltrated the program. Mira Schor wrote to a friend in 1971 suggesting that Chicago's idea of female empowerment was modeled on men: "She goes too far I think and really wants women to pick up some of the worse characteristics of men, the inhuman driving of oneself beyond one's limits, etc."[115]

Anger and resentment boiled up at the seemingly endless work the students faced, and accusations that Chicago was on a "power trip" surfaced. Such critiques of her as power hungry and exploitative became embedded in Chicago's feminist reputation for years afterward. Once the house "deconstruction" got underway in earnest, LeCocq recalled, "a general uprising of the women in the program against 'the rule' of Judy and Mimi" broke out.[116] Schor was one of its leaders. She resented the workload, felt disempowered by the group dynamics, and was exhausted from her conflicts with Chicago. She had not been a member of the Fresno program and had hoped that joining the FAP would allow her to focus on making her own art, and was not happy, as she saw it, to remake her personality along the lines suggested by her charismatic teacher: "She's a tough, loud, aggressive, messianic, and insecure woman who demands attention and attracts negative feelings from a lot of people. . . . She wants us to give ourselves to her totally and she will lead us to the promised land of independent women artists. But I cannot give my life over to anyone."[117]

The divides between the Fresno and new FAP students broke down as experienced students joined with their new peers to challenge Chicago's authority. Chicago pushed back against student complaints by arguing that the women ought not to be angry with her and Mimi but at "a society that had never demanded that they push beyond their limits, that they reach their potential, that they achieve something." In a strategic reversal, Chicago told the students that their complaints were expressions of their internalized sexism, that they were unconscious manifestations of their difficulty dealing with female authority figures. "Many women have internalized male attitudes and are afraid of women of ambition or strength, seeing them as monsters."[118]

Chicago's response neatly placed her students in a classic double bind, one that haunted feminist groups across the country in the early 1970s and centered on the meaning of equality. The goal of women's equality animated feminism since its inception, even as women active in the movement's "first wave" could not agree on the meaning of women's equality any more than their counterparts fifty years later. Equality for first-wave feminists in the 1910s and 1920s meant neither "similarity to" nor "segregation from" men. Rather, it was about elevating women to positions where their voices had weight equal to those of men.[119]

Chicago's students, active in a different moment of feminism, measured equality through the relationships between women as much as through relationships between men and women. Equality in women-only groups idealized a notion of sisterhood stripped of rank and hierarchy. It was gender communalism, a world of sisters (not mothers) who collectively exercised power and control, liberating all their voices from the tyranny of hierarchy and history. Ideally, this view of sisterhood stripped of rank was a way to move past unavoidable differences in education, confidence, and privilege among women. In theory, if everyone had an equal voice, then no one was silenced. In practice, not every woman felt that her voice was heard, much less valued. Infamously, sisterly communalism made consensus a matter of endurance. Critics referred to this as the "tyranny of structurelessness," encapsulating the chaos and boredom bred of "leaderless" groups.[120]

Chicago wrote about the limits of "family" as a trope for theorizing power among women in the FAP group: "The ways the women had of dealing with us grew out of the parent-child relationship. Either they were children and we were the parents—that is, they were powerless and subject to our control and we were powerful and almighty, or we were all the same, that is siblings. This confusion indicates the level of development at which many women remain because they are always treated either as dependent children or as mothers." According to Chicago, equality was a feminist ideal based in shared humanity, but "in reference to talents, abilities, and achievements, not everyone is equal."[121] In this case, the students' complaints of overwork were met not with a collective rethinking of the schedule for repairs as it might in a truly collective group, but with nods to their sexist upbringings and their poor work habits.

Simply put, Chicago and Schapiro understood what they were doing in the classroom differently than did their students. Rather than establishing nonhierarchical equality as the feminist praxis, they saw themselves as readying their students for a world that required more rigorous and less sexist training for them to succeed. Schapiro explains that they did not "legislate what might be fit subject matter for them" but "urg[ed] them on at every turn of the way to do what ever it was they did best" and in that way, did not belittle or control them. But ultimately, she warns, "urging young women artists to make extraordinary demands on themselves is hazardous."[122] Ties that bind can also cut.

Chicago took the "uprising" more personally than did Schapiro. She found the students' discontentment painful, particularly when the Fresno women joined in. She had given them so much, she mused, but their need to symbolically behead her was part of the process. "At some point in the process, after the initial gratitude for the help, many women turn against this figure who has helped them. . . . Only by understanding this [dynamic of female growth] can we who are offering leadership protect ourselves against the terrible hurt of having a woman you've helped reward you with hate instead of love."[123]

The radical feminist teaching methods employed by Chicago and the FAP resulted in a hotbed of mixed feelings. On the one hand, Chicago practiced some of the most powerful tenets of second-wave feminism: personal responsibility, agency, and self-importance. Students had to be willing to work hard, learn new skills, and sacrifice because art making was not for the faint of heart. More ambitiously, she encouraged each student to delve into her past through consciousness-raising for experiences that shaped her. Through discussion with other women, that material would then be transformed into "content" for a new kind of art, a woman-centered art that would illuminate the experiences of being a woman. In her feminist classrooms, Chicago subordinated artistic technique to content. The techniques for how to render an artistic vision could be learned as needed. But content shaped the art and defined the artist.

This message of hard work and discipline came into conflict with other elements of feminism in Chicago's classroom. The ideal of sisterly equality and speech as a performance of identity, other powerful tenets of second-wave feminism, meant that a woman spoke her truth, and in doing so in the company of like-minded women, she became empowered. Empowered women set their own course. They did not have to glaze twenty-five windows for two months in a cold house in Hollywood if they did not want to. And what, after all, did home repair have to do with making women-centered art? The students, empowered by the process of feminist education, at times railed against the hard work and long hours demanded to bring the project to completion. They pushed hard against their instructors and when they were met with hard limits, they grumbled but ultimately did their work. The house was repaired and ready to be made into art.

The processes of radical feminist education invoked and handled, effectively or not, were multifaceted and complicated. They were material and at times literal (as in building a room, negotiating rides, meeting for groups). They were also psychological and thus deeply personal (raising one's consciousness, defining one's art, confronting one's limits). And the processes took place simultaneously—repairing the house and at the same time raising their own and the group's consciousness; wanting to please their teachers and wanting to be set free of others' standards; wanting to be an artist of note and wanting to be a good sister. Looking back on the difficult and overlapping processes, many of the students discovered that they had gotten much out of repairing the house and the (often contrary) practice of feminism. But the time for assessment would come later. For now, it was time to show the world all they had done.

CHAPTER TWO

Making Feminist Art

Womanhouse *and the Feminist Art Movement, 1972–1974*

THE HOUSE ON 533 NORTH MARIPOSA in Hollywood, California, opened on January 23, 1972. The weeks leading up to the opening of *Womanhouse* were intense as the twenty-three students enrolled in the Feminist Art Program (FAP) at CalArts worked countless hours on the rooms each had designed, either alone or in collaboration. The seventeen rooms had been plastered, sanded, painted, and illuminated. Windows and doors had been repaired, toilets cleared, gardens emptied of trash, steps rebuilt. Now, for one month, the public could walk through their feminist art environment and see for themselves what the group had accomplished.

The months of struggle leading up to the opening of *Womanhouse* had been painful and productive. Pushed beyond their own sense of what they were capable of by their instructors, students nevertheless did not let fatigue and resentment stop them from accomplishing a major artistic feat. *Womanhouse* was an early example of site-specific art, a work attached to a physical place or space.[1] What made this piece particularly innovative was the harnessing of art to radical feminist critiques of women's socialization. The opening of *Womanhouse*, and the year and a half of feminist art education that proceeded it, symbolized the growing force of a new feminist art movement.

The timing was pitch-perfect. Out of the stew of art and activism, a new tactic for challenging the art world emerged in West Coast feminist networks and spread outward: that of establishing a woman-centered or "gynocentric" aesthetics, suggesting a distinctive female creative identity. The additional focus on "women's art," not only art made by women, encouraged Chicago's students to express themselves in ways they hadn't before and, importantly, encouraged audiences, art historians, and critics to turn their attention to what had all the markings of an important new trend.[2] All of these factors—art made by women, "gynocentric art," and interest from the art press—converged as *Womanhouse* opened.

Feminism in the Key of Domesticity

Kinder, Kuche, Kirche.

As the students readied *Womanhouse*, they joined an ongoing feminist critique of domesticity and the roles of wife and daughter unfolding in glossy magazines, popular books, and scholarly articles. Betty Friedan's *The Feminine Mystique*, published in 1963, had examined in detail the ideology of Cold War–era gender roles and their implications for women. For her, the home represented a dressed-up internment camp, a US version of the Nazi imperative "Kinder, Kuche, Kirche." Judy Syfers declared that she too wanted a wife to cook and clean up for her so she would not have to be burdened by the endless and thankless tasks of wifehood. Pat Mainardi framed housework as "political" in an essay published in the widely circulated 1970 anthology, *Sisterhood Is Powerful*.[3] FAP students too had read a range of writing on women's social role, from Simone de Beauvoir's *The Second Sex*, to more radical writing by Valerie Solanas, Ti-Grace Atkinson, and Shulamith Firestone. The message of much of the early feminist writing, coming on the heels of the national Cold War–era celebration of motherhood, stressed it as confining. Not all feminists in the early 1970s rejected motherhood, but many felt the near-mandatory requirement that all "healthy and mature" women mother had to be challenged for women to create opportunities for themselves beyond marriage and the family.[4]

FAP students' choice to make art out of the home, or the home into art, reflected the importance of overturning domesticity in mid-twentieth-century radical feminist theory by white women. Women's reproductive capacities had been so chronically conflated with housework that the issue of domesticity had become, by 1971, a central staging ground for feminist attempts to distinguish cultural meaning of femininity from biology. At the same time, not all feminists viewed the home as a site of oppression. For many wage-earning women and women of color, the home functioned in more complex ways as a site of resistance to oppression as well as a place that problematically nurtured gender roles.[5] Neither did all feminists view motherhood as oppressive. Given the youthfulness of the FAP group, they had yet to have or to mother children.[6] In 1971 they stood at the cusp of becoming wives or mothers (as well as wage earners), unless they managed to extricate themselves from those destinies. It was that destiny, packed full of unacknowledged privileges and assumptions, that *Womanhouse* hoped to disrupt both by exposing the oppressiveness of domesticity and by establishing the women as serious artists. Nowhere in *Womanhouse* were the home and domesticity examined from the perspective that many women had the desire to have and raise children.

Students worked in a rich array of genres that included sculpture, performance, painting, weaving, and ordinary objects made strange. Materials varied from room to room, as did colors, textures, and mood, but the message did not: the tight weave between *woman* and *home* was oppressive. For example, *Nightmare Bathroom* displayed a fragile sand sculpture of a woman in the bathtub, body submerged, head and knees exposed, exuding "a sense of vulnerability."[7] In another room a crocheted web hung from the walls, "linked in form and feeling with those primitive womb shelters." Other rooms obsessively displayed the objects that fill women's lives (bras, lipstick, high heels, aprons), while others played with the oppressiveness of confining roles and miniature lives. *Dollhouse Room* by Mimi Schapiro and Sheri Brody offered a small, well-ordered dollhouse that had "real and imagined creatures" infiltrating it, undermining and unsettling the sense of safety and security typically invoked by a dollhouse; and the gardens by Chris Rush in the back yard of *Womanhouse* invoked a bad acid trip.[8] In exploring the meaning of the home through a wide array of materials and techniques, the students materialized a central preoccupation of second wave feminism in the 1970s: the social and psychological intersection of femininity with domesticity. According to feminist art historian and LA activist Arlene Raven, "Entirely new aesthetic subjects that had until then remained in the distant shadows in suburban American homes burst into the public sphere through the installation and performance art of *Womanhouse*."[9]

Visitors to *Womanhouse* entered an environment designed to transport them into a topsy-turvy world where the comforts of home became the source of oppression to "the angel of the house," in the words of Virginia Woolf, an author read by FAP students. A visitor, who entered the house by the wide front steps of the old Victorian mansion, would walk into a space where the female body was tangibly conflated with the roles and duties of the home. The kitchen, the bedroom, the bathroom, the closet were rendered into extreme exposes of the violence, psychologically if not actually, done by roles to women. As the imagined visitor moved into the foyer, she could look up the grand staircase to see a bride, with flowing veils and lacy gown, literally embedded in the wall. In *Bridal Staircase*, Kathy Huberland captured "the bride's failure to look clearly where she is going."[10]

The visitor might move to the kitchen, a room done collaboratively by Robin Weltsch, Vicki Hodgett, and Susan Frazier (*The Kitchen*, *Egg to Breasts*, and *Aprons in the Kitchen*). Earlier in the process, as they began to plan their room, the group had difficulty imagining what sort of kitchen they wanted to build. Schapiro suggested a consciousness-raising session about their feelings about kitchens from their childhood. They focused on the kitchen as a psychological war zone between themselves and their mothers over the giving and receiving of food. When Schapiro reflected on the process, she wrote from the vantage point of the mother. The kitchen "was an arena where ostensibly the horn of plenty overflowed, but where in actuality the mother was acting out her bitterness over being imprisoned in a situation from which she could not bring herself to escape, and from which society would not encourage such an escape."[11] The students also wrote about the process, but not as mothers. They focused on the kitchen as a place of negotiation with the powerful mother. Hodgetts explained the group process.

> We had a consciousness-raising session on kitchens. Some people saw kitchens as fulsome, warm, nurturing. Others saw kitchens as dangerous with hot stoves and sharp knives ("Viciousness in the kitchen—the potatoes hiss"). I had a fleeting image of fried eggs stenciled over everything—walls, ceiling, floor—and some people saw breasts. Breasts were nurturing—kitchens were the extension of mothers' milk. I felt a little railroaded. I still wanted eggs. And then Robin said, "Why not have a transformation from eggs to breasts," and we were all delighted. And that's very important, because although I was the one who finally carried through that aspect of the kitchen (in the main) the idea was really a collective one. It simply would never have existed if women had not tried to work together.[12]

The group painted the kitchen—every piece of it—"a store bought pink," from the walls, ceilings, and floor to the toaster, sink, and stove. They papered drawers with collages of distant places, signifying the longing of the mother to escape and the daughter to dream past the confines of the room. Walls textured with fried eggs that morphed into breasts as they moved up the wall amplified the impact of the cloying uniform color pink.

Schapiro explained: "On the ceiling and walls, fried eggs were attached which transform themselves into breasts as they travel down the walls. Five molds were made from clay showing this transformation, and they were created in a spongy material and painted realistically. The reality of the woman's condition that is epitomized by this kitchen, coupled with a consistently high level of quality art-making, makes the experience of walking into our nurturing center breathtaking."[13] The conflation of the color pink with women quite literally whitewashed the room, a powerful testimony to the group's inability to think about women of color. Many young white Americans at the time embraced a liberal notion of color-blindness as an effective tool for antiracist action; to paint the kitchen white, tan, or brown—anything but baby-dress pink—would signify race, not gender. FAP students adopted such a stance for *Womanhouse*. For them, the breast, be it brown or pink, was the universal referent signifying womanhood, and as such the feature that they believed had the most significance. Pink stood in for the heterosexual matrix of female bodies, reproductive sexuality, and normative femininity they critiqued throughout the installation. This kind of feminism, circa 1972, prioritized gender while leaving other pressing categories like race and sexuality problematically unexplored.

The final part of the kitchen trilogy further underscored the kitchen-as-womb symbolism. Susan Frazier's *Aprons in the Kitchen* occupied a butler's pantry—narrow and long—lined with cabinets overhanging a counter. Five aprons hung on the wall, each one pillowed with a female body part: one with pockets made into breasts, another with large lips running the full length of the skirt. Frazier's catalog entry, done in stream of consciousness, captured the woman's ambivalence at being both a symbol and server: "I must work harder to sustain life for you, to meet your biological needs, feed your habits with habits . . . I am a habit to you! I am not a habit! Release me, let me go, you don't know me, you don't own me. I am a human being, not just a source of cheap labor for lazy people. I want to undo these apron strings, to see what the rest of the world is doing, to see if I can help . . . to see myself once again."[14]

The visitor might follow the journey of the food from the kitchen to the dining room. Created by seven women, including Karen LeCocq, Faith Wilding, and Mimi Schapiro, it was the most collaborative of *Womanhouse*. The large table, built by the students, dominated the space, its place settings crowded by an assortment of food sculptures. Using photographs from cookbooks, the artists made bread-dough sculptures of ham, a turkey, "an irresistible pecan pie," and a salad bowl with overflowing lettuce. The catalog explained, "The vinyl glasses and wine bottle on the table were all leaning on each other, in sensuous contact as though drunk on their own crystalline beauty."[15] Over the table hung a large homemade vinyl chandelier that LeCocq had wired herself. The floor sported a stenciled rug, the windows lemon-yellow curtains, and the back wall a mural of "sensuously painted" peaches, watermelon, freshly baked bread, eggs, and a vase of flowers.

Climbing up the stairs and passing the bride who was "encased in gaiety, in lace, in flowers, in dreamy sky blue" and intended to stress the view of marriage as "eternal protected bliss," the visitor might find herself in one of three bathrooms. Chicago's *Menstruation Bathroom* became notorious for being one of the more confrontational rooms in the house. This bathroom emphasized women's monthly periods as moments when, in the words of art historian Arlene Raven, "signs of womanhood appear and must be hidden behind a locked bathroom door." The room, painted pristine white, displayed feminine hygiene products neatly lined up in their carefully double-wrapped boxes on the shelves. The whiteness of the room made the impact of the overflowing trash basket filled with bloody sanitary products all the more powerful. In the bathroom, blood and "woman" represent each other, but instead of pride, women feel shame. Chicago described her room as "very, very white and clean and deodorized—deodorized except for the blood, the only thing that cannot be covered up. However we feel about our own menstruation is how we feel about seeing its image in front of us."[16] *Menstruation Bathroom* recalled the artist's earlier work, a photolithograph titled *Red Flag*, of a woman pulling a bloody tampon from her vagina. "That's a big mess," reported one man for a 1972 film of *Womanhouse*. "I don't understand it. Is it supposed to be funny?"

In addition to *Menstruation Bathroom* and *Nightmare Bathroom*, *Lipstick Bathroom* by Camille Grey emphasized the performance of a commodified femininity enacted through makeup. Everything in this room had been painted red, from the stockings, bras, and panties that hung from racks to the walls, floor, ceiling, towels, mirror, and its surrounding lightbulbs. A wall of two hundred lipsticks drew the viewer into the relentless ritual of face painting. The overall effect alternated between claustrophobia and horror.[17]

The theme of objects that obsessively represent "woman" continued in a series of closets on the second floor. *Shoe Closet* by Beth Bachenheimerm filled a narrow space with three shelves and displayed approximately forty pairs of women's shoes, each individually treated. For example, a pair of stilettos or "spike" heels "is decorated with real spikes, driven all around the bottom of the shoe."[18] *Linen Closet*, by Sandy Orgel, embedded a female mannequin in a narrow closet stacked with sheets. One viewer quipped when she passed it, "Exactly where women have always been—in between the sheets and on the shelf." In the catalog, the artist reminded her visitors that, "It is time now to come out of the closet."[19] The mannequin literally was on her way out, with one long leg stepping down over the drawers toward the floor.

People touring the house could move through three bedrooms on the second floor. Shawnee Wollenmann furnished *The Nursery* with oversized child toys, including a rocking horse and rag dolls, and clearly intended to make the viewer see through the eyes of a child. Another, by Jan Lester and titled *Personal Space*, might have been the room of an older occupant, perhaps a sloppy teenager. Littered with clothes strewn about and an unkempt bed, the room opened into a "secret room." Lester explained that she realized that "the inner room represented the art that never gets made, the richness that most people, especially women, keep locked inside themselves."[20] The master bedroom, *Lea's Room*, completed the bedroom trilogy. Done collaboratively by Nancy Youdelman and Karen LeCocq, it included a performance piece based on *Cheri* by French novelist Colette. The conventional bedroom was intended to be one of "lush beauty and suffocating oppression." Dominated by a double bed and a crowded dressing table, the watermelon-pink room was adorned with lacy curtains and surfaces covered in lacy doilies, the bed with a satin bedspread and pillows. LeCocq and Youdelman had arranged for an antique dealer to lend them the Victorian-era ornate wooden furniture for the duration of the show. At the dresser, an aging courtesan desperately tried to "save her fading beauty" by applying layer upon layer of makeup, removing it, and starting over again.[21]

Visitors could opt to leave the mansion through a garden installation by Chris Rush titled *Necco Wafers*. Designed to be utterly unconnected to the natural world, Rush painted the ground turquoise, pink, blue, pale green, yellow, and lavender. "I wanted the ground to sort of float in the garden and seem unreal." Artificial clouds, done in a style the artist may have done as a child, added to the fanciful garden.[22] It was motivated, reported Mimi Schapiro, by the artist's fear of crocodiles and her "animal terror."[23]

Actual viewers engaged with the art of *Womanhouse* in many ways, touring the house in their own time and following their interests. The students did not hand out maps or advise viewers in what order to move through the rooms. Part of the force of the house was the sense of surprise as a person moved through it. More than a gallery or a museum, the environment of *Womanhouse* was completely saturated, the art not contained as an object set apart from the viewer on a wall or pedestal but in the surrounding atmosphere. When people stepped into *Womanhouse*, the world they entered offered a psychologically rich and visually textured view of the meaning of mothers and home for daughters of all ages.

Performing Feminism

> A cock means you don't wash dishes. You have a cunt. A cunt means you wash dishes.

The performance pieces that ran every night represent another important expression of the feminism of *Womanhouse*. Artist Suzanne Lacy recalled how the group assembled at Fresno and later at CalArts moved into performance art. Chicago assigned her students to feel their way into provocative situations by posing questions like, "How do you feel when you're walking down the street with men leering at you?" and into emotional states, like rage, their feelings about mothers or about other women. Lacy recalled that "People turned to performance almost intuitively. It wasn't as 'sophisticated' as some of the conceptual performance works at the time. For the most part, we didn't know anything about that work and I don't think Judy knew a lot about it either. We were doing what I'd call skits. She intentionally steered us away from anything that was conceptual, that was removed from a direct engagement with our feelings. We made art of our experience."[24] In her memoir, Chicago explains that performance offered the women of *Womanhouse* a direct way to access and express their anger at a world that restricted them. According to Chicago, men expressed anger directly if not always appropriately and at times with dangerous consequences. But women, she argues, "were not allowed physical expression of anger," and had few socially accepted outlets to express anger directly. "Women prohibited from the direct expression of anger, are thereby also denied the creative aspects of anger." Performance proved an important release for "debilitating, unexpressed anger" of the students as they processed a new political understanding of their own consciousnesses and social roles. "Once in an environment that accepted the expression of anger as natural, women found it quite easy to release their rage symbolically, through performances."[25] The "skits" at *Womanhouse* were early expressions of what would become a vibrant movement of feminist performance art installations.[26]

The living room constituted the house's main performance space. Audiences sat on the floor in the large room, often crowding the performers, who stood inches away from them. These theatrical events took place in the evening, when the number of visitors peaked. Some pieces were set apart from the flow of the house and, as such, became organizing events, with people stopping their tour to grab a seat as the show started. Other "skits" ran continuously. Two silent "maintenance" pieces examined the theme of women's unseen housework. One involved a woman dressed in a housecoat who sets up an ironing board and irons a sheet; a second featured a woman with a bucket who scrubs the floor. A third ongoing silent piece took place, as already mentioned, in *Lea's Room*, with Karen LeCocq playing the aging courtesan. These silent performances nevertheless packed a punch. The woman endlessly ironing or endlessly applying make-up testified to the wasted time women devoted to tasks that ultimately signified little. They appeared as empty tasks for an empty life.

Three fully developed pieces embodied the didactic style of performance feminism at *Womanhouse*: *Cunt and Cock*, *Waiting*, and *Birth Trilogy*. Each took up themes central to early feminist theory: sex roles, pathological femininity, and the power of women's bodily difference. Each had obvious designs on their audiences, intended to bring the viewer through a series of feminist insights. The shock effects of the performances came in part from the baldness of the feminism expressed.

The context of unexamined sexism in the early 1970s is lost to contemporary readers, making it difficult for those who did not live through those years to appreciate the amount of effort early second-wave feminists devoted to make it visible. Readers today often see pieces like *Cunt and Cock* and *Birth Trilogy* as embarrassing, oversimplified, and melodramatic; they criticize such displays for using the blunt force of a sledge hammer where a well-placed poke might not only work just as well but better suit readers living in an age that prefers its feminism to be playful.[27] *Cunt and Cock* in particular is anything but light and easy. Its initial silliness quickly vanishes as the division of labor at home between a man and a woman takes on life-and-death dimensions as the man sees just how threatening a liberated woman is to the psychological infrastructure of heterosexual marriage.

Chicago wrote *Cunt and Cock* in 1970 when teaching at Fresno. She used it as a consciousness-raising piece, but it soon evolved into a fully scripted play. Two women, Faith Wilding and Jan Lester, appear on stage dressed in black leotards. The SHE character's costume features a gigantic pink vagina and the HE's, a satiny oversized penis. SHE speaks in a high squeaky voice and waves her hands near her face; HE speaks at a low pitch and struts around the stage, often lovingly cupping his penis. The action begins when SHE asks HE to help her wash the dishes. Outraged, HE retorts, "A cock means you don't wash dishes. You have a cunt. A cunt means you wash dishes." SHE answers that she doesn't see that rule written anywhere on her body. Getting angry, HE yells, "Stu-pid, your cunt/pussy/gash/hole or whatever it is, is round like a dish. Therefore it's only right for you to wash dishes. My cock is long and hard and straight and meant to shoot like guns, or missiles. Anyone can see that." HE becomes aroused from singing the praises of what his penis can do, and the two begin to have sex, at his urging. "Speaking of shooting, I need to shoot—off, that is, you know—I *have* to; I *have* to; you know; *come*, that is. I *have* to no matter what—*I have to come!*" The slippery slope from housework to sex, from social power to sexual power, is exposed, and along with it the interpenetration, so to speak, of the arenas society artificially divides into public and private realities. After the two copulate, SHE says she wishes she could have an orgasm, too. HE flips out, accuses SHE of wanting to castrate him, and proceeds to attack SHE. Chicago's stage notes explain, "As they run, they knock dishes off the sink, pull bedding off bed until SHE sinks to her knees in a pile of bedding. HE keeps beating her fiercely until SHE slumps and dies, lying straight out with the bedding twisted around her."[28]

Rejecting all subtlety and lacking any of the whimsy that the art of *Womanhouse* invoked, the play nonetheless underscores a dominant strand of early feminist thought in its view of gender roles as psychological prisons, with men invested in their power simply because they have it. In this drama, women are imprisoned by their habituated acceptance of the mythical-biological difference that was supposed to explain their lack of power and lack of interest in power. The play awkwardly gropes toward making the body social by the plastic genitals and their obvious artificiality when placed on two similar, or same-sexed, bodies.

The piece worked effectively as a consciousness-raising exercise in both feminist art programs and on Chicago's visits to women's studies classes around the country. On such visits, Chicago divided the group into two subgroups; each group would play the part of HE or SHE, and then alternate. Afterward, the groups would gather to discuss the experience. "Usually the problems that developed in the process of performing the piece indicate the difficulties women have in being assertive, their own sexuality, being used by men, sharing housework." At *Womanhouse*, audience reactions to the play alternated between shock and fascination. According to Chicago, the impact came from "bringing the private into public view." Change could only happen when "women bring the deepest level of psychic reality of the bedroom, and in this case, onto the stage, where culture itself can be confronted, rather than a single male representative of that culture, as in heterosexual relationships where one woman struggles with one man."[29] In the words of Arlene Raven, "the play leaves no doubt in the minds of its audience that the personal and cultural uses to which biological differences have been put have had dire, indeed mortal consequences for women."[30]

Waiting, by Faith Wilding, takes up normative femininity as well but addresses it as a kind of psychological illness. In this piece, Wilding takes a seat onstage, wearing a simple long dress with her hair parted neatly down the middle and pulled into a bun. With her hands in her lap, she begins to rock. As she rocks, she starts a monotone litany of all the ways she has waited. Raven, who watched the opening, later described Wilding as exemplifying "the consciousness-raising effort of the women's movement of the time—breaking silence by speaking, and thus revealing women's bitterness as a chorus of single voices."[31] It is not clear if the woman rocks to soothe herself from the agony of waiting or to hold back the fury she keeps inside.

The piece starts at childhood: "Waiting for someone to hold me; waiting for someone to feed me; waiting for someone to change my diaper . . . waiting for Mommy to brush my hair . . . waiting to be pretty; waiting to sit on Daddy's lap. . . . Waiting to stay up until seven o'clock; waiting to be a big girl." The waiting moves to adolescence, where she waits to menstruate, to wear a bra, to have a first date. She is "waiting for life to begin; waiting to be beautiful; waiting to be somebody." Soon she is a wife and eventually a mother, where she enters a new universe of waiting:

> waiting for sex; waiting for him to give me an orgasm . . . waiting for my baby to come; waiting for my belly to swell; waiting for my breasts to fill with milk . . . waiting for my baby to stop crying; waiting for my baby to sleep through the night . . . waiting for some time to myself; waiting to be beautiful again . . . waiting for my life to begin. . . . Waiting for him to tell me something interesting, to ask me how I feel . . . waiting for fulfillment, waiting for the chil-

dren to marry, waiting for something to happen, waiting to lose weight, waiting for the first gray hair, waiting for menopause, waiting to grow wise.[32]

Eventually she waits for death. By the end, the utter passivity of this everywoman, the sense of a life deferred, leaves audiences stunned. The unstated implication of *Waiting* is that men do not wait and are agents of their lives in a way that women, as currently constituted, are not. In this way, Wilding's play perfectly captures the critique of social roles developed in early feminist groups, notable for its clearly demarcated and stable binary categories.

The Birth Trilogy takes up the power of women's biology, another important theme of early feminist theory. In this way, the trilogy captures the newly politicized appreciation for women's uniqueness finding voice in the early 1970s. The work emerged from consciousness-raising sessions. In her memoir, Chicago explains that interested students met at her house during the construction of *Womanhouse* to develop pieces that would be "related to the rest of the environment and provide a clearer sense of the entrapment that the house meant for many women." Breaking from her usual role, Chicago acted as both group leader and participant. The group began to "play around" to get ideas flowing. "One night, we all lay down of the floor and began pretending we were in labor. We lay on our back, legs spread, crying: 'Puu-uu-uush, puu-uu-uush,' until we were all laboring together, pushing together, until we felt this strong emotional connection with each other and with all women who had ever borne children." One of the group members got upset and cried, recalling her sense of abandonment by her mother. The group hugged her and talked about the sense many of them felt of not being nurtured enough. "We began to play with that feeling, crawling around on our hands and knees, eyes closed, like infants, crying 'Mommy, mommy, mommy.'" This became the germ of the performance piece on women's experiences of "birth, nurturing, and fulfillment."[33] The process of generating performances closely paralleled the process of consciousness-raising sessions—breaking through fictions of self and individuality (isolation) to get to a deep sense of identification with the group (collectivity).

The Birth Trilogy depicted five women, dressed in simple black leotards and red head scarves. In the first section, the five stand close together in a line with their arms wrapped around the woman in front of them and their legs spread. The *Womanhouse* catalog explains that, "using the space between their spread legs as a passageway, they gave 'birth' to each other in a beautifully symbolic way. As the 'babies' emerged from the 'birth canal' they lay down on the floor and then, after the mother figures sat down, began to crawl toward them, to be picked up, held and comforted." The final section begins as the women kneel in a tight circle with their heads touching. The women, "in an ancient ritual," began to chant and sing, "as the Mid-Eastern women do when they want to signal danger." The chanting grew progressively louder and louder, bringing up "memories of early human life, women giving birth, and finally, at the end, reached a peak of ecstatic sound which signaled joy, freedom and release."[34]

The slippage between "ancient ritual" and "Mid-Eastern women" problematically captured the all-too-common maneuver in 1970s feminism to center modernity in the white European-US world.[35] The performers, as white US women, could visit the mysterious past of "early human life" via the chanting Mid-Eastern woman, assured that it only embellished, not undermined, their universal view of womanhood. By extension, the audience too could come in contact with a world of women who birthed and temporarily transcended time and place; birth became an imaginary resource to bolster a view of women across culture and history as united. With no other references to non-US culture in *Womanhouse*, *The Birth Trilogy* stood out for its disinterest in understanding the lives of non-US women.

For Chicago, the trilogy was a form of consciousness-raising that had the power to touch women in direct ways. In her memoir, she recounts using it at an eastern college to help twenty-six students to understand "their own very special capacity to project emotion directly in ways that men know little about" and to feel themselves and other women "as women, doing something together that women do."[36] *The Birth Trilogy* struck a nerve for audiences, as well. Raven, a lesbian feminist, read it as a Wiccan initiation ceremony. As new members pass through the canal, "A coven member places a knife at her breast, saying, 'It is better for you to rush upon my blade than enter with fear in your heart.' The initiate responds, 'I enter the circle in perfect love and trust.'"[37] For Raven, the significance of the trilogy was its transformation of a secret, women-centered ceremony into a public art performance, rendering women's culture visible.

The performance pieces at *Womanhouse* connected individual choices made by women, alone or in relationship to men, to the realm of the social and the political, or in the words of radical feminists, the "sex class" of women, where the truth of one woman held in miniature the story of the whole. Whether the woman ironed, applied make-up, gave birth, or waited, the performances moved viewers to see themselves as part of the group "women." In *Womanhouse*, this identity was not merely biological, but political. This rhetorical move, done through performance (but also by the space of *Womanhouse*), was the same move being done in feminist practice across many sites, by many texts, and constituted one of the primary ways nonactivist women and the public were introduced to the ideas of 1970s feminism.

Evaluating *Womanhouse*

> Warning: 533 N. Mariposa Ave. may be hazardous to the ego of Male Chauvinist Pigs.

Womanhouse opened twice: first for a weekend conference of women artists January 21 through 23, and then to the public on January 30. After the openings, the exhibit remained opened for four weeks. Audiences could walk through the house, enter the various rooms, listen to other viewers' reactions, catch a performance piece, and perhaps sit on the spacious front porch and ponder when and why domesticity had become political.

The initial opening coincided with the first West Coast Conference of Women Artists, a conference designed "to end the overwhelming oppression and isolation of women artists."[38] The idea of a conference emerged out of a newly formed network of women artists, the West-East Bag or WEB. Cofounded by Chicago, Schapiro, and the art historian Lucy Lippard, among others, WEB was part professional organization and part activist group. It shared information about happenings and events by women artist groups; organized actions to improve the status of women artists in museums, galleries, and schools; and collected slides for registries of women's work to be used by researchers, art historians, students, and collectors, all to promote women's visibility in the art world.[39] Each month a different city's chapter published a newsletter. The conference in January, organized by the San Francisco and Los Angeles chapters of WEB, drew artists from around the state and the Southwest in what *New York Times* critic Grace Glueck called "a sort of mammoth consciousness-raising bee."[40] During the conference, Chicago and Schapiro gave a talk on the essential features of women's art, FAP student Jan Lester presented a slide show on the Woman's Building from the 1893 World's Columbian Exposition in Chicago, and attorney Isabel Welch updated the group on the investigation into institutional sexism at the University of California, Berkeley.[41]

Between 150 and 180 women converged on *Womanhouse* over the weekend to see the rooms and performances.[42] Chicago recalled that the women artists' responses were overwhelmingly positive, particularly when compared to that of general audiences after the house opened to the public: "The actresses could hardly get through the lines of the *Cock and Cunt* play, the laughter and applause was so loud. During the *Three Women* piece, women cried, laughed, and empathized, and the *Waiting* play caused a profound silence—everyone was deeply moved. After the performances, the acting group was ecstatic, and our ecstasy lasted until our next performance the following week, which was for a mixed audience. Through the evening, there was inappropriate silence, embarrassed laughter or muffled applause." Chicago despaired at the response of men to the performance pieces, fearing that having men in the audience compromised women's ability to "respond directly" to the feminist content. Her husband at the time, artist and CalArts faculty member Lloyd Hamrol, disagreed. He saw the men as "so overwhelmed by the experience of the house and the performances that they didn't know *how* to respond." Chicago asked a handful of men about their responses to *Womanhouse* and concluded that, while there were men who did not like the house or the performances, "there were other men who responded deeply, but who did not know how to show their response. Many men, accustomed to images of women that were quite different from those we presented, felt somewhat shocked by the new information they were receiving about women and women's point of view."[43]

As the first event of the newly formed Feminist Art Program in CalArts, *Womanhouse* grabbed an impressive amount of media attention. *Time* magazine, in an article titled "Bad Dream House," estimated that four thousand viewers came at its opening day to see the "mausoleum, in which the images and illusion of generations of women were embalmed along with their old nylons and spike-heeled shoes."[44] During the month *Womanhouse* was open, over ten thousand visitors came through. The *Los Angeles Times* reviewer, William Wilson, in his review "Lair of Female Creativity," captures the patronizing tone that many art critics brought to their review of *Womanhouse*, an art environment he sarcastically describes as "pervaded with the spirit of comfort and magic that women bring to living, their endless inventiveness, bottomless energy and gentle persuasive humor." In a statement both mocking and off the mark, he explains that, in *Womanhouse*, "We are made to understand that women, simply in their being, are creative. Their houses, meals and children represent art out of masculine reach. *Womanhouse* reminds us that the female is our only direct link with the forces of nature and that man's greatest creative acts may be but envious shadowing of her fecundity."[45]

Wilson appears to miss the overt feminist message that the restriction of female creativity to their "houses, meals and children" was precisely the problem exposed by *Womanhouse*. Critics of *Womanhouse* questioned its separatism, the isolation of female artists in their own environment, with one reporter suggesting that it was a "cop out" for Chicago and her students to avoid direct competition with men. Chicago responded that the "cop out" was manmade: "women have been segregated from the human race for 2,000 years. We have to segregate now to strengthen ourselves because of the damage done by being segregated!"[46] Deliberate and strategic separation based on gender flew in the face of the enshrined liberal view of the public sphere as equally available to all citizens, a space that was both color-blind and free of gender barriers. WEB and other activist groups of women artists in the early 1970s struggled to make clear that the dream of the open and free public arena, at least in the museum world, was just that: only a dream.

Frankly feminist reviewers and audiences unpacked the layers of feminist signification in the process and product of *Womanhouse*, noting that women artists utilized a unique vocabulary that had not yet been displayed in art. The feminist journal *Everywoman* wrote that *Womanhouse* used a "very female vocabulary to create a kind of art that has not been created by men."[47] Notable feminists mingled with the crowds. Anaïs Nin, author and avid supporter of Chicago, toured the house and took in the performances, seeing in it a "life-giving energy and broad vision [that] will give birth to woman's pride in herself."[48] Karen LeCocq recalled how Nin's visit had made her feel like the house and all they had worked so hard to accomplish mattered. "I can still see her standing in the doorway of Lea's Room, a look of delight on her face. She had loved Collette's books[;] she told Nancy and me that our room was a wonderful depiction of Lea's room."[49] Journalist Gloria Steinem recalled that walking through *Womanhouse* was the first time she had seen a woman-centered art and was "where I discovered female symbolism in my own culture for the first time."[50] A year later, after Steinem had cofounded the glossy magazine devoted to popular feminism, *Ms.*, Lucy Lippard invoked *Womanhouse* in an article on the power of feminist aesthetics, writing that "many women artists have organized, are shedding their shackles, proudly untying the apron strings—and in some cases, keeping the apron on, flaunting it, turning it into art."[51]

Feminist or feminist supporters also appeared in unlikely places. A more sympathetic piece is Betty Liddick's "Emergence of the Feminist Artist" for the *LA Times*, where she contextualizes the *Womanhouse* in a broader women's art movement and the house's critique of domesticity as a more serious challenge.[52] Marilyn Wachman's review in *California Apparel News* offers a tongue-in-cheek warning with a headline that announces, "533 N. Mariposa Ave. may be hazardous to the ego of Male Chauvinist Pigs." She notes that while men might dismiss the house, "women take the lipstick bathroom, pillow room and fried egg kitchen ceiling as facts of their lives. *Womanhouse* is not a satyr or paradox . . . it is taken seriously . . . not only by the artists but by all liberated women."[53]

Schapiro hits a similar note in a 1972 interview published in *Art Journal*. She believed that women who visited *Womanhouse* understood its significance "instinctively": "At *Womanhouse* women, particularly, walked into what was essentially their 'home ground,' knowing instinctively how to react. They cried when they saw the cosmetic performance piece. They gasped at the kitchen. They shook their heads wisely when they looked at the bridal piece. The shoe closet was familiar, the menstruation bathroom belonged to them, the stockings were theirs; and the aesthetic distances provided by the controlled environment of *Womanhouse* allowed them to respond with fullness to the honor, joy, and beauty of the house which, in the end, was really theirs."[54] The "instinctive" understanding that the stuff of a house comprised women's "home ground" was foundational to the feminism of *Womanhouse*. Identifying the home and domesticity as both a metaphorical and a literal expression of women's socialization and social roles, the art and performances strove to act on audiences as a consciousness-raising event. Chicago explained to the *LA Free Press* that the house was a way to change consciousness and the world. "I want to change the world," she said. Schapiro concurred, "I want every woman strengthened."[55] Evaluating the attempt to grab the audience and make them think like a feminist determined the kind of review it received. To critics, the feminist designs on viewers made the art conceptual, driven by ideas or, even worse, politics and not aesthetics. For supporters, the feminist design worked beautifully with the art to reveal "women's experience."

As Chicago's biographer Gail Levin notes, "*Womanhouse* turned out to be more important than Chicago and Schapiro ever imagined." At the time, the mainstream press ran pieces on it, including *Time*, *Life*, the *New York Times*, the *LA Times*, CBS, and NBC news, as well as left-leaning papers like *Ramparts* and *Everywoman*.[56] Two documentaries aired, one by local Public

Broadcasting Service affiliate KCET and another by Johanna Demetrakas.[57] The art world took notice, as well. Art historian Linda Nochlin spoke about the project at a women's meeting during the College Art Association annual meeting in 1972. Curators from major museums attended, including Maurice Tuchman from the LA County Museum of Art, who sat through the performances. Chicago wrote in her diary that Tuchman was "kissing up to me. I felt exalted because I've waited a long time to see those 'macho' guys have to acknowledge me."[58] However, only six members of the CalArts Art Department bothered to visit, and two of them were the husbands of Chicago and Schapiro.[59]

Overflow crowds turned up for the final weekend of *Womanhouse* in February. The group kept a few of the pieces and sold others, including Schapiro's *Doll House*, to the Smithsonian. A thief stole Wilding's crochet *Womb Room*.[60] The FAP students held a giant farewell dinner for themselves before they walked away from *Womanhouse* for the last time. Karen LeCocq spoke for many when she explained that, "When *Womanhouse* was over, I experienced a great sense of relief, combined with a tremendous sense of loss."[61]

Students had mixed feelings about their time at the FAP and about the giddy enthusiasm in and difficulties of making *Womanhouse*. For some, the materials they used and skills they developed opened new possibilities. Dori Atlantis said the most important message she took from her time at FAP was that "women artists had value [and] that the materials women chose to use for art were acceptable."[62] Robin Mitchell found the construction skills useful. "The *Womanhouse* experience taught me to accept responsibility and to develop construction skills while developing the foundations of a feminist art."[63] To Mira Schor, the practice of feminism mattered the most, specifically "consciousness-raising with the goal of developing subject matter for art by women, researching the history of women artists, collective art projects, and the over-all experience of a group of women trying to critique and analyze patriarchal authority and come to terms with power dynamics within the feminist group."[64]

Group collaboration taught the students an enormous amount, yet their own work, put off for months as they worked on *Womanhouse*, called loudly. Wilding writes that many students "longed to get back to their individual work."[65] Schor felt the experience had been too isolating. Nevertheless, her evaluation of the FAP stresses the time as an important feminist awakening: "Every new step into feminism is like putting on a new set of prescription glasses and this past summer's set was particularly strong." She goes on to say that, even with the moments of "joys—new friends, funny times," the group process unleashed for her "a great deal of unpleasant stuff." Despite the psychological stress, she concludes that practicing feminism through group processes, "perhaps . . . has been even more valuable than the first, intellectual exposure to the ideas of feminism."[66] Schor, LeCocq, and Wilding went on to careers as professional artists, as did a number of other FAP graduates.[67]

Personalities—who had them or needed one, whose were reconstructed and whose not—shaped the FAPs. Chicago herself inspired mixed feelings in her students. For some, only time allowed them to appreciate what could be described as a complicated relationship. Writing to Chicago in 1973, Karen LeCocq explains the roller-coaster feelings she and others had about her: "You know, Judy, a lot of women in our past and present groups sort of 'worshiped' you setting you up as an idol, and when they saw through the 'image at the human—they were crushed, the idol made mistakes, you weren't perfect and therefore let them down . . . I hated you and then loved you, seeing you were human and extremely vulnerable, then I hated you and then loved you, over and over—never indifferent."[68]

Bad feelings, mixed feelings, and confusion, along with rising confidence, giddy excitement at what they could do, and enjoyment of sisterhood characterized the feminist classroom as run by Schapiro and Chicago. Nancy Youdelman found that her subsequent art came from many of the themes she first explored in the FAP, but she recalled her sense of relief to be finished with it. For her, the program could not "get beyond personalities" and so could not reach its full potential.[69] Robbin Schiff dismissed the whole experience as a "political boot camp. It had nothing to do with my development."[70] Shawnee Woollman likened it to being in a cult.[71] Janice Lester and Loudelman agreed that it had been "one of the hardest and most exhilarating experiences" they ever had.[72] Arlene Raven, on the faculty of CalArts and a leader in the LA feminist art scene, hit the right note: each contributor to *Womanhouse* "felt taken apart and put back together, but altogether differently."[73]

For Chicago, the end of *Womanhouse* marked an important turning point in her life and her work. The impact of the project on her rising reputation as a player in the West Coast art scene was tangible. Her visibility was at an all-time high. The lessons learned at the FAPs and in the making of *Womanhouse* added up to the conviction that women needed their own alternative institutions to bring about change. They needed art programs that taught students about women's art history; they needed instructors who valued the artistic rendering of women's unique history and experiences. They needed places to show women's work and networks of informed viewers and reviewers to connect women's art to women's communities. The necessity for change was enormous, but the times were right for ambitious dreaming. Networks of women artists now existed. *Womanhouse* proved that audiences would come to see art by women and feminist performances. Chicago found herself surrounded by a group of feminist artists who shared a vision of a transformed art world. The question on Chicago's mind as *Womanhouse* drew to an end was whether CalArts could accommodate the ambitious plans for educating and promoting women artists. It was, after all, an institution controlled by men and by the very forces—such as promotion, curriculum, and male faculties—that required change to promote feminist art practice.

Like her students, Chicago was also worn out from the intensity of the group processes she had been engaged in for the previous two years. Hurt by the criticism of students she had devoted herself to, suspicious of Schapiro's efforts to incorporate the FAP deeper into CalArts by dropping anything hinting at "cunt art," and ready to capitalize on the buzz swirling about her, Chicago contemplated leaving CalArts.[74] She too had been changed by the experience. She had intuitively felt that she needed feminist group process to connect herself to her embodied female experiences.[75] Her work with students at Fresno and CalArts had helped her to get past the ethos of modernism, with its sterile focus on technique. Chicago had at last found the content and community for her own art. On November 30, 1972, Chicago turned in a letter of resignation to CalArts, effective at the end of the 1973 spring semester.

Building Alternatives

Somewhere during those years the I became a we—and I'm a part of a We now.

Chicago's involvement with the feminist art movement was far from finished as she tendered her resignation. Chicago left CalArts to devote more time to her art and more energy to building innovative women-centered institutions. In many ways, she deinstitutionalized herself to better enact the goals she and others had for feminist art.

The goals of the West Coast feminist art movement for Chicago and her peers constituted a multipronged attack on the institutional art world. The first element centered on enfranchising women as artists. This included deliberate efforts to increase women's access to the means of artistic production—to art schools, to a range of material skills and techniques, to a history of art that included women—and to the avenues through which women artists could display and sell their work, which included galleries and museums, as well as private collections, auction houses, and the art market. The second element involved altering the definition of "significant art" to include art not only made by women but also based on that still-emerging idea of female "aesthetic values," in other words, to "aesthetically enfranchise" work historically dismissed as "feminine." This required revising the distinctions between *craft* (needlework, sewing, fabrics, china painting, collages) and *art* (historically understood as painting and sculpture), content (meaning) and form (aesthetics), and personal (expressive) and political (social).[76] Third, the feminist art movement focused attention on gathering an audience for women-centered work and thus to displace the unstated ideal of the "male viewer" invoked habitually by the art world. Taken together, the feminist art movement in the early 1970s asserted that art and aesthetics could be liberating by allowing previously marginalized people to represent themselves apart from the confining aesthetics of the dominant group.[77]

Chicago's feminist art education programs participated in identifying the problem of equality of access and opportunity in the museum world. At the same time, she (and others) also practiced a more radical form of feminist activism that pushed hard against the lines dividing private from public subject matter, the individual from the group, and sexuality from politics. Both strategies—the liberal goal of representation and the radical goal of female empowerment—poured into the movement, giving it dynamism and broad appeal. Chicago's efforts to build empowered female artists, controversial in its attention to a student's "personality" and socialization, targeted the learned passivity of female art students. How else to address the nagging reality that while female students flocked to art programs in the 1960s, few became professional artists?

Chicago's programs attempted to disrupt that historic pattern. The FAPS applied radical feminist practices of consciousness-raising, critique-self-critique, separatism, and group collaboration to connect women to gendered experiences that could provide them with authentic (rather than imitative) "content" for their art. By producing art that emerged from experience, Chicago and her feminist art students participated in reconstructing the criterion for the entire enterprise of art evaluation. Feminist art as practiced by Chicago at times subordinated technique, valued in modernist art as the basis for determining the aesthetic importance of a piece, to content, the meaning of the piece as it communicated to audiences. In this way, feminist artists and their supporters challenged the separation between social considerations (such as sexism) and aesthetic ones (what counts as art). Further, feminist art education practiced radical feminism through its cultivation of a view of the artist as a member of a community and art as a vehicle for that community. *Womanhouse* came to symbolize the overlapping requirements of the new feminist art movement: new art, new artists, new audiences, new networks, new spaces.[78]

This mix constituted the blend of liberal and radical sensibilities that characterize US feminism at its most effective. Art activists organized to include women in the existing recognition-and-reward system of the art world as well as constructed alternative networks of institutions, publications and organizations to nurture talent and audiences.[79] But change in the art world moved at glacial speed. Impatient and talented, radicals in the women's art movement called for immediate change by creating their own institutions that would prefigure the transformations they hoped to bring about in the art world. Toward that end, two alternative West Coast feminist art institutions formed in 1972: Womanspace, a woman-owned gallery, and the Feminist Studio Workshop (FSW), an art school. In 1973, they jointly rented a two-story building in downtown Los Angeles, where they established the most ambitious women's art community center to date, the LA Woman's Building.

On March 20, 1972, a month after the closing of *Womanhouse*, *Time Magazine* published a "Situation Report" on women and the arts. It reported that of the galleries showing modern art in Manhattan, women owned 20 percent; women artists made up 9 percent of the Museum of Modern Art collection and only 6 percent of the Corcoran Gallery of Art in Washington, DC.[80] The Conference of Women in the Visual Arts, held at the Corcoran Gallery in 1972, brought together East and West Coast feminist artists and art historians to strategize, including June Wayne, Miriam Schapiro, Linda Nochlin, Adelyn Breeskin, and Chicago. According to historian Mary Garrad, "Many of the women who came together in Washington were radicalized on the spot."[81] Around the country, women's art groups determined the first order of business was to raise funds to build gallery spaces for women to show their work. The first board of Womanspace shared the sense of urgency. The board included a number of artists from *Womanhouse* (Chicago, Schapiro, Faith Wilding, and Wanda Westcoast), wealthy women interested in the arts, and women knowledgeable about the museum and gallery world.[82] Six months later, in October 1972, interested women gathered to convert an old laundry on Venice Boulevard into an acceptable gallery. Their renovations included building a space large enough for community lectures, screenings, and performances. Reflecting its commitment to support all women's art, they designated one unjuried space called the "Open Wall" as permanently open for any woman who paid the $16 membership fee to display her work for a week. The organizers of Womanspace prioritized showing the work of minority women and collective decision making.[83] They intended that this structure would reflect the feminist value of power sharing, with no one person assuming "authoritarian control" over the group. Wilding reported that such leaderless structure sounded good "in theory," although in practice, "many of the leaders held conflicting views about the goals of Womanspace and often left abruptly rather than attempting to work towards a resolution of differences."[84]

Womanspace opened to the public on January 23, 1973, exactly a year after *Womanhouse* had opened to the West Coast Conference of Women Artists. Several thousand people attended the opening. Buoyed by the enthusiasm, Womanspace worked hard to reflect the women-centered values of the founders' feminism. They offered a range of programs that included lectures on women's art history, regular Friday night discussions on feminist topics like lesbianism and mother-daughter relationships and women-made films. The goal was to "provide something women artists had never had before: a comfortable public place where they could work, debate, socialize and share vital professional and personal information." Womanspace curators regularly chose to explore a theme rather than a single artist, clustering individual works that together illuminated the subject, another expression of the movement's suspicion of the ideal of the isolated (male) genius/artist. One of the more successful shows was "Black Mirror," which showcased the work of five African American women artists. Others included "Taboo," on forbidden topics like rape and witchcraft, and "Opulence," about women's involvement with "glittering, glamorous, tinsel world of fame, fortune and fashion."[85] Each show was accompanied by a full month of related programming, such as slide lectures, discussions, meals, and performances, to enhance the community participation in the art. Womanspace grew rapidly, confirming its mission of giving women artists a gallery of their own.

Despite the impressive accomplishment of the group in so short a time, struggles over funds and, even more devastating, over leadership sapped Womanspace. Fights over what art to show, over whether men could make "feminist" art, and over whether only professional artists should show their work, tore whatever workable consensus had carried it forward. In its preemptive efforts to guard against elitism, the structure of Womanspace left little room for effective leadership to emerge. Control followed commitment; those who put the most time and energy into the group had the loudest voices and determined the collective's direction. Experienced women with ideas about what should happen, women with strong personalities or reputations, wealthy women who donated to the arts and were accustomed to weighing in on major decisions, and straight women intimidated by the lesbian feminists among them became casualties to feminist infighting.[86] Womanspace lost many of its supporters and paying members. A leaner Womanspace reconstituted itself.

At the same time, Chicago and two other feminist luminaries from CalArts, art historian Arlene Raven and designer Sheila de Bretteville, hatched plans for a new unaffiliated alternative art school to be called the Feminist Studio Workshop (FSW). Responding to the same need women artists had for material and community support that motivated Womanspace, FSW too waded into the fraught waters of feminist institution making. The initial plans called for approximately thirty women who would each contribute $750 for their own studio space in a shared building. In a November 1972 letter to friend and art historian Cindy Nemser, Chicago laid out her vision of a broad feminist art educational center: "If Arlene and I can make this work, it would mean women from all over the country could rent spaces, start programs to train young women, make enough money to survive, have control over our own educational programs, determine our own values, not have to beg for crumbs from men."[87]

Chicago, Raven, and de Bretteville agreed on much of the organizational structure of their new art program. "Our purpose," they stated in their initial recruitment brochure, "is to develop a new concept of art, a new kind of artist and a new art community built from the lives, feelings, and needs of women."[88] Yet differences between them also existed. Chicago, eight years older than Raven and four older than de Bretteville, practiced a kind of art apprenticeship model of teaching where, in the words of Chicago biographer Levin, the "apprentices learn skills from a master, who supplies overall vision and design." On the other hand, Raven and de Bretteville "conceived of art more as collaborative work among equals."[89] Despite differences in approach, they launched the program and held their first classes in de Bretteville's living room. By the fall of 1973, enrollments had grown enough for the program to lease space in a two-story building on Grandview Avenue in downtown LA. With this move, the FSW joined the newly formed Woman's Building, named for the Woman's Building at the 1893 World Columbian Exposition, designed by architect Sophie Hayden.

The Woman's Building soon became an important center for the diverse and vibrant communities of women's groups that made up the Southern California feminist movement. The Woman's Building not only included art groups such as Womanspace and FSW but political groups like the liberal LA chapter of the National Organization for Women and the more radical Women's Liberation Union. Cultural groups like the Associated Feminist Press, publisher of five feminist journals (*Sister*, *Momma*, *Womanspace Journal*, *Lesbian Tide*, and *Women and Film*), leased office space in the building, as did a branch of Sisterhood Bookstore, which featured books by feminist authors, weekly readings, and a range of hard-to-find feminist journals.[90] Within a few months, it became home to three additional gallery spaces besides Womanspace: Gallery 707, owned by Anait Stevens, and Grandview Galleries 1 and 2, owned and operated by a collective of forty women artists. With five shows running every month, the Women's Building soon made up a significant percentage of the LA art scene. According to Suzanne Lacy, even that fact did not inspire the mainstream art world to take note. Writing for the staid *Art in America* in 1974, she noted that few "art establishment figures," either artists or curators, "had yet to darken the doors."[91]

Unfazed by the disregard of curators who ignored them anyway, women artists and women interested in the arts flocked to the Woman's Building and partook of its expanding offerings. The Center for Feminist Art Historical Studies, an affiliate of the FSW that included the Los Angeles WEB slide registry, offered an interdisciplinary approach to the study of women's art history; the Performance Project coordinated local women's performance groups and connected individuals to auditions; the Women's Graphic Center offered women access to printing machines and classes on printmaking. A restaurant opened to give women a place to unwind and chat.[92] Chicago, who displayed a selection of her series on historic women titled "The Great Ladies" at the opening of the Woman's Building, wrote passionately in her journal about the ways the Woman's Building made manifest her deeply felt desire to be part of a women's art community: "[The values] were all there in microcosm in that funky community theatre [in Fresno]—and now we're here—and I say *we* advisedly—because somewhere during those years the I became a we—and I'm a part of a We now—and I can't believe I've done it. I mean that I've realized my dream to be part of a We—in the sense of a social, not a personal context."[93]

The Woman's Building came to embody one of the principle philosophical underpinnings of the feminist art movement, the creation of mutually supportive communities of women artists. According to historian Laura Meyer, "In opposition to the popular mythology of the lone (usual male) creative genius, the leaders of the feminist art movement contended that broad based community support was a necessary condition of creative productivity and set out to build the kind of support systems—both material and psychological—that women artists historically had lacked."[94] LA was uniquely suited to launch such an undertaking. With much of its formal art institutions "standing at attention facing east," in the words of Nancy Marmer of *Art News*, the geographical isolation of artists in the sprawling city and the relative unity of the region's art scene in contrast to New York's enormous and multiple art worlds, made the alternative art institution immediately significant to the city.[95] Coupled with the intensity of the feminist movement in 1972 and 1973 nationally, and specifically in California, the LA Woman's Building became a beacon.[96] News of it spread throughout the state and to cities beyond through feminist networks, marking Southern California as a magnet for women artists.[97]

With a new location and growing interest, the FSW added faculty, including performance artist and former Fresno student Suzanne Lacy, graphic designer Helen Alm Roth, art historian Ruth Iskin, and writer Deena Metzger.[98] The techniques first tested in the FAPs became the basis for FSW classes: students and teachers sat in a circle to foster equality; groups practiced consciousness-raising and frank talk; instructors encouraged collaborations and resource sharing across classes. Cheri Gaulke, as student, explained that "you weren't just there to develop your creativity, your intellect, but also your emotional self."[99] Initial assignments involved building repair and restoration and studio making. Ann Isolde remembered her surprise at discovering that after she had paid a hefty tuition to the FSW she was stuck plastering walls and sanding floors. She finally gave in, finding over time that she took pride in the fact that she could "make stuff."[100]

By 1974, only a year into the FSW, Chicago wanted out. She longed for her own studio and time in it to produce her own work. She struggled to find time for all the projects with which she was involved or asked to affiliate. Since starting the FAPs, she had been on a national lecture tour, visiting art schools, women's studies programs, and cultural centers. She had finalized a manuscript of her memoir and had been in discussion with publishers to get it in print, all this while teaching classes at the FSW and making art. Chicago's strong personality, her national reputation, and her at times abrasive style of group participation led to predictable conflicts in the FSW and in the broader community of the Woman's Building. Exacerbating matters, she was increasingly identified with advocating a model of female aesthetics organized around the female body or "central core" imagery she and others, including Mimi Schapiro and art critic Lucy Lippard, saw as defining a uniquely female art aesthetic. This view of an identifiable "female art" was controversial in the feminist art movement and became a major and, at times, divisive debate among feminists.[101]

After a particularly brutal conflict with a student and a group accusation that Chicago was "copping out" by spending time in her studio, choosing "art over the women's movement," Chicago decided to leave the FSW in December of 1974. She felt that the other faculty members had not contained the hostilities toward her effectively and was fed up with what she saw as the tyranny of equality among women of unequal talents. In her journal, Chicago processed the fallout, framing it in the lessons she had learned in other feminist classrooms: "The main growth step in female education comes when undeveloped women are disallowed the possibility for shitting on women of achievement as a way of rationalizing their own basic lack of achievement—BASIC—FUNDAMENTAL rule of the programs I've been involved with is to help women break out of their oppression by stopping the chain of oppressing other women as a way of not taking responsibility for one's own inadequacy."[102] Chicago's desire to spend more time in her studio and to cultivate her place in the art world motivated her to pull back from a community she both identified with and took pride in. Critics saw in that move a deep-seated desire to be recognized by the very art world she criticized, to be the token woman in a world where men still controlled the rules and the resources. Supporters understood her decision as her desire to make art.

Disagreements between women over the best strategy to transform the art world were inevitable, particularly between wanting recognition and reward from the art world as it currently existed and wanting to restructure that world by altering its criterion for inclusion.[103] Chicago straddled the contradiction. On the one hand, she wanted to change "the DNA" of the art world, but on the other, she understandably wanted acclaim and to produce notable, even historic, work.[104] Whatever Chicago's motive, the network of feminist artists with whom she maintained strong affiliations continued to devote their energies to their community work and to sustaining the vibrancy of their alternative feminist art scene. Chicago had lent her time and her name to that effort, but her heart was no longer in it. She was ready to make history, literally, in a monumental piece soon to be known as *The Dinner Party*.

CHAPTER THREE

The Studio as a Feminist Space

Practicing Feminism at The Dinner Party, *1975–1979*

IN 1974, CHICAGO BEGAN what turned into a five-year project on a monumental work, *The Dinner Party*. For over a year, the artist had been working on historical themes in her art. As her thinking about women's history and about women's exclusion from the grand sweep of art history evolved, Chicago settled on the idea of a dinner party seating thirty-nine women with three table wings representing time periods, each seating thirteen guests. Under the table, a porcelain floor with the names of 999 women would show a long history of achievement—traditions of accomplishment building over generations. Eventually her vision included opening banners, religious staging, and historical documentation. As she imagined *The Dinner Party* in 1974, she took inspiration from the writing and erasures of European history and she expressed her feminism by inserting women into the understanding of that history. At the same time, Chicago continued to practice feminism as she had at FSC, CalArts, and the Feminist Studio Workshop. By 1979, *The Dinner Party* project had become one of the largest cultural feminist art groups of the decade, involving four hundred people over a four-year period.

Chicago infused her practice of feminism with a sense of history and historical mission. No stranger to historical research, Chicago had been involved in researching prominent women since 1970, when she and her students in Fresno logged in hours researching women artists and Chicago and Schapiro presented their new feminist art history to groups across the country. When she lectured or wrote about her new project, Chicago offered the image of a lone female researcher piecing together a fragmented record of women in the dark and inhospitable male-centric library of Western history. Her sense of being alone in the process of "doing" women's history, while salient as mythmaking, was not an accurate portrait of either the state of women's history as a discipline or her own efforts to locate expert advice for her new project. The history generated by Chicago and her students and later, by *The Dinner Party* project workers, moved in tandem with a growing interest in women's history within the women's liberation movement more broadly. As with other social protest movements of the 1960s, feminists saw politics and history as deeply related endeavors and routinely blurred the distinction between activist and academic. In 1974, Chicago found experts in the new field of women's history to augment her research, soliciting syllabi from Joan Kelly-Gadol at Sarah Lawrence College and Vern Bullough of California State University, Northridge.[1]

That Chicago was not alone in her passion for a new history of women does not detract from her innovative use of that history. Her contribution in *The Dinner Party* would be a visual representation of women's history circa 1975 that symbolized and contextualized the female body, stressing both its essentialism and its changing social meaning. Chicago represented a version of women's history that reflected the feminist moment she occupied, representing gender as a heritage, a social role, a set of images, a psychological way of being, and as unmarked by race, nation, or religion. *The Dinner Party* reflected Chicago's version of radical feminism's view of women's history, with all its brilliance and with all its flaws. At the same time, Chicago invoked history in a different sense. She viewed herself and her studio as historical, as having significance to the history of women, to Western art, and to the feminist revolution. In letters to other feminists, in her personal journal, in her memoir and in other accounts of *The Dinner Party*, Chicago stressed that her new piece would reveal both the record of women's accomplishment and its historical suppression. The efforts at the studio to make *The Dinner Party* mattered, according to the artist, because those efforts would produce a work of art that would be the ultimate form of consciousness-raising—raise women's feminist consciousness by helping them understand their lost history.

As Chicago left the Feminist Studio Workshop and began her new project, feminism itself was changing. For women like Chicago, who had been engaged with exploring the psychological consequences of women's secondary status for five or more years, as she had in Fresno, CalArts, and the LA feminist art scene, feminism as a theory and practice had new priorities. By 1974 the first blush of radical feminism, where discovering and naming sexism and discrimination was a primary praxis, had passed, and groups of feminists moved toward establishing women-centered institutions where they could enact feminist principles and lifestyles.[2] Awareness of the limits of heterosocial political groups that had inspired the women's liberation movement in the 1960s were still at play in the mid-1970s. But as cultural feminism came into its ascendency (as an expression and extension of feminist radicalism), women like Chicago hoped to use new and autonomous male-free spaces like the newly formed Woman's Building to enable women to come together and express themselves and express feminism. They also viewed "women's culture"—defined as symbols, rituals, and objects made by women as well as "women-centered" values—as supportive of feminist political activism, not in opposition to it or as a replacement for it.[3] With this, Chicago placed herself firmly within the cultural branch of 1970s feminism, the one that emphasized personal insight as a road to social change, woman by woman.[4]

In tandem with this evolution in the women's liberation movement and as a consequence of her time in her feminist classrooms, Chicago recreated her *Dinner Party* studio to better suit her ambitious artistic plans. By 1976, she remade her once-private and near-sacred private studio into a space divided into distinct areas where people could work alongside her. As with the feminist art programs at FSC and CalArts, people who came to work at the studio would learn the value of work and discipline and, in addition, have the chance to work on a major piece of feminist art in a feminist environment. Unlike at Fresno and CalArts, Chicago determined to move herself out of the role of teacher and into the role of muse-in-chief. Process, not an emotional relationship with the artist, would transform participants.

Chicago's decision to establish the studio as a collaborative, feminist-inspired space expressed the complex reality of her goals. She wanted *The Dinner Party* to represent a record of women's accomplishments. Yet she was also a teacher and leader, gifted at inspiring people. At FSC and CalArts she had pioneered applying feminist practices like consciousness-raising to teaching. Chicago drew energy from working with other people and, particularly in times of stress, relied heavily on others' senses of her when her own sense of herself fragmented. For these reasons, opening her studio proved essential to her ability to complete the project.

At the same time, Chicago had concrete, material goals for opening her studio. She needed help finishing a huge and ambitious undertaking. Pulling in people to help her was not only an expression of her feminist commitments but an absolute necessity to completing the work. With no money to pay for help, Chicago offered the women who came to the studio payment in the form of a feminist experience and a chance to work closely with her on a major work of art. For many of the women and the few men who joined Chicago, working at the studio was an intense and transformative experience, one they made sacrifices to have and which they valued highly. For some, it was their primary or only encounter with feminism. For others, it was an extension of their budding feminist awareness. For all of them, it was an experience set apart from their ordinary lives, where they could "do" sisterhood, with all its ambivalences, and participate, for a bit, in the revolution.

Defining Feminist Art

Feminist art reaches out to people, especially women, with a communicated truth.

The step from the domesticity of *Womanhouse* to the materiality of women's history in *The Dinner Party* proved easy for Chicago to take. Her interest in the skills women applied in their homes, homes that in *Womanhouse* entrapped women quite literally, led her to china painting, a skill dismissed by the art world and practitioners alike as "craft" and hobby. According to Chicago, it was a "technique usually associated with old ladies and not taken seriously. I wanted to push it into 'art.'"[5] In 1972, the year she began to plot her exit from CalArts, Chicago began formal training in china painting and found a teacher, Miriam "Mimi" Halpern, who shared Chicago's interest in pushing the staid craft in new directions.[6] Chicago had done this kind of skill-intensive training before. After college, she had attended auto body school to learn to spray paint, the only woman among 250 men. Later, she took a boat-building course in Long Beach, California, again to master spray painting, a technique clearly apparent in *Domes* (1968) and *Pasadena Lifesavers* (1969–70). Chicago's interest in smoke as an element for large sculptures led her to train as a licensed pyrotechnician with the only fireworks company on the West Coast that had the technical expertise she needed.[7]

Yet this turn to china painting, a craft that was profoundly gendered, was not without risks. Modernism in the LA art scene broadly celebrated abstraction, painting, and slick finishes and viewed the artist as a transcendent force, not a product of the environment. Chicago's undertaking—to take the dismissed crafts of china painting and, later, needlework into the fine art world of the museum—coupled with her view of art as an expression of women's collective and historical identities, set her on a collision course with the male-dominated art world.

In her account of the making of *The Dinner Party*, Chicago recalled her fascination with the community of women drawn to china painting, particularly the intensity of effort they devoted to a tightly constricted and undervalued art form. "The china-painting world, and the household objects the women painted, seemed to be a perfect metaphor for women's domesticated and trivialized circumstances. It was an excruciating experience to watch enormously gifted women squander their creative talents on teacups." Her characterization of painting teacups as "squandering" of talent reflected Chicago's identification with the mainstream art world, particularly what counted as art and what did not. As feminist art historians noted, as early as 1972, the binary of art and craft itself rested on unexamined gendered categories.

Yet for Chicago, the fact that so many of the china painters had gone to art school when they were young, and only took up china painting after marrying and having children, meant that china painting was as much a testimony to women's limits as it was to their talents. "They looked for a way to express themselves that did not require—as it did for so many professional artists—a choice between their family and their work." Chicago recalled visiting the home of one woman where all the chairs were adorned with needleworked cushions, the pillowcases hand-embroidered, the walls covered with her oil paintings, and the plates hand-painted in flower patterns. "This woman had done all that work, trying as best she could to fit her creative drive—which could probably have expanded into mural-size paintings or monumental sculptures—into the confined space of her house."[8] Chicago recognized a similarity between herself, her students, the multitudes of female artists who worked in obscurity in their home studios, and the unappreciated china painters. Untouched by the feminism percolating around the students of *Womanhouse*, the china painters nonetheless embodied a kind of sisterhood, a female world that lovingly passed the techniques of china painting from mother to daughter, which appealed to Chicago and helped her articulate her interest in traditions that preserved and passed on gendered knowledge.[9] Chicago studied china painting for a year and a half.

During the course of that study, Chicago continued to develop her ideas about "female art," specifically the importance of "central core imagery" in women's creative expressions. She first explored the idea of a female aesthetic during her teaching at FSC and CalArts, where she and her students explored the role of the female body in their own art. The debate, however, was far larger than just Chicago and the LA art scene, even as her views on "female art" quickly gained a national audience. In a 1973 interview, Chicago explained her view that many female artists shared what she called "central core imagery" in their work, "a central focus (or void), spheres, domes, circles, boxes, ovals, overlapping flower forms, and webs" that invoked female biology.[10] Her first significant work using the idea of the central core was *Through the Flower* (1973), a large painting of a flower with red-orange petals that opened to a radiant blue-green center. The painting invoked the feeling of being inside a very happy vagina or moving through a birth canal. Even more forcefully, *Let It All Hang Out* (1973), another large painting, had rings of pink and violet paint that appeared to be pulsating like the contractions of an orgasm. She connected history to these abstract central core images in two series also done in 1973, *Great Ladies* and *Reincarnation Triptych*. In these, Chicago enclosed the images of radiant central cores in bands of handwritten texts that identified the female monarchs and intellectuals, respectively. These informed her evolving ideas about the china plates she wanted to make for *The Dinner Party*.

Chicago's experiments with central core images placed her among a group of female artists who shared her interest in using the female body as a template for their art.[11] The vibrant LA feminist scene supported their body-based art, yet not all feminists, particularly those on the East Coast, approved of what they dismissed as "cunt art." The debate among feminists over aesthetics, specifically if an identifiable "female aesthetic" existed, became important in defining broad goals and tactics for the women's art movement. Much of this debate took place in the short-lived alternative art journals produced by feminists.[12]

Writing in *Everywoman* in 1972, Chicago staked out her views. She argued that central core imagery had existed throughout art history yet has been barred from being recognized as such by simple prejudice. "[Y]ou see cunts in Bontecou, and cunts in Barbara Hepworth, and cunts in Georgia O'Keeffe, and cunts in Miriam Schapiro's paintings and cunts in my work. What happens then when that work is looked at? Cunt is a symbol of contempt, i.e. 'she is a dumb cunt.'" Men, she went on, reacted to such images out of their learned dismissal of anything affiliated with the feminine or with women, and the institutional art world reified that view into art world's tools of evaluation. "A woman's work cannot be perceived accurately and will never be perceived accurately until women are perceived accurately, with the exception of work by women who are attempting to paint or make art like a man, and who have accepted the framework of art-making as dictated by men and by what serves men."[13]

For Chicago, female imagery—central cores, vulvas, dark hidden spaces—reflected the experience of living in a female body, and as such, ought to be granted equal status in the art world. To deny "cunt art" was akin to denying the unique aspects of women's embodied existence. Chicago and curator Dextra Frankel of Cal State Fullerton articulated this new "bio-aesthetics" for an important exhibition that opened at the Long Beach Museum of Art in the spring of 1972 titled 21 Artist Invisible Visible. The style on display—some of it "cunt art"—in the show used the form of women's bodies but was not mere empty formalism. Chicago and Frankel argued that these artists "used a formalist framework to express female subject matter. A great deal of the work we saw articulated emotional reality, described states of feeling, or life as it is lived in kitchens, living rooms, and bedrooms—the woman's environment."[14]

Marjorie Kramer, writing in *Women in Art* in 1971, dismissed the idea that a recognizable "female" art existed. "To say that women paint cunts doesn't ring any bells in my head." Yet she did believe in "feminist" art. Feminist art, she wrote, "comes out of feminist consciousness." It rejected the modernist credo of "art for art's sake." Rather than being art in a "closed system of rich collectors, trustees, and a few superstar artists whose audience is the former . . . feminist art reaches out to people, especially women, with a communicated truth."[15] For Kramer, the circuit between artist, art and audience, each informed by feminist consciousness, was the crucial aspect of "feminist" art.

Pat Mainardi, writing in *Feminist Art Journal* in 1972, also viewed feminist art as more clearly affiliated with the political messages of feminism. "Feminist art is political propaganda art which like all political art, should owe its first allegiance to the political system," she wrote. For Mainardi, the message and its designs on audiences made a piece of art "feminist," not the kind of genitals the artist had. "Since feminism is a political position and feminist art reflects those politics, it could even be made by men." She viewed artists like Chicago and Schapiro, who embraced the vulva and central core imagery as primary symbols of female art, as reactionary: "To put it bluntly, I think the whole thing is opportunistic. It is reactionary because it is going backward into some form of biological determinism at a time when the most progressive women and men are fighting their way out of repressive ideas that one's humanity should be defined and limited by the location of one's genitals or the color of one's skin."[16] Writing for the student magazine at CalArts, Judith Stein argued that no limits whatsoever ought to be placed on feminist art since its major goal was to articulate the varied and diverse views about women's liberation. "It seems to me that in striving towards a feminist art *we would not want to limit women artists in any way.* We would want to make women as free as possible to discover those means of expression and authentic art making of which we have so long been deprived." For Stein, striving for success in the formal art world was another way of emulating men. *Process*, not product, mattered, and the struggle to define "female art" distracted women from the more pressing task of changing social systems.[17]

The debate over female aesthetics reflected the large issue in the women's movement of the 1970s and in twentieth-century feminism more broadly over what status to grant women's bodily difference. According to Chicago and others, women as social actors experienced the world differently than did men because of their female bodies. That lived difference required recognition and validation. For others like Mainardi and Kramer, women entered a world unjustly shaped by cultural investments in marking them as different; gender, as a system of predetermined distinctions, had to be dismantled, not reified. The feminist art movement—or the broader political woman's movement for that matter—never reached a consensus about the status of women's difference, even as the question of female aesthetics became a major arena for feminist theory-making in the 1980s and 1990s. As a reviewer writing for the feminist journal *Signs* in 1975 noted: "The answer to the question of whether, indeed, there is something definable as a 'female aesthetic' is ultimately less important than the fact that the issue has been raised. . . . It is too early to tell what still unimaginable aesthetic may then evolve. What is clear is that the history of art will no longer be the same."[18]

For Chicago and other feminists writing in the early 1970s, the debate over the status of the female body provided an opportunity to articulate their views on how to bring change to the art world. Both positions offered viable tactics and existed simultaneously if uneasily in the 1970s. Feminists and women artists could celebrate women's art as cunt art while also picketing museums for discriminating against women artists on the basis of their bodies without having the contradiction paralyze them. Striving for equality and celebrating difference shaped this moment of the feminist art movement as well as Chicago's art. In *The Dinner Party*, she would mobilize both strategies.

Remaking the Studio

I'm living on pennies. I don't even know if I can pay the rent next month.

Ready to start work on *The Dinner Party* by 1974, Chicago turned in earnest to the tremendous task of making plates and designing the tablecloth, the first iteration of what would later become runners for each place setting. She worked alone for the first year, firing test plates and nearly finalizing the guest list of notable women to be seated at the table. However, as Chicago faced her second year of making plates—imagined now as more three-dimensional and requiring a difficult and technically challenging style of ceramics—the scope of the work ahead impressed on her the need to bring in assistants and collaborators.[19]

But it was more than just the sheer amount of work that led her to reconsider the modernist narrative of the solo artist. It was the crushing solitude of that myth that burdened Chicago. Rather than relishing it, which she had previously (and would again), she entered a period of great doubt over her choices and questions about her abilities. In a July 1975 journal entry Chicago worried, "are my choices right? Will the piece work when it's all put together? Will I have the money to finish it? . . . Can I work it out technically?" In October 1975, she confessed that "I am very upset tonight and overwhelmed. I have completed the main part of the D.P. [*Dinner Party*] that I can do myself. . . . What it boils down to is that I need . . . the help, the support, the resources to finish something that challenges the values of society."[20]

Chicago's understanding of the solo artist was an early casualty of her changed awareness of gender and history, yet the full measure of that change only appeared after a year and a half of long hours working alone at the studio. Her encounter with feminist groups at FSC and CalArts changed what had once been an intensely pleasurable part of being an artist for Chicago—working alone, having a vision, and working it through. Her classroom adventures in FSC and CalArts, though draining, had offered her competing pleasures of collaboration. For this new project, Chicago needed a context that would make the risks required of her monumental effort visible and valuable. Without eyes watching her, without a historical sisterhood validating her, Chicago's vision of herself and her effort seemed dangerously fragile. She connected her struggle to her historical studies, writing in her journal, "My knowledge of history and women's defeats, especially combined with my own experiences, can't help but make me worried. My struggle this time is with myself: Can I go forward in the face of all the risks, the probable debts, the uncertainty, the shaky support. Can I just go forward? Can I just keep on plugging away, no matter how frustrating or unsure or shaky the whole project might seem some days?"[21]

Through public talks and the publication of her first memoir in 1975, Chicago found a steady stream of people interested in working with her. Three stand out as central to the success of *The Dinner Party*. Leonard Skuro, a graduate student in ceramics at UCLA, agreed to work with Chicago in 1975. Skuro, long the only man in the studio, helped Chicago work through the process of making plates. Despite his bringing "with him all the difficulties of dealing with men," he and Chicago worked diligently to solve the seemingly intractable problems posed by three-dimensional plates.[22] Chicago's journals reported her experiments with Leonard to find different clays that might better withstand the numerous firings, her efforts to find a kiln that would fire at lower heats for longer periods of time, and technical strategies for carving plates. With much angst and anxiety, and amid piles of broken plates around them, Skuro and Chicago resolved the technical issues, and by August 1977, Chicago gratefully reported a higher success rate.

The second crucial person for the project was Susan Hill. A commercial photographer transitioning into art photography, Hill offered her services for *The Dinner Party* after hearing Chicago lecture in San Diego in 1975. Relatively early in her tenure with the project, Hill suggested using runners for the place settings instead of an embroidered tablecloth.[23] Her mother, grandmother, and aunts had helped Hill develop her embroidery and sewing skills as a child, but she had not considered needlework as art. Together, the talents of Hill in stitching and Chicago in conceptualizing merged in the runners. This innovation proved central to the conception of *The Dinner Party*, enabling Chicago to design specific place settings that foreground the historical era of each dinner party guest. Hill became the head of needlework and supervised "the Loft" in Chicago's studio where teams of people worked on runners.[24]

The final person whose efforts proved absolutely essential was Diane Gelon, an art history graduate student at UCLA who first met Chicago at the opening of the Woman's Building in 1973. After the two met again at a 1975 gathering, Chicago asked if Gelon was interested in doing a few weeks of research to come up with the 999 names to be used on the floor of *The Dinner Party*. Gelon started working on the project two days a week, but then dropped out of graduate school to work full-time as Chicago's assistant. Eventually, she managed the daily administration of the project.[25]

By 1976, these three had been joined by others: Ann Isolde, Karen Schmidt, and Ruth Askey were helping Gelon with historical research; Kathleen Schneider, Karen Valentine, and Robyn Hill were helping Hill in the loft; and Judye Keyes was helping with ceramics. With this augmented team, Chicago had begun to address the pressing problem of help. But she still struggled with money. Chicago had barely enough funds to keep herself in clay and thread. She strategized continually over how to keep the project afloat, agonizing in her journal that "I'm living on pennies. I don't even know if I can pay the rent next month."[26]

Gelon took over the time-consuming task of searching for and applying for outside funding.[27] She recalled that she and Chicago took out credit cards and alternated maxing them out to fund Gelon's travel to potential donors.[28] During the next two years, Gelon taught herself to become a feminist fundraiser—researching the granting institution or person, networking and following up on contacts, and learning to navigate the nonprofit world.[29] She sought out women in granting institutions, explaining that "most of the support, outside of the NEA, has come as a result of having women in a leadership capacity in the foundation, the donations are almost entirely from women."[30] They won nearly 50 percent of the grants they applied for.[31]

Over time, Gelon found clever ways to involve potential donors in *The Dinner Party*, such as asking them to sponsor place settings for women close to their cause. For example, donor records from 1977 record a fund-raising event in New York where *Ms.* magazine gave $500 to fund St. Bridget, Planned Parenthood of New York City gave $500 for Margaret Sanger, and writer Anne Roiphe and actress Joanne Woodward each gave $500 for Elizabeth Blackwell and Theodora, respectively.[32] Well-known feminists like author Marilyn French, and women's studies professors Carolyn Heilbrun and Catharine R. Stimpson, also donated funds to support *The Dinner Party*.[33] By 1978, a steady stream of small donations arrived from women who read about the studio and *The Dinner Party* in local and national newspapers and magazines as well as in small, local feminist newspapers and journals, with checks ranging from $1 to $100.[34]

As Chicago and Gelon struggled to keep the studio funded, the team at the studio scrambled to support themselves in whatever way they could. Gelon recalls that, when she first began as Chicago's assistant, she was on unemployment before taking a job as a school bus driver for ten to fifteen hours a week, while devoting between fifty and sixty hours to the studio.[35] Throughout her nearly ten-year tenure as chief fund-raiser for the studio, Gelon supported herself, accepting no money from Chicago or the project. Hill worked part-time at a dentist's office; Ann Isolde worked part-time as a paralegal.[36] Eventually, both drew a small stipend from the project.

Money, however crucial, was merely one thread of a complex web of support that the project required. It was hard to separate the need for money from the equally pressing need for more willing hands to do the work. Chicago and the people working at the studio (sometimes referred to in the archival materials as "core staff") eventually came to see that the experience of working in a feminist environment like Chicago's studio was itself a potential asset on which to capitalize, particularly to women interested in experiencing feminism in a more direct way. Partly a solution to chronic shortages in money and labor and also part of the larger project of stitching *The Dinner Party* to feminism and to history, the decision to call for more volunteers came with risks. Chicago was experienced at leading groups. But Chicago did not view this project as a joint endeavor, and did not view the group gathered at her studio as a collective. This time, neither she nor the art would be subordinated to other women's psychological or artistic processes.

Personal and Political Transformations at the Studio

Will you help us?

In March 1977, Chicago and the core staff recognized the enormity of the task they had undertaken and after a dramatic evening rap session, determined to bring in more people, streamline the studio, and build an alternative "grass roots" financial support network. Formal team leaders for each department (research, ceramics, graphics, and needlework) volunteered to take more responsibility to permit Chicago to focus on the carving and painting of plates. Henry Hopkins, the director of the San Francisco Museum of Modern Art and longtime supporter of Chicago, agreed to show the work and worked with the artist to schedule the opening, which was pushed back a few times as the full extent of the time and effort required to finish *The Dinner Party* became clear. With a new opening date in 1979 secured and a more formalized structure in place, people at the studio breathed a collective sigh of relief. Ann Isolde wrote in her diary, "At last we have a real support structure, one in which even the leader can collapse temporarily while everyone else continues to work. I'm so relieved we will have more time because now we'll be able to do a more thorough job."[37] On March 31, 1977, the first core staff meeting took place with Gelon (administration and fund-raising), Ken Gilliam (industrial design and fabrication), Susan Hill (needlework), Helene Simich (graphics), Leonard Skuro (ceramics), and Ann Isolde (research).[38]

One key component of the reorganization was a two-tiered strategy to bring in volunteers. The first strategy involved a formal workshop structure where interested people paid for the opportunity to have a feminist group experience and to work on a major feminist art project for a limited time. The second strategy was less formal and involved creating an ongoing, weekly schedule where interested people could participate based on clearly laid-out time commitments. Volunteers could apply to join the studio if they could offer needed skills and could offer the studio a minimum of sixteen hours a week.

To inspire women to volunteer, the studio emphasized that those who came to work on *The Dinner Party* would experience firsthand the techniques and benefits of feminism. The flyer they put together read, quite simply:

> Will you help us? Come work with us on the project. Grow with us, develop your potential as an artist, work in a supportive environment, acquire new work modes. Consciousness-raising groups, open rap sessions, and sharing with other people are amoung [*sic*] the benefits in this unique experience.
>
> In addition, intense workshop programs will be offered beginning May 1978. Participants will work in a unique professional environment that employs feminist education techniques. This will produce and [*sic*] opportunity for people to work co-operatively and make a contribution to women's history. . . . Consciousness raising and art-making sessions will be available to both men and women.[39]

Through rap session and consciousness-raising groups, participants could experience "sharing" and working "cooperatively" with others and by doing so, contribute to "women's history." For women who did not join the hundreds of small feminist groups that sprang up across the country in the late 1960s, who did not take part in speak-outs on illegal abortions and rape, who had not joined NOW or any other formal feminist group, who might feel too old or too married to join anything, but who nonetheless found something compelling in the language of feminism, such an offer was appealing. Here was a chance to "do" feminism for a few weeks or a month, to reap the benefits of "consciousness-raising," to experience sisterhood directly by working among other women, and to participate in the larger sweep of history by contributing to Chicago's monument to women. A steady stream of volunteers, almost entirely women, came to Santa Monica to work on the project.

Summer workshops ranged in length and cost. An eight-week workshop cost the participants between $150 and $175 (some received university credit for participating), and a special three-month intensive on weaving cost $400. The one-time weaving workshop run by the San Francisco Tapestry Workshop (SFTW) in the summer of 1977 proved particularly helpful for Chicago. After winning an NEH grant to fund a workshop in Aubusson weaving, Chicago offered twelve people the opportunity to train in the technique. For a $125 fee, the workshop participants learned the old European skill by making the five opening banners for *The Dinner Party*.[40] They worked in San Francisco rather than at the studio in Santa Monica. But three eight-week workshops ran in Santa Monica that summer, transforming the studio into a lively, bustling place. Between 1976 and 1979, anywhere from fifteen to thirty people worked in the studio at any given time. Numbers dropped during the winter to half that, with five or so workers doing needlework in the loft and about eight at the studio doing ceramics, graphics, and research.[41]

In many ways, Chicago re-created the atmosphere of the Feminist Art Programs at the studio. Orientation materials for the volunteers laid out expectations and routines: "During your eight weeks with us you will be expected to work forty hours per week. The actual hours are somewhat flexible since the studio is open 7 days per week from 8 am to 10 pm." To ease the volunteers into the studio, the staff assigned each newcomer a "guardian angel/big sister" who would "help make the transition to the studio a little smoother."[42] The studio expected workshop participants to arrange for their own housing and meals on top of the fee—ranging from $75 (in 1976) to $175 (in 1978)—they paid to the project.[43] Many of the participants came from the region or lived in LA, while others came from out of town and arranged their own accommodations. One woman who wrote to tell the studio when she was arriving announced that "I will be bringing my pack and sleeping bag and will only need someone's lawn or nearby campground to tent in."[44] Another reported that she had found an apartment to rent for two weeks.[45] Many wrote asking for advice as to where to look for apartments, what bus routes would bring them to the studio, and general orientation to Santa Monica.

During summer intensives, the core staff shuttled to the airport and bus terminal, and managed the steady stream of requests for information and the ongoing need for housing. They pushed the responsibility for workers' arrangements squarely back on volunteers' shoulders, underscoring the message that everyone who came to work on the project was expected to fend for themselves and contribute without requiring a lot of hand-holding. The housing requirements varied from needing to be put up for three days or eight weeks, to more permanent and open-ended arrangements. One woman wrote to ask, "Is there a YWCA in Santa Monica? Is it within walking distance or easy bus line of the studio? Or is there someone I can room with for a reasonable rate? I can arrange child care with my folks for my son so there would only be me and I'm easy to get along with."[46] Another explained that, "I have enough money to live on for about 2 months, but I might get a job and stay until the project is completed—as long as I can contribute I'd like to, because it will be quite a learning experience for me."[47] Participants who needed housing funded their stays in a variety of ways. Some relied on their husbands to support them while they volunteered. Others dipped into savings and contracted for only as long as their money held out. A few applied for welfare and food stamps. The 1977 *Dinner Party Survival Manual* for the studio had a section devoted to applying for welfare and other subsidized city and state services.[48]

Volunteers came from around the country: from Washington, DC, Kansas City, Cleveland, and Boston. But the majority came from California. The robust feminist art scene in California lent it distinctive networks of friends, former lovers, and formal and informal groups that pumped a steady stream of workers into Chicago's studio.[49] Of the thirty-five volunteers who joined the studio in 1977 and who filled out information sheets, twenty-four arrived there through these networks. Twelve found their way to the studio after hearing Chicago lecture or after reading about the project in the art press.[50]

When taken as a whole, the group of volunteers who moved in and out of the studio between 1976 and 1979 had certain commonalities. Studio volunteers were all women except for six men.[51] They were overwhelmingly white. No information about the volunteers' racial identity exists based on studio records for 188 of the 400 volunteers. Based on photographs and personal memories, Michelle Davis appears to have been the sole African American in the studio, and Winifred Grant and Cherie Fraine the studio's only Native Americans. Susan Hill recalled that at the studio no one spoke about race or felt self-conscious about not speaking about it.[52] For the racially diverse city of LA, characterized by tense race relations in the wake of the 1965 Watts riots, the volunteers' reluctance to discuss race testifies to their strategic erasure of their own whiteness.[53] Versed as most were in civil rights and labor activism, volunteers nonetheless relied on the simple and hope-infused term "woman," not *European*, *African American*, or *First* woman, as they cultivated the studio's feminist community.

Many of the workers—52 of the 188 volunteers between 1976 and 1979—listed their occupations as "artist" or in art-related fields such as graphics or art education. Art teachers ranged from pre-K and high school art teachers to college instructors. Of the twenty-two volunteers who described themselves as "unemployed" or as housewives, nearly all qualified those categories by noting that they made art without financial remuneration. Thirty-two volunteers were full-time students, including many art or women's studies majors. One was a fourth-year medical student on "a summer vacation with time to kill."[54] The majority of volunteers—sixty-two—listed a range of female occupations for their work, from waitressing and bookkeeping to secretarial work and building management.[55] One, Aurelia Morris, seventy-three, listed her occupation as "feminist."[56] The women who wrote down a paid occupation on their forms might not have felt entitled to claim "artist" as their occupation, whether they viewed themselves that way or not. Likewise, an unemployed person might be quicker to list "artist" as an occupation when applying to work at *The Dinner Party* studio. Such nuances simply cannot be vetted based on the archival record. What we can know is that some of the women who worked on *The Dinner Party* did not see themselves artists while others did, no matter how they earned a living.

Many of the volunteers who came through the studio left only a few sentences scattered in the archive about what the experience was like. For example, two women from Washington, DC, arrived in July 1978 to volunteer for a few weeks. Both had attended a lecture by Chicago and felt so moved by what they heard that they wanted to participate. Margaret Litchfield, a thirty-five-year-old psychiatric social worker, wrote that *The Dinner Party* project "has been important to me for a long time even before I imagined I could participate in any way." Once she arrived, she found the studio to be welcoming: "Never before have I encountered a project of such vision and scope which is by nature so generous. The openness, the willingness to be inclusive makes it extraordinarily accessible. The concept and its execution are a celebration to me in themselves. I have a real emotional investment and conviction regarding the value of the Dinner Party being seen out there in the world."[57] Aldeth Spence Christy also arrived at the studio in July 1978. "Most personally what I have wanted since that first lecture was the chance to make some stitches with an appropriate reverence and as anonymously as fits the concept; to make a contribution because I so believe in this staggering work. I think this is a religious event though I have no religion."[58]

Orientation forms asked newcomers about their expectations for their time and efforts, and their answers reflected the diversity of wishes that drew them to the studio. Some wanted to hone their artistic skills and work habits. Jenny Stern, adult education teacher, said she hoped to gain "Discipline, more confidence in my talent, skills, and vision; to function as a constructive, positive artist. . . . To grow as a woman, artist, feminist."[59] Nancy Macko echoed her sentiments: "a better working discipline so I don't waste so much time when I do my own work, more feminist energy to carry around with myself, new ideas and attitudes to pass on and share with other women."[60] Others wanted the experience of working with a group of women. Michelene Reed, a painter and calligrapher, wanted "the experience of working with a group, something new to me—feedback, exposure, and a sense of accomplishment."[61] Similarly, Roberta Rothman, an unemployed artist, wanted "a rich experience of working collaboratively on a large scale project, a sense of seeing something through to the finish, in a museum, print and film. A sense of closeness to a warm group of special women and a chance to do something great on my own one day."[62]

Others had explicitly feminist aspirations. Ruth Crane, fifty-two, and experienced at needlework, worked from December 1977 to February 1978; she wrote that *The Dinner Party* studio "seems to be an opportunity to be in an unique feminist project that is not likely to come my away again."[63] Carol Bromberg, twenty-six, came to the studio with already developed feminist ideas. She saw the call for volunteers in the feminist journal *Chrysalis*, and wrote that she hoped to gain "a sense of what it is to work with women on a woman-identified project."[64] Linda Preuss, from Cleveland, wrote that "I see myself as being part of a piece of art that is going to have an enormous impact on the image and history of women."[65]

Those who crossed the studio doorway had their own reasons for doing so. The path Juliet Myers, who became a stalwart member of the core staff, took to *The Dinner Party* studio represented the all-too-common experience of gender discrimination in the art world and its role in pushing women toward feminism. While working toward a master's degree in printmaking at the University of Missouri in Kansas City in the early 1970s, Myers studied under one of the department's few female faculty members. She recalled being impressed by her teacher and by the handful of female students in her program, all whom had a determination to make a name for themselves despite the fact that few female artists appeared in their art history books or course materials. After finishing her degree, Myers took a position teaching art in the Kansas City public schools, but after a few years she felt listless and bored. She dressed the part of the good art teacher, yet was drawn to the counterculture around her. In 1976 she left her tenured job and with her retirement funds set out for "points unknown." She arrived in Los Angeles and heard from friends about Chicago and her studio: "I arrived in LA and Judy's name was like a beacon. Just to know that there was this person, I knew she was important and that she was a rebel. She was not in any of the art books. . . . I heard that there was a project and all these women are working on it, and I said wow, I want to do that."[66]

Her first attempt at working at the studio was rebuffed. But in the spring of 1977, Myers went to the open house the studio held to attract new volunteers. She immediately agreed to do historical research to identify the 999 women of merit for the Heritage Floor. Uninvolved with feminist political activism, Myers was nonetheless drawn to be a part of the group of women at the studio and to work on a project about women's history. Scouring old histories for accounts of women who shared a desire to make more of themselves and to challenge limits brought Myers's own quest into a new context.[67] She worked for Chicago for nearly twelve years over the next two decades.[68]

Chicago's lecture about *The Dinner Party* and the group of men and women working at the studio proved to be one of the best ways to pull in new volunteers. A group of twenty-five women in Cleveland, Ohio, organized funds to bring Chicago to speak in the spring of 1977.[69] They called themselves the Cleveland-Chicago Connection. Out of this group, three women—Dorothy Goodwill, Cindy Waronker, and Linda Preuss—arranged to live in California for a few weeks to work on the project.[70] A fourth, Jeanne Van Atta, told her mother, Bette Van Atta, about the project. Bette's and Dorothy's experiences capture the unexpected sense of excitement many nonactivist women found in the practice of feminism of the studio.

At sixty-seven, Bette was in the process of moving from Cleveland to a retirement community in Arizona, but at the encouragement of her daughter she sent a letter of inquiry to Susan Hill with samples of her needlework. Hill liked what she saw and quickly responded, "When can you join us? We'd love to have you stitch with us." Bette left for Santa Monica in early February 1977 and had the distinction of being the oldest person working at the studio. She wrote to her daughter that she felt terribly intimidated by the work atmosphere at the studio: "I can't possibly sew well enough to meet the high standards they expect here. The runners are so beautiful and so perfect and so delicate and minute in detail it seems as though they couldn't have been made by anyone."

Not one to avoid a challenge, she bought a new pair of bifocals and a magnifying glass and announced to her daughter that "Lo and behold. I can do it." She was sewing a runner for Italian Renaissance princess and art patron Isabelle D'Este. According to her daughter, "suddenly she was talking about how she absolutely had to see the finished piece when it was exhibited. . . . Then she wrote that she was going to a CR group at night and out to dinner with different women who are involved in the project. Each letter was more enthusiastic than the last." At the end of February, Bette wrote her daughter about feeling sad that her time was at an end and that she had to return to her responsibilities in Arizona: "'What responsibilities?' I had to ask. 'You are retired, you have no dependents, you get a social security check every month, and you can do whatever you want—probably for the first time in your whole life.' The reply: 'I have decided to stay on longer. I will be moving in with a woman I met here, her husband, his mother and three cats in a big old house.'"[71] Bette particularly liked the experience of joining a consciousness-raising group and the process the studio established to let the workers solve whatever problems arose. According to *LA Times* reporter, Barbara Isenberg, Van Atta explained during the reporter's visit to the studio that she "originally came here because of the stitchery but got involved in both feminism and consciousness-raising activities."[72]

Dorothy Goodwill, one of the founders of the Cleveland-Chicago Connection, spent two months at the studio, leaving her three teenage daughters and husband to fend for themselves in South Euclid, Ohio.[73] Goodwill, experienced in needlework, had worked on liturgical vestments and altar hangings for Episcopal churches in northern Ohio. She arrived at the studio and was set to work on the runner for medieval abbess and mystic Hildegarde of Bingen. She researched the medieval and ecclesiastical embroidery style, Opus Anglicanum, known for its gold and silver couching.[74] With her training and interests, Goodwill was perfectly matched to work on the Hildegarde runner, another sign of Hill's skill in assigning the right person to the right task.[75]

Like other volunteers, Goodwill participated in the lively group meetings and consciousness-raising groups at the studio and reported that the experience was "transformative." The Cleveland press proudly covered Goodwill as a talented and perky mom on an extended field trip to sew. However, the impact of her time at the studio reached beyond stitching. After Goodwill's two months in LA, Gelon and Goodwill continued to enjoy a close friendship, with Gelon frequently staying with Goodwill and her family during her long cross-country fund-raising trips.[76] Dorothy developed romantic feelings for Diane Gelon, the studio manager, feelings that took her by surprise. Goodwill struggled with the implications of her attraction. On December 18, 1978, Gelon wrote in her diary that she had "talked to Dorothy—she's having a hard time in Cleveland."

> She writes me of how it feels to "live in a foreign country" and to "have a black pit" in her stomach. I am trying to be there for her but I have a relationship here that I care about and so I can only proceed with what [I know] will not cause conflict. I am Dorothy's friend and want to maintain that—I am sorry it is so hard for her. I hope that in the end it will be for the best that I provided her with a safe space to deal with her feelings for me.[77]

Goodwill's questioning of her sexual orientation echoed the experience of many women who joined feminist groups, participated in consciousness-raising groups, or who read the books, articles, underground media, and novels of feminism that asked if traditional heterosexuality could be made to accommodate truly liberated women.[78] Goodwill might have spoken to feminists at the studio who openly viewed heterosexuality as a form of male power over women; if she dipped into the suggested studio reading list at all, she most certainly had been introduced to this style of lesbian feminism. However she came across it, Goodwill appeared to have experienced the often jarring transformation of her ordinary and taken-for-granted consciousness by the ideas of feminism or by spending time in a feminist environment where other women lived quite differently than she did.[79] Her heterosexuality had become a foreign land, even if only temporarily.[80]

Shannon Hogan also found the studio enlightening as she plotted how to escape her domestic confinement. When she arrived to volunteer at the studio, she was in her midthirties, the mother of three boys and wife to a husband who looked askance at his wife's budding feminism. "He didn't want me to volunteer. He agreed only if I was sure to have dinner on the table each night," Shannon later recalled, rolling her eyes. Hogan cultivated her artistic skills by working on a series of projects while raising her sons and tending to the family home in Los Angeles. She found it inspiring to watch Chicago follow her own creative process.[81] She listened closely to the other women who shared their experiences about art and feminism and participated in Thursday night rap sessions.[82] Years later, Hogan attributes her ability to open her own graphics company and divorce her husband to the lessons on self-sufficiency and self-worth she learned at the studio.[83]

For Goodwill and Hogan, the studio introduced them to unfamiliar aspects of 1970s feminism. In contrast, Ann Isolde had already had a feminist awakening before she arrived at the studio in 1977. Ann earned her MFA at the University of Colorado and was living with her husband in Boulder in the early 1970s. When her husband announced that he wanted an open marriage, Ann reacted with a mix of hurt and anger. Open marriages, or marriages where both partners could enjoy sexual relationships with other partners either with or without their spouses, enjoyed new visibility in the straight sexual revolution of the 1970s. Ann describes her husband's experimentation as "heart-breaking," and the couple separated.[84] Through friends, Ann found her way to a women's collective and moved in. Outside the confines of a nuclear marriage, she began to reevaluate her marriage and her life. She joined a consciousness-raising group sponsored by NOW and also discovered a feminist art organization called Front Range Women in the Visual Arts, a group of university-trained artists living in Boulder.[85] When one of the other women in the collective and her new boyfriend announced that they were relocating to LA, Ann decided to join them, excited by the prospects of participating in the vibrant feminist art scene there. The three of them took off for the West Coast in October 1975, and Ann enrolled at the Feminist Studio Workshop, where she heard about Chicago's new project and decided to volunteer.[86]

The kind of volunteer Chicago drew to the studio—the artist, the housewife, the office manager—testified to the broad appeal of *The Dinner Party* project itself. For the women who came to work, the opportunity to participate in a feminist group and make woman-centered art was worth the effort. If they worked intensely for two months, every weekend for a year, or twice weekly for six months, the women who worked on *The Dinner Party* rearranged their lives to do so. The structured, welcoming atmosphere of the studio reflected the willingness of Chicago and the core staff to tolerate newcomers. Hill recalled that after long winter weeks with only a few people working at the studio, seasoned workers welcomed the influx of summer volunteers, happy for the extra hands and the new surge of energy into the project.[87] As more volunteers arrived, Chicago's studio became as much a dense web of relationships as a literal workspace. Together, Chicago's vision of women's history, the workers who wanted to participate in something larger than themselves, and the group's focus on making high-quality art made the studio an unusual and personally transformative feminist space.

Practice and Process

Judy expects a great deal from DP workers—in this way each of us has learned to expect more of her/himself.

As with the making of *Womanhouse* in 1972, Chicago strove to practice feminism in the making of *The Dinner Party*. The process by which the piece came into existence became as much of an expression of feminist values of collaboration and enlightenment as the piece itself. Practicing feminism was not always comfortable, as Chicago's experiences in feminist art education and institution making had proved. The women's liberation movement, with its mantra "the personal is political," rooted its vision of female liberation firmly in the realm of relationships, relationships made up of equals. Feminists cast relationships—between men and women and among women—as the medium through which oppression could be studied and liberation practiced. They studied personal interactions with men for signs of sexism, and with women for signs of male identification or "power trips," in the vernacular of the times. Group dynamics among women in the years of feminist activism were a principle site for the practice of female equality and empowerment.

However, as the experiences at FSC, CalArts, and the Woman's Building demonstrated, feminist groups did not always attain the goals of equality and empowerment, and these lapses shaped the experience of feminism in the 1970s as much as did the admirable goal of harmonious sisterhood. Attention to personal dynamics and relationships often made group processes difficult or tedious, and at times, painful. A deep ambivalence about power—who had it and who did not—crippled many groups. The highs and lows of group processes riddled groups and institutions throughout the history of the women's liberation movement, often paralyzing meetings and driving members away.[88] This blend of empowerment and disempowerment in feminist group dynamics also played out in Chicago's studio, but in terms that were unique to the unusual setting. Group processes mattered, but not as much as they had in the FAP, and the more seasoned studio workers did not question Chicago's leadership in the ways that the younger and untested students in the FAP programs had. Most centrally, the mission of the group that gathered in Chicago's studio never waivered: they gathered together to make *The Dinner Party*. Women artists volunteered and did their own art before, during and after their time at *The Dinner Party* studio, but building their careers was not the purpose of the group.

Even with the differences between the women gathered at FAP and *The Dinner Party* studio, Chicago felt committed to the techniques of feminist art education and applied them. Workers could expect to participate in groups and activities outside of the studio where they would encounter feminist methods of personal change directly. Studio orientation materials explained that

> Part of your work time will also include feminist education sessions, group raps and exchange of knowledge . . . there is a group that runs on the beach 3 mornings per week—we are in need of more runners (so to speak—you will get that joke once you arrive—) so bring your sweat pants. In addition we have regular Thursday night meetings for everyone involved in the project. A tentative schedule of events is attached. You will also be involved in a Consciousness Raising Group with the members of the workshop—together you will decide on a time to meet. . . . These function independently of the studio and will be held outside of the studio in your homes/apartments, etc.[89]

Volunteers were also given a reading list in feminist theory. This included such titles as Simone De Beauvoir, *The Second Sex*; Robin Morgan, *Sisterhood Is Powerful*; Mary Daly, *Beyond God the Father*; Lucy Lippard, *From the Center*; and Virginia Woolf, *A Room of One's Own*, a veritable canon in the fast-growing field of women's studies.[90]

Gelon oversaw two kinds of studio groups: consciousness-raising, done in groups of eight to twelve people; and Thursday night "rap sessions," where anyone working at the studio, or who had worked at the studio, met collectively around the huge ceramics worktables, pushed together family style, to share potluck dinners and conversation. These gatherings enacted the goals of feminist education: to enhance everyone's involvement by soliciting ideas and feedback; to address group dynamics in the studio in an honest and direct manner; to explore the significance of women's lives and women's history; and to connect the work at the studio to the larger efforts to bring women's history to light. On a more practical level, Thursday night full-studio meetings also proved critical in coordinating what could be quite a large group. Together, the small consciousness-raising groups and the large Thursday evening meeting provided the weekly structure that kept the project moving forward.

Consciousness-raising in the studio became a foundational practice and one of the experiences that left volunteers feeling that they truly had encountered feminism. Orientation materials explained the process:

> CR is not group therapy. The underlying assumption of CR is that we are healthy people responding to the crazy-making social structures we live in. The purpose of CR is mutual validation so that we do not feel like we are alone in the world with our problems. Another purpose to CR is to make sure each woman "takes her space." This is accomplished by structuring the discussion around a specific topic (chosen weekly) and requiring each participant to speak to the topic twice, in turn, for five minutes. Women in CR groups together become very close and offer tremendous strength to each other. If you plan on being at the studio for more than a few months it is strongly recommended that you join one.[91]

Volunteer L. A. Olson explained that these groups were "one of the bonuses" of the work. "By following the structure for consciousness-raising meetings, which includes letting everyone take space, listening to each person, being non-judgmental and supportive, we had developed a strong support group within the eight weeks." Consciousness-raising groups were workshop specific, and when those workshops ended, women who stayed on at the studio joined other groups. Olson, who found her participation in an eight-week intensive so compelling that she took a leave from her full-time job and moved with her husband to Santa Monica, reports that it was through her experience of consciousness-raising that she came to see elements of her personal relationship with her husband as connected to privilege and power. "I expect the privilege of being able to let our relationship suffer some neglect and of having Neil carry some of the nurturing burdens that a wife usually carries; but this is no more than many husbands (including mine) expect when they decide to pursue their goals and go to law school."[92]

Consciousness-raising groups targeted the ways that the identities of wives and mothers often stood in the way of women reaching their full potential. Dorothy Goodwill from Cleveland reported that while "the most important thing that I got personally out of this project was the validation of my own skills . . . I also realized that I am a lot more strong and secure than I thought I was because one of the most important reasons for coming out here for me was to get in touch with myself and an individual instead of myself as a daughter, wife, mother, member of groups from church all the way down to kindergarten."[93] A woman who participated in an eight-week workshop wrote to tell Chicago that once at home she began to apply skills she practiced at the studio. "My husband and children were too dependent upon me for things that were not necessary. As I have observed in the workshop how people perform tasks to the best of their ability independently and then if in doubt ask for help, I now feel the assertive strength to ask that my children rely on their own reasoning more and facilitate my family modeled after the workshop."[94]

The dovetailing of the workshop structure with feminist principles and a tremendous workload made group meetings, small or large, a time when team members pushed each other to work harder and to take their contributions to the project seriously. Some found the pressure transformative. "Judy expects a great deal from DP workers—in this way each of us has learned to expect more of her/himself. The process of the DP has encouraged self-esteem (sadly lacking in many women) and maturation. Human growth is what the DP is all about and Chicago has provided a safe environment for the hardy and fragile to become whole human beings."[95]

But the process of becoming "whole human beings" came at a cost and often led to resentment. Terry Blecher, a recent college graduate and skilled textile artist who worked for two and a half years at the studio and wrote a master's thesis for Goddard College about her experience, described her dislike of the guilt and pressure put on workers to give more, do more, and stay longer. Blecher's impressive needle skills coupled with chronic fatigue made her feel particularly conflicted about the physically demanding work of stitching.

> I began stitching immediately upon entering the studio. I had trouble sitting still and working for long periods of time. My eyes became strained from close work. Each day while I was packing up to leave, Susan Hill, the head of the

> needlework loft, tried to talk me into staying longer hours and setting higher goals for myself. Susan and Judy were very demanding of me and my energies from the time I began working at the studio. I explained that I was sick and my energy level was low. I felt I was being pushed and pulled and was angry at their demands on my time.[96]

Having her work evaluated by Hill and her work habits made public in the group setting led Blecher to wonder whether she was working as hard or as well as she might. "I felt intensely vulnerable, exposed and lost all at once and I didn't know where to turn. I began weekly therapy to help sort out the feelings revolving around my fantasies about myself, my poor self image, my problem integrating my successes, and my resistance."[97]

A testimony to the stress of the studio and the often personally challenging techniques of consciousness-raising, Blecher's soul-searching was indicative of the atmosphere not only of feminism in the 1970s, but broadly in the alternative self-help movements spawned by the counterculture.[98] Personal growth and self-development had emerged as touchstones by the mid-1970s, touchstones that became more and more commodified as the context that linked lifestyle to left-leaning political activism faded.

Feminists had long criticized conventional therapy for its personalizing and trivializing of power relations, and Blecher, committed to feminism as she was, concluded that her individual therapy could not give her the larger framework of history in which to couch her experience. Ultimately, she found that her consciousness-raising group helped her feel more confident and gave her a way to confront her "role conditioning" more effectively than did therapy. "I was surrounded by women who were struggling with the same issues in their lives (authority, work, self image, and relating to people). Sharing these struggles brought us out of isolation so that we could feel safe with our painful and joyful discoveries. Bringing these issues into the community of The Dinner Party Project was a first step towards positively communicating our private experiences as women in the public sphere."[99]

Not all the women who came through the studio found it positive or empowering. Blecher identified a pattern she saw among the women who volunteered. Women started with lots of enthusiasm, which was then followed by resistance and reluctance, and for some, retreat.

> When women see that they will not be taken care of in ways they are accustomed to, and that demands are being made on them, which involve work, commitment and participation in a new way, they often become angry and

> resistant. This stage is filled with painful and/or joyful political and personal realizations. People who are not willing to deal with these intense feelings, or are afraid, may withdraw and even leave the process at this time. The third stage is characterized by a catharsis, bringing the individual closer in touch with their personal power, which is the goal of feminist education.[100]

Being pushed to work diligently at the studio led some to appreciate their own capacities more. Adrienne Weiss, youngest of the regular workers at seventeen, wrote that "one of the main things that I've learned here (or begun to learn) is how to endure and do things even if I don't want to. I also feel a lot more powerful here than before I came here."[101]

Another woman noted that, "I realized last night that I have never really tested my limits and so I always feel more limited than I am."[102] The pressure to do more, and be more responsible to the group set the studio apart from other work environments and what, for Elaine Ireland, made the studio empowering: "I have rarely if ever experienced support from any other working environment to excel or be strong, serious or decisive. There were always orders coming down to obey. There was never any need to be disciplined, or aware, centered or focused. There was never anything to be responsible to other than filling someone's glass or typing some else's words. I never had much of a chance to be who I am with those characteristics, but many chances to be who I could be without them."[103]

One of the most important expectations of the studio was that volunteers take ownership of the work they contributed, be it on one runner, doing graphic design, or sweeping. The cooperative atmosphere of the studio supported this goal and promoted a view that every person could and should participate in problem solving and, to some extent, decision making. However, a person had to put in the hours and do the work if she or he wanted to have authority in the studio. Work was the coin of the studio realm, a status open to anyone, no matter the person's skill level. This gave many women a sense of collaboration and responsibility and kept them engaged in what was often tedious work. Marti Rotchford, a devoted member first of needlework and later, graphics, explained that "each new problem is open to input and whoever comes up with the best solution is responsible for overseeing its implementation. In this way responsibility is shared so cooperation becomes spontaneous. Because of this I can take joy in work that is otherwise arduous, boring, painstaking in detail and taken piecemeal, aesthetically limited." She concluded that, "I can act simultaneously as a leader and co-peer within my working situation. It is the feminist atmosphere in which I work daily that provides me with the perseverance to keep at the work that still confronts us."[104]

While many volunteers reported feeling powerful in the studio, many also recognized that the studio was not a simple place of feminist solidarity. The work was physically difficult, the immersion in one part of one runner intense and myopic, tension among workers thick, and anger at the demands ever-present. One woman wrote in the group journal that "I think I feel better each and every time I come in—despite the fact that I am always SO TOTALLY guilt-ridden about not putting in enough time!"[105]

Feelings toward Chicago seesawed from admiration to rage and back again, creating rich fodder for Thursday night rap sessions about the emotions inspired by women in positions of authority. The studio and Chicago herself tried to contain these feelings in abstract discussions. But on less theoretical levels, the feelings of love and resentment made the studio's atmosphere charged. One woman wrote, "I love Judy for who she's been, is, and what she is giving me"; another that, "When I first came to the studio I was afraid of Judy, then I was in awe of her, and now I love her." Few written records exist for those who found her too demanding, or the work unrewarding, or who simply left. According to Blecher, women who came to the studio with an "inflated sense of their skill level would be confronted with reality, couldn't cope with the truth, and would leave."[106] One brave woman signed her name to one of the few written critical comments in the community journal: "Once more I feel oppressed by Judy Chicago. Laura Elkins."[107] Stated and unstated tensions appear in passing comments. For example, Thelma reported that she often knew something had happened at the studio when she wasn't there: "I can feel the tension. Although I am not usually directly involved in whatever confrontation has taken place the tension builds up in me and there are times when I get home from the studio that I have to lie down."[108] An unsigned entry in the collective journal announced that "people are starting to go crazy again."[109]

Thursday nights constituted an important staging for the practice of feminist group process. These sessions provided moments to clear the air in the studio and often helped to restore a necessary sense of context and history. In addition to process meetings, Chicago and Gelon arranged for guest speakers—historians, feminists, and artists—to present their work on Thursday nights. Orientation materials explained these were "either brown bag or pot luck (as announced every week). They are also either semi-structured around a guest speaker or they are open raps about random but timely topics."[110] They also scheduled potluck dinners one Thursday each month for talking, laughing, and relaxing. One worker, Fay Evans, describes a particularly high-spirited dinner in the fall of 1976: "We started throwing spaghetti at one another, why not it was cold by now. Some were jumping on top of the table. Stomping the wilted salad and the best part was squishing the butter through our toes. Only a few of us got to do that; and some people think that sex is the best activity in the world, try butter toe squishing. . . . We're getting to be more and more like a family."[111]

That the studio was family-like was both positive and problematic. Bonds of sisterhood, forged in relation to Chicago as mother-goddess, made feminism intimate and cozy at some points for some participants, but for others, the moments of confrontation between project members, between team members, and with Chicago were too visceral to be easy or comfortable. One exchange particularly captures this tension. Robyn Hill wrote to Chicago about her feeling about their interactions and her "fear of speaking up—exercising my voice," and feeling that she needed some control over her work in the studio. She let the artist know that she viewed this letter as "only a start—it is intentionally brief because lengthy explanations have been very agonizing and incoherent in past aborted letters to you."[112]

Chicago struck back, characterizing Robyn's tone as "defensive and untrusting."

> As to speaking up, the entire structure of the studio is set up to help each person to grow to the point where she can express herself openly and the degree to which a person can't do that is her responsibility. I believe that all we can do is provide an environment for growth, creative work and personal integrity. . . . I'm not particularly interested in your arriving in the fall to "do a job" but rather in your coming based on your decision that you have something to give and something to get from working here.[113]

These painful moments in the studio were as much a part of the feminist environment as were the joyful ones. Yet within the dominant narratives of feminism, with its emphasis on sisterly solidarity and appreciation for strong women, these ruptures in relationships were hard to incorporate or appreciate. Group dynamics had no simple meaning, but rather reflected the value feminists in the 1970s placed on process. Group processes functioned as a form of prefigurative politics, a way to practice equality, respect, collaboration, and personal growth even as those involved saw themselves as unfinished feminist works in process. Studio processes, like all group dynamics, were unstable and shifting, continually changing as women came or left, bonded with the group or felt pushed beyond their limits. Yet even with all the emotional ups and downs, most of the volunteers reported that immersion in group process with other women, be the group a needlework team or consciousness-raising gathering, comprised the best part of their studio experience.

The Muse of the Studio

Alone and apart from the mythic "Judy Chicago."

With her quiet studio transformed into a group workspace, Chicago's sense of self strengthened and fragmented. While Chicago submerged herself in a collaborative creative enterprise, her journal entries record her ongoing rebellion against abandoning the deeply engrained myth of the isolated artist. As her dependence on others for emotional support and artistic work grew, and as she grew more comfortable in having people in her studio working alongside her daily, she simultaneously struggled with a commitment to her professional success and to the goals of the feminist art movement. After all, she was the artist. Her name brought people from around the country to work with her. Her reputation was at stake.

Throughout the four years of making *The Dinner Party*, Chicago confronted the gap between herself as feminist icon and her inner perception of herself as limited, irritable, and increasingly exhausted. In January 1976, she despaired over the situation she had brought on herself. "In a way, all these people, with all their ideas about the importance of the piece and their raving about it, make me feel intimidated. Instead of feeling more connected to it, I get afraid of its implications." Later that summer, she again returned to the sense of being torn apart by the gap of competing self-conceptions: "It seems that if I am not with Diane [Gelon], who sees me as I see myself, or in the process of working on the piece with the other people who believe in me, my own belief falters and I begin to lose my grasp of who I am and what I'm capable of." She went on: "So today I am alone, and my self is capsizing. I think there is a growing gulf between my own belief in myself and how I present myself to the world. A crack in the wall . . . it is getting harder, not easier." She confessed in a July 1977 entry to needing to find space "where I can be alone and apart from the mythic 'Judy Chicago.'"[114]

When the dynamics were good and work went smoothly, Chicago felt strong and connected to her past and to the larger feminist movement. She drew positive connections to her time in Fresno in September 1976, writing, "Last night I felt the power of what I've created: fifteen women were there—assertive, eager, committed to the Project. I've built an environment again—like in Fresno." She took pride in creating an environment that enacted her feminism. "The studio atmosphere is wonderful," she wrote in the winter of 1977. "People are growing as a result of the permission the Project and the studio afford. It's great to see. If growth is not stunted and people are allowed some space, they expand and fill it, assuming their expansion is not seen as a threat by those whose space it is." The members' positive responses often gave her a needed boost of perspective. In her journal from August 1977, Chicago wrote of the overall successful environment of the studio, "What a long way from Fresno and even from *Womanhouse*. I see the progress finally—fusing my own art making with an educational context that allows me to operate fully (if not with as much private space as I'd like) while providing a context in which women can grow."[115]

However, Chicago was not always able to see the large group as a sisterhood. At times, she found its dynamics challenging. Chicago reported that, "I try and remind myself that all these people are working with me for nothing, and I try to be responsible for their growth and needs—but sometimes it's hard." Sometimes the cost of paying people with the experience of feminism felt too high, required too much of her, and infused her studio with emotional drama she did not want. She reported that Thursday nights often became gripe sessions that wore her out. She longed to drop what she felt to be the heavy burden of leadership and responsibility for the project and for the feminist process she had set in place. "I felt that people took too much from me, that I had to be artist, organizer, and energy source all at once when I could hardly keep myself together. I brought this all up at our Thursday night meeting."

Relinquishing some control over the daily operations of the studio, particularly to Hill and Gelon, certainly helped to enact Chicago's dream to create a kind of feminist community. At the same time, Chicago's separation from the group resulted in discomfort among the workers who had been moved to participate by Chicago's forceful vision of her place in art history. Many wanted a heroine, not a sister. Chicago noted the group's ambivalence in a March 1977 journal entry that "people are struggling to emerge from their fantasies and misconceptions about me—from seeing me as 'up there,' the authority, to allowing me to be a person among them."[116]

As with the making of *Womanhouse* in 1970, the process of making *The Dinner Party* from 1974 to 1979 emerged from the practice of feminism. The processes established by Chicago and project members through which the literal piece came into existence were shaped by the values of self-empowerment through work and the importance of women-centered alternative groups. The studio, as a space and as a set of relationships, enacted the principles and goals of feminism; the dramas that unfolded there highlight the ways that those goals played out, positively and negatively, in women's groups.

Foremost, the feminist message promoted by Chicago and the studio environment reflected the mid-1970s emphasis on individual women and the centrality of self-perception to feminist empowerment. The terrain of the psychological, politicized by radical feminists in the late 1960s, continued to shape cultural feminism, but in distinctive ways.[117] The focus of mid-1970s feminism as it was practiced by predominantly white and middle-class women was on individual women's transformation in the face of crippling gender socialization. While socialization happened to women as a group, and as such where feminism retained its attention to politics, the emphasis on change in cultural feminism highlighted individual women and emphasized activities like personal growth, insight, and expression. For women like Chicago and the project members, a woman changed by feminism was an emboldened political actor, ready to take to the streets, cast the right vote, or confront others in her life for underestimating her. In this way, cultural feminism never surrendered the realm of politics.

At the same time, by continuing the focus on the personal as political but embedding it in individualism, cultural feminism problematically embraced a therapeutic model of change. An empowered woman might as easily opt not to participate in politics. She might find cultural consumption—buying women-centered books, music, art, or activities—more than political activism to be the best way to express her individual style of feminism.[118] More troubling, when harnessed to individuality, cultural feminism could easily support a myopic view of power and help mask the deeper structures of inequality that forged unwanted collective experiences of discrimination based on race, class, and sexuality.

The people who came to Chicago's studio embodied some of these troubling tendencies of an individualized, therapeutic, and culturally oriented feminism. Each had to have enough financial support to volunteer. Not all were comfortably middle-class, not all had families that could help them, and not all enjoyed a college education. Yet their various privileges, be they from race, class, or marriage, nevertheless permitted them to work without pay at Chicago's studio. As a result, for many of them, personal growth became the most relevant terrain of feminist empowerment. Some used the experience to bring about change in classrooms, in the teaching of art history, in the representation of women in the media, and in the overall treatment of women in a male-dominated society. Some applied their new feminist insights to their child-rearing practices and their marriages or divorces. Some looked to buy or make women-centered cultural products. For all of them, no matter if they consumed feminism or organized under its banner, the studio had been a place where they experienced feminism and made it relevant to their own lives.

CHAPTER FOUR

Joining Forces

Making Art and History at The Dinner Party, *1975–1979*

BETWEEN 1976 AND 1979, Chicago headed a significant cultural feminist art studio in Santa Monica, California. She had succeeded in drawing people to help her complete a monument to women's history, *The Dinner Party*. As the studio expanded, Chicago grew more comfortable with the process of cooperation that enabled the work-intensive project to proceed. The sheer amount of art being made each day made it nearly impossible for all decisions to run through Chicago. Workers consulted with each other over how to address the range of problems or issues that came up. At the same time, even as volunteers took responsibility for their work and tackled many questions on their own, the structure of the studio was unquestioningly hierarchical: Chicago was never far away or far removed from the daily flow of decisions in the studio. She had the power to decide if a volunteer's work on a runner had to be altered or if the glaze on a plate hit the right color. She did so in dialogue with others in the studio, but it was very clear that all final decisions rested with Chicago. This dynamic—of empowerment within hierarchy, where individuals claimed authority and responsibility through their clearly demarcated roles in a tiered system—characterized the way Chicago practiced feminism in *The Dinner Party* studio. Volunteers could learn from her and participate in an ongoing fine art project. They could give their time and effort and take all they could get from the experience. Responsibility for the piece, however, its symbolism and metanarrative of Western women's history, its potential to make or break her career, remained Chicago's.

That said, the meanings of the feminism practiced in the studio extended beyond Chicago and cannot be measured simply by *The Dinner Party*'s effect on Chicago's career or even its role in the larger feminist art movement in the 1970s. Given its unique production conditions, understanding the feminist meaning of *The Dinner Party* must include an examination of the feminist ideology that infused each design decision and Chicago's translation of a "new" history of women into art.

Like other cultural feminists in the 1970s, Chicago's feminism was bound by limits in both imagination and resources. Multicultural accounts of women had yet to be written; accounts of poor, laboring, or enslaved women were only just beginning to be published by new feminist historians. Culling a history of women from traditional sources, Chicago's team of researchers inadvertently reproduced many of the biases that later generations of historians have corrected. Even within the limits of their day, the researchers were informed by the first stirrings of what would become cornerstones of the vibrant fields of women's studies and women's history. They read, discussed, and absorbed bold new theories about the role of patriarchy in capitalism, the suppression of women's education and spiritual authority, and the prevalence of rape in history.[1] Chicago and her team were not driven by the desire to offer global, transnational, or non-European histories of women as they might have been if they had been working ten years later. Rather, contemporary US gender politics and the themes held most dear to (white) US feminists in the early 1970s shaped the overarching vision of history Chicago told through *The Dinner Party*.

Like other US feminists of her generation, Chicago witnessed a host of related contradictions in women's status in the United States. Women attended college but were unwelcomed in the professions; women worked for pay but in positions that offered little chance for advancement or potential for leadership; the term *glass ceiling* would not appear until 1984. Women enjoyed the right to vote, but few held positions in political parties, the judiciary, or in local, state, or national halls of power. Women of this generation came of age participating in the struggles to challenge US racism and watched the enshrinement of color-blindness as a form of antiracism go hand in hand with ongoing discrimination. Black women continued to earn less in any job classification than did other workers. US women watched the Cold War–era commitment to female domesticity transform to a widespread celebration of female sexual availability, the freedom to divorce coupled with rising rates of female poverty, the programs to end poverty again targeting black mothers for special scrutiny.

These nesting contradictions shaped the wide-reaching goals of 1970s feminists, from mandating civil rights, equal pay, and abortion rights, to protesting the harnessing of women's bodies to commodities and corporate profits.[2]

Activists moved on different priorities. Liberal feminists targeted the public culture of institutional sexism that limited women's economic and political opportunities. Radical feminists pointed out the sinister fact of patriarchy, its simple-minded obsession with controlling women's bodies and sexuality, and the power women could mobilize if they would recognize their membership in the sex class "woman." Women of color feminists pioneered analyses of simultaneous and overlapping modes of oppression and called for coalition politics with male allies.[3] All feminists declared the personal was political even if they did not embrace an imagined community of like-minded sisters.

Concern with establishing women as a class of people discriminated against because of their female bodies—a view articulated predominantly by white middle-class women—was woven into *The Dinner Party* while other concerns (welfare rights, women of color feminism, lesbian and gay discrimination, to name a few) were not. As a result, the history of women offered by *The Dinner Party* is incomplete. However, its incompleteness does not change what *The Dinner Party* did communicate; rather, it highlights the specificity of its understanding of what women's liberation required. Despite its invocation of "woman" unmodified, its utopian hope to speak to and for all females around the world and throughout time, *The Dinner Party* offered a view of the world filtered through the preoccupations specific to its own historical moment. As such, it is best read as a symbolic genealogy or a useable past for 1970s feminist theory, an expression of a culturally oriented US feminism that drew selectively from the past to support a particular vision of the future, not as an account of global women's history. When we look closely at the main artistic components of the exhibit, design choices become windows into the literal embedding of 1970s feminist theory, with its glaring blind spots and brilliant insights, into *The Dinner Party*. The embroidered runners, the ceramic floor, the china plates, and the staging of the piece each distinctively embodied a feminist insight about history and women that, when taken as a whole, constituted a material rendering of 1970s sisterhood at its most ambitious.

Women's Culture and the Runners

Pitch in and stitch!

The Dinner Party runners, which Chicago initially viewed as a backdrop to the plates, which she saw as the main event of the party, became one of the most powerful visual and educational elements of *The Dinner Party*. The sheer amount of time each required also made the runners the most labor-intensive aspect of the work. The process of making the runners, coupled with their role in the larger narrative of *The Dinner Party*, transformed them into a central expression of Chicago's understanding of "women's culture." "Women's culture," a controversial element of 1970s feminism, explained that women had forged an alternative value system, a distinctive moral code and unique social history out of their unique role as mothers and their unique historic experiences of marginalization.[4] Of all the elements that comprised *The Dinner Party*, the runners became the site where ideas about women's culture and women's history intertwined.

Project workers encountered 1970s feminist ideas of a universal "women's culture" most directly by working on the runners. First, sewing and needlework, quintessential elements of women's daily life in the past, became central activities in volunteers' own daily or weekly lives, and this shared activity fostered a sense of transhistorical sisterhood in the needlework loft. Second, since the runners literally embodied the tremendous, orchestrated, and sustained effort by many people over many months and years to complete *The Dinner Party*, they became testimonies to the value of women's collective work to accomplish great deeds. Last, through their efforts with the needle, volunteers learned that, if women's culture was inspiring, it was also potentially disabling. Newcomers faced efforts by team leaders to keep them on task and focused, and in some cases to help them "unlearn" aspects of "women's culture" that stood in their way: women's tendency to chat, the impulse to put down their own work to help someone else, and a reluctance to take ownership and thus responsibility for their actions. Since women allowed other women to sustain these self-abandoning behaviors, the negatives of "women's culture" occupied the same status as what Chicago had earlier called the "personality structures" of her FSC and CalArts students. These "personality structures," framed here as debilitating habits that women nurtured in themselves and in one another, had to be addressed to get the volunteers to work effectively. Since much of this learning took place through needlework, the loft became the source for much of the rhetoric of women's culture that infused the studio.

Susan Hill oversaw and engaged in all the needlework for *The Dinner Party*. She first heard about Chicago from her memoir, *Through the Flower*. In 1976 Hill traveled three hours to hear Chicago lecture on her pyrotechnic work and *Womanhouse*. Chicago concluded her talk by saying she was looking for help with *The Dinner Party*; the next day Hill wrote to volunteer.

Hill had been introduced to feminist ideas in a way typical for nonactivists: she had read Betty Friedan's *The Feminine Mystique* and Germaine Greer's *The Female Eunuch*, which had been published by two large, mainstream publishing houses (Dell and McGraw-Hill, respectively), and *Ms.* magazine.[5]

Yet Hill too experienced the contradictions in women's social status she read about. As a professional photographer, she regularly dealt with prejudicial views of her abilities in her interactions with clients, other photographers, and her boyfriend. She recalls that while potential clients and galleries complemented her work, they tended to doubt if she could carry equipment and they rolled their eyes over her subject matter. "You take lovely photos; they remind me of Walker Evans, but I can't understand why you keep taking pictures of women and children."[6] Adding to her sense of needing a change, she and her partner of ten years ended their relationship. For Hill it was time to start a new chapter in her life. Part of that involved moving to Los Angeles to work with Chicago. Hill recalls that she wavered on whether or not to wear eye make-up for her first meeting with "the great feminist." She did. Chicago assigned her to research. Yet, according to Hill, she was so bad at research, despite graduating from Wellesley College, that Chicago bluntly asked her, "What *else* can you do?" Stuttering and nervous, Hill racked her brain. "I was getting a little desperate. So I tell the great feminist that I can cook and sew. She says, 'you can sew?!'"[7] Chicago immediately reassigned Hill to the tablecloths, a job that suited Hill's long years sewing and embroidering with her women relatives. This, along with her family's loving attention to dinner tables as a gathering place, gave her a deep appreciation of Chicago's vision of a women's dinner party.

The individual runners that came to be one of the main achievements of *The Dinner Party* came about because of a design problem in Chicago's initial conception. Chicago envisioned embroidering the name of each woman around her plate along with a brief identifier, such as "Gaea, the earth as feminine."[8] The needlework would be applied to the sixty-foot-long linen tablecloths covering each wing of the triangular table. Chicago purchased a Bernina embroidery machine for this stitching (since the artist had never mastered needlework), and Hill taught herself how to use it.[9] However, the sheer size of the planned tablecloths and the peevishness of the Bernina, which jammed easily, made that plan unworkable. Once Hill and Chicago realized they would have to cut the cloth to embroider it, the idea of placing an embroidered "runner" over a white tablecloth was born. They modeled the runners on "fair linens," large panels of white linen used on the altar cloth during church sacraments, building on the idea of *The Dinner Party* as the Last Supper. Hill took Chicago to see ecclesiastical embroidery done by embroiderers in the Episcopal Church's Altar Guild and to see the Judaic textiles in the Skirball Museum (now the Skirball Cultural Center).[10]

Chicago wanted to design the runners, not stitch them. That task fell to Hill, who apprenticed herself to Marjorie Biggs, a teacher for the Episcopal embroiderers, to learn the elaborate and varied needlework skills necessary for what Chicago had in mind. The world of traditional needleworkers echoed the world of china painters that Chicago had studied with as she prepared for *The Dinner Party*. It was at this point, according to Hill, that "We discovered the world of embroidery, which, like china painting, has a long and special history. Looking back on it, it seems as if all the information came together at once, and Judy—in that very quick, true way she has—saw the narrative possibilities of presenting the history of needlework through the runners, echoing the chronology of the women on the table."[11] Together, Chicago and Hill moved toward reinventing the runners. According to Hill, this dynamic became indicative of the ways the two women drew inspiration from each other: "I have this very practical idea or suggestion and Judy then sees how to employ it. I never would have on my own envisioned the runners. But I knew the history of embroidery. I showed it to Judy and between us there was that great . . . that's how collaboration works, how it gets bigger than either of you."[12]

A final contribution solidified the design parameters of the runners. Pearl Krause, a needlework designer and owner of an antique textile shop, hit upon the idea of embroidering the runner using design elements from the plate, eliminating "the problem of the embroidery fighting with the plate."[13] In addition, it was decided that each runner should be long enough for nearly a full drop on both sides of the table, nearly covering the white tablecloth underneath. With detailed embroidery both on the side nearest the eventual viewer and on the "back" side of the runner, viewers have both a close-up view and a distant view of the embroidered runners as they move around the tables. These two details augmented significantly the overall effect of *The Dinner Party* on viewers.

Once these decisions had been made, Chicago turned to translating her designs to needlework. "I approached needlework as I had approached every other media I'd used—in terms of what I wanted to express." In this case, Chicago's inexperience in textiles actually proved beneficial to the process since she had "no preconceptions of what could or could not be done."

Neither woman would have anticipated the effort required to make thread do what Chicago did with paint–layer, fade, and shimmer. With the help of a few textile majors from nearby colleges, Hill and Chicago assembled samples of types and styles of stitches into what became the studio's "Embroidery Sample Book," a virtual encyclopedia of embroidery. This established a visual vocabulary for design. Chicago studied it "endlessly, trying to determine how the marvelous visual qualities of these different types of embroidery could best be utilized."[14]

As Chicago discovered the medium's tremendous potential and rich history, the idea of the runners, and its place in the overall message of *The Dinner Party,* expanded. The creation of the sample book, with its traditional symbolic patterns and multiple examples of stitches and techniques, moved Chicago toward seeing embroidery itself as a part of "women's unrecognized heritage." "I decided that—in addition to using embroidery to identify the women on the table and extend the imagery on the plates—I would express something about each woman's experience, environment, or context through a combination of symbolic and literal images which create a narrative on the backs of the runners. This led to an expansion of the iconography of the runners generally."[15]

With this, the newly envisioned runners could capture salient elements of the social and cultural context in which the commemorated woman lived; this in turn clarified the plate as representing the woman's essential self, condensed and abstracted. Each runner would employ fabrics, techniques, and stitching appropriate to the status and era of the woman symbolized on the plate. Chicago explained that the relationship between the runners and the plates would "reflect the varying position of women in different periods of history." Sometimes the "plates dominate the runners," visually recording moments, particularly in prehistorical times, where women were affiliated with the mysteries of nature and the power of the divine. At other points, the runners would "encroach" more forcefully on the plate, reflecting periods of social repression of women's creativity and strength, particularly in the second wing (beginnings of Christianity to the Reformation). By the third wing of the table, marked by the beginning of the nineteenth-century "women's revolution," the runners would break free from the rectangular form to represent "women's growing struggle towards freedom."[16] The runners, once seen as backdrop, were now poised to be one of the more forceful articulations of Chicago's feminism.

Along with their new prominence, the runners now became the most time-consuming element of *The Dinner Party*. Studio members sent anyone who came to volunteer without any specifically useful experience like woodwork or ceramics to the loft. As Hill recalled, "If you didn't come with a skill, we gave you one." "Pitch in and stitch" became the studio mantra. By 1977, as news spread that Chicago wanted help on her project, managing the steady stream of visitors to the studio became a major part of Hill's workweek. The studio set a steep requirement about the hours they expected each person to give (a minimum of sixteen hours a week) in an attempt to separate the merely interested from the truly committed.[17] A few times between 1977 and 1979, the Woman's Building organized weekend *Dinner Party* events where a relatively large group descended on the studio to help. These blasts of newcomers were hardest on Hill. Too often visitors had unrealistic expectations for what they would do for the project in the course of one weekend, a situation that left some local feminists critical of the studio and fed rumors that Chicago exploited her workers.

Once volunteers were assigned to the loft, Hill and others well-versed in studio standards evaluated their needlework skills or taught them basic stitches and set them to practice. Many women spent two or three eight-hour days practicing until their embroidery met Hill's exacting standards. If a volunteer could not master a consistent stitch, she was put to other studio-related tasks: managing supplies, updating the notebooks on each runner, sewing backs on runners, and cleaning the studio. Ann Isolde noted that the studio did not saddle short-term volunteers with housework. "We were expected to take turns emptying the trash, sweeping the floor, and answering the door . . . even the most skilled workers did a share of the dull jobs."[18] At any given time between 1977 and 1979, the loft housed between six and twelve large frames where workers stitched. Every aspect of the making of the runner drew the embroiderer deeper into the meaning of the piece, down to the smallest detail.

Chicago redesigned traditional embroidery frames to hold the long runners fully revealed—not rolled—to fit her feminist vision.[19] She wanted the needleworker to view the runner as a painting and herself as not just following Chicago's design but actively constructing it. The guidelines for needleworkers, written by Hill, underscored this message. "DO NOT PAINT BY NUMBER . . . meaning, don't just imitate the mock-up, following the lines of the pattern, even if they seem wrong. *Stop* and *ask* if you don't think what you're doing looks good."[20] Chicago empowered the needleworkers, many of whom were artists, to bring their own creative sensibilities and hands-on experience of the design to bear on each runner.[21] This approach to embroidery required that the worker be able to see the piece in its entirety, something traditional frames do not permit.[22] Volunteer Millie Stein designed and built large frames that rested on specially built tilting stands designed by the project's fabrication designer, Ken Gilliam. Together, the stand and the frame allowed the needleworker to tilt and turn the runner in a variety of positions.[23] This feminist infrastructure, of course, is not discernible in the finished runner.

Hill strove to make the loft a quiet workplace. Part of her concern in keeping chatter to a minimum came from the space the studio occupied. The loft was an open second floor above the ceramic studio and the graphic and research areas. Everyone in the studio could hear every word spoken, whether or not he or she wanted to.[24] Hill and other core staff encouraged the loft workers to keep on task and not interrupt each other unnecessarily. "We ask you to please work quietly, to have the juicy conversations about abortion or the ERA during a Thursday night rap or at lunch."[25] During the day, Chicago expected no one to speak to her beyond what was absolutely necessary. She would interrupt a person who wanted to chat with her with a tart, "Excuse me, I'm working. Save it for Thursday night."[26] The guide to the loft explained that while "we want our work environment to be one in which people do not have to stifle any dimension of their personal being . . . work and working is taken very seriously."[27]

Minimizing unnecessary chatter also encouraged the group to think about what they were doing. Hill hoped the workers might see stitching as a practice that transcended the gap of history between themselves and the woman whose runner they worked on. In the "Needleworkers' Information Index," an essential orientation and guidebook for new needleworkers, Hill wrote,

> I hope that as you stitch or weave some of the ancient, repetitive rhythms of the work will come to you. Think of the women who make the pieces that are the sources for our needlework: the lace, the alter [*sic*] cloths, the doilies, the mourning pictures, the dampler, bed curtains, tapestries, handkerchiefs, coverlets, silk gauze, gold robes, tiny hems. Embroidery, during its history, was a symbol of great power, used to aggrandize men. We are now building the old patterns and stitches into a new power for women, to honor the women who went before us, and to create a place for women in the future.[28]

Through these materials, the view of women's culture—what women did in the past, their "ancient" rhythms of stitching, their historic subordination to men—oriented volunteers not only to how to behave in Chicago's studio in 1977 but to the studio's feminist vision of women's heritage and a past handed down from woman to woman. Embroidery, once used to "aggrandize men," would now be reclaimed as a "new power" for women.

More than any other element of *The Dinner Party*, the runners united the practice of feminism with the feminist meaning of the piece. Part of this involved volunteers stepping up to new challenges, including translating historical research into a design.[29] Hill would post a meeting for specific runners on the studio calendar; anyone could sign up for the meetings (one runner per day) with the expectation that, in advance of the meeting, they would have done some research on the subject, her times, and circumstances, as well as popular fabrics and designs for the woman's status, traditional symbols, and historically appropriate embroidery techniques. Some runners drew as many as thirteen volunteers, while others only two or three.

At least one highly skilled long-term studio member was always assigned to a runner's team, creating a situation where a handful of women worked on multiple runners. Pat Akers worked on eight, Elaine Ireland twelve, Connie von Briesen seven.[30] On the scheduled day, the group gathered around a large piece of white paper at one of the large ceramic tables on the studio's ground floor and began to brainstorm with the artist. Once Chicago's design emerged, a runner-sized piece of white cotton fabric became the mock-up and was adorned with paint and other fabrics or ornaments to approximate the final design. The mock-up and sketches along with the photocopies of the designs from the meetings went to the graphics studio to become an exact full-scale pattern for the runner. A studio graphics person then transferred the design to the linen of the actual runner as a reference for line and measurements as workers produced the runner.[31]

Karen Valentine explained the cooperative design process as her team began a runner for Sophia, the Gnostic representation of feminine wisdom: "The Sophia runner started to become special on the first day we all sat down at the table to begin the design. We had a pile of multi-colored scraps, and we began to cut petals and arrange them in color sequence. Chicago asked if any of us knew who Sophia was; no one did. While we were working, she read to us about Sophia and what she represented."[32] Out of design meetings, a "runner mother" emerged to lead the team until the runner was finished. Orientation materials explained that "A mother is a person who loves and respects the runner, who cares for her runner by supervising the work with a sharp but tender eye."[33] Mothers assembled and managed other needleworkers who stitched "her" runner. Once the runner had been completed, or "birthed," in the lexicon of the loft, the women paused to celebrate the accomplishment. When a team completed a runner and Chicago signed off on it, Hill washed the runner. She arrived early on those days to submerge the runner in a specially designed wash box on a ceramics table. The runner air-dried in its frame, in its stand in the loft, before being cut off. Women who worked on the piece from beginning to end had their full names embroidered in white thread on the white back of the runner before it was packed away; those who worked on the runner for a limited number of hours had their initials embroidered on the piece. Hill and Chicago used this kind of memorializing of the labor to disrupt the longstanding practice in ecclesiastical embroidery of not acknowledging the artist-craftswomen whose stitches adorned the sanctuary.[34]

Chicago believed that teaching women to commit to sustained work was "a time-consuming but important aspect of the Project" and was key to overturning self-limiting elements of women's culture.[35] During a Thursday-night rap session, captured in the documentary *Right Out of History*, Diane Gelon explained that "All you have to do is to come in when you say you're going to come in and do work, and you've got yourself a track record. This is not a collective; there is a hierarchy in this project, but it's what I call a flexible hierarchy in that anyone can move into it *if they work*. It all comes down to that four-letter word: *work*."[36] Work was the coin of the studio realm. Chicago's emphasis on cultivating good work habits was a direct legacy of her feminist educational practices; women, in this case the white and predominantly middle-class women in the studio, had too often been socialized to not take themselves seriously. Most volunteers worked in service-oriented or support jobs and reported that they had grown accustomed to thinking their work did not matter.[37] According to Hill, the work ethic in the studio confronted "the way women had been dismissed and dismissed themselves as interchangeable or replaceable. It was a part of them not taking themselves seriously. A kind of learned infantilization."[38]

As head of the loft, Hill did much of the teaching and provided much of the work support. She developed a keen sense for matching volunteers to tasks and to knowing whom to push. As she explained, "I have to know whom I can push, and when, and how. I have to be sensitive to who is willing to grow, who is doing the best possible." At the same time, she also found herself in the uncomfortable role of taskmaster and often felt personally "unsupported in the job of doing all the challenging, all the demanding, making all the calls for a quiet work space, faster work. That is a terrible drain."[39] Hill grew dismayed at the ease at which women could put down their tasks to talk or do something for someone else. She came to see this as a part of a set of behaviors culled from women's historical experiences of caretaking. Writing in the orientation guide, she framed this tendency as an element of women's unique culture. "Deep in our heritage is the idea that people gathered around big sewing frames gossip, swap remedies, do CR . . . while away the time with warm and sociable chatter." This "heritage" made keeping the needleworkers on task difficult at times, particularly when Hill confronted their unexamined attitudes about sewing as just "women's work" and therefore insignificant. "I continually fight the whole tradition of the wonderfully soft work pace of women sitting and sewing together. Somehow it is *my* energy that counteracts that whole behavioral set that was delivered to us when we took on embroidery."[40]

The challenges Hill and others faced working with volunteers are apparent when we examine how the Amazon runner was produced. Chicago designed the letter A in the Amazon runner with a double ax, the weapon Amazon warriors carried into battle. Artist Cherie Fraine wrote an account of their group process in March 1978 for the studio. She recalled that a new person eagerly signed up to work on the ax, which required both stitching the handles in thread and figuring out how to attach the metal ax blades to the runner.

> She came every Saturday, had a limited amount of time, and was happy to have a small project to do from start to finish. She was hypoglycemic, and very sociable. She ate many times during her few hours, extending the breaks into visits. Every Saturday she needed a pep talk from me to get going and I spoke to her when the snack breaks became avoidance. The ax handles were a two-person effort. (A year or so later, long after she had moved away, I got a letter, thanking me for my part. She said she hadn't understood discipline or its importance in work at the time, but had come to appreciate what I had tried to show her.)[41]

A second volunteer who had signed up to work on a few additional components of the runner went missing. Fraine explained that "she called to say how guilty she felt, and explained how busy she had been. She asked me to tell her it was okay to leave without finishing; I didn't." The team completed the Amazon axe after project member Elfie Schwitkis took the problem to her husband, an engineer and metals expert, who fashioned the ax blades of titanium, a strong silver metal that would not tarnish or discolor.[42]

Fraine's account of making the Amazon runner included a narrative of her own process, specifically her frustration at being unable to make Chicago's design work and then negotiating with Chicago about changing it. Looking at oneself as part of the creative process meant studying feelings, frustrations, and other psychological dimensions of experience: "Kathleen and I were frustrated with the progress of the runner, and unhappy with the results of the applique. We wanted to make some pieces over, but Judy showed us that our own frustration and compulsion were hindering the work. Instead of giving space and encouraging this process of trial and error, we were generating negative attitudes. So we pulled back. Eventually, when we were still unable to make good shapes in appliqué, Judy agreed to change the technique to embroidery."[43]

Chicago's request that the group study their own "frustration and compulsion" and that they engage in a process that allowed for "trial and error" was less about finishing the runner than about enabling the women gathered to be fully present to the process of art making. Chicago ultimately accepted the changes requested by the workers. But the process inevitably entailed difficult confrontations. Schneider describes feeling crushed when, having "worked steadily and without stopping on the Amazon runner,"

> Judy told me to rip out all of my work—and rightly so, for I haven't been looking at my edges, nor measuring the widths of my couching. 1/16th of an inch makes a big difference on something so small. It looked terrible and I knew it. So I spent the day ripping out what I'd done, reshaped the lines, and am now ready to spend the night re-stitching, very carefully and exactly, never putting down my ruler. I felt so stupid when Judy, at first glance, saw all of my mistakes. Hopefully she hasn't lost confidence in my capabilities and judgment.[44]

The Amazon runner, like most of the thirty-nine runners, took over a year to complete, in part because of the studio's commitment to process-centered feminist practice.

For Hill and Chicago, the process of individual feminist empowerment came about not just from sisterly camaraderie but also from confronting oneself and one's limits, real or perceived. Despite efforts to make the studio a "professional work environment" that rewarded high levels of skill, concentration, and responsibility, many women found "working in this way was new, and in many cases, threatening." People who were unused to working on a set schedule or enduring the physical demands of long hours with the needle simply dropped out. As Hill noted, oftentimes women's culture supported weakness as much as it did strength: "We nurture each other in very self destructive ways: we understand that it's hard on the neck or the eyes to sew, it is hard not to be at home in the evening, not to have the groceries bought; it is hard to work when you have cramps; hard to work on art when you could be making money; hard to work on a feminist project when the very concept is threatening. Worse still than the permission given to women to quit or slow down or take a vacation under these circumstances, is the real refusal to change."[45]

Refusing to change or to even show up on time affected the schedule and work rhythm at the studio. "I am angry and upset," wrote Karen Schneider in the studio's collective journal. "People, it's time to look around and see that others working with you are affected by your actions—do something about it."[46] Volunteers wanted to be transformed by the studio, but the romance of feminist rhetoric faded as the reality of deadlines and the stress of too much work set in. For *The Dinner Party* to be completed, the studio required people who would take ownership over the piece they worked on. The ease with which individual women could evade taking charge of their part challenged the whole idea of enacting feminist education in the face of a huge task with looming deadlines. "It is very hard for most of us to sustain the idea that we are important or powerful," Hill noted.[47] In the loft environment, embroidery became both a symbol and practice of the discipline and effort required to achieve.

Volunteers either adopted the ethic of work as transformative or they left. For those who stayed, the content of *The Dinner Party* and process of making it merged. For example, needleworkers took very seriously the idea of textile history as women's social history. Making the materials in the way that historical women made them forged a link between past and present. For the Primordial Goddess runner, Kathleen Schneider and Hill could not locate suitable pieces of leather or hide for this first and necessarily unadorned earth-bound goddess. Schneider had studied the crafts of North American Indians at the University of Wisconsin as an undergraduate and knew how to tan deerskin, bead moccasins, and carve bone needles. She convinced Chicago that "tanning our own deerskin was a symbolic act that couldn't be passed up since I possessed the knowledge and the deep desire to perform this ancient craft—traditional women's work."[48] She wrote her former professor and, within a few months, received a box of fresh deer-skin from deer killed on the highways of Wisconsin. She gleefully reported in the studio's collective journal that, "This morning I begin the task of de-fleshing the deer hides—removing all of the meat and flesh from the hide so it doesn't rot before we begin the tanning process." After hours of scraping in the alley behind the studio, Hill and Schneider found that the hides were too infested with maggots to use. They reluctantly purchased a finished hide. Undeterred, Karen later successfully made needles out of cow bone, following ancient techniques. She wrote in the journal that "The first bone needle was created yesterday with great success, much work, but oh so satisfying to see the transformation of a rather smelly, marrow-filled cow leg bone, into a delicate, smooth, white, ivory like tool."[49] They stitched the needles onto the Fertile Goddess runner, alongside yarn they made at the studio using the ancient technique of the drop spindle.[50]

Many needleworkers reported a budding identification with the woman on whose runner they worked, often coming to see the historical woman as a role model. Studio rituals and rhetoric supported this view of a trans-historical sisterhood. Stevie Martin, who worked on the Sophia runner, describes problem solving not only with her fellow needleworker Karen Valentine but with Sophia herself. "If we disagreed, Sophia would tell us which way to go."[51] Valentine wrote in the journal about the strong feelings she had when she looked at the completed runner. "She's been a hard task mistress—demanding our best—demanding our love, our intellect, our souls. She fed on our blood, our energy, she gave in return a deeper understanding, a fuller awareness." When Chicago suggested covering the bright colors with a veil to symbolize Sophia's muted power, Karen donated her own wedding veil and her investment in the runner intensified. "The suppression of ages came like a flood of pain and frustration when we covered our gentle goddess in a shroud of silk and net, but her wisdom is only diluted to those who haven't known her." She signed the entry, "In reverence to her, Karen V."[52]

The historic women seated at the table became friends, mentors, and spiritual members of the studio for some longtime workers. Hill recalls that the general mood of the studio darkened when they worked on certain runners: "It is an interesting thought to me that the very bleakest days of the Project and the most tedious runners fall in the same period; Petronilla de Meath, Anna van Schurmann, Hypatia, to name some, were wrung out of us then. Our holding it together through the worst seems to parallel their experiences."[53] It is no wonder the studio's mood soured as they worked on these runners: Hypatia, a Roman scholar who advocated female deities, met "an agonizing death" at the hands of the Christian archbishop in 415; De Meath was burned to death in the thirteenth century for being a witch; and the very intellectually gifted van Schurmann retreated to a monastery in the seventeenth century when her calls for women's equality were resoundingly dismissed.[54] Each of these women's stories also hit on favorite themes of 1970s cultural feminism: the villainy of the Roman Catholic church, witches as victims of patriarchy, and the nunnery as a feminist space.[55]

Working on the runner that represented Mary Wollstonecraft's death in childbirth upset everyone at the studio. Chicago's aunt Dorothy Polin noted that, "Working on Mary Wollstonecraft was an emotional experience for me. I was moved by the charm and beauty of the front of the runner, and deeply saddened as the death scene began to take shape."[56] Adrienne Weiss recorded the process, which had started with Weiss reading a biography of Wollstonecraft: "That summer when I returned from school to work on the project, Judy thought that I would be the perfect one to take a major portion of responsibility for Mary. All along I had thought that stump work seemed like a nutty idea but Judy was always the most fun at her nuttiest. So after some initial resistance . . . I was game.[57]

Stump work was a difficult, abandoned technique. It had been popular in seventeenth-century England with embroiderers who used it primarily to make densely filled "needle pictures" and to decorate home items such as boxes, frames, and cabinets. Its major characteristic was the padding or stuffing of various parts of the design. Women made these raised elements separately and then sewed them onto the surface. Historically, much of this work was done by young girls as part of their embroidery training, making Adrienne Weiss, as the youngest studio volunteer, an obvious if humorous choice for runner mother.[58] Weiss enlisted anyone who entered the studio to help her with the tiny pillowed forms, with the result that pieces of stump work arrived at the studio from around the country. "Often women from out of town who worked at the studio for only a week or so would take some stump work with them and mail back the finished work to us. We have flowers and butterflies from Sacramento and much of the lace on the dolls dresses was sent to us by Bunny Christy, an artist in Washington DC." By the end, "almost everyone in the studio had done a little stump work! (I could never get that Chicago to sit down to stitch though!)."[59] The work required many hands because of its oppressive detailing. Even the studio bathroom graffiti commented on the needleworkers' dislike of stump work.

While Weiss oversaw the many detachable parts of the runner, Julie Brown worked on Wollstonecraft's three-dimensional pillowed form as she died from childbirth, unique among the runners for its portrayal of maternity as deadly. She recalls asking Chicago to look at it before she stitched it onto the runner:

> She looked at it for a while, then said that Mary looked too relaxed and at peace; she should seem ill and weak, her hair wild, oily and sweaty, her gesture exaggerated to express her exhaustion. Chicago manipulated the fabric, crushing the blanket and making it look as if it were about to fall off the bed, crumpling the pillows and pushing them askew. At her urging, I restitched the face with light and dark gray thread to give it a haggard expression, using Chicago's technical drawing as a guide. Instead of a woman in restful sleep, the finished bed scene was a graphic portrayal of the horror and tragedy of Mary Wollstonecraft's death.[60]

The death scene, where a river of blood soaked the bed, stood in stark contrast to the hyperfloral femininity of the runner's top and the assertive plate, done in rich reds, oranges, and greens, that honored Wollstonecraft's forceful 1792 feminist masterpiece, *A Vindication of the Rights of Woman*. Chicago explains that she wanted the stump work "to serve as a visual symbol of the confining environment in which Wollstonecraft, like most of the women of her time, lived."[61] Chicago's message is clear: women's shared biology could not be escaped, even by the most brilliant.

Studio members came to see their own efforts to make the runners paralleled the stories of *The Dinner Party* guests to shape their societies. The psychological hurdles of not taking themselves seriously or of feeling unimportant, which the volunteers had to clear to be able to complete their tasks, paralleled the struggles of *The Dinner Party* guests. These points of convergence between past and present, along with the material details of houses, children, food, jobs, and time that workers had to arrange to simply get to the studio, became the feminist meaning of *The Dinner Party*. Hill explained that, "the runners are very beautiful to me as physical objects, but if the runners are seen as the culmination of a work process that demands and supports change in women's lives, they are truly monuments to power and achievement."[62]

While personally empowering for some workers, the practice of feminism at the studio also had its limits. Unlike the Woman's Building or the feminist classroom at FSC or CalArts, where groups of women gathered to nurture their own art, this group gathered for a single purpose—to create *The Dinner Party*. In Chicago's own words, the group at work on *The Dinner Party* was not a collective; "It was a community only inasmuch as people worked together on one idea, my idea."[63] The sense of shared collaboration between themselves and Chicago on a runner at times led to conflicts over the extent of Chicago's authority over the work. Terry Blecher expressed a sense of confusion over ownership of a runner she had worked on extensively. As the date for the museum opening loomed in the winter of 1978, Blecher took charge of the runner for US birth control advocate Margaret Sanger. She understood what Chicago wanted the runner to look like, but Blecher had made the thousand small decisions to bring it to completion. She felt deeply connected to it and chafed at submitting her needlework to Chicago. "I felt a conflict of ownership for the first time. Was it my piece or Judy's piece or half-and-half? Who should have the final say? These thoughts went through my head for a week as I prepared the techniques I would present to her. I was angry at Judy for having the final say at *The Dinner Party* when I had made all the decisions on the piece, and I was angry at myself for giving her that power and not feeling the confidence to just do it."[64]

The hierarchal atmosphere that supported responsibility and growth on the one hand subordinated all final decisions to Chicago on the other. For Hill, it was a price she was willing to pay. She felt keenly that "they had been entrusted with this history," not just for themselves but for "future generations."[65] The meaning of *The Dinner Party* and the making of the runners was enough to connect her and many other volunteers to both the imagined intimacies of a "women's culture" and the grand sweep of women's history.

The Liberal Promise of the Heritage Floor

Our heritage is our power.

If the runners articulated a view of women's culture, the Heritage Floor represented Chicago's understanding of women's historic accomplishments in Western civilization and as such, quite literally symbolized the salvaged past *The Dinner Party* sought to memorialize. Unlike the vulva/butterfly plates that dramatically represented *The Dinner Party* guest's identity as a vagina-bearing "great" human, the names of women on the floor represented an equally impressive but lesser-known history of women's effort and accomplishment. No longer standing on her own accomplishments in the bright light of history, each guest at *The Dinner Party* stood on the shoulders of generations of women, just as *The Dinner Party* tables quite literally stood on the Heritage Floor. The Heritage Floor, with its 999 golden hand-painted names of women of merit, restored this lost tradition. And because of its centrality to women's empowerment, the floor had to be luminous, eye-catching, and dramatic.

While the notion of restoring an unrecognized legacy upon which women of accomplishment relied constituted an important feminist intervention into the male-centric story of Western European history, it also reproduced the class privilege that great men had enjoyed in the past. The labor of hundreds of thousands of servants, slaves, and workers—male and female—that elites relied on over time and across cultures remained invisible in this new record of women's history. With this, the Heritage Floor enacted the limits of liberal histories based on recognized public accomplishment and left in the dustbin a more radical reenvisioning of women's history generated by Marxist-informed social historians of the 1960s and 1970s.[66]

Chicago's investment in history expressed a deeply held conviction of many liberal feminists in the 1970s that the psychological damage done to women by male privilege could not only be measured by their wage scale or by job discrimination alone. Its true measurement was the self-imposed repression women learned, the thousand acts of silencing they inflicted on themselves in the name of womanhood. Making history in such a context was not an esoteric undertaking. Rather, it was central to repairing women's sense of themselves as accomplished, creative, and emboldened actors on the world stage. Chicago explained the connection between empowerment and history as she talked about *The Dinner Party*: "I had been personally strengthened by discovering my rich heritage as a woman and the enormous amount of information that existed about women's contributions to society. This information, however, was totally outside the mainstream of historical thought and was certainly unknown to most people. And as long as women's achievements were excluded from our understanding of the past, we would continue to feel as if we had never done anything worthwhile. This absence of any sense of our tradition as women seemed to cripple us psychologically." Chicago believed that restoring women to the history of Western civilization and, along the way, writing a different record of human accomplishment, would overturn the damage inflicted by invisibility. Nevertheless, Chicago admitted in her journal that "a nagging voice kept reminding me that the women whose plates I was painting, whose runners we were embroidering, whose names we were firing on to the porcelain floor, were primarily women of the ruling classes."[67]

When Diane Gelon arrived in the studio in 1975, Chicago asked if she would locate a thousand names of significant women in history. Gelon agreed, thinking the task would take no longer than six weeks. As a doctoral student in art history at UCLA, she had access to a major research library. She and Chicago also began to collect secondhand books about women's history, since many of them had been written in the 1900s and 1910s as the suffrage movement gained new momentum.[68] Gelon recalled her delight at finding a six-volume biography of 294 women written in 1803 by Mary Hays, a colleague of Mary Wollstonecraft. No one had checked any of the volumes out of the library at the University of California at Los Angeles for over fifty years.[69] The two also talked through Chicago's final decisions on who to seat at the table, for example, going back and forth over French martyr and Catholic saint Joan of Arc and Lucretia Borgia, illegitimate daughter of Pope Alexander the VI and infamous femme fatale, both rejected because Chicago could not see a way to make either story positive enough for her purposes.[70] Gelon, who became Chicago's closest ally and trusted confidant, soon moved out of research and into administration, determined to build the kind of financial and artistic support system historically enjoyed by men to enable Chicago to finish the piece. Ann Isolde appeared at just the right moment to take over research.

Like other artists who found their way to *The Dinner Party* studio, Isolde had not had a female art instructor or seen a single slide by a woman artist throughout her MFA program. But her path through feminism allowed her to see that women could be artists and the formal art world—the educational and museum systems—were at fault for the lack of "great women artists," in the words of Linda Nochlin. While living in Boulder, Ann read Chicago's memoir *Through the Flower* with her consciousness-raising group and Eleanor Tufts's *Our Hidden Heritage: Five Centuries of Women Artists* (1974). Isolde signed up for two afternoons a week to research the seventeenth-century Italian artist Artemisia Gentileschi and the twentieth-century US painter, Georgia O'Keeffe. She then typed note cards and parts of Chicago's notes about the project. Her diary from 1976 recorded her growing commitment: "I told Diane Gelon that after almost ten years of clerical experience, this is the first time I ever typed anything that contributed to female culture rather than male culture. I am beginning to want to spend more time on research and take on leadership responsibilities. Recently, I even volunteered to read to the needle workers every Monday, Wednesday and Friday from *Women and Music* by Sophie Drinker."

By year's end, Isolde recorded feeling overwhelmed by her competing responsibilities. She, and many volunteers, felt that their hours volunteering at the studio mattered and that they were engaged in something larger than themselves. Yet home, work, and the desire of many of them to produce their own art exerted a counterweight to the studio, pulling volunteers back to their own lives and goals. As Isolde expressed it in her diary, "I'm working so hard on *The Dinner Party* plus my part time job that it's really difficult for me to concentrate on my own painting. I'm definitely conflicted about this. However, it may be necessary for me to temporarily put my own artwork aside to contribute to a monumental sculpture that will benefit women on a large scale and help us move forward together."[71] The next year, Isolde became the leader of the eight-person research team, a job she held for two years.[72]

Eventually, twenty women researched for nearly two years to compile information on women represented on the Heritage Floor.[73] In the beginning, Isolde secretly worried that the task of finding "women of accomplishment" simply could not be done, that there were not enough women who had shaped history and so they would have to "make up" names.[74] To everyone's relief, the libraries were in fact full of women's history, scattered in dusty volumes across all disciplines and nationalities. Many were written in the nineteenth century, but volunteers nevertheless studied them for what they could offer. Despite the occasional women-friendly accounts like Mary Hay's *Female Biographies*, the research team discovered that most of the books available to them reproduced the devaluation of women they were trying to combat. The books rarely focused on women's accomplishments. If a book noted a woman's accomplishment, the authors typically folded it into the history of the woman's husband, son, father, or brother, or vilified it as a monstrous anomaly of a power-hungry woman. Isolde notes that most books did not adequately connect a woman to her historical context. "Women are represented like bonbons in a candy box, all beautifully wrapped and each one tasting different. The material is confusing because the women are not presented in any logical order or in terms of a fabric of historical events."[75]

The research team scrutinized information about women in conventional history for sexist assumptions and distortions. Isolde recalls that "we were desperately trying to learn what had been left out."[76] The team understood part of its task as developing, according to Katie Amend, "its own historical framework in order to relate individual women to each other and to some context." Amend explains that the group had to "reevaluate and reinterpret most of the available material and reread and rethink what had been written in order to redefine women's achievements from our own point of view. We then needed to place these women in a historical context which emphasized that each of them was not solitary and unique, but rather an inheritor as well as an originator of a long tradition of female achievement."[77] Researchers honed the skill of reading like a feminist, training themselves, in the words of Isolde, to "read through" the biases and "ferret out" useful, neutral facts. These facts were then typed onto four-by-five-inch note cards and cross-filed alphabetically by country, century, and profession.[78]

By the fall of 1978, the group had consulted over a thousand books and researched nearly three thousand women. Juliet Myers expressed some dismay at all the information they had amassed: "I was overwhelmed by the volume, the variety, and the extent of women's contributions and achievements throughout history. And, frankly, I was puzzled as to how we as women could have allowed the obscurity, the trivialization, the belittlement to go on for such a long, long time."[79] Isolde too felt shock at what they had uncovered: "I'm educated, I have a master's degree in art history. Why didn't I know this? What happened to this history?"[80] The group then began what was essentially a very, lengthy seminar on women's history. Over a successive, intense weekend sessions at the big table used for Thursday-night rap sessions, the group, along with Chicago, worked through which women's names would be on the Heritage Floor. They did so using three criteria established by Chicago: "(1) Did the woman make a significant contribution to society? (2) Did she attempt to improve conditions for women? (3) Did her life illuminate an aspect of women's experience or provide a model for the future?"[81]

The evaluative terms the group applied—the importance of a woman making a "significant contribution" and trying to "improve conditions" for all women—as well as the notion of role models, underscored the liberal values of the larger feminist movement of the mid-1970s. These terms were designed to insert women into existing models for recognizing accomplishment and by doing so, offer a more robust account of women's place in society. In this way, the floor visually created a representation of the sex class "woman" and, once that was established, demonstrated its accomplishments.

In addition to the three criteria for inclusion, researchers strove for the Heritage Floor to represent "a range of nationalities, experiences, and contributions." They explained that they were not trying to "*define* women's history but to symbolize it—to say that there have been many women who have done many things, and they deserve to be known."[82] The team took care to select scientists, aviators, mathematicians, doctors, artists, writers, musicians, intellectuals, and goddesses from the obscure (the mythical Siberian goddess Ajysyt and the fifteenth-century French fortune-teller Catherine Deshayes) to the well-known (Chilean educator Isabel Pinochet and US journalist Ida B. Wells).[83] Each name selected for the floor also had to relate to one of the guests in some way, either by region, contribution, or interest. Some assignments were obvious, like the stream of names for political leaders. For example, the names streaming under Egyptian Pharaoh Hatshepsut plate included the beautiful wife of Akhenaton, Nefertiti; wife of Amenhotep III and mother of Nefertiti, Tiy; Assyrian Queen Nitocris; and Roman Queen Tanaquil; the names leading up to and streaming away from US poet Emily Dickinson included other literary giants such as Jane Austen, Charlotte Brontë, Elizabeth Barrett Browning, George Eliot, Christina Rossetti, and Susanna Rowson.[84] Other streams reflected efforts the volunteers made to address American race relations. A cluster of "race pride" women ran under the plate for African American activist Sojourner Truth, such as singers Marian Anderson and Josephine Baker, New Deal activist Mary McLeod Bethune, and anthropologist and writer Zora Neale Hurston.[85]

Isolde's diary sheds light into the ways the team struggled with how to represent an assimilated history of women, or in her words, to avoid a "separatist situation." To help them decide into what "stream" to place selected names, the team adopted religious language, language that also testified to *The Dinner Party*'s underlying religious metaphors of the Last Supper and the Sistine Chapel. The seated guests became "apostles," and the names flowing beneath them "disciples of the apostles." This language helped them approach the often vexed question of where to place each woman's name.

> For example, Mary Church Terrell is the Black woman who worked with Susan B. Anthony on suffrage in a prominent way, so we moved her into that group. We put a 20th century Bolivian doctor with Elizabeth Blackwell due

> to the breakthroughs she had made in that profession and her later dates. We put Augusta Savage (Black artist) in with Georgia O'Keeffe but kept Edmonia Lewis (Black sculptor), with Sojourner Truth, largely due to her dates and the content of work. Lorraine Hansberry went with Virginia Woolf, but Phillis Wheatley went back with Anne Hutchinson. So, we moved them where they made a significant contribution and/or lived at a time closer to another apostle than to Sojourner Truth. That way we preserved a sort of cohesive identity without locking all Black women into a ghetto situation.[86]

By showing the woman of accomplishment as being a sister in the struggle, the floor ideally complicated the "great (wo)man" model of history and in its place offered a more "holistic, unified view of women's history."[87] It also strove to show women's common struggle across race and nation, uniting women's diverse experiences under the harness of bodily similarity, a strategy that Chicago and the research team hoped would effect a shared experience of the category "woman." By the late 1970s, this strategy, adopted by studio workers with progressive intentions, came under pressure by a range of women, some of whom became vocal critics of *The Dinner Party*.

All told, the history offered by the Heritage Floor represented a liberal tradition of achievement, not a radical vision of feminist sisterhood. The women represented on the floor struggled to accomplish great things without a formal women's movement from which to draw support. What support they did have came from their families and communities of women—mothers, sisters, and friends—with whom they lived, loved, and endured. The language of women's culture nurtured by the studio regularly invoked these social and familial networks of women in the past and present as an explanation for women's resilience. The names on the Heritage Floor marked a history of discrete individuals that together constituted a tradition of women's public accomplishment. Studio workers imposed or created the idea of sisterhood as they gathered the names into a useable feminist past.

Yet in crucial ways the women gathered at the studio had successfully made themselves into a feminist sisterhood, an accomplishment they directly linked to women's history. Katie Amend was quite explicit about the connection. Amend had been teaching women's studies classes in Northern California when she learned about Chicago through Johanna Demetrakas's documentary *Womanhouse* and moved from San Francisco to LA in 1978 to volunteer. She viewed what was happening at the studio as a crucial moment in time, akin to the suffrage movement.[88] For her and others, women's history was a new frontier. "We were explorers, interpreters, and discoverers all in search of the same thing. We celebrated our discoveries by sharing them with one another. There was a continuity and a deliberateness to the research—a constant effort to reinterpret historical material, to revitalized it and discover parts of women's history that had been lost. Research was never done in isolation, for it contributed to piecing together a jigsaw puzzle more gigantic than we could ever have imagined."[89]

"Jigsaw puzzle" proved to be an apt metaphor. In terms of research, the team worked together to assemble the pieces of a lost women's history and to represent and re-present it on the floor. But less metaphorically, the research they uncovered had to be rendered into a literal floor, itself a jigsaw puzzle of dizzying dimensions. Chicago anticipated the floor being made of approximately two thousand twelve-inch porcelain triangle tiles with the names of the selected women painted in gold letters; by the end, the number of tiles reached 2,400. These would be assembled into a large triangle, forty-eight feet on each side, on which the tables would rest.

Once the list of names was final, the research group dispersed to apply—literally—what they had gathered to actual physical objects. Some helped produce large illustrated Heritage Panels that presented the names of women on the Heritage Floor under the place setting for *The Dinner Party* guest to whom she was affiliated.[90] Volunteers adorned these large panels with dense collages of biographical information, photographs, and illustrations of related art and artifacts. Chicago wrote passages that contextualized in broad feminist strokes the historical circumstances and social life of women in the past, retelling her narrative of women's history as a struggle against patriarchy. These were designed to accompany the show. Others worked on the floor itself. Ceramicist Evelyn Appelt made the triangular tiles, a job that took nearly two years to complete at a cost of $12,875; the team readied themselves for painting names on the tiles by first tracing stylized letters onto paper.[91]

This task fell to a handful of women, the most dedicated being Shannon Hogan and Marti Rotchford.[92] When Hogan arrived at the studio, she discovered that only ninety names had been copied into paper. The work was mindless, she recalls. "The letters were drawn out in Judy's handwriting in a certain size and then Xeroxed. So we had stacks of A's, B's, C's. You grabbed what you needed and Scotch-taped them together."[93] Eventually, paper streams of names hung down the walls in the studio. Shannon was often the only person working in the graphics area on the first floor of Chicago's studio. "Compared to the other concerns I had in my life (my husband, three children, painting and trying to promote my work to galleries and a dollhouse booklet I was writing and publishing), this seemed lightweight."[94] It took four months to transfer the names to paper.

Once the 999 names had been rendered onto paper streams, the team moved into a large temporary space in a high-rise building in Century City to lay them out. Ken Gilliam, a design engineer, helped with this major design task. "The goal was to get the names to flow, to come in from different corners, converge but not make a vortex."[95] Some plates, particularly those on the second wing of the table representing medieval Europe, had long names streaming from them, while other streams consisted of shorter names. Gilliam rigged the ceiling with a platform on which Chicago perched to see how the flow of names looked and from which she directed the team to move this or that name. It took six weeks to get it right. Isolde used the metaphor of childbirth when she announced on June 25, 1978, "the design for the Heritage Floor was completed at 4:00 pm. I felt absolutely wonderful! The image of women's history that finally emerged was simple, yet very organic and dynamic. It flowed like an energy field with channels in between. . . . When the last name was lain in, it was like cutting the umbilical cord, the life-support system. Now the design could be sustained by its own energy."[96]

Yet, like a newborn, the completed design was far from self-sufficient and proved to be just as exhausting as all the previous steps had been. Once laid out in the proper form, the names had to be painted on twelve-inch porcelain tiles and fired in a kiln, a job that took another three months.[97] The team worked ten- and twelve-hour days, seven days a week. Gilliam made a long sliding platform on which the women could lie to paint names at the center of the Heritage Floor. Painting on their stomachs was hard, so they swapped out every few hours.[98] A wealthy art collector and early supporter of Chicago, Stanley Grinstein, donated the gold paint, exorbitantly expensive at $100 an ounce. Against the glossy white tiles, the gold paint radiated light. The tiles fit together to make the large triangular-shaped floor. Gilliam color-coded each tile with a number to facilitate its breakdown and setup, and used a custom-shaded grout to secure the tiles.

One of three men who worked for an extended amount of time on the project, Gilliam found his work at the studio challenging both creatively and personally. His job was to design the specialized objects, tools, and machines needed by the studio as well as the complex lighting that traveled with the piece.[99] He first heard of Chicago from his friend ceramicist

Leonard Skuro, who worked with Chicago on the plates. Gilliam enjoyed the sheer array of design issues he tackled at the studio, from retooling the jigger machine used for throwing the heavy three-dimensional plates, to building embroidery frames, to sorting out how best to illuminate the Heritage Floor. He and Chicago became lovers, adding a degree of strain to the relations among the predominantly female volunteers. Gilliam too found the work and responsibility transformative. "I came into the project having no experience in really taking responsibility, with no one to turn to when I "finished my part." He found that the studio kept him from "thinking that my value grew out of how much I was making financially as opposed to what I was contributing." He found the process meetings hardest to accept. "Admitting my weakness or vulnerability, remaining open to input and criticism about my ability to operate with other people—this is what I've had the most difficulty with."[100] Gilliam was truly a jack-of-all-trades by the time he left: he had carved a three-dimensional plate (Ethel Smyth), designed reinforced *Dinner Party* tables (to withstand the heavy china plates), and had created a lighting system that made the table look as if it were "levitating."[101]

In the midst of the porcelain tile-painting blitz in the summer of 1978, six months before the scheduled museum opening, Chicago and the team faced renewed concerns that *The Dinner Party* represented only white and elite women. The bubble of imagined sisterhood nurtured at the studio burst when a group of five Chicana women met with Chicago to request that a Hispanic woman be included at *The Dinner Party* table. Their request testified to the central role representation played in liberal feminism and the realities of feminist activism in the racially diverse city of LA. Chicago, Gelon, Hill, and Isolde met with the group to discuss their proposal for including Mexican Sor Juana Inés de la Cruz (1651–1695), a nun of New Spain (Spanish settlements in North America) whose writings mark the first Mexican literature written in the Spanish language. The group threatened to picket the opening of *The Dinner Party* if Chicago did not meet their demand. Chicago commiserated with the women's request, particularly the gap in historical representation between minority and white women. Yet practicalities were foremost on Chicago's mind. She explained that adding de la Cruz would require removing another woman from the table, designing a new plate and runner, reorganizing the names of the women around the plate, and rewriting a section of the book to be published by Doubleday around the time of the exhibition opening. She did agree to include more

Hispanic women on the Heritage Panels. The encounter left *The Dinner Party* group shaken. Isolde wrote in her diary that "I'm still reverberating from the studio meeting with a group of Chicana women on Friday. So many feelings and impressions are still going through my mind. I became very aware of how complicated the women's movement really is. The minority women have a double battle as women and as members of oppressed racial and ethnic groups. I have a great deal of respect for their fighting spirit because they are up against so much."[102]

The liberal history Chicago embraced had limits, limits that were not of Chicago's making, but through which she could not see a way past. All around the studio, historians actively crafted new multicultural and international accounts of women's varied contributions, but these came too late to influence the Heritage Floor. *The Dinner Party* research team's conventional research unintentionally replicated conventional hierarchies of social power.

Chicago understood that she could do her part toward righting one historic wrong, but not all wrongs. She designed the floor to showcase a lost female tradition and to provide a broader (tangible) context for the great women sitting at the table. In this way, the Heritage Floor underscored a central premise of US liberal feminism, that women required self-knowledge, which included a useable past, to make a place for themselves at the proverbial table. The floor literalized this past in the form of knowledge, names dropped from the male-generated record, and demonstrated, according to Chicago, that "the women at the table had risen from a foundation provided by other women's accomplishments, and each plate would then symbolize not only a particular woman but also the tradition from which she emerged." Summing up the place of history in women's empowerment, Chicago made a case for why a feminist history matters: "To make people feel worthless, society robs them of their pride; this has happened to women. All institutions of our culture tell us—through words, deeds, and, even worse, silence—that we are insignificant. But our heritage is our power; we can know ourselves and our capacities by seeing that other women have been strong. To reclaim our past and insist that it become a part of human history is the task that lies before us, for the future requires that women, as well as men, shape the world's destiny."[103]

As with the runners, the floor was a monumental undertaking in its own right. Transferring the names onto paper, and then to the thousands of porcelain triangles, assembling them properly and lighting them effectively comprised another tremendous effort. Working on the Heritage Floor, with all its symbolism, sustained the workers by inspiring them.[104] Chicago wrote in her journal that, "As the researchers learned about their history as women, their sense of themselves changed. Their initial lack of confidence was replaced by an understanding of their historic circumstances and a determination to share the information they were finding with other women." They too felt like the encounter with history mattered. Isolde wrote that her "whole attitude about history and women's place in it had changed immensely after two years of intense research."[105]

The Feminist Essentialism of the Plates

I want them all to have vaginas.

If the runners embodied a view of "women's culture" and the Heritage Floor, a liberal view of accomplishment, the plates represented Chicago's ongoing interest in central core imagery or "cunt art." The fourteen-inch places, each requiring carving, painting, and numerous glazings, represented the most technically challenging aspect of *The Dinner Party* and the element that depended on the fewest number of workers to complete; handling the clay was difficult, falling "somewhere between skill and alchemy," Gilliam explained.[106] The plates became the single most controversial element of *The Dinner Party* and the aspect that generated the most commentary and criticism in subsequent debates about the piece. The central core, vulva imagery of the plates represented a direct and undeniable expression of Chicago's radical feminist view of women's difference and her primary symbol of human liberation in a female form. The plates had always been at the heart of Chicago's thinking for *The Dinner Party*. While she was still teaching at the Feminist Studio Workshop (FSW) at the Woman's Building in LA, Chicago described her vision of the plates in a 1974 journal entry: "I want to make butterfly images that are hard, strong, soft, passive, opaque, transparent—all different states—and I want them all to have vaginas so they'll be female butterflies and at the same time be shells, flowers, flesh, forest—all kinds of things simultaneously."[107]

As Chicago started to design the plates for *The Dinner Party*, debates that had begun in the early 1970s over "cunt art" raged on. Artists like Judith Bernstein, Shelley Lowell, and Colette Whiten, as well as Chicago's former CalArts colleagues, Miriam Schapiro and Faith Wilding, produced art with frank references to female genitalia.[108] Art critic Anne-Marie Sauzeau-Boetti, writing in *Studio International* in 1976, defined the emphasis of these artists, including Chicago, positively as "an explicit female iconography."[109] For those for whom images of caves, flowers, shells, and dark hidden spaces put the female body into a visual form, the notion of central core imagery was an effective intervention into the sexism and prejudices of the art establishment. Yet this was by no means a consensus viewpoint. A number of art critics and feminists viewed the notion of a female form language as problematic.[110] They viewed it as unable to effectively disrupt the tight web of gendered meanings associated with female bodies, even though women artists represented those bodies as part of a feminist project.

Chicago, however, was not all that interested in debates among feminist art historians, critics, and activists over how best to represent women's interests. After 1975, she was immersed in her own artistic process. Further, defining feminist art was not a debate to Chicago. She viewed her images as female centered and as such part of overturning the erasure of female experience in Western art. She also understood feminism to be about nurturing individual agency, practicing consciousness-raising, and establishing alternative female-dominated spaces. As in Fresno, CalArts, and FSW, Chicago's style of feminism tethered studio practice to female-centered images. According to her, female artists who made art from their own experiences, from the materials of their own lives, supported by other women, and in spaces that permitted them full and unfettered expression constituted feminist art, with or without central core imagery. Chicago essentially retreated from these debates as she worked in her studio. She saw the image of a butterfly/vulva to be an invocative female form. And she wanted a formal, repeating, yet varied image to carry through all thirty-nine plates. With her interest in female forms, Chicago saw herself as a direct descendant of British writer Virginia Woolf and US painter Georgia O'Keeffe, both whom the artist recognized as working in a distinctively female expressive language. Of Woolf she wrote, "Her work, like the lighthouse in her most famous book, illuminated the path to a woman-formed language in literature," and of O'Keeffe, "her work provides a foundation upon which we can build a universal language to express our own point of view as women."[111] As a result of their powerful inspiration to Chicago and her personal sense of being in a shared lineage with them, these two women held the final seats at the end of the last table and represented, for Chicago, the pinnacle of *The Dinner Party*.

Chicago's ambitious plans for the plates involved building the clay on the plate, then carving, painting, and firing it numerous times. She made the design for the plates before working out how to make them. The technique to make three-dimensional plates was not clear or straightforward, and she improvised. More plates cracked in the kiln than survived. It took Chicago nearly two years to figure out how to fire them, particularly the heavier plates. The Susan B. Anthony plate weighed an astonishing thirty-eight pounds.[112] Leonard Skuro and Ken Gilliam worked with Chicago to retool the jigger machine, the device they used to throw plates. They tinkered with the kilns to ensure they would fire evenly and allow the built-up plates to survive the process. During the trial-and-error period, Chicago despaired of ever getting ceramics to do what she wanted it to do. Skuro too recalled a deep sense of foreboding: "Everything was so difficult and I didn't know what I was doing. I had never built a jigger machine, never made fourteen inch porcelain plates, and everyone told me I couldn't do it."[113] Eventually they found a kind of clay that withstood the multiple firings and their production rate improved.

The unpredictable process took an emotional strain on the artist. Elation and disappointment went hand in hand. For example, on May 2, 1977, Chicago proudly reported that, "I got my first finished, painted, carved plate out of the kiln today. At last—after a year and a half!" A few hours later, her excitement died as the plate cracked. "We have been working and working and working on getting the electric kiln to fire well, and I had just done three or four firings with two test plates that were perfect. Then I put in the real ones and wham! The Boadaceia plate that broke was the second version—the first broke in almost exactly the same way. It really made me depressed—not just because the plate cracked, but also because I just suddenly felt overwhelmed again."[114]

Skuro and Chicago pitted themselves against the clay and the kiln, day after day, working closely together, sometimes hunched over the same plate as they carved. They relied on and learned from each other. Skuro described their collaborative process while working on bird wings for German astronomer Caroline Herschel's plate: "We would see things very differently and yet see the same thing. Judy would be seeing it as an image, and I would be seeing it as a shape. This is my training."[115] They enjoyed working together, but the time demands became unmanageable for Skuro. As Skuro ended his working arrangements with the studio, Chicago found help from two other ceramists. Judye Keyes, an art student from Kansas City, arrived in the summer of 1977 and became head of ceramics after Skuro left. Sharon Kagan arrived in 1978 and become Chicago's assistant, carving and painting side by side with the artist. Together, the ceramics team spent their days making plates, carving, sanding, and painting. They worked closely together, sometimes with one of them painting an entire plate and at other times taking shifts on the same plate. No one tracked whose plate survived the kiln, since each version followed Chicago's design. No one knew if the plates they had spent hours working on would survive. Hill recalls the sense of anticipation the entire studio felt when the ceramists checked the kilns in the morning after the overnight firing.[116] Others recall screams of despair when a plate emerged from the kiln cracked.[117]

While the ceramicists at the studio followed Chicago's designs, they also actively participated in solving design and production problems. The guiding philosophy among them all was to "not be inhibited by preconceived notions of what clay would do and what it would not do."[118] Keyes described her work on the sixth-century Byzantine empress Theodora's plate:

> I had a lot of preconceived notions about how mosaics should be done. I researched different mosaic techniques which had been done by placing single stones side by side and grouting. But that wouldn't work in ceramics, so I had to devise a new way of working that was more applicable. I worked with templates and more or less laced the plate, expanded it outward and worked on sections at a time. I must have done about four or five test plates before getting something that I was satisfied with. It took four months to work it out and get one out of the kiln without cracking.[119]

Each person working on the plates learned what Chicago wanted and how to deliver it. For Kagan, this became a personal tutorial with Chicago about painting. Kagan was not alone with this feeling; many longtime workers particularly valued working with Chicago and learning from her about technique, color, design, and process: "After a few hours of work Judy picked up my plate, wiped off the bulk of the pigment, and began to paint. She talked about working with the underlying color and enhancing it rather than covering it up. She talked about building layers of wash and applying different colors over the existing color. When I went back to the plate I realized that I hadn't been painting—I had merely been laying on color. What I was learning while I painted those plates was to trust myself as an artist and to take risks."[120]

In December 1977, with the San Francisco opening bearing down on them, the ceramics team did a weeklong "blitz" to complete the test plates for Susan B. Anthony, Virginia Woolf, and Georgia O'Keeffe, the three most difficult because they were the most ornate and sculpted of the table. These three embodied Chicago's celebration of women's political aspirations and artistic accomplishment. For Chicago, the task of completing the plates represented what women could accomplish when they joined forces. She described the support she and the team received from the studio: "I have never had a more wonderful creative experience with the Project before. Six days this time, from waking to sleeping. We've had people cooking for us and running errands, so we've had no interruptions. The energy has been incredible." In February 1978, she reported that only one of eight plates broke in the kiln. She worried about the two plates she had painted for Sojourner Truth, since she had poured so much passion into them. "At any rate . . . the energy of my little china painting team is carrying me past whatever tiredness I might feel if I were alone in there."[121]

When completed, the plates, with their recurring butterfly/vulva image in a variety of shapes, colors, and textures, were impressive and affecting but also left Chicago open to charges of essentialism. The charges were not incorrect: each guest at *The Dinner Party* had a single area at the center of the plate that appeared to recede into darkness or marked an opening to an area that was clearly closed or protected. Each of the thirty-nine plates represented the central core differently. From the artist's point of view, the essentialism she deployed was tactical. It was a form of feminist essentialism intended to highlight the oppression women experienced because of their bodily difference, their "central cores" that patriarchy could not get past. The message of the women's history Chicago's researchers unearthed established that despite variation by culture, era, and nation, women's oppression always hinged on the fact of their vaginas. Bodily difference might not define women, yet it did most certainly confine them. At the same time, part of Chicago's feminist essentialism involved viewing female difference—represented by the vulva/butterfly/shell—as a source of women's knowledge and thus became a positive symbol of women's uniqueness. Chicago wanted the human experience to be filtered through women's experience, and as such, represented by female bodies. The plates of *The Dinner Party* captured this tension in Chicago's feminism—and cultural feminism more broadly—between viewing women's difference as a source of their oppression and as a source of their uniqueness.

When laid out together, the plates communicated Chicago's understanding of the wide diversity of women's circumstance and their enduring resilience. As they moved from flat plates to three-dimensional sculptures, the plates reflected the artist's view of women's collective beauty and discontentment, their efforts to shape society and the psychologically and physically violent suppression of those efforts. The Primordial Goddess and Georgia O'Keeffe sat side by side at the triangular beginning-ending of *The Dinner Party*, a testimony to Chicago's understanding of all that had changed and all that remained the same for women.

Staging the Goddess at *The Dinner Party*

Equality for me was seeing the divine through the feminine.

The final way Chicago embedded feminist theory into *The Dinner Party* was through the work's dramatic staging. Chicago brought the major artistic components of *The Dinner Party*—the needlework runners, the Heritage Floor, and the carved and painted plates—together under the rubric of restaging the Last Supper as a first supper, a religious ritual for and about women. The religious staging involved both practical and aesthetic aspects of the installation. Practically, this meant moving crowds around an installation that appeared to be a sanctuary, with dimmed lights, long altars, and low protective rails. Artistically, the staging embedded a female-centered origin story into the viewing experience. For example, each setting had a hand-crafted porcelain chalice fit for a queen's hand or for a Communion ritual; each of the three corners where the wings joined had elaborately crocheted millennium vestments marking the transition as sacred. When combined, these elements of Chicago's staging of *The Dinner Party* ideally enhanced the ritual significance of the art and the transformative experience of encountering it. The six opening banners and the staging implicitly offered a mythical past freed of patriarchy, where goddesses ruled and divinity found expression through female forms.

The staging of *The Dinner Party* reflected the artist's engagement with a major branch of cultural feminism that centered on women's spirituality and the search for feminine images of the divine. Chicago read Mary Daly, the most radical of the feminist theologians in the early 1970s, author of *The Church and the Second Sex* (1968), *Beyond God the Father* (1973), and "God Is a Verb," published in *Ms.* in 1974. When *The Dinner Party* debuted, it did so alongside of a bumper crop of goddess-centered titles: Merle Stone's

When God Was a Woman (1978), Elizabeth Davis's *The First Sex* (1978), Starhawk's *The Spiral Dance: A Rebirth of the Ancient Religion of the Great Goddess* (1979), and Margo Adler's *Drawing Down the Moon* (1979), to name a few.[122]

Chicago herself neither practiced feminist religious rituals nor embraced goddess worship.[123] Rather, for her, a feminist spiritual tradition, be it mythical or actual, mattered because it promised to dissolve the internalization of female inferiority nurtured by male-centered religions. Without the potential of the road not (yet) traveled—in this case a spiritual tradition that honored both sexes as representatives of divinity—women could not imagine themselves into a new future. In a 1978 interview with *Mother Jones*, Chicago laid out her belief that religion had a place in a woman's revolution: "I don't believe that economics pre-dates everything. I believe that *myth* pre-dates everything. . . . I believe that *myth*, at its base, has to be challenged before economics or sociology or philosophy will change." Chicago and other cultural feminists argued that women needed female-centered origin myths to see themselves as powerful and that religion, as a primary source of myth, had to expand enough to represent the feminine as holy. Only then would women know a deep existential equality. Chicago explained that "I like thinking of the world being created by a female deity. It makes me feel important. I look up there at the Sistine Chapel and I see Adam and God and I feel excluded. I want to feel included."[124] She hoped that *The Dinner Party*, as a feminist Sistine Chapel, would restore the feminine to its rightful place at the altar and women in seats of authority. "Equality did not mean having a woman priest leading services to a male god. Equality for me was seeing the divine through the feminine."[125]

The most tangible elements of Chicago's desire for a female-centered religion came in the staging of *The Dinner Party* and its opening banners. But in her original conception for the work, she had a far more ambitious goal. Chicago wanted to make a female Genesis story in the form of an illuminated manuscript to go along with *The Dinner Party* that would give women a female-centered myth. In an unpublished mission statement of sorts written in 1976, Chicago articulated the void she hoped *The Dinner Party* could fill: "There is an underlying lesson that we learn in school and all the women's studies courses in the world will not change that lesson. THE LESSON IS THAT WOMEN ARE NOT IMPORTANT, OUR IDEAS ARE NOT IMPORTANT, OUR ACTIVITIES ARE NOT IMPORTANT, OUR FEELINGS ARE NOT IMPORTANT . . . AND THEREFORE, FOR ALL INTENTS AND PURPOSES, WE DO NOT EXIST. . . . AND HENCE WE DO NOT HAVE THE BASIS UPON

WHICH TO FORM A STRONG SELF-IMAGE." Echoing a message first delivered in her feminist classroom, Chicago stressed the importance of "self-image" and individual transformation to lasting social change. To that, she added women's spiritual empowerment. "*The Dinner Party* is a work of art that is women's history; women's religion; women's metaphor. It gives women something they never had—a history, a mythology, a religion, a cultural identity that is their own." Liberal reform with its focus on politics simply missed the bigger stakes. "Without this changed self-image, as I mentioned, the changed laws are as meaningless as winning the vote was . . . there has to be a new self-image to replace the old one, an alternative way of seeing oneself that sweeps away all the powerlessness and substitutes a powerful self for a helpless victim."[126]

As Chicago formulated the theoretical and historical foundations of *The Dinner Party*, her plans for an illuminated manuscript of a female Genesis story grew. She imagined that the manuscript, "Revelations of the Goddess," would be published when *The Dinner Party* opened; it would function as the spiritual underpinning for the history represented at *The Dinner Party* but also act as an inspiration to anyone who opened it.[127] Many of the women and goddesses seated at the table made an appearance in the text, thickening the overlaps between the art and the metanarrative. Chicago's proposal to Diana Press described the book as "a reinterpretation of Genesis from a feminist perspective written in Biblical language," with hand-drawn capital letters, marginal drawings, images blending with text "like a Blake poem," and "elaborately drawn" frontispiece, all done by the artist. The artist hoped Adrienne Rich would write the opening poem. Chicago also proposed that the publisher work with the International Institute of Experimental Printmaking in Santa Cruz for a limited, high-priced run of a hundred boxed books with loose-leaf pages of handmade paper.[128] In August 1976, Coletta Reid of Diana Press drew up a contract with the designer Sheila de Brentville to ready the manuscript for publication.[129]

Chicago continued to revise her manuscript between 1976 and 1977, eventually retitling it "The Heavenly Banquet." Following the narrative of the creation of the universe in Genesis, it began with the universe giving birth to planets, followed on day two with the creation of the Vagina Primera, out of which "came the ovum of life." Women's bodies become the foundational template for the earth. "And the blood flowed out of the center of the Earth, out of the Vagina Primera and it formed the oceans and the rivers and the Moon caused the oceans and the rivers to ebb and flow. And still the blood flowed and the Earth was nourished and the body of the Earth rose up and her thighs became the mountains and her belly formed the valleys and from her breasts issued the white milk of light which illuminated and nourished all that she had created on the second day." Once the world was made, all human cultures honored women for their abilities to give life and women held all positions of spiritual and political authority. Inevitably, "the men" became jealous. They asked women, "why is it given to you to have this knowledge and to bring forth life? Are not our bodies as holy as yours?" and later threatened, "if we cannot bring forth life, we will take life."

A full-on sex war ensues where women battle men for control of the world. On the brink of victory, "the women" cannot slaughter the men and stop the battle. As women wail over the lives wasted in the battle, men bind and subjugate them. At this point the Great Goddess concedes defeat, saying, "Oh children of my flesh, formed in my own image, we are vanquished and feminine wisdom will be banished from the Earth. But, it shall not be forever, for some day we shall be redeemed. Until that day, your daughters and their daughters shall be my Disciples and my Apostles, as their mothers were before them. And it shall be the mission of my Disciples to keep the pure white light of our wisdom burning throughout all of the generations."[130] The disciples are the thirty-nine guests at *The Dinner Party*, and the apostles are the 999 women named in the Heritage Floor. The story then tells of the new millennium when women's sacred power is reestablished and the Great Goddess heals the earth of environmental degradation, warfare, poverty, and suffering, the legacies of patriarchy. Importantly, many men recognize their participation in these terrible acts and embrace women and the goddess as allies. Now honored for their unique contributions, men join women in the new Eden.

The book was never published. Diana Press had few resources to produce the ambitious proposal, and mainstream publishing houses were uninterested in a book on goddesses and sex (class) wars. They wanted a book on the art of *The Dinner Party*.[131] Doubleday, with its deep pockets, won the day, and Chicago shelved the manuscript. Chicago's decision to sign with Doubleday for an entirely different book, with the promise of significantly more publicity, distribution, and profits, left her vulnerable to criticism from those who saw the artist as self-serving and her feminism as opportunistic. Yet although the manuscript was shelved, all vestiges of "Revelations of the

Goddess" did not disappear from *The Dinner Party*. A female-centered origin poem adorning the six introductory banners became the most lasting reminder of Chicago's belief in the importance of myth and the potential of the goddess to represent divinity in a female form.

Like all other aspects of *The Dinner Party*, the material production of the banner tapestries embodied Chicago's practice of feminism. And, as with all aspects of *The Dinner Party*, the artist relied on the creative engagement of those gathered to help her. Ann Isolde, herself an accomplished artist, helped Chicago design the fifth banner and described their collaborative process in 1978. It started when Chicago lay on the floor with a large sheet of graph paper and began sketching. "I knew I had the option to be involved if I wanted. I hesitated at first, and then I knew I had to get right down there on the paper too. I got the pencils, the markers, the eraser and went into the drawing with her. It was incredible."[132] Once the banners were designed, Chicago recognized that the studio would require specially trained workers to produce them.[133] The studio contracted with the San Francisco Tapestry Workshop under the direction of master weaver Jean Pierre Larochette to teach volunteers the difficult Renaissance-era Aubusson style of weave, selected for its centrality in the history of embroidery.[134] Aubusson weaving also represented to Chicago the ways that women's artistic contribution to European art had been erased: the densely woven tapestries that adorned medieval homes and churches never gave attribute to the female hands that did the work. Chicago intended to disrupt this erasure by rendering her goddess myth in the dominant style of the male church.[135]

In 1977 Gelon issued an announcement for the workshop that would take place in San Francisco.[136] Eight of the twelve people who signed up paid $125 for the three-month workshop, and *The Dinner Party* studio paid the tuition for the remaining four attendees.[137] Each woman agreed to work five days a week, nine to five, during the workshop and to continue until they finished the six banners. The estimated budget for producing the banners came to $30,000. The San Francisco Tapestry Workshop built six specially designed looms for the project, each six feet in width and each costing approximately $700. Each banner required forty-five pounds of wool thread, at the cost of $4,500 for each banner. Gelon applied for and received a NEA workshop grant for $15,000, leaving the studio to pay the rest, part of which it recovered from the workshop admission fees.[138]

Finished in bold color and densely woven, the tapestries that would greet every visitor to *The Dinner Party* invoke the goddess and the sex class woman unabashedly.

> And She Gathered All before Her
> And She made for them A Sign to See
> And lo They saw a Vision
> From this day forth Like to like in All things
> And then all that divided them merged
> And then Everywhere was Eden Once again[139]

The poem oriented the viewer to "She," the Great Goddess and promised that a vision strong enough to unite "all things" as "like to like" awaited them when they entered the installation. The banners functioned as an invocation or blessing and a new female-centered spin on this oldest of stories.

But the spiritual dimensions of *The Dinner Party* continued well beyond the banners. Once viewers moved under the banners, they stepped into a dim space illuminated only through the floor under the table. The table, with its three wings, simultaneously invoked the image of altars and of the Last Supper table and the nightly ritual of meals women oversaw over time and culture. The richly embroidered runners, the chalices, and the broad plates referenced the Christian Communion altar, while the place settings, waiting for the guests, a family-styled dinner. The staging elevated the domestic work of dinner making to a religious ceremony. With these details, *The Dinner Party* staged a cultural feminist celebration of women and the unremarkable and underappreciated roles they played in family life.

Together, the structure of the studio, the experience of the workers, Chicago's aesthetic decisions, and the metanarrative of *The Dinner Party* combined to make the piece a monument to a particular moment of US feminism. By any measure, the conditions of its production mark it as unique. At the end of the four years that it took to complete *The Dinner Party*, four hundred people had worked on it, a few for a week or two but most for years. The studio had functioned as a classroom, library, community center, consciousness-raising group, graphics shop, needlepoint guild, and a ceramics studio all at once. Each arena of production introduced workers to Chicago's understanding of feminism—the promise and perils of women's culture, the suppression and resurgence of women's history, the dilemma of women's bodily difference.

The feminism of *The Dinner Party*—both its art and its production process—was also marred by the limits of the moment. It suffered from elitism, Eurocentrism, and essentialism; in short, from the limits of much 1970s feminist theory. And like many of the groups and collectives of seventies feminism, the piece was made by women whose material circumstances permitted them to volunteer their time or to work for a stipend. These realities of *The Dinner Party* manifest what is now recognized as "white" US feminism, not a universal "women's culture."

In March 1979, as Chicago and the studio members prepared for the first museum viewing of *The Dinner Party*, they saw it as a "threshold" piece: a beginning, not the end, of a long, productive, all-inclusive feminist art movement.[140] Chicago took the history she found and put a distinctive spin on it. She made the insights of feminism of the early 1970s into a women-centered symbolic installation she hoped would restore pride in women's accomplishments. It was now up to museums, audiences, and critics to decide what it all meant.

Design meeting at the studio, 1977. Note the carved plate on the table and the black and white tracing paper as well as snacks on the worktable. Volunteers signed up to work on specific runners and, through discussion, helped Chicago create her design. Bottom row from left: Stevie Martin, Helene Simich, unknown, Roberta Rothman, unknown. Top row from left: Judy Keyes, Judy Chicago, Sharon Kagan. *Courtesy of Through the Flower, housed at the Penn State University Archives.*

Celebrating Christmas with a potluck dinner and dance at the studio, 1977. Ann Isolde standing at the table, Judy Chicago dancing with Ken Gillian and Susan Hill with Diane Gelon. *Courtesy of Through the Flower.*

Ensuring that the work stayed on task, on schedule, and up to the studio's sense of excellence fell to Susan Hill. A master of assigning the right work to the right person, she coordinated, at times, a large number of fellow needleworkers and thousands of details. Here, needleworkers stitch the Petronilla de Meath runner. Note the paper design hanging on the wall and empty needlework frames stacked under a reminder for workers to stop and ask questions. From left, Laura Nelson, Kathy Miller, Susan Hill, Elaine Ireland, Janice Hanson. 1977. *Courtesy of Through the Flower.*

Enjoying some rare downtime, 1977. From left: unknown, Martie Rochford, Stephanie Martin, Judy Chicago. *Courtesy of Through the Flower.*

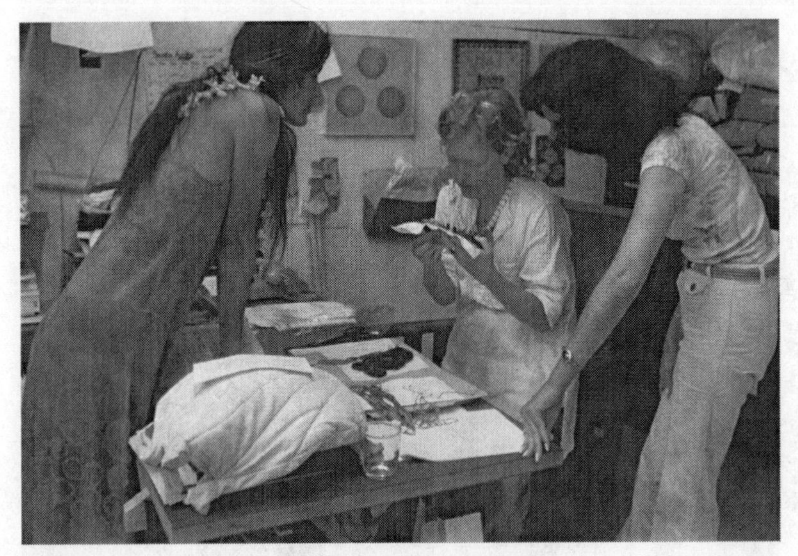

Stephanie Martin, Susan Hill and Shelley Mark examine possible stitches for use in a runner at the loft, 1977. Tremendous care went into matching stitches, thread, and color to most effectively convey Chicago's design and to ensure the historical accuracy of the embroidery. *Courtesy of Through the Flower.*

The loft was crowded with large embroidery frames where workers could see and evaluate the runner as a whole. The frames and stands, made at the studio specifically for the runners, disallowed a common practice of rolling up large work on a small frame and stitching small sections at a time. Note the hanging runners in the background. Each runner was covered and stored at night by Susan Hill. From left, Pat Akers, Susan Brenner, Terry Blecher (1977). *Courtesy of Through the Flower.*

From left, Susan Hill, Marjorie Biggs, Constance von Briesen in consultation over the Caroline Hirschel runner, 1978. Note the layout of the Heritage Floor behind von Briesen, in the upper right. *Courtesy of Through the Flower.*

Researchers logged in many hours at local libraries for information on possible names for the Heritage Floor. They taught themselves how to "read past" biases in the historical record to craft a feminist history of women specific to *The Dinner Party*. From the left, Karen Schmidt, Anne Isolde, Katie Amend, Anne Maire Pois, Juliet Meyers (1977). *Courtesy of Through the Flower.*

Researchers typed information onto index cards that were then cross-referenced for the woman's era, country, profession or expertise, and the source of her authority, 1977. In the predigital research era, the task of finding, recording, and organizing information was time-consuming and labor-intensive. *Courtesy of Through the Flower.*

Ann Isolde, head of research, acted as an informal seminar leader in marathon meetings in 1977 to finalize the list of names for the Heritage Floor. Long debates became opportunities to clarify the feminist message the researchers hoped to represent. Chicago, an avid student of history, actively participated in these conversations and finalized the list. *Courtesy of Through the Flower.*

Once the list of names for the Heritage Floor was finalized, the work shifted to graphics. Workers spent months in 1978 stenciling names on paper and attaching them to plastic sheets that Chicago then used to design the flow of names on the Heritage Floor. From left, Bergin Ruse, Shannon Hogan, Martie Rotchford. *Courtesy of Through the Flower.*

Helene Simich, head of graphics, posting a to-do list on the information board, 1977. Less formal exchange of information among workers appeared in the studio's collective journal and sometimes as graffiti on the bathroom wall. Note the announcements of studio workshops above and a message from Susan Hill below. *Courtesy of Through the Flower.*

Ceramics involved the fewest workers because of its technical difficulty. Here, two women prepare a plate before the clay is carved. Plates become more complex and three-dimensional from the first to the third wing, and, as a result, Chicago lost many to the intense firing process required to produce the depth of color and brightness of surface she wanted. *Courtesy of Through the Flower.*

Expert weaver Jan Marie DuBois and Judy Chicago cut an entry banner off its frame at the San Francisco Studio Workshop in 1978. Opening banners, done in the Aubusson style of weaving, required specialized skills that many volunteers learned in order to complete the work. The banners commemorate a history that might have been, had patriarchy never existed. *Courtesy of Through the Flower.*

CHAPTER FIVE

Going Public

The Dinner Party in San Francisco, 1979

THE SCHEDULED OPENING for *The Dinner Party*—March 1979—loomed large over the studio. The group worked a grueling schedule to finish, their lives outside the studio seeming to shrink as the opening date approached. Yet in the face of the tremendous task of completing *The Dinner Party*, keeping the studio financially afloat also required a tremendous amount of energy and sacrifice. That story—of the finances of *The Dinner Party*—warrants historical attention. It too represents the ways that the women involved in the project practiced feminism. The feminism practiced in this arena was not cultural in terms of its orientation. It was far too focused on the nuts and bolts of money, museums, and donors to consider goddesses and ritual. But the story of the money that funded Chicago testifies to the ways feminism in the 1970s connected women in networks that ran across business, culture industries, granting agencies, and city politics. It also testifies to the ways that money—from donations to ticket sales—spoke loudly and clearly for the public's interest in feminist art.

Sacrifice (not only money) shaped this history. Six core *Dinner Party* workers drew a small salary to keep them (barely) afloat; the artist herself worked without a salary or health insurance. She sold her paintings and sketches and gave supporters and workers her art or traded it for much-needed services. She contributed all her royalties from *Through the Flower* to the project. These funds, as well as the large grants Gelon helped secure, kept the studio doors opened. But it left Chicago without any safety net or plan B if *The Dinner Party* did not secure her a financial backer in the shape of a major gallery, patron, or museum tour.

As Chicago began working on *The Dinner Party* in 1974, the monies flowing through the studio were relatively small. Chicago's accounting records from 1974 show her raising money by selling work (for example, US author-activist Rita Mae Brown bought a drawing for $600 and Barbara Seaman for $1,000), lecturing for a fee between $200 and $350 at colleges and universities, and running a two-day workshop for $1,000. Donations came in the form of cash ($100 to $200 each) or materials.[1] A generous supporter set up an account for the artist at a local art store to keep her in supplies.[2] Chicago took in just under $15,000 in 1974.

In the next four years, Chicago's earning and expenses grew in tandem. Between 1975 and the opening at San Francisco in early 1979, Chicago earned $23,130 from lecturing, ranging from $200 at UC Irvine in 1975 to $1,000 at Fresno in 1978; all of it went into *The Dinner Party*. Chicago also steadily increased the amount of money she took in from selling her art. As her reputation grew, her earnings from selling her work nearly trebled, from $6,610 in 1976 to $17,470 in 1978.[3] At the same time, the amount of materials she required also grew, keeping the studio running on the thinnest of margins. Chicago sold her drawings of Hypatia for $800, Boadaceia for $1,250, and Sojourner Truth for $1,500 in the year before the opening. In 1978, the artist's sales, lectures, and royalties amounted to $32,000, all of which she put into the studio.[4] Subsequent accounting for the cost of making *The Dinner Party* never included the overhead costs of the studio, salaries, or the value of the art Chicago sold or gave away.[5]

To get *The Dinner Party* ready to go public, much had to happen and all of it required money. Chicago's promotional lectures and art sales alone could not fund the studio fully. Monies had to be raised and audiences cultivated. Between 1977 and 1979 these things became deeply intertwined, foremost through the efforts of Diane Gelon. She took over fund-raising and promotion after the studio restructured itself in 1977, and she spent the next two years leading up to the San Francisco opening in a whirlwind of activity. She lectured to groups of women, students, and art groups in various venues: in university lecture halls, art museums, bookstores, and living rooms. She gave interviews, or scheduled Chicago for interviews, with local and national newspapers and with feminist and art publications; she scheduled studio tours with notables, including prominent museum curators, feminists, and politically connected people in city, state, and national women's organizations. She wrote hundreds of personal letters to potential donors, to directors of galleries and museums who might show *The Dinner Party*, and to groups of women asking for information about the project. Along with two other studio volunteers, in 1977 Gelon staffed a *Dinner*

Party booth at the International Year of the Woman Conference in Houston, where she tapped into networks of liberal feminist activists. All told, Gelon's efforts between 1977 and 1979 achieved two critical goals: to bring in enough money into the studio each month to finish the work, and to create a sense of anticipation in potential audiences of what they would see when *The Dinner Party* toured.

Gelon's skills at promotion, coupled with Chicago's for inspiring audiences, combined to make *The Dinner Party* the first feminist art blockbuster. When it opened in 1979, it broke museum attendance records, was among the first shows to initiate the use of ticket and audio tours, and helped catapult art exhibits into a commodity audiences would both wait in line and pay additional fees to see. For these reasons, the story of financing and marketing *The Dinner Party* goes hand in hand with an account of its popularity. Money, in the form of personal and corporate donations, sales of sketches and test plates, tickets to the museum show or related lectures and symposia, made visible the public's interest in *The Dinner Party*. As the San Francisco opening loomed, Gelon's new role as feminist fund-raiser put her at the center of a different set of efforts, efforts that had little to do with art making, to prepare *The Dinner Party* to go public.

Networking Feminism

Every single dollar takes so much work.

Gelon's path to feminism threaded first through Judaism and then through the arts. In 1970, while working on a doctorate in art history at UCLA, Gelon found employment in LA's thriving Jewish community as a camp director and by 1971 as a teacher at a religious school. A notice about a conference of Jewish American feminists to be held in 1973 in New York City caught her eye, and she secured funding to attend. The gathering of five hundred women, including Bella Abzug, awakened Gelon to the first stirrings of feminism across all branches of Judaism, including Orthodox Judaism. She returned and formed the Jewish Women's Project through UCLA, organized a small conference, and started a consciousness-raising group.[6]

Gelon's art historical studies and her feminism ran on parallel tracts until a course offered by Ruth Iskin on women artists at UCLA (though not through the Art Department) joined them. During the class, Gelon decided to redefine her dissertation topic to include a focus on women artists. Iskin literally connected Gelon to the city's feminist art scene by inviting her to the opening of the LA Woman's Building in November 1973, where she saw Chicago's one-woman show. "I wound up buying the cheapest work in the show—$300 for a drawing, which still hangs in my office, out of the Great Ladies series."[7]

When she came to pick up the piece, Gelon and Chicago talked. Iskin also introduced Gelon to Arlene Raven, who, along with Chicago, taught at the Feminist Studio Workshop. Gelon became the archivist for the newly established Feminist Center for Art Historical Studies at the Woman's Building under the direction of Iskin and Raven. At the same time, Gelon nurtured her Jewish feminist connections. She attended a second national conference in the city of Chicago, where she and a small group of radical women, including Cheryl Moch from New York, founded the Jewish Feminist Organization with the intention of staging more conferences and building a constituency for Jewish feminist activism on both regional and national levels. Her feminisms came together briefly when in 1974 Gelon hosted what she suspects was the first feminist Seder on the West Coast. Iskin and Chicago, along with others from the Woman's Building, gathered at Gelon's parents' home and used their own woman-centered Haggadah.[8]

The move from administering summer camps and Jewish feminist conferences to managing *The Dinner Party* project came easily for Gelon. When Chicago asked her to help research 999 names for the Heritage Floor, Gelon agreed and shortly after withdrew from graduate school. Within a year, she had fashioned a new role for herself as project manager. Versed in art history, she understood that many successful male artists in the past and present benefitted from the support of assistants and apprentices who freed the artist to focus on the art. Gelon wanted to provide Chicago with such support. She took on the day-to-day administration of the project, focusing her considerable talents on promoting Chicago by mobilizing networks of feminists and interested audiences in the goings on at the studio. And, critically, she took over fund-raising.

In the fall of 1977, Gelon, along with studio researcher Juliet Meyers and Meyer's girlfriend Peg Wood, attended the National Conference on Women in Houston, a gathering of feminists of all stripes—women active in Republican and Democratic Party circles as well as radical women and lesbian feminists. The National Commission on the Observance of International Women's Year (IWY Commission)—set in motion by President Gerald Ford in response to the UN General Assembly's designation of 1975 as International Women's Year—organized the Houston conference. The IWY held its first international conference in Mexico City in 1975; organizers hoped the Houston gathering would continue to build momentum and set policy agendas for what appeared to be a committed and mobilized feminist movement.[9] Houston was a beehive of activity. Gelon described the opening in her diary:

> The opening session of the conference was . . . well it's hard for me to write about. I cheered and cried, felt joyful, sad, angry. What got to me, emotionally, was seeing the women who were sitting on the dia walk in—(Bella) Abzug, (Gloria) Steinem, Barbara Jordan, and the three first ladies—Carter, Betty Ford, Lady Bird—all sitting together—all assembled for the same reason—women's rights . . . I cried . . . it's been such a long fight—not over yet. I knew Susan B. was in the arena with us—and then when they said that they were using Susan B's gavel that she used at the Women's Rights convention in 1898 I wept.[10]

The 1977 convention allowed Gelon and Meyers to network with a range of interested women. Ken Gilliam rigged up a continuous slide show on the activities taking place in Chicago's Santa Monica studio. Meyers and Gelon handed out flyers asking for volunteers and donations. Activists and nonactivists wandered by, stopped to watch the images, exchange a laugh with the outgoing Meyers, ask for information from the more studious Gelon, pick up materials, and perhaps donate a few dollars. The steady stream of people, conversations, and enthusiasm for feminist causes gave those who attended an infectious sense of confidence that anything was possible. Gelon felt particularly moved by the convention's vote to support lesbian rights. She wrote in her diary that the vote for sexual preference "was wonderful." "I never thought it would happen until I was old and grey that a group of women as wonderfully diverse as these delegates—young, old, rich, poor, minority women and white women would vote so solidly for a resolution to end discrimination for lesbians and homosexuals. Betty Friedan was great when she spoke that she has been known to be against gay rights but supports this resolution because all women must come together . . . the place went crazy and after the vote there was yelling and dancing and embracing."[11]

The exuberance on display at Houston confirmed what Gelon and Meyers understood to be the historic mission of *The Dinner Party*: the times were at last right to offer a new monument to women that would enshrine their long struggle for recognition and celebrate their individual and collective resilience in the face of systematic and pervasive discrimination. Here was the audience for *The Dinner Party* whose support would open the museum world to women's art.

While working the crowds in Houston, Gelon made important connections to liberal women active in publishing, in the arts, and in politics. Two booths away, the Washington, DC–based liberal feminist group National Women's Political Caucus hosted a steady stream of visitors, and Meyers struck up a conversation with the director of development, Lael Stegall. Stegall proved to be a particularly important person for Gelon to meet because of her connections to liberal activists in Washington, and to potentially interested feminists in funding institutions, including the National Endowment for the Arts and the Ford Foundation. By the end of the conference, Stegall had invited Gelon to Washington to present *The Dinner Party* project to a group of well-connected political and cultural women.[12] Among the contacts she made through Stegall was Bess Abell of Second Lady Joan Mondale's staff; Gelon started an eight-month lobbying effort to get Mondale to visit the Santa Monica studio, which she did in the spring of 1978. Abell wrote to Gelon announcing, "You have captured our interest."[13] Gelon also met Ellen Malcolm, a donor who gave seed money to support women running for political office and who eventually founded Emily's List. Malcolm made an anonymous donation to *The Dinner Party* and introduced Gelon to well-connected women in New York and Washington who proved instrumental in building a wider circle of support for *The Dinner Party*.

Gelon traveled extensively in 1978 and 1979, speaking to groups and meeting with potential donors and people interested in bringing *The Dinner Party* to their local museums. Through her travels, Gelon moved along overlapping networks of well-connected professional women in cities around the country, a testimony to the impact second-wave feminism had in establishing women in the world of business. It also spoke to the ways that supporting a feminist-themed cultural product like *The Dinner Party* brought together women who may have had little else in common or few investments in the formal women's movement. In May 1978, Gelon attended an event hosted by the Washington Women's Art Center (WWAC) to build support for bringing the exhibition to the District of Columbia. While there she met with people at the National Endowment for the Arts and National Endowment for the Humanities, and with Charles Millard of the Hirshhorn Museum. A few months later, in New York City, the Sarah Institute held a cocktail party fund-raiser on December 2, 1978, hosted by *Ms.* editor Gloria Steinem and artist Alice Neel. The Sarah Institute donated funds to women in the arts and humanities who had been denied equal access and support for their talents. Their Second Floor Salon provided gallery space for exhibitions, performances, and lectures for the New York feminist community.[14] Over the next few months, Gelon's frequent visits to New York City included meetings with Gail Counts at the Ford Foundation, Barbara Haskell at the Avon Foundation, Christy Hefner at the Playboy foundation, designer Diane von Fürstenberg, and supporters at *Ms.* magazine.[15]

Gelon worked enthusiastically in her new self-created role as feminist fund-raiser. In January and February of 1978 alone, she flew to Boston to meet with John Walsh at the Museum of Fine Arts, Helen Reese, cultural affairs officer at Boston City Hall, and Gary Berger of the Massachusetts Council on Arts and Humanities; then a quick stop in New York City before continuing to Washington, DC, to meet with Abell; to Denver where she gave a lecture at the Denver Art Museum and met with its director; to San Francisco to meet with people at the Hewett Foundation; to Cleveland, where she met with the director of the Cleveland Museum of Art, feminist supporters in the Akron-Cleveland area, and lectured at Case Western Reserve University; and then back to LA to give a lecture in Fresno.[16]

Gelon traveled to small and large cities to meet with groups, some affiliated with cultural institutions and some not, that expressed interest in *The Dinner Party*. As always, she generated the funds required to support her travels. "I did not want to take money from Judy," she recalled.[17] Gelon wrote in her diary in April 1979 that, "Sometimes it feels like all I do is spend time in airports and on airplanes. But I love it—all the traveling, being out in the world, lecturing, promoting the project. I'm good at it and enjoy it. Judy and I make a perfect team. She does the creative work and I do the PR and fund-raising."[18] Throughout the months leading to the San Francisco opening, Gelon crisscrossed the country, visiting Milwaukee, Seattle, Indianapolis, Minneapolis, Pittsburgh, Chicago, Phoenix, Rochester, San Jose, Los Angeles, and Cincinnati.[19]

Yet despite her tremendous efforts, in the summer of 1978, six months shy of the March opening, the project was still short $35,000.[20] Gelon mused in her diary that raising that kind of money "seems both impossible and easy. I've raised about $80,000 in the last two years and it seems like since we made it this far *only* $35,000 should be easy—but every single dollar takes so much work."[21] As the opening loomed, expenses were considerable, even with so many volunteers defraying the costs. Rent, phone, utilities, and five $200 monthly salaries added up to $2,000 a month in operating costs.[22]

New York, as the hub of the art and media worlds, was a particularly important city for Gelon to cultivate. Its wealthy, vibrant, and diverse feminist scenes intersected episodically, typically when galvanized in support of the era's key legislative battles for the ERA and abortion rights.[23] Bringing *The Dinner Party* to New York became one such point of convergence, temporarily coordinating the interest in seeing the piece among women politicians, professionals in publishing, journalism, and education, wealthy philanthropists, struggling and established artists, and audiences interested in feminist cultural and artistic production. When networking in New York, Chicago's editor, Loretta Barrett at Doubleday, quietly supplied Gelon with a small office and access to a phone, copy facilities, and the elegant corporate dining room, where Gelon and sometimes Chicago met with potential donors and supporters. David Rockefeller's son informally interned with her. Under the umbrella of selling Chicago's books, Loretta directed a steady flow of Doubleday's vast resources to support Gelon's efforts to promote *The Dinner Party* art project. She did so despite facing considerable blowback from the publisher, Sam Vaughan, particularly when he became cognizant of the imagery Doubleday had agreed to publish.

On January 31, 1979, less than eight weeks from the San Francisco opening and as the accompanying book on *The Dinner Party* moved into production, Vaughan angrily fired off a memo about the offensiveness of the vaginal imagery of Chicago's plates. Shocked at what he saw in the page proofs, he rifled through his paperwork to see what, exactly, he had agreed to publish. "I can find nowhere in the descriptions any indication of the nature of the art work, except for its technique or of the steady symbolism, which in some renderings is less symbolic than gynecological." How, he asked, could these plates tell the "story of women's history unless this artist's idea of the history of women is centered entirely in one place." Not only would conservative librarians refuse to buy the book, he went on, but the entire Doubleday sales force ought to have been alerted to the fact that the plates have "sexual symbolism." He worried about putting workers in the Manufacturing Department in an uncomfortable position: "We don't for example, ask any of our employees who might be deeply religious or offended by scatological language to proof read galleys emerging from such writing. Do we have any regard for the people along the line who have to handle this book? What I want to know is: why weren't we told what the center or the essence of this book is?"[24]

Angela Cox, who readied the proofs, reminded the publisher that *The Dinner Party* had the markings of becoming a major cultural event.

> When we presented the book to Pub Board, it was based on the fact that Judy Chicago was a Doubleday author, that she was a leading feminist painter and this was an exhibition of considerable prestige: We had three firm museum commitments, articles in major California papers and an impressive list of backers—from David Rockefeller to NEA. And our proposal indicated that this sculpture should get such attention. The book was to be the story behind its making—five years of work by over 250 men and women, including the most conservative of china painters, grandmothers from the Midwest, college students and dedicated artists.[25]

Barrett added her voice to the debate. Chicago's memoir had proved itself as a steady seller, and Barrett would be willing to present the book to the sales force herself. Further, she wryly noted, librarians should not be in the position to censor what the public could read. She presciently articulated what would become an outright culture war in the 1990s over federal support for the arts. "In terms of problems with the Manufacturing Department, how does one protect people from art?"[26] The flap over the art of *The Dinner Party* and its relationship to women's history died down, and Doubleday had copies of "*The Dinner Party*": *A Symbol of Our Heritage* for sale in March as the show opened to the public. Barrett and Cox read the tea leaves correctly, as the book sold. Within its first year, *Publishers Weekly* reported that *The Dinner Party* (1979) and its companion *Embroidering Our Heritage* (1980) had sold over 30,000 copies.[27]

Gelon's busy schedule of networking acted as a catalyst to mobilize a range of financial support for *The Dinner Party* art project. It led to invitations for Chicago to lecture; Chicago's lectures generated interest in her memoir, generated more inquires about bringing *The Dinner Party* to local venues, and inspired donations to the studio, large and small. Gelon's lectures worked similarly. Arriving in town to meet with philanthropists, corporations with a feminist on staff, art directors, museum board members, or university and college groups, led to coverage of *The Dinner Party* in local newspapers, art newsletters, and campus publications. Such happenings, taking place between 1977 and 1979 across the country, combined to create buzz about *The Dinner Party*, elevating it into a newsworthy if quirky feminist cultural event. They also harnessed individual consumption—a person's willingness to spend money for access to a cultural event or object—to *The Dinner Party* project by inspiring people to buy Chicago's memoir or a preliminary plate sketch, or, crucially, to give donations directly to the project. Gelon recalled that, "We sold everything."[28]

When the final accounting was done, *The Dinner Party* cost $250,000 to make. Money to finish came from multiple sources: The NEA awarded the project $17,500 in a matching grant and the Ford Foundation $10,000. Between lecture fees and royalties, Chicago gave approximately $85,000 over five years to *The Dinner Party* project. She also took out a $30,000 loan from Los Angeles Women's Bank.[29] Gelon brought in $110,000 through fund-raising.[30]

Gelon's fund-raising resulted in money coming in from an odd assortment of companies, organizations, and places where Chicago's publicity materials and Gelon's solicitations landed on sympathizers' desks. Not surprisingly, feminist organizations gave support, including the NOW Legal Defense and Education Fund, the New York Women's Fund Joint Foundation, and the Marin County National Women's Political Caucus; more surprisingly, a range of organizations and companies donated after receiving a letter from Gelon, such as the Lucius and Eva Eastman Fund (N.Y.), the Liberty Hill Foundation (Calif.), H. F. Coors Ceramics Company (LA), Westland Graphics (Calif.), and Hanovia Hobby Products (N.J.). Record giant Warner Brothers Records also donated, a savvy public-relations move in the wake of a feminist boycott of the company due to its sexist representation of women in 1976 and 1977.[31] The denim company Levi Strauss and the giant oil corporation Exxon declined.[32] The studio refused money from the Playboy Foundation despite Gelon's courting of Christy Hefner after a long discussion at a Thursday-night rap session at the studio about Playboy's objectification of women.[33]

While Gelon's fund-raising with wealthy and professional women garnered substantial individual donations, ranging from gifts in the hundreds and thousands of dollars, her publicity efforts also produced a steady stream of small individual donations and gifts from women ranging from one to twenty dollars. In 1977, all these donations, large and small, were bundled with the NEA matching grant and run through the San Francisco Museum of Modern Art (SFMOMA), whose charismatic director, Henry Hopkins, had long been a supporter of Chicago. Hopkins was the formal recipient for the grant. Monies came through the museum and then were paid out to

Chicago. Similarly, the hundreds of small donations sent directly to Chicago were forwarded to the museum for processing. Coming from women across the country, these small donations were actively cultivated by Gelon through a number of innovative strategies for encouraging potential audiences to give money. In August 1977 she sent a letter to supporters explaining the necessity of raising $17,500 in individual contributions to order to receive the $17,500 NEA matching grant. The letter broke down what each donation could contribute, particularizing the gift and personalizing the effort:

> $5.00 will provide funds to make a porcelain tile for the floor
> $10.00 will provide an embroidered napkin
> $25.00 will provide a porcelain chalice
> $50.00 will provide a porcelain fork, knife, spoon
> $100.00 will provide for one place setting including napkin, chalice, flatware
> $250.00 will provide for an embroidered runner
> $500.00 will provide funds for one china-painted porcelain plate.[34]

Many of the small personal donations to the studio came with notes explaining what motivated the gift, as in this note from Phyllis Lichenstein of Florida, which accompanied her $100 donation: "It is still difficult for me to express my feelings. *The Dinner Party* is a monumental tribute that makes me even more proud to be a woman. In itself, despite its heroic preparations, it is a work of amazingly delicate beauty. But I am equally moved by the way in which it has come about, the hours of work by so many and diverse skilled hands, the near lost techniques which have been revitalized and used, and above all, the spirit of cooperative effort that reflects the many facets of unity expressed in the finished piece."[35]

Without personally laying eyes on the artist or seeing images of the work, people regularly gave money based solely on hearing about the volunteers' hard at work at the studio or reading about the feminist history that Chicago hoped to memorialize. That winter, for example, Tom and Chris Drow from Wisconsin sent $10, Mitzi Trachtenberg from California $25, Faye Evans from San Francisco $25, Julie Gale from Louisiana $25.[36] Artists from California, Maine, Massachusetts, Ohio, and Colorado sent donations ranging from one to ten dollars. A woman-run picture frame company sent $100.[37] Rounding off winter donations in 1978, the Portland Center for the Visual Arts sent $50, and an anonymous donor using Philip Morris stationery $1,000.[38] The sheer volume of these small contributions threw the SFMOMA accounting office into disarray, set up as it was to process large grants, not hundreds of personal checks in small amounts. Hopkins suggested that Chicago establish a nonprofit organization to manage these funds, which she did in 1978; Through the Flower was the result.

Other fund-raising efforts included direct mailings sent to anyone who expressed interest in *The Dinner Party*. One such appeal went out at the end of 1978 and explicitly cast financial support for *The Dinner Party* as a form of feminist activism. It read: "GIVE THE WORLD WOMEN'S HISTORY FOR THE NEW YEAR: A Personal Appeal from Judy Chicago."[39] Such appeals were not always met positively. For example, F. Maloff wrote to tell Chicago that her appeal to an imagined community of like-minded women sorely missed the mark. She sent her complaint on the back of the above letter on December 12, 1978: "Dear Ms. Chicago, I note that you have expended much time, skill and funds on a work of great magnitude. But I regret that you have seriously limited its significance because of its religious connotation. In my opinion, this represents just one more example of unaware reinforcement of the oppression of non-Christian minority members like myself. I hope that your future feminist achievements will be of an all-inclusive scope. It is very unfair to feel shut out."[40]

Maloff's letter anticipated what would become a steady stream of criticism over the lack of multiculturalism at *The Dinner Party* from audiences. Kathy Hyatt from Minneapolis also complained about Chicago's assumptions of female unity in the letter. Her response came in February 1979 on stationery proclaiming WOMANPOWER in boldface, with the symbol of women's liberation in the letter O: "I received your appeal last December. I confess that I have very mixed feelings about it. As much as I valued what you are doing, I was so offended by one of the statements made in Judy's appeal, that I have hesitated to contribute. 'If we do not finish *The Dinner Party*, it will mean that we have not yet reached a time in history when women's achievements are valued.' I interpreted this to mean that I, personally, do not value women's achievements if I don't shovel out some dough to this project, specifically." Hyatt did "shovel out some dough," acknowledging that, despite the pretense of the appeal, she viewed the work as pioneering: "I do appreciate the energy and sacrifice that is going into *The Dinner Party*. I *want* to participate in this effort, if only to contribute money. When *The Dinner Party* is completed it will be an important contribution to the consciousness of the world."[41]

These explicit criticisms of Chicago's habitual conflation of women's status with the fate of *The Dinner Party* highlight the dangers of her broad appeals to "women" and her project's capacities to represent them as the piece stood on the brink of going public. Appealing to "women" to support "their" history by supporting *The Dinner Party* raised expectations among Chicago's audiences that they would find images of "themselves" at the party. Yet, as the artist was soon to discover, and as these few critical comments anticipated, the audience for feminist-themed culture was far from coherent or unified in its desires.

But in 1977 and 1978, the entire studio team, including Chicago and Gelon, spared little time worrying about audience reactions. With the help of Henry Hopkins, a national tour was falling into place. By 1978, the Seattle Art Museum and the Memorial Art Gallery at the University of Rochester had agreed to show *The Dinner Party* following its San Francisco exhibition. Stephanie Spencer, associate curator at the Memorial Art Gallery at the University of Rochester, wrote enthusiastically to Hopkins in April 1978 that, "The director, senior curator and I are all in agreement that we want the exhibition, so please consider this a firm commitment. I am so pleased that *The Dinner Party* will be coming here. There is already quite a bit of local interest—a result, of course, of Judy's visit here a few weeks ago."[42] Letters of interest before the SFMOMA opening flooded the studio mailbox. Queries from the Los Angeles County Museum, the University of Cincinnati, Rochester Institute of Technology, Aldrich Museum of Contemporary Art in Ridgefield, Connecticut, and the Contemporary Arts Center in Cincinnati confirmed that the publicity campaign had worked and that museum interest had materialized. Once the show opened, even more queries arrived, including from the Peabody Museum at Harvard, the University of Wisconsin, the Wright State University Galleries, the Tucson Museum of Modern Art, the Minnesota Museum of American Art, the John Michael Kohler Arts Center, and the Galleria Dei Bibliofila in Milan, Italy.[43] By the end of 1979, Gelon had answered at least forty requests for information regarding showing *The Dinner Party*.[44]

The materials the studio sent in response to these queries laid out more than costs and calendars. Since 1977, Chicago and the studio workers had been imagining the museum tour as more than a conventional opening where viewers saw the art in a tightly scripted cultural context created for them by the curators and within the long (sexist) tradition of art historical knowledge. Instead, they imagined *The Dinner Party* as embedded into a thickly feminist and a more robust community art context than what was typically provided by museums. Ideally, viewers would encounter *The Dinner Party* as part of a series of events and talks on women's history and artistic accomplishments and, in the tradition of 1970s feminist event planning, organized with the realities of actual women's lives in mind.

A 1977 letter sent to Christina Orr, assistant curator at the Norton Gallery of Art, West Palm Beach, laid out a picture of their ambitious plans for the exhibit, which included a mandatory child-care center, bookstore, and local women's community announcement board, all of which they hoped the gallery would agree to. "One of the goals for the piece is that it involves the community."

> We are very interested in making contact with women in the area to put together a series of activities to coincide with bringing *The Dinner Party* to their area, such as a festival of women in the arts, some kind of conference on that theme, working with artists, needleworkers, and/or china painters in the community to set up exhibits and demonstrations of their work. . . . We receive mail from people around the country who have already heard about the piece and are hungry for more information, not only on what we are doing, but also on women's history and culture generally.[45]

Viewing *The Dinner Party* in a context made up of local women's community groups, as well as one that celebrated a longer and lesser-known tradition of women's arts and feminist history, would help audiences connect the piece to the heritage it strove to commemorate. Viewing *The Dinner Party* in this way would also embody the kind of synergy between art and audiences for which Chicago had long advocated: art that spoke directly to audiences, whose symbolism and meaning were easily accessible, whose relevancy was obvious, not coded. *The Dinner Party* itself had come about from a studio community effort, with a community of interested women and men imagined as its audience. Offering that community a popular or nonelite version of a women's studies seminar would strengthen the circuitry between artists, art, and audiences that was at the heart of the feminist art movement. Those first efforts to bring the women's community to the museum and to make the museum newly relevant to audiences were on display as the exhibit opened in San Francisco in March 1979.

Opening in San Francisco

Seeing it in its entirety was exhilarating.

The first public viewing of *The Dinner Party*, scheduled for March 14, 1979, represented the finish line for Chicago and the project's staff and volunteers. No one had yet seen it assembled in its monumental totality. Installing *The Dinner Party* took two weeks. The studio crew put up the special lighting system to illuminate the Heritage Floor, assembled the floor's 2,400 glossy porcelain triangles, tested and retested the tables to ensure they could bear the weight of the carved plates, and hung the six colorful opening banners, the eight Heritage Panels, and the photo documentation of the studio workers (the Acknowledgment Panels). The linen cloth that covered the tables took hours to iron before the runners could be laid on top and the chalice and flatware secured. Susan Hill tried to warn the museum electrician that running six irons at once might blow the circuits but was brushed off with a "don't be silly." As they got started, the entire floor went dark.[46] On and off during the installation, Hill's anxiety got the best of her and she would run to the nearest bathroom to throw up. Hill reported that the runners and the lace millennium triangles that covered the table's three corners were "finished at 10:00 pm (exactly) on Saturday March 10, as the security guards (hired to stay late with us) were closing up the museum. It was four days before opening, and the needlework was finally finished. We went dancing."[47] Seeing it assembled for the first time proved to be an emotional experience for Chicago and the other workers. Hill experienced it "like a blow to the gut." She and ceramicist Judye Keyes "were stunned . . . I was terrified and overwhelmed and had to stretch to accept it, literally learn to internalize it all."[48]

Supporters, fans, and friends of the artist and workers crowded the March 14 opening night. Former Chicago student Suzanne Lacy and artist and *Dinner Party* studio member Linda Preuss invited women around the world to hold dinner parties in honor of *The Dinner Party* and to honor historical women in their local communities, called "The International Dinner Party." The artists explained that, "We see this as a 'living art work,' in which all of us will be performers in a gathering together and honoring of women from around the world. . . . If each of our dinner parties occurs on the evening of March 14, we will form a continuous 24 hour celebration around the world."[49] Lacy sent out 1,200 announcements with a simple request: "On the evening of March 14, 1979, women should dine together, choose women to honor and describe the event." Telegrams poured in during the opening, and Lacy and Preuss pinned small red triangles on a map of the world on where dinner parties were held.[50] Moira Roth, former CalArts student of Chicago, described the event for *Art in America*:

> In Ghana, West Africa, a group of women dine together and honor women of their choice. From New Zealand comes news of another such dinner at the same time. The guests of honor in Houston are Kathe Kollwitz and Artemisia Gentileschi; in Cornwall, Ontario, "Mary Mack, first Cornwall woman alderman," and in Ohio, Lora Sebrina 1881–1974, quilt maker. Edinburgh feminists dedicated their dinner to women's struggles in Iran, and women sitting at an Athenian dinner table compose a cable to Suzanne Lacy, the organizer of this international dinner party: "In Greece women write their difficult story stop every day is hard work stop deepest appreciation for your movement stop."[51]

Women in two hundred cities around the world participated.[52]

Poetry readings, panels, and workshops ran throughout the weekend. Chicago lectured to a sold-out crowd on Friday. On Saturday, an all-day conference titled "A Celebration of Women's Heritage" took place at a nearby Holiday Inn. Art critics Lucy Lippard and Jan Butterfield, art historian Ruth Iskin, Lacy, and Gelon led a panel discussion in the morning on the subject of "women's art as a vehicle for social change."[53] Afternoon talks included those by Susan Rennie on witches and Amazons, Valerie Mathes on American Indian women, Raye Richardson on Sojourner Truth, and Arlene Raven on Natalie Barney and the "feminist lesbian tradition." Three scholars from Stanford—Harrianne Mills, Marilyn Skinner, and Bella Zweigh—discussed women in the ancient world, and M. J. Hamilton from Cal State University presented on the "alternative lifestyle" of medieval nuns.[54] A workshop ran for children on the art of *The Dinner Party*.[55]

Most impressive, by any measure, were the crowds who lined up to see the exhibit. For much of its run in San Francisco, people waited for three, four, or five hours to see *The Dinner Party*. All told, *The Dinner Party* broke the museum's previous attendance records. Over ninety thousand people came during the twelve-week exhibition, more than doubling attendance records for two of the museum's most popular shows, Jasper Johns and Robert Rauschenberg.[56] Audience anticipation, particularly in California, had been building for months as a direct result of Gelon's publicity and fund-raising efforts. That, coupled with steady regional press coverage, set the conditions for what became a major event. Hopkins recalled in a 2007 interview that the show saved the budget that year. "I think at that moment, it was the biggest attendance we had ever had at the museum. Lines of people coming in every day. People very deeply involved in the arts, people involved in ceramics, people involved in fabric work and things, with the runners on the table, feminists. But there was a big male audience, as well. Events outside the museum of people protesting, and giving support, and it went on and on."[57]

During the long wait times, the lines sometimes erupted into spontaneous temporary feminist communities. Jean A. Rosenfeld, from Carmichael, California, described her experience of being in line for three hours: "I began chatting with the woman behind me—and the chatting became sharing—personal and political and useful talk. And then as we rounded the corner to the final waiting hall a small group of people began to sing. They sang quietly and beautifully and were surprised by the applause. Then the singing spread to the people around them—and then everyone was singing. All the people waiting gathered into the final hallway and sang. Several hundred people singing in harmony—church songs, Hebrew songs, children's rounds, 60's songs, spirituals. It was glorious." Rosenfeld reported that she had brought Chicago's memoir to pass the time with. Holding the book while in line with other women who, like her, had committed the time, energy, and the cost of ticket admission to see *The Dinner Party* intensified her sense of personal participation in the event. "As I was holding on to *Through the Flower* I could feel it vibrating. The walls and the floor and the air were vibrating! I was almost reluctant to enter the long awaited exhibit and leave the singing."

Rosenfeld's experiences waiting in line were more positive than her initial experience of the art. She found herself disturbed by the vulva images on the plates and wondered why some plates made her feel fearful. "At first I disliked symbolizing women by cunts, but as I passed from one plate to another my uncomfortable feeling finally congealed into meaning. The vaginas made me feel vulnerable. . . . This opening into our bodies—the insides that we never see—how frightening to be blood and bones and glands . . . I wonder if this feeling of vulnerability is what frightened male artists—made them so aghast at your work." For Rosenfeld, the unifying central core image on the plates pulled her into a new identification with other vagina-bearing people, the "insides we never see," a truth about embodiment ("how frightening to be blood and bones and glands") that women were singled out to bear in a male-dominated society. The whole package—the memoir, the ticket, waiting in line, singing, and the art—combined to make the viewing of *The Dinner Party* "thrilling" and "exhilarating."[58] Other women who saw it in San Francisco reported a similar experience. Jane Whitehead from Santa Monica reported that waiting in line for over three hours created a feeling of community among the women, a feeling that was bested only by seeing the piece itself. "The camaraderie that developed among the women in the line was surpassed only by the marvelous feeling of pride, beauty, and awareness of women's history that your wonderful exhibit gave us! Thank you so *very* much!"[59]

The anticipation of seeing the piece contributed to the excitement for those who waited in line. But many who had only moments before pressed eagerly forward slowed to a crawl as they stepped into the dim gallery, creating the long lines and long waits. People positioned themselves on the viewing side of the guardrail and started forward in the snaking line to see the first wing of goddesses and the shimmering floor and the golden stream of names. *The Dinner Party* catalog, purchased for less than a dollar, gave more details about what they were seeing, connecting the names on the floor to the seated guests. Heads bent as viewers moved closer to take in a detail, paused to look across the Heritage Floor, gazed at the back of a runner, or lingered over a particularly vivid plate. Some took advantage of the guardrail to kneel and to study the embroidery of a runner. Marsha G. Harris explained the impact of the staging made her burst into tears: "I entered the DP and saw the names all there together in one place for the first time in my life and I wept with joy . . . Why did it take so long? Why did we have to unearth these women buried and obliterated? Why do the power-holders even now try to keep such beauty and such strength and such worth unvisible [*sic*], denied?"[60]

A journalist from *Newsweek* reported that women comprised 75 percent of visitors to the San Francisco exhibit, noting with an air of surprise that, "They seem to take palpable pride in the work. They joke a little about the vaginal imagery and admire the art. They seem to fill in the empty place settings, making the table their own. Many, when they recognize Chicago, go up to her and say, 'Thank you. Thanks very much.'"[61] The imaginative act of "filling in" the empty place settings with themselves, "making the table their own," noted by the journalist, captures the sense of engagement many viewers had with *The Dinner Party*. Witnessing the current between the audiences and the art, SFMOMA director Hopkins took heart from it. He told the *San Francisco Examiner* that, "*The Dinner Party*'s appeal to me became even stronger as I watched during the twelve weeks the power it held. It remained in pristine condition; no one tried to touch it. The audience found it a real experience. That's art."[62]

Touring the Party

And She made for them a Sign to See.

Chicago's intention to create a powerful and transformative experience for anyone who saw *The Dinner Party* hinged on two related visual strategies. Viewers would encounter what Chicago saw as the primordial essence of women and the female experience literalized in the vagina plates. The plates, each uniquely informed by the age in which the woman lived, shared the fundamental structure of a central core image, with layers of texture, pattern, and color giving the sense of depths now revealed. The second representational strategy led viewers to see what the artist understood as the buried tradition of female power and leadership revealed through the form of *The Dinner Party* itself. The rubric of gathering together of the lost sisterhood in a last (and now, first) supper brought the viewer into a new appreciation for the contributions of women.

At the same time, Chicago took care to create an experience for her viewers that would move them to see the world through a prism of feminism. The history Chicago tells through *The Dinner Party* highlights a 1970s view of the trans-historical patriarchy against which these outstanding women struggled and which still dangerously threatened to curtail contemporary women. This explicit history could be accessed in a variety of ways, including an audio tour (available after 1980), *The Dinner Party* book, or the Heritage Panels. Together, the iconography of the plates and runners, the golden names illuminated on the floor, the structure of the Last/First Supper, and its account of patriarchy made *The Dinner Party* didactic, dramatic, and engaging.

Visitors stood in queues for anywhere between one and five hours for most of the initial showings of *The Dinner Party*. While waiting to enter the gallery, they might spend time looking at short video clips and the Acknowledgment Panels, a set of panels covered with photographs detailing the production of *The Dinner Party*. These images of blue-jean-clad women, with sleeves rolled up, holding needles or hunched over the jigger machine, seated around a table covered with books or a potluck dinner, invoked the literal community of women that had gathered at Chicago's Santa

Monica studio for over three years. The visitor might see older women like Marjorie Biggs, Thelma Brenner, and Constance von Briesen side by side with college-aged Adrienne Weiss and Kathy Miller, androgynous women like Catherine Stifter next to the well-coifed Elaine Ireland, male workers like Peter Fieweger stitching a runner or Ken Gilliam up on a ladder, and Chicago, with her distinctive cloud of hair and aviator glasses, working alone or side by side with her crew. Group shots captured serious discussions, a head thrown back in laughter, and moments of sustained, concentrated effort.

These images, prominently displayed during the opening and subsequent tour, underscored that volunteer labor mattered to Chicago and mattered to what the viewer would soon see. Each person who worked at the studio—for two days or for two years—had their name listed on the photo documentation panels. In this way, Chicago broke with the tradition of apprentices whose work commonly went unnoted and unrecorded. These snapshots also oriented audiences to the range of technical skills employed to bring *The Dinner Party* to completion, ideally readying them to see with new appreciation the art, not just the craft, of the needleworker and the china painter.

The experience at the Brooklyn Museum today must be much the same as it was in San Francisco in March 1979. Once a visitor has passed through the documentation panels, she moves under six densely woven banners with lines invoking a female-centered origin myth that position *The Dinner Party* as both a vision of a time without patriarchy and a record of women shaped by unchecked male power. She then enters a dark space where the only light comes from the installation itself. After a first glimpse at what may appear to be levitating altars hovering over a bright floor, the visitors queue up alongside the low railing to file past the place settings. The railing, the dim lights, and the slow-moving line combine to give the feeling of being in a religious sanctuary. The visitor might encounter the overt feminist meaning by way of the written and audio narratives. In these various ways, *The Dinner Party* offers viewers a preferred reading of itself and a specific way to make sense of the images and names. In short, it presents them with a feminist standpoint that they can resist or embrace.

As viewers begin their slow walk around the installation, they confront the beginning and the end of *The Dinner Party* as the first and third wings of the table intersect in front of them. On display at the point of intersection is the first of three millennium (*M*) triangles to mark the transition as sacred. This first triangle displays a capital letter *M*, the thirteenth letter of the alphabet, a number significant for the piece's religious message. Thirteen guests sit at each wing, just as thirteen guests sat at the Last Supper. Yet here the *M* also stands in for a time in the future when, according to Chicago, "the double standard—which defines men's rituals as not only significant but sacred, while rendering women's invisible—will end, and all human effort will be honored for its part in the richness of human experience."[63] The *M*, at its greatest height at the beginning and done in contrasting black and white cutwork and petit point, fades into obscurity as the viewer proceeds around the table to the second and third millennium triangles. Only when the viewer finishes the tour and returns to this first-last millennium triangle does the full narrative significance of the white triangles become clear.

The first guest seated at the table is the Primordial Goddess. According to Chicago's 1980 audio tour, this goddess represents the earliest point in human civilization, when the earth and the creative principal is considered feminine and powerful. The plate, she explains, has a "hot center, the center of the earth or of oneself, the center of women from which all life emerges."[64] The plate's vulva folds, yellow, green, and orange, surround a pulsing red center, with the hint of a yellow opening just below the surface, as a darker red encroaches on it. The plate sits on a runner with animal skins and shells and a spiral marking the first capitalized letter of the guest's name. A series of goddesses follow, including the Fertile Goddess, who symbolizes woman as the source of creation; Ishtar, goddess of ancient Mesopotamia; Kali, Hindu mother goddess; and Snake Goddess, associated with the matriarchal religion of Minoan civilization.

With the Sophia and Amazon plates (the sixth and seventh plates), the parade of female goddesses ends. Sophia as the symbol of sacred female knowledge marks the downfall of female religious power and the rise of Christianity, a pivotal turn in the history of patriarchy as told by *The Dinner Party*. The runner colors pale the closer they are to the plate to represent how "life paled for women after the downfall of the goddess." Chicago explains that she modeled the plate on traditional representations of Sophia as "a single delicate flower, a spiritual whole in which the material world is transcended." Made with six delicately shaded pink, green, and purple flower petals or wings that emanate from a tiny receding point, the plate gives the impression of light flowing both in and out of the form.[65] In contrast, the Amazon plate and runner, which follow Sophia, consist of hard edges and clearly established boundaries, all circular. Breasts with gold plates float over strong thighs; an egg, the ancient symbol of fertility, sits at the plate's center; its far edges join in the image of the double-headed ax, the symbol of Amazonian warriors. This plate testifies to the power of women in groups, the collectivity of a female society and the past existence of female authority.

The remaining six plates on this wing of the table display historical figures who influenced or ruled their communities—the Egyptian queen Hatshepsut; the Hebrew heroine Judith; the poet Sappho from the Greek island of Lesbos; Aspasia, teacher of Greek philosophers Socrates and Pericles; British queen Boadaceia, representative of the "tradition of warrior-queens extending back to ancient times"; and Hypatia, the Roman mathematician and philosopher and appointed head of the University of Alexandria.[66] The plates and runners work together to elaborate the woman's place in the unfolding larger narrative of *The Dinner Party*. Boadaceia's plate's central core image emerges from the play of contrasting shapes, with flat, solid blocks circling a curved helmet that, in turn, holds a circular heart image with a narrow black center opening, a reimagining of Stonehenge as a vulva. The runner draws on legends of Boadaceia as "splendid in a fur-lined, embroidered cape and woolen tunic," and embroidered handmade felt and Celtic jewelry repeat the plate's curvilinear motifs. Roman scholar and philosopher Hypatia is "the last representative at the table of female genius and culture in the classical world."[67] Painted in strong colors, the leaf forms on the plate "pull away from the center, suggesting the events of her life," her death at the hands of an angry mob.[68] The bright orange and red scalloped wheel at the center of the plate seems to spin energetically; woven bans of wool patterned on Coptic tunics adorn the runner.[69] Jan Marie DuBois wove the back of the runner in colors that capture the intensity of Hypatia's suffering when she was punished for her "revival of goddess worship."[70]

This plate marks the end of the first wing of the table. According to Chicago's audio, the images on the second wing appear to rise and fall as a "metaphor for women's desire to become free. But is also a metaphor of women's experience as a symbol of the larger human experience." As the artist notes, not only women suffer from social restrictions. "Most peoples' lives are limited by their race, their class, or their life circumstances."[71] Chicago felt strongly that women's lives too often became identified with particularity, not universality. Here she actively inserts woman as human in her audio tour, an intervention she hopes will inform viewers as they moved forward.

This turn, literally changing direction, from the first to the second wing produces a sense of movement, if not progress. One steps into a new age as the angled tables meet. A second white millennium triangle elevates the site as significant. The letter M on this ornate triangle, done in white thread and placed on white linen, blurs the M into its larger triangular context, another symbol that the recognition of women's power is fading. While it attempts to capture what is almost out of sight, the stitches themselves are eye-catching. Marjorie Biggs included techniques traditionally employed in ecclesiastical embroidery to produce this gloriously textured and delicate altar cloth.[72]

The second wing lacks the drama of mythology that shapes the first and instead focuses on notable women from the beginnings of Christianity to the Reformation in Europe. The guests Chicago selected for this wing reflect the concerns of her own moment in US feminism and its focus on issues of women's spirituality, access to education and leadership, and treatment of their bodies. The guests include Marcella, founder of the first Christian convent in Rome and later declared a saint by the Roman Catholic Church; Saint Bridget of Ireland, whose association with the Celtic goddess Brigid represents the incorporation of paganism into Christianity, and along with it, the loss of female power to a male-centered story of God the father and his son; Byzantine empress Theodora, who initiated reforms that prevented the mistreatment of women, including the death penalty for rape; and Hrosvitha, German nun who wrote plays about women's purity and spiritual steadiness and whose plate setting captures the space of the convent as a female-dominated place that nurtured women's creativity and spirituality. The runner for Hrosvitha pays tribute to her contributions to literature and poetry and draws from the needlework style *opus teutonicum*, which involves complex geometric patterning and counted thread work. *Dinner Party* worker Marny Elliott learned the stitch in 1966 from an eighty-year-old Orthodox nun in Greece.[73] The table continues with Trotula, the Italian physician who specialized in gynecology and obstetrics and who wrote a treatise on women's diseases that was used for centuries until it was forgotten; Eleanor of Aquitaine, medieval queen of France and later, England, imprisoned by her husband, Henry II, for sixteen years; and German Hildegarde of Bingen, a twelfth-century abbess, scientist, scholar, and musician. The plate for Petronilla de Meath, an accused German witch, also references the diminishment of female authority in Europe. Its cauldron-shaped form in the shape of a penetrating candle symbolizes a Wiccan ceremonial candle or a stake on which accused witches burned. Animal motifs, specifically the hare and the cat, also appear on the runner.[74]

The ninth guest on the second table, French writer Christine de Pisan, marks an important turning point on this wing. According to Chicago, de Pisan's book, *The City of Women*, expressed de Pisan's "desire to stand up for women who were being maligned during the Renaissance." Consisting of biographies of five hundred famous women, the book records a history of women that Chicago classified as "lost" when she started her research.[75] Underscoring the centrality of forgetting to the feminist message of *The Dinner Party*, De Pisan's place seals an important change in the dynamics between the runner and plates. Now, the runners begin to intrude more forcefully on the plates, a shift that Chicago explains as representing a point at which "history began to intrude on women."[76] "History," in this instance, stands for patriarchy.

The wing reaches its conclusion with Anna van Schurman, Dutch artist and writer. Van Schurman's plate sits on a runner designed as a needlepoint sampler. Samplers, once used as a "personal dictionary" of styles and stitches, had become, by the end of the seventeenth century, formalized as tools "used to teach little girls—to teach them how to think small, to deal with tedious tasks," according to Chicago's audio. Driving home the emphasis on the debilitating aspects of women's culture broadly and the emphasis on the psychological in 1970s feminism specifically, Chicago explains that samplers "became a real tool of role conditioning." A quote from Schurman's 1646 book on the right of women to be educated, done in cloying cross-stitch on the runner, might easily be mistaken for a passage from Betty Friedan's *The Feminine Mystique* three hundred years later: "Woman has the same wish for self-development as man, the same ideals. And yet she is to be imprisoned in an empty soul of which the very windows are shuttered."[77] Female confinement rendered in the key of domesticity functions here to unite present and past. The final millennium triangle, done in crochet, a quintessentially "obsessive" style of needlework, renders the letter *M* all but invisible.[78]

The final wing runs from the American Revolution to what Chicago calls "the women's revolution." Yet, for such a triumphant preamble, the beginning of the wing starts at "a low point in women's history."[79] The artist explains that this final wing "begins with an expression of grieving for this loss of women's power." The runner for Anne Hutchinson, British settler to the Massachusetts Bay Colony in the seventeenth century, "mourns what has happened to us."[80] Chicago's strategic deployment of the word *us* underscores the subject position that *The Dinner Party* produces for viewers (sisters in the struggle), the standpoint from which they do an "ideal reading" of the art (we mourn our lost power and restore it by viewing our collective past). Chicago adapted the runner from mourning pictures after the death of George Washington. The runner is adorned with a weeping willow, which alone took three workers three months of stitching to complete. The stitch they used—the downward stitch—emphasizes the mood of sadness and loss. Like the runner, the plate is saturated with death. It depicts a "shawl-like form" that resembles a shroud, symbolizing Hutchinson's devastating excommunication from her Calvinist religious community for her bold and controversial preaching.[81] The plate has ghostlike tendrils that fold into themselves, tracing long shadowed crevasses in the white fabric. The whites and ivory colors give the feeling of coldness, adding to the impression that one is looking into the face (or vagina) of Death.

Place settings for Native American guide Sacajawea and British astronomer Caroline Herschel follow. Kathleen Schneider stitched forty thousand brightly colored blue and gold seed beads into the runner for Sacajawea, one of two US women of color seated at *The Dinner Party*.[82] The beadwork reiterates the Sioux-inspired colors and pattern of the plate.[83] A cradleboard form breaks out of the rectangle runner, a reference to the child Sacajawea carried on her back during her time with Lewis and Clark, rendering her a role model for empowered (and pointedly nondomestic) maternity. Herschel's gloriously bright runner celebrates her discovery of eight comets and her drawing of the Milky Way; from her plate, a simple eye with a penetrating view refuses to surrender eye contact.

Mary Wollstonecraft's place setting follows Herschel's and represents the point of highest tension between the runner and the plate and thus the greatest alienation between male-dominated society and an exceptional woman like Wollstonecraft. Chicago's audio tour explains that the Wollstonecraft plate "is very strong and assertive, its form, twisting and lifting, so much so that its edges begin to break from the circular form." The visual impact of the plate is powerful. From a series of more abstracted places that precede it (Sacajawea and Herschel), this one is starkly vaginal. The vulva folds are yellow with alternating bands of spring green. For Chicago, Wollstonecraft "stood at the threshold of modern feminism" and is "a symbol of trying to break loose." The strong and assertive plate stands in "stark contrast" to the "obsessive and trivializing needlework of her runner," representing the contrast between this exceptional woman and her repressive environment.[84] The back of the Wollstonecraft runner, done in stump work, depicts her death in childbirth, a jarring conclusion for a runner that so proudly proclaims "The Vindication of Rights of Woman" in needlework on brightly colored and shiny satin.

The Sojourner Truth plate, easily the most controversial of all the settings, embodies another stark contrast. Each plate at *The Dinner Party* shared the motif of the central core, a strategy that enabled a view of women's difference as being cause and effect, as rooted in the female body and in the shifting cultural meanings attached to it. The Truth plate is made of three faces that share a single body, and the runner blends design features from African masks and American quilting. The brutal history of slavery is both mythologized and memorialized: Chicago explains that the face on the left, with a prominent tear falling, "weeps for the suffering of slaves"; the highly stylized face on the right "reflects the rage experienced by black women but expressed only at the risk of harsh punishment—sometimes death." The center face, a "highly decorated mask, symbolizes the concealment of the real self required not only of black women but of their white sisters as well."[85] The shared "concealment" of white women and black women, between free and bonded women, immediately breaks down under scrutiny. Chicago's (naive) assertion is, nonetheless, her heartfelt attempt to bridge differences among women by emphasizing the discrimination they face because of their shared female bodies. This reading of history, however, depends on viewers not seeing the reality of Truth's racialized body. Given the symbolism of the vulva as representing unity among women, Truth's lack of a central core image translates poorly. If central cores represent real selves, what or where is the truth of Truth?

The literalness of the Sojourner Truth plate, with its clear faces, is comparable only to that of the Ethel Smyth plate, a few places away. Smyth, a British composer, dressed in men's clothes and in so doing, stood in the tradition of the mannish invert, a style adopted at the end of the nineteenth century by affluent women who desired other women. Neither the Sojourner Truth nor the Ethel Smyth plate has a recognizable central core. Smyth's plate is made up of a miniature black grand piano rising off the plate with a "lid [that] threatens to totally compress the form."[86] A keyboard to the right grounds the image in a bird's-eye view, while the curve of the piano lid hints at a space down under. One can only see tragedy in the plate as Smyth's desire to make music—something ethereal and in perpetual motion—has become entombed in the piano's rigid and unchanging form. The plate communicates Smyth's sense of being stymied. Smyth was indeed angry at the prejudices she faced, and her anger drew her to suffrage activism. She composed "The March of Women," which British suffragists sang when demonstrating and imprisoned.[87]

The absence of the central core images in the Truth and Smyth plates marks them as unusual. But the difference is made even more striking by their positions between very powerful vaginal plates. To the left of Truth is the very dramatic setting of Susan B. Anthony. Anthony's plate, in the words of Chicago, "is one of the most active struggling and angry forms" at the table.[88] It is deeply carved to imitate the patterned crevasses of shells. The curves reach up aggressively from a glistening dark red central core that looks ready to give birth or reach orgasm. The shell/vagina struggles to "lift up from the surface of the plate with great force in a vain effort to escape its confines." It is "raw and angry," but also voracious, pushing the limits of Chicago's aesthetics of abstraction.[89] For Chicago, Anthony is the "Queen of the dinner party table" for her role in first temperance, then abolition and suffrage. The runner stresses her place in the history of the feminist revolution, which casts her as a flag-bearing patriot and an ax-wielding Amazon, done in red to reference the red cape worn by Anthony on her suffrage lecture tours.

To the right of Smyth is the setting for the US birth control advocate, Margaret Sanger. This dense plate, Chicago explained, appears to be "reaching down underneath the plate in a struggle to lift itself off." Through efforts like those of Sanger, who called for voluntary motherhood, Chicago explains that "women were helped to break loose from their containment."[90] Chicago based her design for Sanger's runner on an image of the female reproductive system. The plate, assertively muscular, appears to pulsate before one's eyes, bringing the physicality hinted at in the runner to new heights. Bands of blood-red, flesh-like mounds are tightly woven together, as if to imply the muscles of the human abdomen. "Her plate," wrote Chicago, "proclaims women's bodies as their own."[91] Her central core is a weave of muscles that protect what lies underneath, clearly communicating that visitors are not welcome.

The plate for Natalie Barney, an openly lesbian writer and salon hostess, offers viewers a refreshing blue pool in which to cool off after the strenuous struggles of the previous plates. Shaped as a starfish with lovely breasts, art deco–styled violet curls decorate the boundary between inner and outer, but Barney appears not to have policed her borders too vigorously. The plate invites one to look. Unlike those of previous guests, Barney's place and runner are in "congruence," marking her as one of the few women at the table who was able to "create a world where she could live as she desired." She supported other creative women by running "a salon in Paris for sixty years where women shared their work and celebrated their sexual preference."[92] Her runner is an elaborate beaded butterfly, and appears to slide and wink.

The last two guests, Virginia Woolf and Georgia O'Keeffe, are the culmination of the feminist narrative of *The Dinner Party*. These two, explains Chicago, "represent that point in time when women began to regain their power through the creative act," each woman represents the long-awaited for moment in history "when women began to have their own language for the first time."[93] Woolf through writing and O'Keeffe through painting create a "female form language," clearly a legacy Chicago places herself in. The plate for Woolf is highly dimensional, with petallike vulva folds that open to a central core populated with fruit, reminiscent of the Fertile Goddess plate on the first wing of *The Dinner Party*. But its petals also refer to the Sappho plate. Chicago modeled the plate for US painter Georgia O'Keeffe after her 1926 painting, *Black Iris*. The aesthetics of this plate literalize the struggle both to embrace and to transcend the vagina, the "central core" of women's identity. The plate's three-dimensional "mysterious space" echoes the Primordial Goddess plate, linking the first and last place settings, which meet at the first intersection of the tables.[94] The runner, which combines needlework with painting, is meant to show the ways that by this point in history, women fought their way into the mainstream of society by moving out of female-dominated spaces and crafts (like needlework) and into painting, a male-dominated form. This, Chicago concludes, "is what *The Dinner Party* is all about." The Primordial Goddess and Georgia O'Keeffe sit side by side at the triangular beginning-ending of *The Dinner Party*.

The art displayed in San Francisco—unusual, unprecedented, and, for some, disturbing—generated spontaneous conversations among visitors before, during, and after the 1979 viewing. Some left the exhibit and found a place to talk, others moved slowly toward the door, immersed in their own thoughts. Some entered the museum gift shop, and some of those people purchased mementos of their experience—postcards, posters, slides of the art, small embroidery kits, pins, or bumper stickers with *The Dinner Party* logos. The shop also sold Chicago's memoir, *Through the Flower* (1975), and *"The Dinner Party": A Symbol of Our Heritage* (1979). After 1980, the second book about the exhibit, written with Susan Hill, *Embroidering Our Heritage: "The Dinner Party" Needlework*, was also available. In San Francisco, the museum store sold so many *Dinner Party* items that the staff received a much-needed salary increase.[95]

When *Judy Chicago: "The Dinner Party"* opened at the San Francisco Museum of Modern Art on March 15, 1979, two women described the event in the media. Marilyn Woodsea, writing for *Womanspirit*, described a conversation she and a friend had with a "pleasant matronly" docent. The docent reported that, despite the training she and other volunteers received before the opening, many of them felt uncomfortable with the "obvious vulva symbolism" of the plates. The trio proceeded to discuss what it was that troubled them. "We all agreed that female genitalia is so taboo a subject that many of us never even examine our own bodies." Woodsea told the docent about the San Francisco Women's Health Center, where women used speculums to look at themselves. "I felt good about *The Dinner Party* if only this one woman overcame her 50 years of patriarchal conditioning and went home to look at her vulva with a mirror." The vulva symbolism, in this instance, stood for a female reality rarely discussed and provided a point of connection between vagina-bearing strangers. Woodsea concluded that she was not so different from the matronly docent. She, a "counterculture lesbian-feminist," had only the previous year herself grabbed a speculum, and, when she did, she too felt "I was looking at quite a foreign territory."[96] *The Dinner Party*, from this micro, individual perspective, links viewers through their experience of their bodies as both intimate and foreign, as theirs and as part of history. In this way, the experience of viewing the art—coming to see the art, watching others see it, discussing it—forges a temporary feminist community based not on activism but on cultural consumption.

The second media report about the opening came from feminist art critic Lucy Lippard, who particularly noted the crowds' enthusiasm and the event-ness of the weekend:

> The openings were attended by thousands; lines formed around the block; the brochures were gone the first week; when Chicago spoke in the 900 seat Herbst auditorium, hundreds were turned away; reporters for TV, radio, the national

> magazines were much in evidence; every event—two lectures, a panel, a colloquium, films, concerts by Margie Adam, a local artists' studio tour—was filled to capacity; posters, buttons, and the expensive, profusely illustrated book published by Anchor/Doubleday were selling out, hopefully putting a dent in the project's $30,000 debt to the LA Women's Bank and even helping the museum out of a financial bind.[97]

"Even [director Henry] Hopkins was not prepared for the excitement seen and scope of the five-day celebration around the openings," she reported in *Seven Days*.

Lippard's review highlighted two competing frameworks for understanding the exhibit that would shape its reception for years to come. On the one hand, the review subtitle, "A Feminist Counterpart of the Sistine Chapel," underscored the monumentality and historicity of *The Dinner Party*. The association between Michelangelo and Chicago carried water for Chicago. It lent credence to the practice of artists relying on the labors of apprentices in the past, thus wrapping the studio workers and the piece's unique production conditions in a cloak of tradition. By invoking the Sistine Chapel, Lippard also highlighted the sense of near-religious reverence the staging of the exhibit created and audiences embraced. Yet, on the heels of this analogy with the Sistine Chapel, Lippard noted enthusiastically that *The Dinner Party* was no mere golden idol but also a cash cow. The lines of admission-paying visitors brought much-needed money to the museum. The museum purchased a new cash register for the event and named it Judy, since interest in her art had it ringing continually. It was hard to miss that the elements that made viewing *The Dinner Party* so dynamic—the sense of sacredness in its exhibition, the crowds, and the years of publicity—also made it a market powerhouse.

Woodsea's and Lippard's descriptions of the San Francisco opening, one published in a small feminist San Francisco journal and the other in a major national art magazine, capture the diverse and converging experiences that made—indeed, still make—viewing *The Dinner Party* unique. Individual women wrestled with its feminist implications; crowds testified to the public's interest; money and ideas were exchanged. The networks Gelon traveled to find the funds necessary to complete *The Dinner Party* and the publicity campaign she single-handedly waged laid the groundwork for launching it as a major museum exhibition.

Yet the buzz around it, however impressively apparent by the crowds, also gave critics fodder to challenge its status as fine art. Some commentators and museum boards saw the circuitry between the art and the audience not as proof of its artistic effectiveness, as Hopkins did, but as religious in a cultish, almost slavish way. Other critics staged an opposition between *The Dinner Party* as art and as commodity, suggesting that it was cheapened by the crass commercialism of its promotion and ongoing fund-raising. Some deemed the display of vulva images pornographic. Such debates over the status of *The Dinner Party* embedded a set of oppositions into its cultural history. No one could see *The Dinner Party* without wading through a set of questions and a certain amount of controversy: was it a sacred icon or cash cow? Art or commodity? Fine art or feminist politics? Whatever one concluded about the piece, if one "filled in" the piece with a longing for community or found it tasteless, *The Dinner Party* had officially arrived. But, as the event of the next few years make clear, the doors of the museum world proved hard to keep open.

CHAPTER SIX

The Tour That Very Nearly Wasn't

The Dinner Party's *Alternative Showings, 1980–1983*

DESPITE THE CROWDS and the enthusiasm on display in San Francisco, the formal gatekeepers of the institutional art world did not embrace *The Dinner Party* either before or after its brilliant opening in 1979. That spring, the next two museums scheduled to show *The Dinner Party* reneged on their agreements, leaving Chicago and Gelon scrambling to find alternative spaces to show it. News of the cancellations was a terrible blow.[1] For Chicago, the popularity of *The Dinner Party* was a powerful testimony to audiences' connection to the piece and justification enough for museums to show it. Yet museum curators, boards of directors, and art critics judged art on terms driven by aesthetics, cost, space, and schedules, not popularity. That *The Dinner Party* proved to be popular among audiences did not, on its face, guarantee that a serious discussion would ensue about whether to display it. The story of the tour that very nearly wasn't broached critical questions about the connection between art and audiences first raised by the feminist art movement in the early 1970s and increasingly relevant in the 1980s and 1990s as government funding for the arts came under congressional fire. Ironically, the very elements that made museums uneasy about showing *The Dinner Party*—its size, its content, and its controversies—set the stage for it to become an infamous icon of the feminist art movement.

It was with an element of comeuppance, then, that *The Dinner Party*'s status as feminist blockbuster came about as a direct consequence of the collapse of the museum tour. Revenge, as is said, is a dish best served cold. Like the piece's unique production, its US tour—consisting of two museums and five community shows between 1979 and 1982—became noteworthy precisely for its unconventionality and the indefatigability of its success. As community groups stepped forward to build a US tour, public enthusiasm for *The Dinner Party* was as much on display as the art and vividly demonstrated the piece's unusual ability to cross the heavily patrolled boundary between museums and community spaces, between fine art and "craft," and between elite and popular reception.

Community showings of *The Dinner Party* required tremendous effort and years of organization to pull off. Organizers had to reproduce, on their own, the material support routinely offered by a museum: create a climate-controlled, well-lit gallery with guards and docents, paid support staff, and paid installation staff; and come up with funds for publicity and insurance. Without these things, groups of interested audiences worked from the ground up to build alternative museum spaces to show the art they wanted to see, extending the grassroots feminist art movement geographically beyond the hubs of LA and New York and chronologically into the 1980s. Regular local newspaper coverage generated ongoing buzz around *The Dinner Party* as a culturally significant event and brought audiences from near and far to see it. From audience responses, it appeared that no one apart from museum curators and art critics disputed that the art of *The Dinner Party* was visually arresting. Each community show drew unprecedented numbers of viewers and each made a profit that the community—not the artist—kept and distributed.

The unexpected success of its non-museum tour spoke unmistakably of the appeal of *The Dinner Party* and its feminist message to audiences. One explanation for *The Dinner Party*'s success despite its across-the-board rejection by elite cultural institutions can be attributed to its translation of feminism—specifically, women's right to a heroic past—into an engaging message that spoke to a range of women not typically found under the banner of feminism. It did so as a form of symbolic feminism designed to inspire viewers, not to map out a course of action. The meanings of the piece—which included women's underappreciated contributions to Western civilization, the practice of women's culture, patriarchy as a force in women's history, the shared commonalities among women—resonated with many kinds of people. Seeing women from across history and culture as members of a single sex class, even if only for the time it took to walk around the exhibit, moved many who might have come just to see what all the fuss was about but who left feeling inspired.

In this way, community shows suggest a way to chart the cultural impact of feminism in the late 1970s and 1980s in terms other than those of a social movement, a particularly important vantage point as whatever fragile political consensus that held the women's movement together fragmented in these years. When *The Dinner Party*'s feminist message became a cultural commodity, an experience one had for the price of a ticket, the piece actively constructed an imagined community of women and a literal audience for women's art. Despite real and enduring social divides between women, those who came to see *The Dinner Party* became part of the very community invoked by the art. In this way, temporary allegiances—momentary sisterhood—became part of the experience of viewing *The Dinner Party*.

But in 1979, none of this was clear. *The Dinner Party*'s status as feminist icon was far from secure and its future looked bleak: in the wake of the museum cancellations, Gelon and Chicago found themselves improvising. For all either of them knew, the ride was over.

Packing It Up

What does it mean if a museum refuses to be responsive to an audience?

In June 1979, Gelon described the enthusiasm of viewers in a letter from San Francisco, where she was disassembling the exhibition: "The lines all week long have been overwhelming—over a three hour wait to see the show with the lines forming at the museum by 8:00 am every morning."[2] Audiences' willingness to put up with long lines at the SFMOMA surprised even the museum director, Henry Hopkins. For Gelon, the crowds represented long-awaited affirmation that she hoped would translate into a major national tour. In a letter to the National Gallery of Canada in Ottawa, she stressed the profitability of the show through admission fees and sales of books, posters, and postcards: "It's clear to me from the amount of mail we are receiving every day and the number of phone calls still coming into the SFMOMA that there is great interest from people to see the show."[3]

Under the crush of opening, a June 1979 letter from the Memorial Art Gallery of the University of Rochester canceling its exhibition seemed almost inconsequential.[4] A response from Gelon written on June 15, 1979, expressed her confusion as to why Rochester pulled out of its "firm" promise of the previous April. The museum appeared to have taken offense at Chicago's reservation of the right to create a learning environment for the piece, as she had done at SFMOMA. Educational programming by necessity would have involved joint planning and publicity between Chicago's nonprofit Through the Flower and the staff of the Memorial.[5] A follow-up letter from Rawsay Lawless, president of the board of managers at the Memorial Art Gallery, tried to explain the cancellation: "I can assure you that the Gallery tried for many months to negotiate a contract with Ms. Chicago. Unfortunately, her demands escalated over that period of time to a point where there was no hope of accommodation. The unresolvable problems were not only over costs but also involved other aspects of the arrangements. At no time during these negotiations did Ms. Chicago indicate a willingness to modify her terms and assume a more reasonable stance."[6]

Chicago's "unwillingness" to let go of programming was not the only or even the most pressing factor in the decision to cancel. The abrupt change in curatorial direction at the gallery came in part from a key staff turnover.[7] The director who agreed in 1978 to show *The Dinner Party* left as the exhibit opened in San Francisco. Taking his place was a fiscally cautious interim director, Bruce Chambers. When faced with concerns from a conservative board of directors, Chambers was well within his rights to rearrange the gallery schedule. Contract elements regarding the show had indeed changed. With the almost full year delay in the San Francisco opening, shipping costs had doubled from the October 1978 estimates.[8] This, coupled with Through the Flower's more clearly articulated claim over publicity and management of the display, contributed to the breakdown of negotiations.

But the true impact of Rochester's cancellation hit home only when, in early July, the Seattle Art Museum confirmed rumors that it too was canceling its planned exhibition of *The Dinner Party*. Gelon was stunned. She had cultivated a relationship with director Charles Cowles over two years, noting in her diary in 1978 that when Cowles visited the studio, "he seemed to be very impressed by the work" and the number of people working.[9] The museum had arranged to use the larger Seattle Science Center to display *The Dinner Party*, but its director abruptly preempted the space, leaving the museum without a venue.[10] Even with this setback, Cowles might have rescheduled *The Dinner Party* but opted against doing so. His change of direction sent shock waves through the studio. The *San Francisco Sunday Examiner and Chronicle* was the first to cover the story and Chicago's reaction to it. Shaken by the news that *The Dinner Party* would go into crates and be stored after its tremendous San Francisco debut, Chicago criticized the museum world for its apparent indifference to the wishes of its female audiences: "One thing I set out to do with the piece was to test the system, to find whether or not it will respond to women's culture. The San Francisco museum welcomed it and responses were heart-warming, but if *The Dinner Party* meets such resistance elsewhere, what does that mean in society? Is it an anti-feminist backlash? . . . What does it mean if a museum refuses to be responsive to an audience?" Whether the museum cancellations indicated an "anti-feminist backlash" as Chicago believed was not clear. The same article claimed that neither museum director at Rochester or Seattle found the "feminist" aspect of the exhibition offensive. However, Hopkins, also interviewed for the piece, implied otherwise. "I was not upset by the sexual symbolism theme—if you want to call it that. This museum has no problem with that, although there are pockets in the country that do. We are more open in attitude than some institutions and people. That is good for us and sad for other areas."[11] The word "feminist," in this case, functioned narrowly as a code word for unapologetic display of the female body or "sexuality," an association that would dog *The Dinner Party* throughout the 1980s as debates over obscenity in art, in pornography, and in public culture escalated.[12]

What was indisputable was that *The Dinner Party* was big, expensive, and provocative. Part of what captivated audiences was the piece's monumentality. *The Dinner Party*'s scope, scale, and size quite literally pushed against the conventional spatial limits of most museums, which divided their floor space into smaller, more intimate galleries. In addition to space issues, the cost of shipping and installing it was also daunting, more akin to a multiwork exhibition than to displaying a single piece. In fact, *The Dinner Party* was not simply a single piece, but multiple pieces, each of which required expert help in packing and installing. The piece traveled in seventy crates in two large trucks and took three full-time staff people two weeks to install properly. Budget estimates from 1979 put shipping costs between $8,000 and $12,000.[13] When it first began to tour, insuring the piece cost $15,000. In 1978, Fred James and Company valued the work at $700,000. By 1983, the insurance valued the piece substantially higher, at $1,294,000.[14] None of these costs distinguished *The Dinner Party* from other major museum shows, but the costs did force the issue of perception: *The Dinner Party* required all the infrastructure, financially and materially, that other major works of museum-quality fine art commanded.

At the same time, *The Dinner Party* included components that distinguished it from other major museum exhibits: a *Dinner Party* brochure (to be produced at 28 cents and resold for 40 or 50 cents, with profits retained by the exhibiting institution), an educational context about women's art and history to accompany the exhibit, and space allotted for the (non–fine art) Acknowledgment and Heritage Panels. These, coupled with the inherent expenses of mounting a major exhibit, made *The Dinner Party* a lot for some museums to sign up for. And few had. In an interview with the feminist journal *Chrysalis* in 1978, a year before the San Francisco opening, Chicago explained that no curators besides Hopkins had come to her studio to see the work. In the same piece, Gelon explained that she and Chicago understood that they might have to work around an indifferent museum world if *The Dinner Party* were to be seen by the public.[15]

Size and cost represented only the most tangible challenges involved in showing *The Dinner Party*. What became very clear in the wake of the San Francisco opening was that the feminist content of *The Dinner Party* also pushed the boundaries of what museums would show, despite protestation to the contrary by the Rochester and Seattle directors. Needlework and painted china—was it fine art or craft? Plates that looked like vaginas—was it feminist or smut? Panels with timelines and biographies—was it history or politics? No one could dispute that *The Dinner Party* had proven to be financially successful in San Francisco. But neither could anyone dispute that the fare offered by *The Dinner Party* was decidedly unconventional. Whatever the reasons, the collapse of the scheduled museum tour left Chicago's supporters and interested audiences angry and disappointed.

Women in Rochester and Seattle reacted publicly to their museum's decisions to cancel. In Seattle, 150 feminists active with the Feminist Art Project group staged a mock funeral procession on September 17, 1979, to protest the cancellation. The group carried a casket marked with *The Dinner Party* triangle logo up a long hill to Volunteer Park and held a memorial service on the steps of the museum. The director of the Seattle Art Museum, Charles Cowles, defended the distinction between politics and art and the museum's commitment to the latter. "I do not consider this fine art but an interesting project by a group of women whose leader was an artist. I consider this a political statement." The Feminist Art Project returned fire: "Why do we not consider the Lincoln Memorial, Jefferson Memorial and George Washington monument to be political statements as well as works of art? Or does this culture only allow for the celebration of historical men in their works of art?"[16]

The debate played out in the local and national media. A frankly critical local art critic, Michelle Celarier, defended Cowles and denounced the artist and her role in the feminist art movement: "First it was bloody tampons strewn all over the bathroom in The Woman's House [*sic*], a piece of 'art' created by Judy Chicago and a crew of feminists. Now its 39 ceramic, painted dinner plates which, unappetizing enough to some eyes, look like female sex organs. . . . Tack on a line that wallows in matriarchal theories of history and its accompanying biological mysticism and you get what the Seattle Modern Art Museum curator Charles Cowles calls 'a feminist political statement.' And, he told the *Sun* . . . 'we don't show feminist political statements.'"[17] *Seattle Sun* journalist Matthew Kangas also denounced the feminist fervor over *The Dinner Party* in "Burial Act Premature for Seattle Women Artists," where he listed a number of prominent women artists in Seattle and the museum's general responsiveness to female artists. Women artists thrived in the city, he asserted, proving once again that feminists distorted reality in the name of their sour-grapes politics. Angry letters to the editor throughout the fall record the ongoing controversy. A student from nearby Evergreen College invoked radical feminist language of already-liberated womanhood when she described the "womyn of Olympia (and all of Washington state)" as "all furious" at the cancellation.[18] Another read about the cancellation in *Ms.* magazine and wrote the editor: "I live about 20 miles south of Seattle and was very disappointed (and angry) to read Seattle cancelled the exhibit. Please let me know where the exhibit was to be held and the proper people to contact. I want to protest the cancellation."[19]

Unwilling to relinquish hope, groups of women in both cities began to meet to identify other venues to show *The Dinner Party*. That winter, Women Artist Group Northwest raised $3,500 to bring Chicago to Seattle to mobilize community support for bringing *The Dinner Party* to the city. Chicago lectured to a sold-out crowd of 250 people in Seattle's Greenwood Gallery. The gallery displayed a selection of the hundreds of photographs taken in the studio between 1977 and 1979. Tickets sold for three dollars. Local journalist Regina Hackett reported that the crowd was not the typical gallery audience: "When asked why they came, most said they were interested in seeing Chicago whom they greatly admired. A sizeable number said they had never been inside a gallery before or do not go very often. Chicago says she attracts people who are not ordinarily found in an art audience. She wants her work to have broad social impact."[20]

In Rochester, disappointed residents organized a letter-writing campaign in protest. The region's feminist newsletter, the *New Women's Times*, published "from the home of Susan B. Anthony," wrote to Bruce Chambers directly to chastise him for canceling. The museum's unwillingness to work with Chicago and Gelon to ensure the Rochester show's success all testified to the institution's sexism, they wrote. "*The Dinner Party* is a revolution in art. This is possibly why there has been controversy surrounding its coming here."[21] Alexandra Speyer, assistant to CBS's national editor, reached the same conclusion. In a letter to Chicago she wrote that, "All the clippings seem to come to the conclusion that Chambers and the Board are simply staging their own version of a power play. The whole controversy is made ludicrous in light of this."[22] The owner of a local gallery sounded the same note. He suggested that the Memorial Art Gallery had canceled *The Dinner Party* out of fear of political backlash. "I like the political aspect of the work. I feel that the work has major significance. I want to see *The Dinner Party* and Judy Chicago in Rochester."[23] Gelon followed up by sending the gallery owner information about the exhibit, including budgets and size requirements, with a note. "The only way to get things done is to dream and then make them happen. I have faith in that."[24]

Chicago's faith, however, was deeply shaken by the collapse of the museum tour. In the wake of the Rochester and Seattle cancellations in 1979, and with no major museum stepping into their place, documentary filmmaker Johanna Demetrakas captured an angry, exhausted, and distraught Chicago.[25] The cancellations marked the beginning of the worst period of her life, she recalled.[26] Gelon refused to concede defeat and sprang into action, determined that *The Dinner Party* would not remain in crates at a cost of $1,000 a month.[27] She redoubled her efforts by writing to museums, galleries, cultural centers, and universities to inquire if they might host *The Dinner Party*.[28] Some directors explained that the exhibit would take up the bulk of their annual budget, others that their spaces could not accommodate it. Some frankly disliked it. The director of the National Collection of Fine Arts at the Smithsonian, for example, politely explained that *The Dinner Party* did not "fit nicely" into their program.[29] The director of the Institute for the Arts at Rice University made it even plainer: "it is not the kind of exhibit that I usually present at Rice."[30]

Artists continually market themselves and promote their work to galleries and museums and by necessity adjust to high levels of rejection; Chicago was no different. She understood that many of the institutions that declined *The Dinner Party* did so from real limits in their spaces and their budgets. What hit Chicago hardest was the rejection of *The Dinner Party* by the country's major contemporary art institutions, what Chicago referred to as "the taste makers." In an interview with the *Boston Phoenix*, Chicago laid out the problem: "Where the resistance is is at the level of the taste-making museums: the Walker, the Art Institute, The Whitney, The Met, the Modern. Those are the museums that control taste and those are the museums we have a reading from now. And the reading is that they don't care about the audience, don't care about the public or the media response. And because they have power, they can get away with it."[31] The resounding silence from the nation's major contemporary art museums appeared to speak with one voice of the art world's rejection of *The Dinner Party*. Their silence sounded all the louder for the thousands of viewers who lined up to see it in San Francisco and for the interest audiences expressed in seeing it come to their cities. With their personal histories rooted deep in the ground of the feminist art movement, Chicago and Gelon never stopped working to connect *The Dinner Party* to those interested audiences.[32] According to Chicago, it had been created to speak to women and for women, and audiences had a right to view it, no matter the evaluation of "taste-makers." Gelon kept up her efforts, visiting "thirty cities in six weeks going literally to every single women's organization or group or individual who said they could bring the piece. I followed every one of those leads. We were in great despair."[33]

Houston

Step aside King Tut.

In 1980, nearly a year after the triumphant San Francisco opening, feminist and bookseller Mary Ross Taylor called the studio to discuss her idea to bring the piece to Houston. Taylor soon became an important accomplice. Along with Gelon, she set in motion a new kind of tour for *The Dinner Party*, one that would stay true to Chicago's vision of feminist art and audiences' desire for feminist-themed culture. Crucially, this alternative tour of *The Dinner Party* would not wait for or rely on the museum world for its success. Yet Chicago did not immediately take to the idea of showing *The Dinner Party* outside of museums. She wanted to change the DNA of the formal art world, not concede to its narrow parameters. It fell to Gelon to convince Chicago to change her mind.[34]

Taylor, a southerner who moved to Houston with her then-husband, ran an independent bookstore in Houston since the early 1970s known for its offerings in the latest books by feminists and women writers. Taylor knew herself to be a feminist well before she had heard the term; while she was a graduate student in English language and linguistics at the University of Texas at Austin, the experience of being overlooked and dismissed as "a married lady" sealed Taylor's feminist leanings.[35] She left the ivory tower, carved a niche for herself as a bookseller in the fast-growing, future-oriented, oil-rich city of Houston, the new home of the NASA Space Center, and divorced her husband. Taylor participated in the arts in whatever ways she could and took note that artists and nonartists alike bought Chicago's memoir, *Through the Flower*. In the summer of 1978, African American Doubleday seller Evelyn Hubbard told her about Chicago's soon-to-be published book, *"The Dinner Party": A Symbol of Our Heritage*, insisting that Taylor would love it.[36] She was right. "The way women of all sorts have gotten going on this . . . it's just knocked my socks off."[37] Taylor, with her networks and knowledge of art, fund-raising, and Houston, proved uniquely suited to head up the efforts to bring *The Dinner Party* to Texas.[38]

In 1978, with the major modern art institutions of the Houston area—the Museum of Fine Arts, the Contemporary Arts Museum, and Rice University—having previously declined to show *The Dinner Party*, Taylor set to work garnering support from local arts and culture groups to find an alternative space.[39] After fourteen months, she found an ally in the dean of the sciences and humanities at the University of Houston at Clear Lake City (UHCL), Calvin Cannon. Clear Lake City, a satellite commuter campus twenty miles southeast of Houston, catered to the community around the NASA facility, earning it the nickname Space City. The towers of the Johnson Space Center literally dominated the town and, metaphorically, the campus with its degree in "Future Studies."[40]

UHCL made odd sense as a place to show *The Dinner Party*. Its newly constructed buildings tended toward the cavernous and already displayed the works of local artists; the responsive dean had a budget; and the community was educated and open-minded. The feminist audience for *The Dinner Party* was similarly ready to be enlisted. In the wake of the IYW Houston conference, local women activists were newly connected and animated. According to Taylor, Houston feminists in 1979 attended similar cultural and political events, temporarily overcoming differences in sexual orientation and ethnicity to enjoy women-centered events. Taylor had contacts with many of the region's women activists and feminist consumers through her bookstore's mailing list. Taylor, along with Barbara Michels and Helen Cassidy, founded the Texas Arts and Cultural Organization (TACO) as a way to grab newly allotted city arts funds from the hotel and motel tourist tax for women-friendly arts and literary programming. Their very first grant proposal, to bring *The Dinner Party* to Houston, won approval. With the venue identified and an interested public willing to see the exhibit, they aimed for opening *The Dinner Party* in the spring of 1980.[41]

Taylor and Cannon pulled together financial support from a variety of people and organizations. Major support came from UHCL itself. The university bore the cost of the space, the attendant utilities, and insurance, and assumed responsibility for part of the publicity for the show. Other monies came from businesses and city cultural agencies. Large businesses like IBM and groups like the chamber of commerce donated funds, as did the Cultural Arts Council of Houston (funded by hotel and motel lodgers' tax revenue), the Cultural Affairs Council of the Clear Lake Area, Friends of the Arts, UHCL, and TACO.[42] Feminist-leaning organizations such as the Clear Lake Branch of the American Association of University Women (which supplied 147 docents), the Houston Area Women's Center, and the League of Women Voters of the Bay Area contributed money, while women's groups (many of them religiously affiliated) donated volunteer staff and sponsored related programs, a testimony to the broad appeal of *The Dinner Party*. These included the Bay Area Welcome Wagon Club, St. Joan's Alliance of Catholic Women, the Memorial Drive Presbyterian Church Women's Forum, and the First Unitarian Church's Women's Group.[43]

Taylor and Cannon divided their fund-raising targets. Cannon solicited private donations ranging from $1,000 to $5,000, which included major gifts from Marilyn Oshman, a supporter of the Museum of Modern Art, and Jacqueline Goettsche, founder of the Women's Fund for Health Education.[44] Taylor worked city networks and brought in donations as small as $10 and as large as $500 in *The Dinner Party* sponsor program she ran from her bookstore. Fund-raising efforts, large and small, connected audiences to the planned exhibit and to its vision of women's history. The Clear Lake City campus newspaper announced that its own professor Jean Quataert was the "first person to pluck down $40" to sponsor four women of merit on the floor, including German feminist Louyse Bourgeois, "one of her favorite women in history."[45] Mary Moore, a senior in humanities, sponsored Pope Joan, explaining to the student newspaper that, "What happened to her captures the essence of what's happened to all women in history."[46] The strong support among university women reached beyond Clear Lake City to the University of Texas Medical Branch Faculty Women's Club, which raised money by screening *Right Out of History* in nearby Galveston.[47]

All told, the people who donated money and volunteered their time represented the wide range of Houston women's civic involvements: political activists, art supporters, professors, staid "ladies who lunch," church women, and feminists.[48] Two hundred volunteers worked on the exhibit.[49] Whether they did so to express their commitment to feminist art, to see the exhibit's needlework, or to revel in its attention to nuns and Christianity, *The Dinner Party* cast a wide net over Houston women, many of whom consumed the range of new woman-oriented products that trailed in the wake of second-wave feminism. The desire for information about and help choosing from the array of new titles in women's studies bookstore sections motivated members of this loosely affiliated community to organize themselves into an informal seminar, "After *The Dinner Party*," that met on Saturday mornings.[50] Taylor helped sponsor the group.[51] The group's fourteen-page reading list of 350 books included "Women, Spirituality, and Myth," "Sexuality and Sensuality," "Abortion," and "Women and Lesbianism" sections.[52] Even with such topics, "After *The Dinner Party*" membership drew heavily from church networks, with the other three sponsors being the women's groups from the local Presbyterian, Catholic, and Unitarian churches.[53]

Taylor's community goals intersected with Cannon's, making their alliance particularly effective. Throughout his tenure as dean, Cannon toiled to raise the visibility and status of the campus and used unusual cultural events to do so.[54] His enthusiasm for challenging art seemed to be boundless. The student newspaper quoted him as saying, "*The Dinner Party* will do for our university what football does for other schools. It will put us on the map."[55] To help convince Chicago to let *The Dinner Party* show at the regional campus, Cannon agreed to split the revenue brought in by ticket sales if more than 20,000 viewers came, the first time this kind of arrangement had been made with an artist, according to the *Houston Post*. The paper quoted Chicago as saying that, "I was overwhelmed. I thought this is a major step in the way institutions look at artists."[56] Cannon's spirit of innovation ultimately cost him his job less than a month before the Houston show opened. The chancellor demoted Cannon from dean to director of special events when news of a violation of university rules about handling donations broke. When asked if the controversy surrounding *The Dinner Party* contributed to his dismissal, Cannon declined to comment, but he was met with a hero's welcome throughout the three-day opening.[57]

The support of Cannon and Henry Hopkins, who also attended the Clear Lake City opening, underscored the ability of *The Dinner Party* to speak to nonfeminist audiences of both sexes. The feminism of *The Dinner Party* literally represented gender as actively creating and re-creating hierarchies that reached beyond actionable workplace issues like equal pay, equal credit, equal access, seniority, and promotion. Art presenting women as "historic greats" who shaped European societies throughout time gave momentary pause to the sexist train of association about women's preferred and naturalized subordination to home and family. Encountering cultural feminism through *The Dinner Party* engaged audiences, male and female, feminist and nonfeminist. Dodging a request from a Houston journalist to comment on the significance of the piece, Cannon explained that he was not the person to judge its artistic merits: "I do not know if *The Dinner Party* is art or not; that isn't what struck me about it. When I first saw it, I was terribly moved. It is clearly important, and it has moved a lot of people in a way few things have."

Hopkins, in the same interview, summed up the ways *The Dinner Party* spoke not only to a desire for equality whether or not one embraced the label *feminist* but to the multitude of ways feminism challenged the very organization of daily life: "In a pure sense, I wouldn't say that I am [a feminist]. I'm struggling with the idea. If by feminist you mean I am for professional equality, then I definitely am one. But it's more difficult at a personal level. I was raised as a male chauvinist. I have always been cared for by women at home, and I like it."[58] Hopkins's acknowledgment that gender differences, with their unequal pleasures, did not evaporate with greater economic and political equality for women spoke to the unarticulated desire to harmonize rather than resolve the promise and perils of 1970s feminism. After all, how could authentic "equality" be measured? This urge to see the power of women's difference and at the same time to dismantle gender discrimination found a resting place in *The Dinner Party*. Audiences, no matter their views on *Roe v. Wade* or the Equal Rights Amendment, could find something that spoke to them at *The Dinner Party*.

The March 9, 1980, opening took place during the Houston Festival, a city-sponsored cultural event designed to draw people downtown and bolster Houston's national reputation as a sophisticated city.[59] The festival championed *The Dinner Party* in its offerings and in its publicity materials, which directed attendees to travel the thirty minutes between Houston and Clear Lake to see the show.[60] More oriented to California than to New York, many Houstonians saw it as "a coup to land a major national, forward-looking, feminist exhibition."[61] Referencing the major museum blockbuster of the 1970s, the Treasures of Tutankhamun, which did not show in Houston, one local journalist quipped, "Step aside King Tut."[62]

While Houstonians saw themselves as modern and future-forward, the actual UHCL campus looked anything but. The building designated for the exhibit, the Developmental Arts Building, was industrial and freestanding, surrounded, according to a reporter for *Texas Monthly*, by "muddy grassland and acres of freshly laid parking spaces," indistinguishable from nearby "structures occupied by NASA or Boeing or Ford Aerospace Communications." Despite the building's lack of eye-catching architecture, it was large and climate controlled. A large red sign hanging outside the building—"THE DINNER PARTY: JUDY CHICAGO"—beckoned viewers.[63]

The Houston opening of *The Dinner Party* reflected the array of institutional, civic, business, and community support the organizers had effectively mobilized. The gallery was filled with a mix of people, many of whom did not typically attend museum openings. A local journalist described the evening: "Inside the black room people were standing transfixed around the shimmering place settings. There were men in tuxes and women in evening dresses, and men in work shirts and women in warm up suits. Husbands in formal attire listened attentively as their wives consulted historical data in an information pamphlet, and one group studied distant details with binoculars." Visitors viewed *The Dinner Party* in one building and crossed a small courtyard to another building to see the documentary panels and to purchase *Dinner Party* products. Through the Flower sold posters, catalogs, jewelry, pins, and bumper stickers. An opening-night wine and cheese party with Chicago at *The Dinner Party* store gave donors a chance to meet the artist. Chicago signed catalogs and posters, shook hands with visitors, accepted praise and hugs from fans, in a hubbub that elicited comparisons to the celebrity enjoyed by Andy Warhol.[64]

All these funding streams, large and small, corporate and individual, contributed to the sense of community, a feeling the organizers had actively cultivated through the months of planning. On opening night Cannon explained that "We could have gotten IBM to give us fifty thousand dollars to pay for the exhibition costs, but we wanted the community to share in this."[65] Taylor too wanted "to create the biggest and most diverse community of women that we could as stakeholders in the project."[66] Chicago took it one step further: "I think it's like the building of a medieval cathedral when everyone in town would contribute a brick."[67]

Communities of women, literal and imagined, were on display in many forms and formats. Although buying a ticket, a poster, or a Through the Flower lunch marked one way to be part of a community, visitors could also partake of events designed to celebrate women's history and culture. The dense schedule included a panel titled "Sexuality or Iconography: *The Dinner Party* Plates," lectures on women's history by George Lipsitz, Jean Quataert, and Evelyn King among others, and by feminist art historians Ann Sutherland Harris, Eleanor Tufts, and Alessandra Comini. Audiences might attend a concert of women's music, the première of *The Dinner Party* documentary, *Right Out of History*, an evening dance with an all-woman country-and-western band, or a quilting demonstration, all of which required tickets, before the June 1 closing.[68]

A letter to the chancellor made a final accounting and showed *The Dinner Party* to have been a huge success. Sixteen thousand visitors bought tickets and 14,000 visited the exhibit on free days, for a total of 30,000 to the unconventional gallery. Income from admissions, sales, and donations reached $107,000, with $87,700 of that covering the cost of the exhibit. UHCL took $13,000, leaving nearly $7,000 to be distributed to five local Houston women's groups.[69] Recalls UHCL faculty member Gretchen Mieszkowski, "the exhibition drew more people to UHCL than have ever attended any event here before or since."[70]

Community Shows

Forget the institutions, and just do it.

The efforts of Taylor and Gelon to bring *The Dinner Party* to Houston set the template used by the other community groups to organize and exhibit the piece in their cities. While five groups were successful in opening *The Dinner Party* (Atlanta, Boston, Chicago, and Cleveland, in addition to Houston) between 1980 and 1983, others tried and failed, some after years of sustained efforts (Seattle; Washington, DC; and Portland, Oregon). Despite being turned away by major art museums, community groups created their own venues in which to show *The Dinner Party*, their own educational contexts in which to embed it, and their own local women's history to include with it. In the tradition of the feminist art movement, the community groups built temporary woman-centered art galleries where feminist art, feminist artists, and audiences could meet face to face.

The first step of creating a nonmuseum show typically began with one, two, or more local women contacting Through the Flower to express interest in bringing the exhibit to their city. Such queries came from a broad spectrum of women. In Boston, three young feminist artists contacted Gelon; in Chicago, the effort was lead by a group of established bankers and development officers (the Rosyln Group); in Cleveland, two women's studies professors and a women's art education group that had been following Chicago since the mid-1970s joined forces. Gelon's first assignment to any group was for them to locate a venue large enough to display *The Dinner Party* in its entirety—certainly the banners, the Heritage Panels, and Acknowledgment Panels—but there were other requirements as well. The space had to be dark to allow the lighting to illuminate as designed, to be in good enough condition to keep the piece safe and dry, to have capacity for hundreds of viewers to move through each day, and to accommodate a small *Dinner Party* store.

While community organizers scoped out places to show *The Dinner Party*, they also strategized about how to fund it, the second pressing matter facing all such groups. Beyond the costs for simply bringing the piece to the city and insuring it, many community groups discovered they needed hefty sums to bring their spaces up to museum-level quality. Some buildings, as with the UHCL, were new, dry, and required few improvements to get it ready. Other groups found that their buildings were in major need of repair. In both Boston and Cleveland, much of their mushrooming budgets came from their own construction costs. Once restored, some of these venues continued as cultural centers (Boston, Chicago) and neighborhood revitalization projects (Boston, Chicago, and Cleveland).

Community groups, once formed, gathered volunteers and launched a barrage of publicity and fund-raising activities. In Boston, feminist networks sprang into action, with volunteers signing up for tasks and working collectively. Volunteers secured local television, radio, and print media coverage; enlisted public relations groups to donate their expertise; organized fund-raising letter campaigns and contact lists; held events like cocktail parties, screenings, and lectures; approached corporations for donations; and wrote grants.[71] In Cleveland, the group formed a board and assigned tasks for members to oversee, eventually hiring an executive director and an assistant.[72] Organizers in each city cultivated large and small private donations from local philanthropists and from city and state arts and cultural councils and explored any way to raise money. In Chicago, the Rosyln Group, consisting of eight professional women, treated the show as an investment in a neighborhood development project, even as they embraced it as an important expression of women's history and culture. Each community show paid for itself and more; Chicago earned no more than a small honorarium for an opening-night lecture.[73] Any profits stayed in the community groups and were spent as the group saw fit. In Boston and Cleveland, the surplus went to women's shelters and rape crisis centers; in Chicago, it went to grants for women artists.[74]

In addition to dealing with costs and location concerns, local groups were tasked by Gelon to create an educational context for the exhibit. She encouraged each community group to find local women's history and include key people in the educational programming. Part of incorporating local women's history took place through the International Quilting Bee, a community art project launched at the Houston show.[75] In advance of *The Dinner Party* shows, local groups invited interested people to send in a 24-inch triangle quilt honoring a woman of their choice. Volunteers then stitched the triangles together into one large quilt. The International Quilting Bee traveled with *The Dinner Party* to all its subsequent exhibitions. A Cleveland newspaper explained that "Women from all over the world have made and donated these quilts as gestures of appreciation and solidarity with *The Dinner Party*. Some of the quilts are crude in their conception and execution. Others rival the main event in their exquisite detail and high quality. All speak of people expressing themselves, making a contribution, feeling committed."[76]

Over the next ten years, quilts poured in to the offices of Through the Flower honoring sisters, mothers, grandmothers, important teachers, and neighbors. Some were made collectively. A group from Nebraska sent in a quilt for one of their city's local heroes, African American Betty Jean Beckham Dederich, who overcame her addiction to become "a philosopher, teacher, role model and mother figure" to the more than 15,000 people who came to her community kitchen.[77] A number of quilts commemorated nationally famous women like Billie Jean King, Helen Keller, Lorena Hickok, Annie Oakley, and Mother Teresa. Young girls sent in quilts, like a third-grader from Berkeley, California, who submitted a quilt to honor Judy Chicago: "She was chosen because she did the Dinner Party and I think it was *real neat*! The sun and moon are to indicate that Judy worked day and night on the dinner party . . . I liked it a lot!!!!!"[78]

By the end of *The Dinner Party* tour, seven hundred women had sent in Honor Quilts from around the world, each with documentation and each telling a story. Amrita Dass, president of the alumnae of Isabella Thoburn College in Lucknow, India, sent in a quilt in honor of the college's first

Indian president, Constance Premnath Dass (1886–1970), whose leadership "broke through barriers of prejudicial tradition"; Israeli artist Miriam Sharon sent a quilt honoring women's resilience during the Yom Kippur War; the Ilinge Gugletu Sisters, a group of women from a black township in Cape Town, South Africa, sent a quilt honoring women who had been "jailed, beaten, and intimidated" for their human rights activism.[79] The quilt became its own expression of women's history, demonstrating the impact one woman could have on a community and anticipating the Names Project AIDS Memorial Quilt, which was initiated in 1987.[80] The International Quilting Bee enacted on a micro level Chicago's macro aspirations for *The Dinner Party* by giving women a way to place their comrades into history.

Chicago and Gelon were on a learning curve about how to have a tour for *The Dinner Party* independent from traditional art institutions. With letters requesting information vying with bills and bank notices, both women felt the pressure of history, specifically about the future (what would happen to *The Dinner Party*?) and the past (what had it all meant?). Gelon seeded possible shows continually and worked simultaneously with multiple groups to see if they could pull together a showing. Obstacles abounded. Two examples of efforts that did not result in a community show underscore the fragility of the process: a large-scale campaign mounted by a very savvy and well-connected group of political and cultural activists in the nation's capital with everything at their disposal, and a bid by a small feminist collective in the Northwest who had nothing but their feminist ideology and elbow grease to bring to the table.

When the Smithsonian's Hirshhorn Museum declined *The Dinner Party* in 1978 after Gelon's yearlong lobbying effort, Chicago's DC supporters turned to the Washington Women's Art Center (WWAC), a network of well-connected women in the Northeast Corridor. Susan Chaires (who had volunteered for two months at the studio), Ellouise Schoettler, and Joan Mister from Washington, DC, used their contacts to urge the Ford Foundation to fund *The Dinner Party*. New Yorker Lael Stegall introduced Gelon to Mary Jean Tully of the NOW Legal Defense and Education Fund, and Tully arranged for Gelon a face-to-face meeting with the Ford people. Much to everyone's relief, critical Ford funds came in just as the exhibit opened in San Francisco. Comfortable in the world of government funding and versed in the DC culture of political networking, Chicago's Washington supporters worked all leads. Joan Mister, the executive assistant to the second lady, wrote Gelon that "Joan Mondale support[s] the idea of it coming to Washington and she will also use whatever clout she has."[81] The WWAC threw its support behind getting funding from the National Endowment for the Humanities for a community showing of *The Dinner Party* that would, by its location in the nation's capital, become a major cultural event.

The WWAC made ambitious plans. Their NEH funding proposal estimated that a showing of *The Dinner Party* in Washington, DC, could bring in sixty thousand visitors, "many of whom may never have previously visited an art exhibition." Its appeal, they argued, lay in both its accessibility and its focus on women. The WWAC did not fear dropping the F word, frankly announcing the exhibition as "feminist." *The Dinner Party* "makes visible feminist ideas and principles which have the potential of transforming society's perception of women's history and illuminating women's present status." The educational context that the WWAC proposed included a two-day symposium on women's "access to culture," four lectures on women's art, minicourses on the history and practice of needlework, china painting "and other traditional women's arts," an exhibit of local women artists, as well as music and dance concerts.[82] When the NEH turned down the grant request, the WWAC abandoned its years of effort to open *The Dinner Party* in Washington. Many of these supporters turned their sights on bringing it to New York City.

In contrast to the well-connected women of Washington, DC, a group of Chicago supporters, called Through the Flower (TTF) Northwest, wrote the studio in 1979 to express interest in bringing *The Dinner Party* to Portland, Oregon. Small and feminist, TTF Northwest had few resources beyond their volunteer labor and their passion. In a matter of months, they ended their bid in frustration. Their repeated requests for guidance from *The Dinner Party* studio went unanswered for too long. They had requested detailed space requirements, guidelines, and anticipated costs of related educational events, and a breakdown of what the "$15,000 museum fee" covered. In a letter to Gelon announcing their decision to drop their bid, the group wrote, "The actions of TTF in not returning phone calls, withholding information, not following through with needed material and advice that was promised and inconsistent communication generally, has led us to this belief [that we must give up]. As this information was not provided in a timely fashion, months of our sincere hard work and planning has been wasted." In addition to information on tangibles like spatial dimensions, the group wanted guidance for organizing on a level that could raise the needed funds. Without that kind of support, TTF Northwest could not begin the process. The Oregon group thought the studio should have been more forthcoming: "We suggest that if you are contacted by other feminist groups such as ourselves to produce the show, that you seriously consider your own limitations and commitments before encouraging this activity."[83]

Mounting a major exhibit outside a museum setting was, by any measure, an ambitious undertaking. The anger and disappointment between feminists in TTF Northwest and *The Dinner Party* studio made the communication breakdown all the more painful. Chicago's response to the Portland group acknowledged this and shed light on the difficulties she and Gelon faced as they worked simultaneously on many potential venues to show *The Dinner Party*. Chicago offered a reason for their failure to be timely: "We are trying our best under extremely difficult circumstances. The expectations you have of an institution are certainly valid; but we are a young, struggling, feminist organization still enduring growing pains. Our resources are constantly being taxed, but we are attempting to meet the challenges. . . . We too sometimes feel like we are operating in a void—and that we, too, lack support as well as adequate funding. In fact, the experience you described with us is quite similar to our everyday reality."[84] Acknowledging that each community show taught TTF something more, Chicago closed the letter with "in Sisterhood."

Four US shows, in addition to Houston, did succeed—Boston, Chicago, Cleveland, and Atlanta. In these alternative venues, tens of thousands of viewers saw *The Dinner Party* in a context that celebrated their region's women's history and the efforts of their organizers to mobilize local support for the exhibit. The community shows succeeded precisely because of the organizers' abilities to draw from a range of interested viewers. The groups in Boston, Cleveland, and Chicago highlight the diversity of women who labored to bring *The Dinner Party* to their cities and the various strategies they used to mount successful exhibitions.

Boston

Everyone knew someone they could call on for help.

The Boston organizers were the youngest, most radical, and least experienced of the successful community *Dinner Party* shows. The Boston Women's Art Alliance (BWAA) opened *The Dinner Party* in July 1980 immediately on the heels of the Houston showing. Gelon connected the initial group of organizers—April Hankins, Virginia Boegli, and Libby Wendt—all of whom were in their early twenties, all connected to the art and feminist scenes in Boston, and all without experience in organizing or mounting major art exhibits. A fourth woman, Cate Bradley, joined them later.[85] The group met each other and Gelon at the Houston show, and volunteers from Houston agreed to help them organize.[86]

Modeling itself after *The Dinner Party* studio, the BWAA issued a community-wide call for volunteers to help "staff our office, do mailings, errands, typing and organizing, to help with publicity and fund-raising by writing press-releases, advertisements and making phone contacts, and to help with the installation and staffing of the exhibit."[87] With no funds in hand but emboldened by their enthusiasm, they handed out flyers at local women's music and literature events, ran notices in the city's feminist publications, and pinned notices on college and university bulletin boards. "The response was overwhelming," Hankins recalled. "Young women and sympathetic men who responded were enthusiastic, ready and available . . . the bulk of our supporters—at the grass-roots level—were young."[88] The organizers each took on the task of managing an area they felt competent to oversee. Wendt took on fund-raising and money management, Bradley oversaw the renovations, Boegli worked closely with the volunteers, and Hankins acted as the liaison between Through the Flower and the BWAA. Hankins described the group as "dysfunctional, but united." She told a *Boston Globe* reporter four weeks before it opened that they felt willing to do the hard work because "its important to everybody—not just to artists or women artists—to see this piece."[89]

The BWAA searched for a large and affordable space for the exhibit, which it found in the Boston Center for the Arts (BCA) in the rundown neighborhood of South Boston. The rotunda-topped building had been built in 1884 and, then known as the Cyclorama, originally housed a cycloramic painting of the Battle of Gettysburg. The city of Boston renovated in 1970 as part of its urban-renewal efforts and renamed it the BCA, which soon developed a reputation as an affordable space for artists.[90] In the spirit of the FAP of Fresno and CalArts, the college-aged volunteers occupied the run-down space, built new walls, resurfaced floors, repaired bathrooms, and built a wheelchair access ramp. Bradley located an architect who figured out a way to cover the central dome to screen out light and protect the exhibit. Like many feminists, she tried to work with women-owned businesses whenever possible.[91]

The BWAA anticipated the total cost of mounting the exhibit in Boston would be $80,000. Funds came from the NEH and the Massachusetts Council on the Arts and Humanities. The Boston Jubilee 350, organized to celebrate the city's 350th anniversary in June 1980, gave funds, as did the Polaroid Foundation and Palmer and Dodge Law Firm. The *Boston Phoenix* lent them $50,000. The rest, according to the *Boston Globe*, had to come from "a large number of small donations."[92] Hankins explained that, "Everyone knew someone they could call on for help."[93] One fund-raising letter explained that, "All over New England people are helping to raise funds to support this effort by encouraging their friends to donate, having dinner parties for 'The Dinner Party' or organizing fund-raisers or joint fund-raisers."[94] The BWAA adopted the "sponsor" program used in Houston. As the opening date loomed, the fund-raising and publicity efforts culminated in a party at the Great Hall in Boston's historic Quincy Market on June 15, 1980, organized by Katherine Kane.[95] Doubleday, the publisher of Chicago's books, anticipated a large crowd and national press coverage.[96]

The Boston opening followed the format established by San Francisco and Houston. Each *The Dinner Party* catalog listed the names of the women and goddesses seated at the table and the names on the Heritage Floor. Each community group wrote their own introduction to the exhibit on the front cover and a history of their efforts to bring *The Dinner Party* to their cities on the back. The Boston catalog reflected the sensibilities of the BWAA and of Boston's vibrant feminist communities. "The Dinner Party serves to expand our cultural awareness by challenging the myths that surround and define women's experience . . . it not only adds to our existing perceptions, but also vindicates the negative image of women so pervasive in our culture."[97] The most distinctive element of the Boston show was its Jasette lecture series on Sundays, when entrance to the exhibit was free. The series promoted itself as a new manner of speech that was both subversive and frankly defiant, a cultural practice of the powerless as they cast off their oppression. Far from the halls of legislative power, this cultural act of subversion was intended to undermine the stable categories of male-dominated society through language, the ground from which all social practice grew. The printed materials for the Sunday lectures defined *jasette*:

> to talk simply for the sake of talking, for the pleasure or the need, like that, to pour out your heart, to find yourself again, whatever . . .
>
> . . . can be interrupted from beginning to end or exchanged while doing the dishes . . .

> On the plantation as Blacks hadn't the right to talk among themselves, they sent their message by song, they "jazzed." Jazz is to Black oppression what *jasette* is to women's oppression; it does the same thing, it plays the same role. It's roundabout. It's talking in spite of . . .
>
> . . . is the speech of the oppressed. Gossiping about our lives has made us conscious of our bonds of experience as women; we then discovered to what degree private life is political.[98]

The spirit of the Jasette lectures embodied a new style of feminist essentialism gaining popularity in the 1980s that was informed by radical French feminists Luce Irigaray and Hélène Cixous, whose newly translated works had recently arrived in US bookstores and classrooms.[99] With its move to reclaim attributes devalued by their historic association with women (such as personal talk, dismissed as gossip), Jasette offered a new theoretical gloss on the 1970s feminist message of *The Dinner Party*. Yet at the same time, Jasette drew on Afrocentric practices designed to celebrate agency and community resilience. Boston's network of black feminists, including Combahee River Collective founder Barbara Smith, Smith's sister Beverly Smith, Gloria Hull, and Audre Lorde, deeply influenced the city's expression of feminism and regularly provided the point of contact between overlapping communities of women.[100] Boston's women's community, steeped in activist and academic feminism, offered *The Dinner Party* as an unapologetically woman-centered cultural event.

The Boston show, like those in San Francisco and Houston before it, put up impressive attendance records. On week four, over three thousand people attended; by week eight, that number had tripled to nearly nine thousand visitors. Attendance totaled forty thousand over the two-month showing, and just over a quarter of all visitors bought the audio guide, bringing in nearly $21,000 to offset exhibition costs.[101] Surprised by their success and "devastated" when it closed, everyone agreed that the Boston organizers had pulled off an impressive feat.[102]

Cleveland

I met people I never would have met otherwise and we became friends.

A year later, in May 1981, *The Dinner Party* opened a third community show in Cleveland, Ohio. In contrast to the ebullience of the already-feminist Boston group, the organizers of the Cleveland exhibition included women touched by feminist ideas but not necessarily by "the movement." Like Boston, the city of Cleveland had a rich history of left-leaning activism and established networks that organizers could mobilize. And, like Houston, Cleveland's isolation from major cultural centers galvanized interested audiences to support a major cultural event. The combination pulled in women who had not participated in organized feminism yet found in *The Dinner Party* a history of women that moved them to participate.

At her monthly women's reading group, Mickey Stern heard about a screening of *Right Out of History*, the documentary on the making of *The Dinner Party*, in nearby Akron. Stern made the forty-minute drive and later reported that she left the showing "two inches taller."[103] She learned that a group of *Dinner Party* supporters in Akron had organized themselves after the city's museum of art had declined to show the installation.[104] Stern immediately joined them and offered her prior experiences in political organizing. Stern's activism started in Cleveland's anti–Vietnam War movement, and from those contacts she eventually found her way to the city's women's liberation groups. An empty nester, Stern threw herself into the pro-choice movement and helped to establish in the 1970s the first clinics in Cleveland where women could receive reproductive care, including having an abortion. Stern applied these organizing skills to *The Dinner Party*.[105]

Marcia Levine learned about *The Dinner Party* through Stern. Levine, like Stern, had found the ideas represented in *Right Out of History* so powerful as to jar her into a whole new awareness. This was her "click!" moment, pulling together a set of previously unremarked upon incidents she had during her social work training and while raising her children as a single woman.[106] Her mother, a longstanding feminist (possibly touched by the first wave of suffrage activism in the 1920s), bought Betty Friedan's *The Feminine Mystique* for her when it came out in 1963, but Levine (who came of age in the conservative 1950s) said it took awhile for her to see herself in its message.[107]

Screening *Right Out of History* changed all that. Levine now felt the heavy hand of history and wanted to ensure that women never fell outside its records again. "The fact that so many women had done so much and we had no memory of them moved me." That there were only a few women she recognized—Queen Elizabeth I and Virginia Woolf—made it all the more poignant to her that she had no meaningful context for them.[108] Dorothy Goodwill, who volunteered at Chicago's Santa Monica studio, also joined the Ohio group. Goodwill described in the Cleveland exhibit brochure her feminist "click!" moment as happening when she heard Chicago lecture in the mid-1970s. "I had worked hard and with dedication at my job as a mother and homemaker. Why did I feel somehow secondary? And alone?"[109] As Chicago spoke, Goodwill recalled that she "leaned forward in fascination and hung onto the seat in front of me, riveted by her story of *The Dinner Party* project and her appeal for workers." Goodwill told that not only had she been personally changed by working on *The Dinner Party*, but she believed that seeing the final product also changed viewers. It "gives to me and my daughters a history of our role models. It gives us back our *heritage*."[110]

Stern, Levine, and Goodwill joined forces with the three organizers from Akron: Tina Bronako, a University of Akron student; and two UA faculty members, Robert Zangrando and Faye Dambrot. Calling themselves the Ohio-Chicago Art Project, they turned their sights to Cleveland when no space big enough could be found in Akron. As did organizers in Houston, Boston, and Chicago, the group immediately began to cultivate the local press. Local papers in Cleveland and Akron ran numerous articles on the group's progress over the next eighteen months, including one in the *Cleveland Plain Dealer* that captured the sense of teamwork among that city's volunteers. "I have a friend who, many times after a long day of work, came home to give her family dinner and then went to The Dinner Party to saw and hammer and paint to get the exhibit ready for its opening. She did it, she said, because she wanted to feel a part of this important undertaking."[111] The group, now at thirteen, also put in their own money. Stern fearlessly pledged all of her retirement funds.[112] Levine recalled that funds and donations came from unexpected places, including local hardware companies and churches. They raised all necessary funds by personal donations and wholly without grants.[113]

Almost immediately, the Ohio-Chicago Art Project faced mounting costs once they turned to renovating the former Jewish temple in Cleveland Heights. The *Akron Beacon Journal* reported that the anticipated cost doubled from their initial estimates to a staggering $120,000. "The group has two months to turn the old Temple on the Heights, in Cleveland Heights, into a museum, including a new lighting system."[114] The group expected to recoup its renovation costs. A study by the Institute for Future Studies at the University of Akron reported in its assessment of *The Dinner Party* that "each attendee at a cultural institution generates about 9–10 dollars in direct economic impact." The report concluded that given even a moderate attendance estimate for *The Dinner Party* of thirty thousand people, fewer than at Boston, the economic impact of bringing the piece to Cleveland would net approximately $300,000.[115] The owner of the building, Temple Associates, also saw this potential. They hoped to make the run-down building into a cultural center and offered to rent the space to the group without a fee, as long as the group did the renovations. Jean Gappert, the executive coordinator, explained that, "By the time we leave, this will be a museum-quality space, and you could plug art shows in here so easily."[116]

A month later, on April 19, 1981, the *Akron Beacon* reported that costs had risen to over $190,000, but the group succeeded in paying their expenses and turning a profit.[117] Final accounting of the Cleveland show included $81,000 in admission fees, $87,000 in retail sales, and $102,000 in fund-raising, for a total revenue of $273,000.[118] Attendance over 12 weeks was 33,000 people, each of whom purchased a $3 ticket, resulting in a $58,000 profit after paying Through the Flower.[119] The Ohio-Chicago Art Project donated surplus funds to women's shelters and a rape crisis center.[120] When the show closed, the group stayed in touch, valuing the friendships they had forged. "I met people I never would have met otherwise and we became friends," recalled Levine.[121]

Chicago

The old girls network has grown up a lot and we now have a lot of access to people in important places.

The community group from Chicago represented a stylistically very different group from those in Boston or Cleveland. Most notably, it was led by a group of midcareer bankers and developers, part of a new cohort of women who broke into once-exclusive male professions in the 1970s. Armed with business suits, salaries, and knowledge of investment banking, the Rosyln Group mobilized various approaches for bringing *The Dinner Party* to Chicago, once more testifying to *The Dinner Party*'s ability to draw women from across the political and cultural spectrums.

The Roslyn Group grew out of a larger women's cultural gathering, the Roslyn Group for Arts and Letters, which described itself as "1300 networking women who want to generate support and recognition for women writers and artists." Sixty members met monthly for a literary salon on Rosyln Place, where they read books written by women and discussed "women's issues." The group read Chicago's memoir and began looking into whether the city's museums or galleries would agree to exhibit *The Dinner Party*.

Initially, prospects looked good. The Museum of Contemporary Art, which did not have adequate space to show it, agreed to help with presentation and publicity in an alternative space if it received $75,000 in advance and another $150,000 in guarantors. The museum canceled this arrangement as renovation costs rose.[122] Columbia College (now Columbia College Chicago) next agreed to show it.[123] Yet the costs to show it at the Navy Pier quickly became prohibitive, as college president Mirron Alexandroff explained to the *Chicago Tribune*: "I think the exhibit is immensely important and I would like to do anything personally or institutionally to see that it gets here. But we just could not pull it off. It takes an enormous amount of space that you have to tie up for a minimum of three months."[124]

At that point, the group decided to move ahead despite these setbacks. "We chose to exhibit *The Dinner Party* ourselves."[125] The *Chicago Tribune* quoted Boston organizer April Hankins's advice: "Forget the institutions, and just do it."[126] Diann DeWeese Smith, a development banker at the South Shore Bank, founded and incorporated the group in 1981. They worked with Gelon for two years to raise funds and find a proper building. They searched over 150 properties before settling on the South Loop site, which a local developer, Columbia Homes/Borg Warner, offered free of charge in hopes of spurring on the potentially gentrifying neighborhood.[127] With the help of three hundred volunteers, they began renovating the thirteenth floor of an old Printing House Row building.

As was the case with the Cleveland temple and the Boston Cyclorama, the space was rough and needed substantial renovation. The large skylight had to be covered to create a dark viewing environment, the roof leaked and the first floor had to be entirely gutted, all of which significantly drove up costs. The *Chicago Tribune* reported that the final price for bringing the show to Chicago was $268,000, a substantial part—some $145,000—in preopening costs.[128] Gelon explained in an interview with the local feminist journal, *Sister Source*, that rising costs were inevitable when women's groups were creating their own cultural institutions: "What's happening here is that a whole new institution is being created. The staff is expensive. Staff might be 15 to 18 people, plus telephones, office supplies, Xerox machines, everything that creates an office environment. Then there's security—museum quality guards. On-going staff, setting up bookstores, doing all the renovations for the space are major costs. The ongoing costs aren't that much; it's the initial costs of creating a bureaucracy."[129]

The Rosyln Group arranged an array of business-centered fund-raising events, including a fashion show by the Chicago retailer Marshall Field's and a benefit dinner party held by Tiffany at its downtown store.[130] Well-connected volunteers worked their professional and city networks, as well. Marilyn D. Clancy, former special assistant to US senators Adlai Stevenson and Alan Dixon and chairwoman of the Roslyn Group steering committee, explained in an interview that the times were tough for such an ambitious cultural undertaking.

> The art world, especially the women's art world is seen as sort of a dilettante. We're sort of at the bottom of the funding pile. But the old girls network has grown up a lot and we now have a lot of access to people in important places.
>
> We know where the money is and we're much better at getting it.[131]

Days before the opening, the Roslyn Group was still short of funds. The group would cover costs if thirty thousand people bought the $4 tickets. They expected to sell double that. Nevertheless, eight members of the group drew $10,000 personal loans to fund the show.[132] The faith the organizers and developers had in the capacity of *The Dinner Party* to bring in crowds never waivered. "I cannot tell you that I'll like it," Diann Smith, director of marketing at the South Shore Bank and one of the community organizers, told a *Tribune* journalist. "But I am guaranteeing my right to see it."[133]

The strong academic feminist regional community lent its support, particularly for the educational events scheduled for the exhibition. The Roslyn Group took advantage of a local conference on the 1893 Chicago World's Columbian Exposition and the tenth anniversary of the Chicago area women's history conference, "Women's Heritage: Celebration and Challenge." Held on November 13 and 14, 1981, at Roosevelt University, the conference showcased the rich history of women in the city of Chicago, a perfect context for viewing *The Dinner Party*. American women's historian Kathryn Kish Sklar gave the conference keynote address. Historian Nancy Cott drew a parallel between the Woman's Building at the 1893 Exposition and *The Dinner Party* in the *New York Times*, writing that in important ways the Woman's Building "prefigured *The Dinner Party*." "Like the later work, the building represented a prodigious collective effort, and also showed to best advantage women's artistry in ceramics and needlework. The kinship between the two works is further apparent on the panels that lined the grand rotunda of the Woman's Building: Listed were the 'golden names of women who in past and present centuries have done honor to the human race,' a roll-call echoed in the names on the floor of 'The Dinner Party.'"[134] Many of the city's numerous women's studies programs sponsored the conference, including the Association of Women in Science, the Chicago Area Women's History Conference, the Chicago Area Women's Studies Association, and the women's studies programs of the University of Illinois, Chicago; Loyola University; and Northeastern Illinois University.[135]

Final calculations for the Chicago exhibit of *The Dinner Party* reached an impressive $220,000.[136] A press release from the South Loop Planning Board proudly announced the show's success. Seventy thousand people came to the "alternative viewing space," approximately five hundred men and women each day for its five-month stay. The press release explained that the owner of the building "gambled that having the exhibit in the new South Loop would attract people to the area and introduce them to Chicago's newest residential downtown district." The South Loop developers had accomplished what they had hoped to: one week after *The Dinner Party* closed, a new show opened, Artists of the New South Loop, securing the South Loop as Chicago's newest art destination. The impact of *The Dinner Party*, however, radiated beyond the building to the larger dreams of gentrifying the neighborhood, which included the completion of two major projects—the city's renovation of the abandoned nearby Dearborn Station and the renovation of a new 294-unit residential building by a *Dinner Party* show volunteer, Russell Barns.[137] Bette Hill, president of the South Loop Planning Board, was all optimism: "[People] have been here now. They found it safe and they discovered the Printers Museum, Prairie Avenue Book Store, Blackies and Printers Row restaurants. They will want to come back to show their friends the Soho atmosphere, introduce them to loft living and see the new show."[138]

The Chicago art scene also stood to reap benefits from the success of *The Dinner Party*. Jean Hunt told *Gay Life* that after the loans had been repaid the Roslyn Group planned on using profits to invest in the city's women's art community by sponsoring other less costly but still ambitious art projects and through scholarships and financial assistance to artists. The paper's criticism that the Roslyn Group was made up of "wealthy, uniformly WASP-straight women who were too busy eating cucumber sandwiches and keeping their white gloves clean to do anything more strenuous than sign checks," Hunt called "balderdash." Rather than society matrons, they were savvy investors who took a calculated risk: "The bulk of the money was raised through individuals. They financed loans—one woman even put up her house [as collateral]. We talked for a year before things were firm.... We expected to make back our investment—we had absolute reason to believe that we would. The show has been successful everywhere it's been, meaning that it has made back its costs."[139] While the Chicago gay press might not have seen enough celebration of lesbians in *The Dinner Party*, such criticisms did not translate into open divides among audiences in Chicago or any other community show. Differences, in this case between white-gloved wealthy straight women and lesbians, continued to shape how women met and socialized. Nonetheless, community shows, however temporarily, brought together interested viewers, many of whom had little in common beyond their desire to see *The Dinner Party*.

Like the style of cultural feminism it came to embody, *The Dinner Party* brought together many kinds of women under the banner of supporting women-themed culture. That these temporary communities, both organizers and audiences, dispersed after the show, speaks to the limits of cultural products to bring about coherent social change. Cultural feminist products like *The Dinner Party* may have inspired viewers to think about women's history and culture broadly defined as a story of oppression and liberation, lesser known but surely no less compelling drama than that of the biblical Moses leading his people out of Egypt. But the path to liberation it offered its "chosen people" remained deliberately and tactically unmapped. In this way, cultural feminist products offered a women-friendly space for many kinds of people and many kinds of feminists to enjoy for as long as they wanted.

One unexpected consequence of the collapse of the museum tour was that *The Dinner Party* built its reputation as a significant cultural event based on its popularity, not on the blessings of the formal art world. Audiences and organizers together created feminist events in alternative spaces. In this way, the context of community-organized shows with their concerted and sustained efforts to draw local interest and resources together under the rubric of "women's art" brought together feminist consumer and community identities. Funders and ticket-buyers, investors and organizers, people who bought books and sent enthusiastic letters to their newspapers, participated in the financial dimension of *The Dinner Party* tour. Together they mobilized local markets to distribute, sell, and consume—show and *sell*—a popular expression of feminism. In doing so, they helped create an unlikely feminist art blockbuster.

At the same time, *The Dinner Party* tour's representations of community, both metaphorical and literal, raised a set of questions about women's status, women's history, and women's activism. Viewers were compelled to ask which community, which history, which women did *The Dinner Party* memorialize and why? Did a woman see herself at *The Dinner Party* and in its attendant communities, or did she confront images of Woman that felt foreign to her? The setting itself also raised pressing questions: what did it mean about the status of women and women-centered art that audiences paid to see *The Dinner Party* in alternative venues, rather than in the mainstream and historically powerful, status-conferring museum? These questions of inclusion—inclusion in women's history and inclusion of women into mainstream cultural institutions like museums—were taken up and debated among critics, feminists, and audiences in every city where *The Dinner Party* opened.

As *The Dinner Party* toured, Chicago herself moved on to new projects and into new ways of working. She remained committed to seeing *The Dinner Party* displayed and properly honored as a major work of twentieth-century art and continued to attend all opening events. For the artist, these included giving lectures, doing book signings, and meeting with local groups of organizers to thank them. But Chicago would never be content to have her creative life or her professional reputation rise and fall with *The Dinner Party*. She took many lessons forward from the experience of *The Dinner Party* studio. Foremost, she had new appreciation for the power of her embroidery design. Along with long-time studio worker and dear friend Audrey Cowan, Chicago began *The Birth Project*, a needlework fine-art exploration of women giving birth. The structure Chicago set up for this project did away with the literal collective of needleworkers and any attendant obligation for a group studio. For this feminist-themed project, Chicago sent her designs to individual needleworkers who met with the artist regularly, making *The Birth Project* more collaborative and dispersed.[140] In the 1980s, Chicago threw herself into her studio and her own artistic practice and explored the gendered dimension of her humanism in new formats. While working on *The Birth Project* (1980–85), the artist began a series on masculinity, *Powerplay* (1982–87), and a collaborative work with her new husband, photographer Donald Woodman, *The Holocaust Project: From Darkness into Light* (1985–93), proving beyond all doubt that both her professional and personal life could survive and even thrive after *The Dinner Party*.

CHAPTER SEVEN

Debating Feminist Art

The Dinner Party *in Published and Unpublished Commentary, 1979–1989*

THE DINNER PARTY OPENED in its second and last major museum show in the fall of 1981 at the Brooklyn Museum. The Brooklyn opening of *The Dinner Party* confirmed the work's symbiotic relationship with the media. Before the museum openings, Chicago and Gelon cultivated media attention as a way to raise money and build audience interest in the piece. As it became clear that museums would not display the work, Chicago, Gelon, and community organizers used the media to build an alternative, nonmuseum-based tour. Ironically, creating a tour for *The Dinner Party* outside of traditional venues required a level of public relations that brought an unprecedented amount of attention to the piece, specifically of a kind that underscored its controversies. In a classic catch-22, the drama around *The Dinner Party* tour made it newsworthy while its very newsworthiness undermined its status as fine art. This cycle of commentary and controversy profoundly shaped the reception of *The Dinner Party.*

When taken as a whole, the published response to *The Dinner Party* in the years it toured in the United States followed no simple pattern. It included praise and criticism from regional newspapers such as the *Cleveland Plain Dealer*, the *Chicago Tribune*, and the *Boston Globe* and from national media such as *Newsweek*, *Time*, and the *New York Times*. Journals, newsletters, and newspapers with smaller and specific readerships like those of feminists and art professionals also covered *The Dinner Party*. Art world reactions, such as those chronicled in *Artforum* and *Art in America,* followed the museum openings in San Francisco and Brooklyn, whereas feminist reactions followed local shows, given the absence of a national feminist press presence beyond a handful of columnists and *Ms.* magazine. These outlets included *Sojourner* in Boston, *Chrysalis* in Los Angeles, *Womanspirit* in San Francisco, and academic journals such as *Frontiers*.

While no consistent pattern emerged to predict a critic's response, with feminists, art critics, and journalists loving and hating it in almost equal measure, the new wave of national reportage after the Brooklyn show nevertheless seared a set of questions into the cultural history of *The Dinner Party*: was it art or politics? Was it a blockbuster commodity or a religious icon? Was it a masterpiece or kitsch? New vistas of controversy also opened up under the bright lights of national media attention. To conservatives, *The Dinner Party* represented a near-pornographic display of the female body. For many feminists, this same invocation of the female body marred the piece as tragically essentialist. For left and liberal supporters of multiculturalism, including feminists, *The Dinner Party* could never represent "women" because of the lack of racial diversity at the table and its chronic Eurocentrism. For critics concerned in defending the museum from market trends, its popularity became a gaudy populism. The reviews of *The Dinner Party* from local and national newspapers, magazines, and editorials, as well as from art and feminist critics, showed it to be under harsh scrutiny from all quarters.

The sole exception to the barrage of criticism was the public, which continued to line up to see *The Dinner Party* in record numbers. Examining the published reviews along with public commentary (in fan letters and comment books) illuminates the strikingly divergent responses to *The Dinner Party* and suggests that a new atmosphere for feminist-themed cultural products had begun to take shape in the 1980s, one no longer in the hands of published feminists or cultural arbitrators. It also suggests that no single group (like museum professionals) or one viewpoint (art critics) dominated the reception of *The Dinner Party*. Rather, the heated—and at times overheated—debates about *The Dinner Party* testified to the fact that no single group could either guarantee or deny its success. The vitriolic and admiring voices battling it out in the print media fed the buzz-worthiness of the piece and inadvertently helped propel it into its status as the controversial icon of the feminist art movement.

Show and Sell

A pop phenomenon on the order of bra burning and *The Women's Room.*

It took years of effort and fund-raising to pull off a New York City showing. Supporters included key people from women's organizations like the Women's Fund Joint Foundation and *Ms.* magazine, businesswomen like Christine Hefner, well-known feminists like Anne Roiphe, and networked women like Lael Stegall of the National Women's Political Caucus and Sarah Kovner and Bobbie Handman of the public affairs firm Arts, Letters, and Politics.[1] Gatherings organized by Ann Rockefeller Roberts, the daughter of New York's former governor, brought an infusion of funds. All told, the group raised $40,000, over half of the total cost to mount the exhibit.[2] Such intense networking and fund-raising generated an eager audience. Forty-five hundred guests attended the Thursday night opening on October 17, 1981, the largest in the museum's history.[3] Lines for the public opening stretched around Brooklyn's Flatbush Avenue. Surprised by the numbers, the museum had to modify its procedures to sell tickets with entry times printed on them. The Brooklyn *Dinner Party* exhibit also introduced an audio tour narrated by Chicago for an additional two dollars.[4] Two hundred people an hour moved through the exhibit, for a total of a hundred thousand over the course of its two-month showing.[5]

Despite its reputation at the far edge of the New York art world, the Brooklyn Museum commanded significant national media attention. Unlike the five community shows that enjoyed intense local media coverage, when *The Dinner Party* opened in Brooklyn in October 1981, the national press corps covered it, as did critics from the country's major art publications. This second wave of national media coverage was particularly hostile to the artist, the art, and the event-ness of *The Dinner Party,* with many journalists finding its very popularity a cause for suspicion and seeing in its clear message politics of the worst sort.

Journalists and professional commentators obsessively scrutinized the crowds and their reactions. "I thought there was undue emphasis on sexual organs," one viewer confessed to a *New York Times* reporter. "But I think it was terrific that so many women worked such long and arduous hours on it." Another turned away, saying, "It made me sick." One female viewer enjoyed the piece's "sensuality," another described it as "almost orgasmic," while a third noted that, "This is aggressive feminism. That's what's impressive."[6] Museum director Michael Botwinick recalled the distinctiveness of the audiences who came to see the exhibit, particularly their penchant for what he called impromptu seminars in the galleries. The visitors defied categorization: "They ranged widely over a far broader spectrum of age, background, origin than we usually saw. And most exciting, they were energized. No parades of bored visitors, eyes glazed over, walking down the middle of the galleries simply because this was the show to see. They came early, they stayed late, they returned again and again, and even when they were profoundly challenged and disturbed by the piece they told us they felt it was important that they had seen it."[7]

Other professional observers characterized the crowds less generously. Hilton Kramer snidely reported in the *New York Times* that, "For aficionados of Feminist art, 'The Dinner Party' is the event of the year—and of many a year."[8] Some came simply to poke fun at the hoopla. An alternative performance ran just outside the museum throughout the fall of 1981. "If you're still hungry after THE DINNER PARTY, try *Maria Manhattan's Box Lunch*." The thirty-nine women of "dubious distinction" invited to Maria's lunch included Patty Hearst, Tricia Nixon, Betty Crocker, Lot's Wife, Minnie Mouse, and Lassie.[9] The Box Lunch brochure even had its own legend, one that blended two favorite critiques of *The Dinner Party*. Its message was heavy-handed and self-serving: "In the beginning I was just another self-centered artist. And then I beheld a vision. And the sign said, 'Look, Maria, already you're in your thirties. You're a good artist, but recognition-wise you're on the other side of the tracks. Capitalize on the Movement! Jump on the Band-wagon! And Lo, I conceived of the Box Lunch."[10] The gamut of reactions in Brooklyn captured in a single snapshot a tangle of debates about *The Dinner Party* that had followed it wherever it was displayed.

Commentary on *The Dinner Party* from local and national media established a vocabulary of debate that followed the piece throughout its US tour. Major art journals, national magazines, and newspapers in cities that opened the exhibit ran numerous stories about *The Dinner Party* and associated controversies. The *Chicago Tribune*, for example, ran nine articles about the efforts to bring the piece to the city between 1979 and 1981 and a handful of reviews once it opened. Critics favorably and unfavorably inclined toward *The Dinner Party* shared a focus on the symbolism of the female body, the significance of the piece's popularity, and its status as art. At the same time, there were glaring differences in coverage. In scathing critiques of *The Dinner Party* from the local and national press corps, reviewers regularly conflated art criticism, denunciations of pop culture or feminism and ad hominem attacks on Chicago. Each complaint could stand in for any other. If the critic disliked the art, he could attack the influence of politics in the museum world; if she disliked the artist she could attack Chicago as a cult figure; if he disliked feminism, he could dismiss the art as trendy. Most striking, the tone of many critics smoldered white-hot and personal. Clearly, the experience of viewing *The Dinner Party* proved provocative enough to raise the critical temperature to unusually high levels. In contrast, journalists positively inclined grappled with the art and artist differently, mainly in interview-style reviews that appeared in the culture or life sections of regional newspapers and in glossy national magazines. In this journalistic genre, Chicago herself—her appearance, her manner, and her reaction to the publicity junket she rode—figured prominently. The phenomena of *The Dinner Party* and its attendant controversies became as important as aesthetic evaluations of the installation. When taken together, the media coverage rooted *The Dinner Party* in the realm of pop cultural drama as much as in art history.

Reporters regularly commented on "Chicago, the woman" and her celebrity; in these pieces the artist's body became part of the coverage and often was a proxy for her art. For example, the monthly magazine *Mother Jones* published an interview between Chicago and Jan Butterfield, journalist and wife of San Francisco Museum of Modern Art director, Henry Hopkins, weeks before the first public showing in San Francisco. In what became typical of the media reportage, Butterfield combined praise and a touch of snarkiness in her description of the artist. She began her interview by describing Chicago as "a cult figure in the women's art movement" and her memoir *Through the Flower* as "a bible" before orienting her readers to Chicago the Woman. "Chicago herself is affectionate, generous and articulate; she can also be, by turns, aggressive, demanding and compulsive." Almost redundantly, Butterfield added that, "it is impossible to spend time with her without talking about feminism."[11]

Mademoiselle followed the same playbook in an article that appeared before *The Dinner Party* opened in Cleveland in 1981. Initially, Gwenda Blair described the artist as diminutive, as "only slightly over five feet tall, lean and limber as a gymnast," with a mere "distant resemblance to the pudgy powerhouse" photographed in her books. This limber woman could be "easily mistaken for Judy Chicago's younger sister." Do not be fooled, dear readers. "But from the decisive voice and the vitality with which she fairly vibrates, it is apparent that this is Chicago herself. After all, who else would begin by reprimanding me for an ill-informed question on her work?" Who else but Chicago the Feminist? In pieces that showcased Chicago as part of the coverage of *The Dinner Party*, her body and manners functioned as an alternate space where critics and commentators negotiated the meaning and limits of her feminism. "In the traditional sense of the word, Judy Chicago is not, in fact, particularly 'nice.' She is not soft-spoken, deferential or self-sacrificing. She has a strong point of view and the abruptness with which she expresses it is off-putting at first. Yet she is also refreshing, engaging and, I gradually realize, sincere, to an unusual degree. . . . As we talk, she seems less a steamroller than someone genuinely determined not to let anyone settle for anything less than her (or his) very best. And that, I begin to conclude, may just be *better* than nice."[12]

What could possibly be "*better* than nice" for a woman? Competing notions of womanhood squared off. Chicago's direct speech, cultivated as key to women's liberation in her feminist classrooms, veered toward the strident when represented in the mainstream media. Interviewers struggled to find ways to acknowledge and contain Chicago's authority, and her appearance became an easy place to deposit any ambivalence. *Texas Monthly*'s Michael Ennis could barely contain his misgivings over Chicago the Woman. He represents the artist as questionably outfitted, her bohemianism a poor replacement for proper hair management: "Chicago at forty is short and trim, with a big mass of long, kinky, gray-flecked dark hair, and she speaks very directly in a nasal Midwestern twang. She wore purple-tinted glasses that matched her purple turtleneck, black cord jeans, and thick-soled sandals over iridescent socks. She didn't go in for vanities like make up or bleaching her mustache, but it looked like her eyebrows had been plucked."[13] Taming the feminist message by sneering at Chicago the Woman spoke to the sense of anxiety she and *The Dinner Party* provoked in some quarters. Arthur Berger from the *Chronicle of Higher Education* explained that he "felt somewhat like Henry Adams must have felt when he gazed upon the dynamo for the first time and recognized it as a symbol of a new order, of a new force that would transform society." That new force, the dynamo of change, "is woman affirming and reveling in her femininity, her sexuality, her generativity and her creativity."[14]

Chicago and *The Dinner Party* provoked strong responses in part because each in different ways represented the reoccurring anxiety dream of 1970s gender politics: men's fear of a full-scale revolt by women, coupled with a terrifying unleashing of female body hair. Chicago and her art stood as interchangeable signs of potential gender trouble brewing just over the horizon. Berger articulated his view of what he called men's "visceral fear" of female sexuality and their hostility to feminism: "For thousands of years, in Western Civilization, there has been a subliminal and perhaps even visceral fear of female sexuality among males. Judy Chicago, with just 39 place setting[s], confronts all the centuries of ignorance and misunderstanding and forces us to deal with them."[15]

A *Boston Globe* editor commented on the different effects the piece had on men and women. He suggested that men tended to see *The Dinner Party* as "a misconceived conglomeration of needlework and ceramic plates dedicated to women they have never heard of," whereas women saw it as validating women's lost history of accomplishment and their taken-for-granted status as hostess to the world's dinner parties. If the artist had wanted to avoid controversy, which she clearly had not, the editor suggested that Chicago might have chosen to honor the well-known women who did not challenge gender norms, such as "St. Theresa, Queen Victoria, Florence Nightingale, Mamie Eisenhower and Marilyn Monroe." The real subject of *The Dinner Party*, then, was not "famous women of the past" but infamous lies, "lies that permeate our history and our present. It is this that makes it controversial. And it is this that gives it value."[16]

For critics bothered by feminism, the plates' distinctive central core imagery stood as the movement's offensive symbol. A reporter in Boston summed it up: "Vaginal imagery is becoming identified with the politics of militant feminism."[17] However, the identification between vaginal imagery and militant feminism was neither new nor an uncontested element of feminist thought. "Cunt art," linked to radical feminism in the early 1970s and particularly in the West Coast feminist art movement, made its mainstream debut in *The Dinner Party*, exposing it to the lion's share of damning media attention. Historically, the display of women's bodies in high art and popular culture triggered controversies about where to draw the line between decency and obscenity. Cunt art of the 1970s, with its tactical use of the female genitals to expose assumptions about despised physicality and women's "tragic" entrapment in the gory realities of reproduction, unquestionably represented challenging fare. Critics entered battles about *The Dinner Party* prepared to shore up the space of the museum as set apart from offensive politics, vulgar marketing, and misguided anatomy lessons.

The most infamous of the attacks came from Hilton Kramer of the *New*

York Times, who wrote that the vulva plates demonstrate a "vulgarity" more appropriate "to an advertising campaign than to a work of art." Yet, he snorted, "What ad campaign, even in these 'liberated' times, would dare to vulgarize and exploit the imagery of female sexuality on this scale and with such abysmal taste?" "For its principal image, 'The Dinner Party' remains fixated on the external genital organs of the female body. Its many variations of the image are not without a certain ingenuity, to be sure, but it is the kind of ingenuity we associate with kitsch."[18] A Cleveland editor couldn't bring himself to use the proper language about what the plates represented: "The center of interest, as I understand it, is the same center of interest that commands the attention of a gynecologist."[19] One reviewer simply dismisses the deeply carved plates of Virginia Woolf and Georgia O'Keeffe as "gross."[20]

While some critics acknowledged that the plates demonstrated "ingenuity" or even "astonishing beauty," for many the vulva imagery veered too close to parody or insult to be taken seriously.[21] Robert Hughes, writing in *Time* magazine, explained that the controversy lay in "Chicago's relentless concentration on the pudenda. . . . To represent Virginia Woolf as a clump of pottery labia majora is on par with symbolizing Mozart as a phallus."[22] The choice of the word *pudenda*, with it Latin roots in *pudere* or shame, spoke volumes about what bothered the journalist and others who found the vaginal plates in poor taste. The *New York Review* described Chicago's plates as "comparable in style and organic form to those ornate psychedelic candles that used to be the rage of Village 'head' shops," their colors "worthy of a Taiwanese souvenir factory." John Richardson of the *New York Review* dismissed what he called Chicago's "vulva artifacts" as akin to "a tropical fruit not much prized even by the locals." The "locals" or the women to whom Richardson referred, in his mind did not see "themselves" when they gazed into the plates. Clearly, Richardson longed for a class of locals who would reject *The Dinner Party*'s view of women. Yet, to his dismay, female audiences lined up to see it: "All the more striking, then, that these women, who would certainly have evinced distaste rather than interest in a display of sex shop paraphernalia, were shuffling past rows of Three D. Beaver, as awed as if they were on a pilgrimage."[23] Pilgrimage to the promised land or to a fraternity stag show? For Richardson, the female body could never shed its associations with a sexuality that could be acceptably displayed only in private.

Critics argued over whether *The Dinner Party*'s representation of the female body celebrated or denounced misogyny. Anita Diamant, writing in the *Boston Phoenix*, gave Chicago room to explain her focus on the body and specifically central core images as a female liberation symbol. She quoted the artist: "Let's play fair. Is everything that sticks into the air a penis? So all these tall buildings, they're only phalluses. I want to know why it's okay for things to be phalluses and be important, but if I make an open form, that's only a vagina and that's no good. That's a double standard right there."[24] Diamant sent Chicago a personal note with the unedited version of her piece explaining her sympathy with Chicago's views: "I wanted to express to you how moving I think your work its, how important for women and for men as well, and how inspiring. The challenge to celebrate vulnerability—femaleness—in a male defined, much-armored world speaks loud and clear to me in what I try and try to do."[25]

Chicago used sympathetic interviews to gain a voice in the published conversation about her vulva plates. She stressed her goal of representing fundamental human experiences in a female form language and the value of both men and women. In the *Boston Phoenix* she explained, "When I make those nice vulnerable centers, I'm talking about the terror of vulnerability that has been deposited in the feminine." Human terror of vulnerability had been "deposited" in disgust of vaginas as overly physical or, in contrast, embodying emptiness in form. "People get upset about the word, 'cunt'. Well, that word doesn't mean to me what it means to other people. I don't have cunt hatred. My work starts with an assumption about feeling okay about being female and universalizing from there." Chicago's unmistakably feminine plates posed a direct challenge to the unstated masculinity of most liberation images. She asked, "Why can't the whole human experience be expressed through a *female* metaphor? . . . In the gesture of liberation and the desire to be free that is expressed in the plates, I wasn't just talking about women. I was talking about seeing the human condition through the female condition."[26] It was not an easy case to make. Images of women's bodies, historically associated with maternity or pornography, remained ensnared in old and new debates about obscenity and privacy; art, fine art or not, displayed in museums or museum-like spaces, was not immune from these larger concerns.

Chicago's challenge to male-dominated spiritual traditions in *The Dinner Party* also incited fierce debate. Her embrace of alternative female spiritual models to bring about a more hospitable place for women linked her to religious women of all faiths and to groups of feminists who throughout the 1970s and 1980s looked for ways to bring women into the center of religious life. This debate took place through commentary about the staging of *The Dinner Party*, through analogies to the Sistine Chapel and the medieval church, and the reverence implied by seating goddesses at *The Dinner Party* table.

The work's religious underpinnings pleased some reviewers and they, like the artist, regularly invoked the medieval church—a time when religion triumphed over science and secularism—to describe it. *Ms.* magazine likened Chicago's *Dinner Party* studio to "medieval monasteries or Renaissance ateliers."[27] The *SoHo News* praised the piece for both its monumentality and its "holiness": "What is the total effect? Commemorative, ritualistic, holy."[28] Others hated the spiritual dimension, which often translated into mocking commentary on the exhibition's chapel-like staging. One reviewer disliked the "pretentious atmosphere [that] infects its shrine-like installation." She reported that a certain Foucaultian disciplinary force bore down on her and insisted on spectator reverence, an experience too close to religion for her comfort: "In front of the place setting celebrating the Primordial Goddess I was again tapped on the shoulder and told 'you can kneel if you want.' This kindly meant suggestion (to kneel on the carpeted rail) allowed for close careful scrutiny of the place settings—which of course is valid and valuable. But in the midst of the quasi-holy atmosphere, it was uncomfortably like an invitation to kneel in prayer to the Primordial Goddess plate."[29] For this journalist, the conflation of feminism with goddess worship and museum with cathedral undermined her experience of the art. Other critics who drew a negative analogy between *The Dinner Party* and the medieval church argued that the piece's didacticism functioned similarly to the early clergy's reliance on images to speak to their illiterate members. Hal Fisher of *Artforum*, used the analogy of the church to couch his scathing criticism. "Chicago's conception originates in her own interpretation of medieval art: just as art taught the Bible to illiterates, so should *The Dinner Party* instruct us. To this end, the presentation is obsessively literal and cloyingly ecclesiastic."[30]

Hostile critics had a heyday spinning out the religious analogy. *Time* magazine called *The Dinner Party* "no better than mass devotional art." For *Artforum* it was "proselytizing," marred by a "self-righteousness that replaces art with cultism and offers literalism under the guise of education." Rather than divine and ritualistic, some critics characterized the staging as tacky. Boston's Art Jahnke complained of its "pompous pseudo-biblical prophecy." The *Boston Globe*'s Robert Taylor found *The Dinner Party* "unappetizing" for its pretense of religion, describing it as suffering the "lunatic obsessive vulgarity of a full-scale model of a Gothic cathedral built from toothpicks." The *Village Voice* called it "a sort of Black Mass of feminism," and Dorothy Shinn of the *Akron Beacon*, "the religiofication of the feminist cause." Religion and feminism became interchangeable terms that added up to bad art. A *Newsweek* review complained that "There's too much message, not quite enough art." The *New York Times* explained that the art failed precisely because of its messianic message: "It is art so mired in the pieties of a political cause that it quite fails to acquire any independent artistic life of its own."[31] In short, the criticism reiterated that devotion to feminism marred the art.

As hyperbolic as the negative reviewers were, positive reviews offered equally dramatic accolades. The *Current* gushed that *The Dinner Party* represented a "masterpiece," "a long needed lesson in history," and a "deep affirmation for women."[32] Kay Larson of the *Village Voice* viewed "*The Dinner Party* is the first epic feminist artwork."[33] *Mademoiselle* called it "the most popular feminist art work ever shown in the United States."[34] If negative reviews testified to the arrival of "proselytizing" feminism to the museum, positive reviews demonstrated that Chicago's message was not too radical for mainstream audiences.

For commentators concerned with the contemporary state of art, *The Dinner Party* and "fleeting" trends like the women's movement violated the sacred space of the museum. This complaint appeared most commonly in attacks against Chicago for her celebrity and her art's popularity. According to the *Chicago Tribune* art critic, "The extraordinary amount of preopening publicity for Judy Chicago's *The Dinner Party* again emphasized the problem of treating artworks as if they were only news."[35] A journalist described audiences as akin to a Hollywood fan club, drawn in by "Judy Chicago & Co.," rather than by art.[36] "Judy Chicago is becoming a cottage industry. There is autobiography, the t-shirts, the posters, the chic opening night parties, and a couple of lavishly illustrated volumes from Doubleday. There are also rap groups, speechless onlookers, gigglers, and those who spend considerable time wondering what all the fuss is about. All this would be remarkable for a rock star; for a contemporary artist it is unheard of."[37]

"The whole Dinner Party project," with its star and her books, films, buttons, and posters, offended some reviewers. One pointed to the tie-ins as pushing the piece to "teeter so precariously on the brink of artistic and intellectual ridicule that one might think a serious museum would fight shy of sponsoring it."[38] Amei Wallach from *Newsday* described Chicago as "a movie star among her feminist following." For her, the "hoopla" around *The Dinner Party* only proved that "it's just as hard and takes just as much work to create a bad work of art as it does a good one."[39] For these critics, Chicago's celebrity, *The Dinner Party* tie-in products, and organizers' use of publicity networks pushed *The Dinner Party* firmly into the realm of pop culture and out of fine art.[40]

The Dinner Party's popularity did not signal compromise and sellout to all observers. A *New York* reviewer saw the crowds as an affirmation of the artist. "There is no denying that Chicago has achieved one of her stated goals: to create a new audience for women's art by making it accessible to people generally uninterested in abstract works."[41] A writer for the Living/Forum section of the *Boston Globe*, Katherine Driscoll-Knoll, emphasized a positive populism in the products and events associated with *The Dinner Party*. For her, the tie-ins spread the message. She confessed that, "I even bought *The Dinner Party* heritage book just to get to know these 1000-plus women and their accomplishments better." She, like many viewers, found the audio tour helpful: "Without the cassette I was overwhelmed by the multiple images, but with the cassette tour, I was enthralled."[42] Rather than dismissing the books and audio tour as part of "Judy Chicago & Co.," commentators appreciated the varied ways into the thickly layered details of *The Dinner Party*. The *SoHo News* praised it for the multiple ways it communicated: "It is polysemic."[43]

Regularly critics read *The Dinner Party* as both too religious and too market-driven and its popularity as symptomatic of the eroding boundary between art and pop culture.[44] *Artforum*'s Carrie Rickey dismissed it for "bringing the Consciousness Raising group into the museum" and, by doing so, making itself into "a pop phenomenon on the order of bra burning and *The Women's Room*."[45] The analogy worked, for reasons above and beyond the writer's intent. Marilyn French's 1977 best-selling novel about a white suburban woman's journey from wife to feminist relied on the therapeutic language of 1970s feminist transformation and was simultaneously beloved and controversial for its exploration of privileged women's psychological suffering under patriarchy. Commonalities linked the feminism of *The Dinner Party* and *The Woman's Room*, but none more saliently than their status as popular blockbusters. For this reviewer, this was exactly the problem. Vulgar politics—"consciousness-raising"—had infiltrated the museum. The *Boston Globe* critic advised people to view *The Dinner Party* as an event, because "as a work of art, however, it is valueless."[46] The *Chicago Tribune* announced that the only art on display was Chicago's ability to convince viewers that her work had significance.[47]

For critics worried about shoring up the boundaries of art against agit-prop or populist blockbusters, "serious" museums existed as a world apart from the market with its constantly shifting desires and innovations. Art stood over or against such short-lived, "kitschy," market-driven cycles of "it"-ness. In this way, critics who rejected *The Dinner Party* because of its "trendy" feminist message or its status as the "must-see" event of the season attempted to protect the museum as a space apart, existing in its own privileged value system.[48] To do so, they aggressively narrowed their stated concerns to aesthetics, which they then opposed to the market and its commodities. This selective focus overlooked the fact that the world of museum art was saturated with shifting tides of money. It also overlooked that "Judy Chicago & Co.," particularly her fund-raising, came into being out of necessity because of discrimination: women had been systematically denied access to the support that would enable them to show and sell their work. Aesthetically, the museum as arbiter of taste hid its own investments in such trends. Defenders of the museum as an alternative value system anointed secular modernism as the highest form of expression. *The Dinner Party*, with its popularity (trendiness), its self-promotion (commodification), and its attention to the divine, rendered in female form (religious) offered many provocations to the art establishment.

Defenders of the museum as a space set apart from popular culture might point to positive media coverage of *The Dinner Party* and Chicago's celebrity as symptoms of a larger crisis of cultural authority; such coverage nonetheless introduced US readers to the debates and event-ness associated with the piece. The controversy of its message, the unconventionality of its domestic tour, and the ongoing fascination with its provocative artist became reason for readers to either love or hate, but definitely to go see, *The Dinner Party*.

Feminist Twister

It's Art! It's Feminism! It's *The Dinner Party*!

Feminist reviews of *The Dinner Party* were as multifaceted as the women who wrote under the label in the 1980s. Particularly for feminists, reviewing *The Dinner Party* in the years between 1979 and 1989 became a game of Twister, with commentators praising some elements while criticizing others, going into contortions to reconcile the message, the messenger, and the notoriety of *The Dinner Party* with their view of feminism. Chicago, in turn, found herself engaged in battles with the very audience she once imagined to be easily mobilized by woman-centered art.

The printed feminist response appeared in women's and art newsletters and journals, and in a handful of national media, with varied levels of readership. Lucy Lippard's reviews in *Art in America* reached a national audience, and Ellen Willis's columns in the *Village Voice* circulated widely in the influential New York metropolitan area, while a writer in the feminist journal *Sojourner*, published in Boston, reached considerably fewer readers. On the whole, the published feminist response to *The Dinner Party* tended to circulate in more specialized networks, networks that did not always or regularly reach a broad audience of interested, feminist-influenced readers. *Ms.* magazine, one of the few mainstream voices of feminism, remained the exception.[49] Coverage of *The Dinner Party* in *Ms.* reached a range of readers who might not have picked up *Women's Art Journal* but who followed feminism in the popular press.

Published feminist responses to *The Dinner Party* addressed many of the same issues that concerned national and local media. But three issues appeared in feminist publications more than in these other outlets. The first involved evaluating Chicago's feminist politics in the studio and in the broader art world. Charges that Chicago exploited her studio volunteers first arose during the Q&A portion of a lecture at the San Francisco opening. Chicago later reported that she was stunned to hear the question.[50] While studio workers immediately refuted the charge, it nonetheless stuck, particularly among feminists.

Feminists also challenged the lack of diversity in the art of *The Dinner Party*. What became clear between 1979 and 1989 was that Chicago's vision, imagined in 1973 as inserting women into the traditional categories of Western civilization, was inadequate to the needs of a feminist movement committed to multiculturalism. The third point that feminists debated was the issue of essentialism. It became clear that women's biological sameness, or in Chicago's words, women's "central core," had ceased to be a politically viable signifier for feminism in the 1980s. Rather than promoting connections among various feminists, images of a universal female experience drove wedges between groups of women. The critical responses to multiculturalism and essentialism went hand in hand. White privileged women and their vaginas could no longer represent all women, over all time, over all nations, races, and religious differences. The white middle-class underpinnings of the category "woman" had been exposed, and there was no going back. Further, after 1976 the antipornography movement had successfully brought attention to the problematic hypersexualization of women's bodies across US culture, which added to many feminists' ambivalence about Chicago's vulva images as possibly too close to "woman-as-cunt" to be political useful.[51]

Other critics addressed issues of essentialism and multiculturalism as limits of *The Dinner Party*, but none more regularly than feminists. Criticism on this front had been reaching Chicago before the piece went public. In a 1978 interview with *Chrysalis*, a Los Angeles journal of women's culture, Chicago defended herself from the charge of Eurocentrism: "I set out to recast Western civilization from a female perspective. I'm sorry, folks, I did not set out to recast all of human civilization. I've been brought up in Western culture, and it's the art I understand, the images I understand, the history I know, the literature with which I'm familiar. I don't even know anything outside of Western civilization. People ask a lot of questions, why didn't I do this and why didn't I do that? I did *this*. I hope it has value." The artist worried that such attacks were attempts to diminish what she had accomplished and to provide another justification for marginalizing her work. "Instead of saying 'My God, I can't believe what you have done,' the work is belittled by saying 'Why haven't you done something else?'"[52]

In truth, Chicago could say little to defend herself from the charge. Feminist reviewers wanted more inclusive and more global representations of women than *The Dinner Party* offered. One journalist from Northampton, Massachusetts, made her political investment in feminism clear for her local paper in a review sardonically titled "It's Art! It's Feminism! It's 'The Dinner Party'!" She was dismayed that the place settings for the only two US women of color—abolitionist and suffragist Sojourner Truth and First American Sacajawea—lacked clearly demarcated vulva forms: "Sojourner Truth, the only black woman represented, is also the only woman symbolized by recognizable faces on her china painted plate. A weeping face, an African mask and angry face with upraised fist—these are clichés rather than reinterpretations of women's history. Some critics have insisted this is an expression of unconscious racism, coupled with the evidence that another exception to the standard circular image is the Native American woman Sacajawea."[53] Sacajawea, in fact, had a central core motif: a brightly colored eight-tipped star encompassed a blue circle, which was divided by a golden line. For this reviewer, however, Sacajawea's central core was not vaginal enough. And given that the central core image stood for "woman," its absence or near absence marked for her a serious omission.

The reviewer from Northampton was not the only feminist thinking that women of color were being shortchanged in terms of their central cores. African American womanist and writer Alice Walker reviewed *The Dinner Party* in San Francisco in 1979 for *Ms.* magazine. Walker mused on the seeming inability of white feminists to imagine that "black women have vaginas. Or if they can, where imagination leads them is too far to go." She observed that "Sojourner Truth certainly had a vagina, as noted her lament about her children, born of her body, but sold into slavery. Note her comment that when she cried out with a mother's grief, none but Jesus heard her. Surely a vagina has to be acknowledged when one reads these words."[54] Walker's criticism reverberated across the feminist print landscape, touching activists and nonactivists alike and becoming a touchstone for subsequent feminist reviews throughout the 1980s and 1990s.

Feminist reviewers addressed *The Dinner Party*'s challenge to the male-dominated art world and, according to many of them, the artist did not take her challenge far enough. Instead of Chicago the Woman and Chicago the Feminist facing off as they had in the mainstream press, here a split between Chicago the Feminist and Chicago the Artist emerged and cast doubt on her feminist credentials. A feminist writing for the *Village Voice* in 1979 highlighted Chicago's approach to "women's crafts" and china painters as a site of rupture in the artist's feminism: "On the one hand, Chicago is delighted that American women have kept the china-painting tradition alive; on the other, she is horrified that women have 'wasted their talents putting roses on plates.' Chicago the feminist wants to give the china painters their historic due. Chicago the artist is offended by the aesthetic of what they have done."[55]

A Canadian feminist, writing in the journal *Broadside*, accused Chicago of both wanting to challenge the art world and to win its approval.[56] Another, writing for *Sojourner*, found Chicago's own celebrity belittled the workers who labored on the piece alongside her. "And all we are told is 'this is The Dinner Party: Judy Chicago,' not about the women who volunteered, not the women whose names were eliminated, not the women whose lives were completely disregarded."[57] Lauren Rabinovitz, writing in *Woman's Art Journal*, also commented on the work's implied elevation of Chicago herself as a "great woman": "Chicago assumes that by creating *The Dinner Party* she becomes as exemplary as the women on whom the piece centers. Once she sets herself up as a role model, her artistic process redeems itself politically and becomes a central part of the project." The *atelier* tradition, justified by Chicago as a "cooperative activity uniting women" for Rabinovitz, failed by "emulating the social and art school practices that many feminists have fought."[58]

The criticism that Chicago was not feminist enough spilled across various topics, but none stuck to the artist or hurt her more than her rumored "exploitation" of the studio workers. Critical feminist reviews cast the workers alternately as exploited apprentices or as duped innocents who would do anything to work on a feminist art project. The first feminist coverage of the controversy over the volunteers appeared in *Chrysalis* in 1978. During the interview, Chicago, Susan Hill, and Diane Gelon described the studio processes.[59] Hill explained that, "People experience themselves in a whole new way in the studio environment. They see large chunks of work they have done and they feel good about it. They can experience themselves as strong, they can experience their opinions as valid—or have their misinformation exposed." Gelon spoke about the professionalism at the studio as "a model for the way women can work on a project together." Chicago spoke openly about the impact of the studio's work ethic on the workers: "You should see these women taking control of their lives, starting to discipline their lives, starting to exercise, starting to make a pattern, a day-to-day rhythm in their lives that will allow them to work, starting to structure their lives around work as opposed to structuring their work around their lives, whenever they have a few free minutes. . . . People have to change when they come to work on the project. If they don't change, they don't stay."[60]

Such sentiments did not sit well with all feminists. The explanations of support and personal transformation sounded to some like the portrait of a manipulative work environment dominated by an overbearing artist. Rumors of this circulated in West Coast feminist networks, where some had firsthand experience with the artist and her leadership style from CalArts, the Woman's Building, the Feminist Studio Workshop, or *The Dinner Party* studio. Some reviewers put into print unfounded rumors as well as their own disappointment with Chicago. Susan Minnicks, writing for *Sojourner*, argued that the contributions of the workers were lost under the "media event" fund-raising spirit of *The Dinner Party* and Chicago's egoism. In one of the strongest accusations in print, Minnick baldly stated, "I suggest here that 'The Dinner Party: Judy Chicago' has exploited women." She built her case through the notion of volunteerism as a form of dependency, akin to the roles women played at home and in conventional work settings. Minnicks wrote, "The volunteers extended their roles in the home to their activities in Chicago's studio. Chicago's journal entries testify that without their support and encouragement the piece would never have been completed. Yet working on *The Dinner Party* did little to build the self-esteem and employability of the volunteers. Although Chicago herself is internationally known, few of the women who produced the piece gained status." Volunteerism, she concludes, "too frequently teaches women to become more dependent rather than teaching them skills and encouraging them to be independent."[61] Clearly, for Minnicks, volunteers could never be full sisters.

Chicago supporters challenged the accusation of exploitation. For Susan Diehl, writing in the journal *Frontiers*, the feminist process at the studio and its impact on the hundreds of women who volunteered, positively shaped the meaning of the piece. Chicago took pains to display the names of all the people who worked on *The Dinner Party* as well as to document their labors, which never would have happened with apprentices of days gone by. "The acknowledgements and documentation showed photo after photo of women with their tools in their hands: tools—not babies or typewriters. A videotape (at the exhibit) pictured interviews with a number of people who were mainstays of the project. Each told a moving story of how she came to the project, why she stayed, and how it had transformed her." The exhibit's ability to bring women together—in the studio, at *The Dinner Party* table, and in line at the museum—constituted an important part of the feminist message to Diehl, becoming a spontaneous women's community as when she went to see the exhibit. "It began with the friendliness of the people in the waiting line. A common orientation overcame reserve: strangers who would have met under no other circumstances worked crossword puzzles together, bought each other programs, and talked."[62]

Feminists and feminist publications found themselves juggling these and other competing concerns in their reviews. What exactly constituted the feminism of *The Dinner Party*? The volunteers? The art? The history? The audience? The artist? As with all things feminist, evaluating the effectiveness of *The Dinner Party*'s feminism depended on how the speaker defined the notoriously complicated term. Ellen Willis, writing for the *Village Voice*, felt compelled to respond to Hilton Kramer's scathing *New York Times* review of *The Dinner Party* where he denounced the piece as "fixated on the external genital organs of the female body." Ironically, like Kramer, Willis also found Chicago's "cunt as dinner plate" problematic, but for very different reasons. For her the symbolism worked too closely with the simplistic sexist belief that "a woman's personality lies between her legs." After denouncing Kramer's "cunt phobia," Willis shifted the lens of her critique off the female body and on to *The Dinner Party* as both failed feminism and failed art. Chicago's swap of matriarchy for patriarchy equaled a confused feminism, according to Willis: "Since she believes that the source of women's oppression was the supplanting of mother-right for father-right, she sees women's struggle more in terms of 'reestablishing the feminine' than of breaking down the masculine-feminine polarity." As art, it was too polished; as a feminist statement, overly "sanitized"; as commentary, wholly without "irony and humor." She went on: "There are no cracks or chips in the dinner plates, no overturned goblets, no real recognition of the devastating human cost of feminine domesticity. . . . Myself, I would have put Lizzy Borden right up there at the table."[63]

Marilynn Woodsea, writing in the San Francisco feminist journal *Womanspirit*, also juggled competing reactions to the piece. She described feeling both "awed and disappointed" by *The Dinner Party*. "The disappointment came from feeling that this piece of art was not relevant to me. Everything was too perfect." Where were the gravy stains, she mused? Yet Woodsea also took issue with the hostile response of reviewers. She proposed that part of the critical ambivalence the piece called out of reviewers could be traced to a deep and unconscious ambivalence about the vagina and its connection to a "primitive" physicality. Woodsea wondered if audiences recoiled from seeing too much. In the same key that Alice Walker sounded for Sojourner Truth's (missing) vagina, Woodsea asked if maybe it was just too hard "to image that Susan B. Anthony had one under all those skirts?" Despite her ambivalence, Woodsea concluded that *The Dinner Party* did important work for feminism: "Where else in art accepted for mainstream consumption have we seen so many female sexual images presented by a woman, and without shame or covertness, and without relating that undiluted sexuality to men?"[64]

After reviewing *The Dinner Party* positively in 1979, *Frontiers* staged a second debate over its meaning for feminism in 1981, reflecting the growing complexity of the debate surrounding the piece. This time, the debate over the vaginal plates included feminists who viewed them as pornographic, a nod to the dovetailing authority of the antipornography and conservative movements. After laying out her liberal feminist credentials, reviewer Lolette Kuby explained that *The Dinner Party* "is profoundly misogynous. Traveling under the guise of an exaltation of the female principle, it is a reduction, once again, of women to vulvas and wombs, seedpods and plants, earth and nether-earth." Had a man or men created it, "women would rightfully have been infuriated. They would have boycotted and picketed." Worse, *The Dinner Party* "hoodwinked" women from their money by a cult of personality around the artist. All the money squandered on *The Dinner Party* could have gone to a true feminist cause: "In Houston, Boston, Brooklyn, Cleveland the huge expenditures of time and money which might have been utilized for supporting the Equal Rights Amendment, and correcting pervasive economic disparities were siphoned into *The Dinner Party*."[65] In short, according to Kuby, rather than staging an epic battle between the feminist artist and the male-controlled museum world, *The Dinner Party* singlehandedly stole feminism and killed the ERA.

Ann Marie Pois wrote a rebuttal. If *The Dinner Party* stole feminism, "why do women of diverse backgrounds, representing a variety of viewpoints, see the work in such great numbers when the reviews range from vaguely nasty and patronizing to outright condemnation?" Pois pointed to the disparity between published critical reviews and audiences who were willing to "defy" the critics to embrace the piece. She asked, "Why are women not behaving as the critics dictate? Has *The Dinner Party* stirred something in the lives of 'the masses'?"[66] Her answer: a resounding yes. That ability to speak directly to "the masses" surely had to matter to feminists.

Other feminist journals staged similar debates for their readers, a testimony to the divergent readings of *The Dinner Party* among self-identified feminists. In these debates, participants weighed in on the meaning of a changing feminist movement as it faced both loyal and disloyal opposition. How far could feminism expand beyond a unified sense of womanhood without splintering? What could hold a movement of women together? *Beacon*, a feminist journal in Cleveland, devoted an entire issue to *The Dinner Party* in 1981 and ran two side-by-side reviews by feminists, one positive and one negative. Two Cleveland area *Dinner Party* workers wrote the positive review: Dorothy Goodwill, who worked on *The Dinner Party* in Santa Monica, and Jeanne Van Atta, who helped organize the Cleveland show and whose mother, Bette Van Atta, was the oldest volunteer at *The Dinner Party* studio. A feminist art historian from the State University of New York at Binghamton, Eunice Lipton, wrote the negative review. The credentials of these two kinds of feminist voices—that of the volunteer worker and the expert—captured opening divides among Chicago's feminist audiences. Whereas the volunteers stressed *The Dinner Party*'s educational mission and effective emotional impact, the expert responded to Chicago's vision of feminism, the female body, and the didactic imposition of its message on the viewer.

Lipton's negative review repeated familiar complaints. First, she found the "religious aura" to be intimidating and controlling: "We are silently directed to tip-toe around. The format directs us." The monumentality insists upon "obeisance" from the viewer, a stance Lipton viewed as completely at odds with its feminism. "Why the reverence, the awe, the overwhelming ambience of authority at *The Dinner Party*? Walk this way, not that! Whisper! Admire! Believe! Where is the invocation to question, to explore, to disagree? To be bad girls, not obedient good girls?" Its essentialism offended Lipton by placing too much attention on admiring "the oldest and most conservative vision of what women are: reproductive organs." She paraphrased what she saw as the exhibit's true message: "Margaret Sanger an inflamed vagina; Virginia Woolf a pea-pod-in-cabbage-leaf vagina; Emily Dickinson, a pink-lace vagina." For these reasons, she concluded that "*The Dinner Party* pays monumental homage to the status quo. Power and women remained male defined."[67]

Whereas Lipton diagnosed *The Dinner Party* as suffering "from the ills of both high art and the worst sectarian politics"—having "no sense of humor"—Goodwill and Van Atta emphasized the ways the information "moved" and "inspired" people.[68] Van Atta explained that *The Dinner Party* had become a literal space of transformation for women akin to other women-centered places, like the Rape Crisis Center she worked in. "I felt that our goals were the same—to build a kind of respect and reverence for women, women's achievements, women's bodies and minds, to create a safe space for women." That space helped women who might have had little contact with women's groups a glimpse of something else. And therein lay *The Dinner Party*'s significance to feminism. "I've talked to people who witnessed women seeing it for the first time who had no background or understanding and it was almost like some kind of religious, apocalyptic experience for them. It's almost like seeing yourself in the mirror for the first time—you've had some kind of awakening process. Women see it and all of a sudden they wake up and say 'I haven't had my history before; I haven't seen art work that viewed things through a female vision.'" Goodwill took a different angle on the feminist meaning of *The Dinner Party*. As a needleworker, she valued that Chicago elevated the "craft" of embroidery by utilizing it in a museum-quality work of art. She also valued the ways

Chicago opened up the process of art making: "Judy's trying to show that art isn't something that's made by an isolated person in some little studio somewhere. She's opening up the process so people can share in the making of it." Lastly, she found the history *The Dinner Party* commemorated to be absolutely central to the power of the piece: "*The Dinner Party* is saying, 'Look at the history we have found that none of us knew. Look at all these people who did important things. How come we didn't know about them before?'"[69]

Stressing the transformative encounter with the ideas of feminism, Van Atta and Goodwill spoke to the emotional and personal impact *The Dinner Party* had on many who saw it. They claimed the right to speak as feminists and to speak back to feminist critics. Lucy Lippard agreed in her 1980 review in *Art in America*, the most sympathetic review of *The Dinner Party* to appear in a major art journal. Lippard addressed the art world's rejection of the piece as too popular, while also offering a spirited counter-argument to feminist critics. To the art world, she wrote, "the capacity actually to *move* an audience through real and specific feelings is denigrated as crude, sentimental and crowd-pleasing by that part of the art establishment that considers an emotionally affective audience as escaping art's proper sphere of influence. (Because if a 'crowd' knows something about what it likes, the control of 'high art' begins to slip away from those who like to *tell* people what to like.) As a political force, Chicago has appeared all the more dangerous in the last six years, since she actively began to encourage male participation in her work."

Chicago's "dangerous" potential to shatter the chronic conflation of feminism with separatism meant, by extension, that her art spoke to male audiences and could not be contained or dismissed as subcultural. To feminist critics of Chicago, Lippard argued that *The Dinner Party* satisfied a "deep cultural hunger" in women for affirming symbols. Lippard defended the feminist spirit of Chicago's Santa Monica studio by accounting for the work process Chicago established: "*The Dinner Party* is unique in having as one of its immediate goals the education and training of women to take command—not only of the project, but, by extension, of their own work and lives." She took note of Alice Walker's criticism of the Sojourner Truth plate. But according to Lippard, Walker missed the true intention of the plate, which showed the strategy of dissemblance by representing Truth's central core as multiple, preserving "hidden feelings" as a way to survive brutal enslavement. This defense did not address the deeper issue of multicultural representation or Walker's point that singling out Sojourner Truth reenacted racialist systems of differentiation. However, in her role as feminist art critic, Lippard foremost defended the ability of *The Dinner Party* to move viewers: "The whole Dinner Party experience, difficult as it has been, has only affirmed [Chicago's] belief that 'art can affect culture.'"[70]

Affecting culture by emotionally engaging individual women, powerful as it was, ultimately could not justify the problematic aspects of *The Dinner Party*. And herein lay a major source of rupture among women who gathered in an imagined community under the banner of "feminism." Writing in 1995, feminist art historian Hilary Robinson recalled the importance of the debate over *The Dinner Party* to feminists as they moved toward rethinking the basis of feminist solidarity. "The debate it engendered amongst feminists clarified the problems of suggesting an essential womanliness through visual representation. Vulva-as-symbol in Chicago's work was reductive of womankind as a category, and of the individual. Although consistent symbolic use of the vulva implied a universality and all-embracing inclusiveness, *The Dinner Party* in fact repeated old exclusions." Primary among the exclusions were nonwhite women, economically disadvantaged women, and women from the global south and east. Robinson wryly noted that, at *The Dinner Party*, "some women, it seemed, were less essential than others."[71]

The fork in the road of feminist unity represented by *The Dinner Party* divided participants along lines that would become one of the hallmarks of US feminism in the 1980s. On one side of the debate were feminists who saw the primary goal of feminism to be dismantling oppressive power structures, including the pernicious blending of racism, sexism, and gender privilege. On the other side were feminists who found the imagined community of "women" to be powerful enough to hold on to, even as divides among women became more pressing. For these feminists, lesbian and straight, brown, white, and black-skinned women, rich and poor women could change the world if they acted—at key moments—as women. Many of the women who viewed *The Dinner Party* in this way—as transformative and generative—wrote to the artist to share what it meant to them but did not participate in the public debate over the work. They did, however, respond to some of the media coverage of feminism, Chicago, and *The Dinner Party*.

Fan Letters and Comment Books

I was a special guest at this fabulous dinner party.

As debates over *The Dinner Party* rolled on in the print media throughout the 1980s, a steady stream of fan mail arrived at the offices of Through the Flower from people who had seen the exhibit and felt moved enough to write the artist. The majority of these letters praised Chicago for her efforts and shared the ways in which the piece spoke to them. These letters offered a glimpse into the reasons *The Dinner Party* became meaningful to viewers. Comment books from community shows offered a different way to track the public response to the feminist blockbuster. These reactions, penned immediately upon exiting the show, vividly testify to which parts of Chicago's message landed and which did not for those motivated enough to write. Fan letters and the comment books from Boston and Cleveland revealed a public versed with the debates and controversies in the published reaction to *The Dinner Party*. Concerns with multiculturalism, essentialism, its feminist message, and *The Dinner Party*'s status as art regularly appeared in letters and comment books. At the same time, both offered testimonies about the power of the art to effect emotional and feminist insight in the viewer, an aspect few published critics valued.

Fan letters and comment books underscore the reach of cultural feminism in the 1980s as audiences engaged in a lively public debate about the best way to represent women. This question was not new for feminist activists, artists, or cultural producers. But by the 1980s a new urgency had entered the debate. In the age of growing conservatism from the right and new commitments to multiculturalism on the left, the question became whether feminism could move beyond its founding notion of an imagined collective of (white) sisters toward a set of shared goals and political objectives. Viewers addressed the issues of feminist unity, multiculturalism, and essentialism, and their responses markedly diverged from those in the published record. The majority of comments and letters were far more positive than published critics about *The Dinner Party*'s ability to function as an ambassador for feminism in the 1980s.

The letters, on whole, tended to be positive and enthusiastic about the art and the artist. Fan letters arrived immediately after the San Francisco opening in 1979 and after every subsequent *Dinner Party* showing. For example, Judy Grosfield from Seattle wrote that when she heard that the Seattle Art Museum had canceled its scheduled showing, she and a friend took a bus to San Francisco. "We rode the bus all night, finished reading *Through the Flower*, we waited in line five hours on the last day of the exhibit and we were totally moved by its power. I cried when I finally stood inside the door and sensed its sacredness and beauty."[72] A woman from Houston described seeing it with her nine-year-old daughter as a "very emotional, almost religious, experience"; Amy Drinker from Boston wrote to say how pleased she was to see her grandmother, Sophie Drinker, a historian of women who worked with Mary Beard, commemorated on the Heritage Floor.[73] Most of the fan letters, like the one from Liz, offered praise and unqualified endorsement of *The Dinner Party*. Donna Anthony explained she felt "awed, speechless *and* terrifically *elevated* at experiencing this work of art." "The historical research alone is so educational, but the tribute to women is so direct, so right straight to the heart that I felt I had something to do with it! I felt proud to be a woman. I felt enriched. Thank you so much for this wonderful act of beauty and creation. We need it, we women!"[74]

The telling move in this letter from "women" to "we women" testified to the ability of the piece to bring viewers into the imagined category of "woman" and by extension, into being a feminist subject. That *The Dinner Party* could speak "straight to the heart" reverberated across the letters. Descriptions regularly included phrases that blur the visual and emotional: "stunned and later sparked," "overwhelmed—moved—inspired," "enthralled and entranced," "wonderfully tearful," "beautiful and brilliantly executed," and "strengthened."[75] Others wrote to share the feeling that seeing *The Dinner Party* changed them: "I recently had the privilege of viewing *The Dinner Party* and I'm certain that I will never again be the same person who entered the museum"; "It gave me chills and inspiration."[76] These emotional descriptions of the experience of seeing *The Dinner Party* reflected many women's sense of personal connection to the piece.

The excerpts of Chicago's diary recording her highs and lows included in "*The Dinner Party*" book and her frankness in interviews encouraged many to feel personally connected to the artist. Liz Adelinau from Brooklyn wrote of wanting to speak with Chicago: "After seeing *The Dinner Party* and reading the book, I was, at the same time, so emotionally drained, overwhelmed, excited, and happy about many of the implications reflected in your work and your writing, that I had to put this all down on paper for myself. . . . There are so many aspects of *The Dinner Party* that I would like to talk about but can't really straighten out in my mind. I hope that one day we will meet and be able to talk."[77] Chicago's emphasis on her own personal transformation hailed viewers to the therapeutics of feminist change, making intimate what might otherwise have felt distant and abstract. Pamela Joy Roper wrote, "You and Virginia Wolfe [*sic*] and my women friends have been important in waking me up to myself. I want to thank you for trying so hard and hope that letters of appreciation such as this one help sometimes where your energy is low."[78] Kathleen Martin wrote to say that, "your honest account of these and other feelings helped me identify their source and attempt your solution—move forward. . . . The support I received from your sharing helped me go forward. Thank you."[79]

Letters noted that the exhibit functioned as a space apart and, as such, became a valuable pause in their otherwise full lives. A woman who saw the show in Cleveland with her forty-nine-year-old daughter wrote about her experience of being in a space set apart from ordinary time: "We went to the Exhibit, rented a tape cassette, with dual earphones so we had the closeness of a mechanical umbilical cord as we walked slowly around the Table. We paused often (shutting off the machine) and enjoyed a good communication interchange about the display. It was a long, remembered afternoon—your Project being the focus of our unique togetherness."[80]

Fans shared the various ways they had found their way to the exhibit; many said they did so by the consumer elements of "Judy Chicago & Co." that so annoyed critics: "Your three books—*Through the Flower*, *"The Dinner Party,"* and *Embroidering Our Heritage* have deeply influenced and encouraged me."[81] Kathleen Martin explained that, "When I saw the book I grabbed it immediately as the next best thing to being there."[82] *Through the Flower*, Chicago's first memoir, also spoke to many women artists who still felt marginal and isolated in the art world. One woman wrote that, in 1980, she had still never seen any example of "women's art": "When I read your book and saw your art—it was like a revelation—you see I never knew I was expressing from my woman-ness, my experiences as a woman! I kept yearning for certain images, sensuous shapes, undulating and layered shells. . . . All of this was coming out of me subconsciously—I never knew why until now. I feel like I have discovered that I'm a cell in a larger organism—one I never knew existed." Another woman also expressed that she felt she had found a deep connection to other women through reading about Chicago's artistic struggles. "I can't even begin to express to you how I feel after reading this book. I cried in so many places to see in print the way I feel. Your book has enlightened me, moved me, touched me like I have never experienced. . . . It's like finding a sister I never knew I had."[83]

Fandom based on emotional identification, in this case between the feminist artist-author and the reader, became a way for a woman without a feminist context to imagine a way into a feminist identity.

The letters documented the impact of steady media coverage on drawing people to the exhibit. Some came after seeing a piece on *The Dinner Party* on television: "I had seen the film of *The Dinner Party* on Public TV and had become very excited by the concept—both artistically and philosophically. The courage, the overcoming of artistic, technical, and emotional difficulties, the sheer size and scope of the project was electrifying. I knew at the time, that I would have to see The Dinner Party in person."[84] Another wrote to say she had seen Chicago on the CBS evening news. "It was a wonderful contrast to the almost totally male dominated point of view seen on tv. Thank you for planting the seeds of hope and feminism in the minds of all the women watching; as well as all the people who see The Dinner Party."[85] Another wrote that, "I fell in love with the concept and tiny bit of *The Dinner Party* visible in *Ms.* Magazine and have felt cheated at the reluctance of museums to give it proper circulation."[86]

Fans regularly complained about the museum world's lack of support for *The Dinner Party*. A woman from Racine, Wisconsin, visiting Boston, wrote to tell Chicago that she had to choose between walking the city's homage to its early history, the Freedom Trail, or *The Dinner Party*, since the latter was not scheduled to show anywhere near her home. She picked *The Dinner Party*. "My conscious and understanding of feminism and the power of being a woman-identified woman has been an exciting process over the past few years, and I want to tell you of the part your work and books have played in that process."[87] Many, having read about the collapsed museum tour, implored the artist to keep showing it. "What a glorious history of women we have! . . . Please try to keep showing *The Dinner Party* no matter what the established art community thinks!"[88]

Critical letters arrived, as well. Some posed questions for the artist, like Margaret Loewen Reimer from Toronto, who wondered why the Virgin Mary wasn't seated at the table.[89] Another woman felt cheated that the audiotape cost extra: "I liked *The Dinner Party*," she wrote, "but I feel there are very few people who can understand [it] without purchasing the tapes. Thus the [ticket] price of $3 is deceptive because it does not include the guided tour. I resent this extra charge for tapes."[90] William Wing, a visiting professor of physics at MIT, complained of Chicago's essentialism: "As either feminine or feminist statements, your works up to now have really a very narrow view of women, rooted entirely as they are in reproductive-system imagery. The same works done by a man would likely be taken as blatantly biased and stereotypic, in effect reducing women to sexual parodies."[91]

A woman from Houston baldly wrote "For shame, Judy Chicago!" She found Chicago's choice of women to honor outrageous: "Folks like Florence Nightingale were delegated to a place on the floor while the first woman to live only as a lesbian sat at the table. . . . If Flo was invited to your Dinner Party, she would surely have declined the invitation."[92] A number of letters criticize the artist for not including more women of color or women from around the world. A woman from Boston wrote to complain about the Sojourner Truth plate: "I don't understand how, with all the research that was done, anyone could have painted Sojourner Truth *yellow*! Don't you know that 'yellow' is one of the worst insults a black person can hurl at another black person? I also didn't like hers being the only plate with a woman's face on it rather than the motif used throughout."[93] Another viewer from Boston complained of the piece's lack of diversity: "What I noticed was no Japanese, Chinese or 'oriental' women represented on the heritage floor or on the places. Did your researchers find no women who contributed to our world from that part of our planet????"[94]

While writers of letters, on whole, addressed themselves to the artist and tended to offer praise and support, comments from community books, in contrast, were not always framed as a dialogue with the artist, and as such, offered a different glimpse into the public's reaction to the art and message of *The Dinner Party*. Comments, like fan letters, were overwhelmingly positive. Yet comments also reflected issues raised in the print responses, including wholesale rejection of the art and the feminism on display.

Like the letters, comment books from community shows vividly testified to the impact the piece had on viewers. The bulk of reviews from Boston were positive:

> Through woman energy like this someday there will be an Amazon nation again.
>
> The greatest work of our time.
>
> Made me proud to be a womyn.
>
> Thank you, Judy. It was one of the most meaningful experiences of my life, to savor this beautifully powerful statement about women.—Karen Scott.[95]

Cleveland visitors also praised the piece:

> This is absolutely the biggest EVENT of all women's history.
>
> Absolutely, positively stupendous—from a person who rarely uses superlatives.
>
> What a terrific experience and it was so much more wonderful to see it with my mom. What a marvelous contribution to the women's movement—keep helping us (all women) come together.
>
> As I walked down the corridor to the dinner party I felt goose bumps all over—as though I was a special guest at this fabulous dinner party. This project was most definitely a work of beauty and emotion. I also felt very proud to be a woman.[96]

As with letters, many comments demonstrated viewers' familiarity with the controversies that surrounded the piece. A viewer from Cleveland wrote, "I have to disagree with those who argue that this is not 'art.' I'm sorry for them." Another, sarcastically, "Congrats Judy Chicago for a didactic work of art." One Cleveland viewer addressed her concern that the time had expired for symbolizing women through their bodies. "I do think there is a change in portraying women as the mystic center of life, the womb, the earth and mother goddesses—I don't want to be mystified any longer. Presenting as a mystique, as incomprehensible beings has only reinforced our otherness." Another asked, "Are vaginal images an effort at getting even with phallic representations throughout the history of art? Is that a good way to represent women's power?" One woman suggested that the images of volunteers at the studio are the most effective representation of feminism offered at the exhibit: "I couldn't help thinking that I saw more life and inspiration in the photos of women (and men) working together than in *The Dinner Party* itself. For me, the main exhibit was a little too hushed, reverent, and static. Still, I like seeing the celebration of women's achievements. How about more black and Hispanic women—more 20th century activist women?"[97]

Some brought fully formed opinions about Chicago the celebrity artist to their viewing. "The beauty and genius of the work transcends the personality of the creator," wrote one viewer from Cleveland. Another, that "It's depressing that such a wonderful concept was executed by Judy Chicago"[98]

Viewers also regularly used the comment books to vent their general response to feminism, sometimes humorously, and sometimes with the same hostility reflected in the critical print reviews:

Stop the ERA!

Less bitching about patriarchy on the tape . . .[99]

I've decided to go ahead with the sex change.

Too many vaginas. Let's see some penises.[100]

While demonstrating their general awareness of published debates over the exhibit, comments also spoke to specific controversies, such as the issue of volunteer labor. Some had heard that Chicago had exploited volunteers and came to the exhibit with serious questions about Chicago's ethics. Others found inspiration from the story of women's volunteer efforts:

> Powerful Wow, I've been watching and waiting for *The Dinner Party* to come to the East Coast and now it is here!!! I questioned the working system—all those people working so hard and only Chicago's name being attached to it—but now I don't know. The results are amazing! The piece is vibrant, wonderful consoling and very encouraging.

> I think I was more moved by the exploration of the group effort than I was by the actual piece . . . I love the idea and I love the vision and the fact that it involved such a group effort.

> Chicago's apparent dominance cannot take away one iota of the skills, confidence, sense of camaraderie and sense of achievement experienced and gained by those who worked on the piece and those who brought it here.[101]

As in the published record, viewers responded positively to the community of women gathered at Chicago's Santa Monica studio. That effort, prominently displayed at the exhibit, communicated the power of women gathered together in a common purpose. Yet Chicago's unabashed leadership over the volunteers and her aesthetic control over the piece did not easily mesh with some viewers' desire for egalitarian collectivity and a longing for a less individualistic model of artistic accomplishment.

A number of comments in both cities criticized the piece for its limited representation of non-European women. These comments, twelve out of approximately four hundred in Boston and sixteen out of nearly nineteen hundred in Cleveland, chart the cultural inroads made by multiculturalism. Like the published feminist responses, comments reflected the reality that, for many viewers, evaluating *The Dinner Party* became a game of Twister, trying to point out what it did and didn't do for feminism.

I feel an immense gratitude for such an aesthetic and historically dignified piece. Truly womyn's work in all its glory (and sweat . . .) I think that it is also *very* important to clear up another myth—this isn't a vision of womyn in western civilization: it *is* a vision of *white* womyn in western civilization. I think it is essential to be honest about the strong racist limitations as well as worth of such a landmark piece.

The tapestry and ceramics are beautiful. I have never been so impressed by artisan talent but . . . this exhibit is so racist by omission. To present a study of women since the beginning of time and include only an incomplete take is racially insensitive and shocking. . . . The racism of this exhibit makes me feel ashamed to be white far more than it inspires me as a woman.—P. Sharp, Montclair NJ [includes her address][102]

A masterpiece, of course, but why no Chinese?

As a young black woman the significance of The Dinner Party is profound; it offers a community of women all joined together overcoming all barriers. I hope we can all achieve the goals she has set forth. Most profound and fascinating.

I believe that women of color were not represented as they should have been. It was essentially a white woman's experience of our history. Despite that the power of what you have shown us is shattering: hopefully a shattering of the oppressing with in and outside of ourselves.[103]

Some felt that the racial exclusions severely constrained its message and by extension, its ability to speak for all women.

Almost a conceit of white folks.

I am an African American woman and also on that score I wish that the Sojourner Truth plate had had more in common with the others.[104]

How can you include Anthony and not Tubman, Chisholm, McLeod? How include Dickinson and not the wonderful artists of Afro American tradition such as Bessie Smith and Billy Holiday? It is this sort of feminism which excludes so many women from the American women's movement.[105]

A boring stupid and racist hustle.

You forgot Angela Davis.[106]

A Cleveland viewer asked pointed questions about Alice Walker's criticism of *The Dinner Party*: "I am still waiting to hear Judy Chicago's response to Alice Walker's article, . . . 'Child of One's Own,' published in the August 1979 issue of *Ms.* Magazine." "As far as I am concerned, the inability to carry through with the theme of the flower i.e. female sexuality clearly displays the lack of sensitivity and consequently the non-acceptance of black women as women. Once again—black women find themselves alienated from the heritage which 'The Dinner Party' so dearly wanted to proclaim."[107]

Spontaneous debates over race broke out in both comment books. In Cleveland, the Ohio Black Women's Leadership Caucus extolled the piece as a "Fantastic idea!" Shortly after, another asked, "but why are all the women except for Sojourner Truth and Sacagawea white?" "Because it's western civ!" responded the next viewer.[108] In Boston a set of dialogic comments began with a few scathingly ironic notes.

> Hurray! The great white way revealed *again* and *again*.
>
> I love the many, many Third world women you've represented here. This is truly an international history with *one* Indian name, *no* African names, *no* moslem [*sic*] names and *no* Japanese or Chinese names. The gold distracts from some of those really beautiful plates and goblets are gross. This is a good idea but not a great idea and it is *very incomplete*.[109]

Following on the heels of these two comments, another viewer defended *The Dinner Party*: "Yes, it has its flaws—no one can deny that. But it is a start, isn't it." "After so many years of history writing us out, there has to be a beginning and I think that this is a great beginning. I would shudder at the thought of this as an end. . . . So the critics may dismiss this and say 'incorrect, incomplete.' Ok, don't leave it there then—correct it, complete it. Show your side, their side. And I do think that, though flawed in execution, it *is* a great idea—and a moving show."[110]

While proportionately small (approximately less than 10 percent of the overall comments), such critiques of *The Dinner Party*'s Eurocentric focus show that many viewers hoped to see a different face for their feminism. If *The Dinner Party* was committed to showing women's history, then the women seated had to reflect the realities of the actual class of women—diverse, dispersed, and too many still outside of history. Commentators did not announce their political leanings or identify themselves as feminists. Yet their concerns reflect the views of some published feminists, and show a viewing public versed in the shifting trends of feminist thought.

Debates over the meaning of the vaginal imagery appeared in the Cleveland comment book more than in the Boston comment book. Comments reflected both feminist and antifeminist views. Approximately 5 percent of the Cleveland comments singled out the central core as inadequate for representing women.[111] Some viewers simply hated the images.

> Vile, corrupt all those vaginal orifices, disgusting.
>
> I agree!
>
> So do I!!
>
> I'm glad I came the hundred miles but I was very disappointed in some of the plates. . . . We all have vaginas; that is not the only important thing about us.[112]

Others sparred over whether the vaginal plates challenged or confirmed the legacy of sexist imagery. These two comments appeared one after another:

> I thought much of the work is beautiful, but I can't help but feel that the centrality to the near exclusion of all else of the vaginal imagery, is an echo of the same type of stereotyping feminism rightly seeks to combat.
>
> Wrong. The vaginal imagery is not portrayed "to the near exclusion of all else." You are obviously threatened/bothered by it, or else merely dense; you are so obviously blind to the unbelievable richness and variety of images and iconography.[113]

Like the critics, viewers appeared to be obsessed with the meaning of the plates' vaginal symbolism. No other aspect of *The Dinner Party* was commented upon as thoroughly:

> The butterfly motif seems as a representation of the female genitalia which seems an inconsistent imagery for a work to celebrate the whole of women's achievements and struggles. Although I appreciate the work and thoughts behind The Dinner Party, I feel belittled.
>
> A woman's genitals are not necessarily sexual—why not go beyond and see them as a representation of our commonalities? Or life bearing abilities.[114]
>
> The redundant vagina imagery leaves me bewildered, overworked unjustifiably. . . . an exclusive jeer at humanity.
>
> Employing the use of the female sexual organs in the plates will only encourage the view of women as a sex object—I object to it.
>
> I am a little disturbed by the overwhelming image of "woman as cunt" . . . if Henry Miller or Norman Mailer had pictured us so we'd have been infuriated (and rightly so).[115]

> Very interesting. A lot of effort. Homosexuality is an abomination in the sight of the Lord. God Bless You.[116]

The fact that viewers, published and unpublished, felt compelled to comment as much as they did on the plates testified to the lack of nonsexualized images of women's bodies in art and in culture more broadly. The plates shocked and delighted viewers because the image of "woman" it offered neither sexually objectified women nor extolled them for their maternity. The vulva symbolism of the plates cast off the two reigning visual paradigms for women and offered a frankly feminist representation of women's essential difference as the basis for their essential ontological autonomy. Without doubt, they presented audiences with an opportunity for combustible conversation.

Despite the concerns over the display of female bodies and the racial exclusions of *The Dinner Party*, the majority of letters to the artist and comments from community shows praised the piece, primarily because of the information about women's history and (to them) the lost record of accomplishment. A resounding theme of public comments and letters was "pride": a new sense of pride in the history of women, in themselves as women, in the successful struggle to get *The Dinner Party* seen. Over and over again, audiences reported being moved by what they learned in viewing *The Dinner Party*. As public testimony demonstrated, aspects of Chicago's feminist vision went "straight to the heart" of many viewers, and they valued exactly that about it.

The emotional impact of feminist-themed culture like *The Dinner Party* offered viewers a specific kind of feminist theory, one that did not necessarily match with the fast-moving evolution of US feminist thought in the 1980s. First, that women's history mattered and should be integrated into the longer record of (European) accomplishment. Second, that some women had enjoyed a form of authority in premodern institutions in which contemporary women now struggled to be included. Third, that women's bodies had been discredited as symbols for either divinity or humanity. The vagina—as an idea and a body part—incited such fear and loathing that using the vulva as a symbol triggered a flood of hostility. That hostility became part of the lesson of viewing *The Dinner Party*. It exposed viewers to the underlying assumptions of patriarchy: that men and masculinity constituted the unbiased representation of humanity, the evaluation for all historical significance and the measure of creativity.

While feminist theorists generated new approaches to dismantling the production of gender as a system of oppressive binaries and renewed their commitment to intersectional identities, consumers of feminist-themed culture flocked to affirmations of their difference and their value as women. *The Dinner Party* joined a range of new feminist-themed cultural products available in the 1980s and 1990s that offered accounts of women that blended their belief in women's difference from men while still advancing the basic feminist call for greater equality between the sexes. The basis for equality, in much of popular feminism, rested squarely on difference.

As feminist thought multiplied and new tensions opened up between professional feminists and consumers, other culture wars brewed. *The Dinner Party* success in the 1980s essentially made it an unelected representative of radical feminist "cunt art," whether or not Chicago's peers supported the art or the artist. As such, in the summer of 1990, it was swept into congressional debates over funding of the arts, specifically of art that an activist conservative movement deemed "obscene."

CHAPTER EIGHT

From Controversy to Canonization

The Dinner Party *in the Culture Wars, 1990–2007*

AFTER THE BROOKLYN MUSEUM OPENING, *The Dinner Party* moved to Chicago, Cleveland, and Atlanta for community shows, and then abroad. Three Canadian museums showed it in 1982 and 1983; huge crowds turned out and made the venues significant and (somehow still) unexpected profits. The international tour became an unbridled success, opening to enthusiastic reviews at the Fringe during the Festival in Edinburgh, the Warehouse in London, and at the contemporary art museum, Schirn Kunsthalle, in Frankfurt, Germany, where the showing was accompanied by a gala women's festival at the city's newly renovated opera house.[1] The final museum show in the tour took place at the Royal Exhibition Center in Melbourne, Australia, in 1988. All told, *The Dinner Party* opened fourteen shows in six countries. Over a million people came to see it. Between 1979 and 1989, an average of 775 people viewed it each day it was on display.[2] At a $4 admissions fee, *The Dinner Party* generated money throughout its tour; when coupled with the audio tour and tie-in products, estimates of *The Dinner Party*'s potential revenue stream to a host institution reached an impressive $1,652,000 annually.[3]

These tangible markers of *The Dinner Party*'s economic heft came into sharp focus as the decade and the tour came to a close. After such extensive touring, Chicago—in consultation with Susan Hill, Peter Bunzick, and others who installed and broke down the piece everywhere it traveled—decided that the piece was showing signs of wear and tear. The time had come to find a permanent home for *The Dinner Party*. Eighteen years later, in 2007, *The Dinner Party* found just that—an institutional, safe, prestigious, and permanent home at the Brooklyn Museum. The journey to Brooklyn was not easy; as ever, the path veered between controversies and neglect, with sudden bursts of national media coverage followed by years of silence as the work stayed crated. The nearly twenty years between the end of the tour and the permanent opening in 2007 inexorably moved *The Dinner Party* into history, a place that proved far more welcoming and restorative to Chicago's initial animating vision than the rough road to get there.

Three historical developments converged in the 1990s to change the reception of *The Dinner Party*. The first unfolded in Washington, DC, where congressional debates over funding for the arts doomed Chicago's efforts to gift the piece to the University of the District of Columbia. Congressional debates in 1990 over whether Chicago's vulva plates constituted "3-D ceramic pornography" followed on the heels of two more widely covered congressional attacks on "obscene" art by Robert Mapplethorpe and Andres Serrano in 1989. This bruising chapter of *The Dinner Party*'s history was a particularly difficult way to end its tour. The piece went into storage with no clear plan of how to return it to display.

The second development that contributed to *The Dinner Party* being recast as a relic of "history" was the rise of postmodernism in feminist art theory. This new form of feminist theory offered a sophisticated critique of the pitfalls of essentialism and specifically the limits of Chicago's 1970s-style feminism. This shift came into sharp focus at a 1996 conference, *Sexual Politics: Judy Chicago's "Dinner Party" in Feminist Art History*, which displayed *The Dinner Party* for six weeks in a show designed to evaluate its place in the ongoing feminist art movement. The conference solidified a new set of oppositions in the viewing of *The Dinner Party*—postmodernism/feminism, gender/woman, performativity/embodiment—that added to the work's status as a relic, falling as it (chronically) did on the less-valued side of the feminist binary. Together with the University of the District of Columbia scandal, postmodern feminist art theory deepened *The Dinner Party*'s invisibility and the perception of its irrelevance.

The third and final element that altered the reception of *The Dinner Party* was the steady growth of feminist-themed popular culture in the 1980s and 1990s. This development proved advantageous for a generational reviewing of *The Dinner Party*. Take, for instance, the growth of woman-centered theater starting with Ntozake Shange, *For Colored Girls Who Have Contemplated Suicide When the Rainbow Is Enuf* (1975), followed by the one-woman stage show written by Jane Wagner and performed by Lily Tomlin, *The Search for Signs of Intelligent Life in the Universe* (1986), and ten years later Eve Ensler's 1996 *The Vagina Monologues* (HBO 1998). In these years, feminist-themed movies appeared with regularity, including Alice Walker's crossover blockbuster novel, *The Color Purple* (1982), made into a film by Stephen Spielberg in 1985. Other popular films include *An Unmarried Woman* (1978), *Kramer vs. Kramer* (1979), *Nine to Five* (1980), *Tootsie* (1982), and *Thelma and Louise* (1991), but these marked only a fraction of new quasi-feminist films available to interested viewers.

Other crossover texts generated a distinctive array of popular feminist culture, most centrally, the chick literature-film-cable hybrid phenomena of the 1990s like Helen Fielding's *Bridget Jones's Diary* (1996, 2001) and Candice Bushnell's *Sex and the City* (1997, HBO 1998–2004, 2008, 2010). Both updated feminist themes for a postfeminist television audience. These cultural products, which narrated feminism in a different way than did feminist theorists and art historians, offered audiences a way into the insights of feminism apart from activism or gender theory. Cultural consumption of feminist-themed products spread the good news of women's equality without mandating any difficult social change. With its less revolutionary but far more comfortable offerings, popular feminism welcomed a diverse array of viewers into its fold and, in doing so, provided a new platform from which to view *The Dinner Party*.

Together, then, the competing frameworks imposed on *The Dinner Party* by different constituencies in the 1990s set the conditions for it to play a central role in the full-scale canonization of the feminist art movement by the 2000s. In other words, after years of marginalization, *The Dinner Party*'s status as "history" finally helped it win a place in the museum world, something Chicago had wanted since first conceiving of *The Dinner Party*. In a 1975 excerpt from her personal journal, Chicago writes of wanting to make a work of such importance that it "will enter the cultural pool and never be erased from history."[4] By 2007, there was no denying that *The Dinner Party* was here to stay.

A Gift, Scorned

Yes, Virginia, vaginas.

The path to finding a permanent home began in earnest in the spring of 1990 when Pat Mathis, a longtime Chicago supporter, former assistant secretary of the treasury under President Carter, and a board member of the University of the District of Columbia (UDC) in Washington, DC, approached

Chicago about establishing a permanent exhibit space for *The Dinner Party*.[5] By early summer, Chicago had determined to gift *The Dinner Party* to the underfunded, working-class, predominantly African American university as part of its newly proposed multicultural arts center. Parties on both sides expressed their enthusiasm for what appeared to be a money-making proposition for the UDC and, for the artist, a much-valued context for *The Dinner Party* that would highlight the common plight of the disadvantaged. Yet, in what now seems all together too familiar in the cultural history of *The Dinner Party*, within months of the announcement, Chicago found herself at the center of a new firestorm of controversy. After eight weeks of a vicious misinformation campaign by conservatives countered by vigorous lobbying by Chicago supporters, the artist abandoned the donation arrangements. Chicago's vulva plates, once the symbol of radical feminist empowerment, had became entangled in the culture wars over the meaning of *pornography* and *obscenity*, two words that a decade of feminist and then conservative activism had established as viable political concerns. The wave of hostility against *The Dinner Party* in the summer and fall of 1990 resulted in the almost complete disappearance of *The Dinner Party* from the art scene.

A brief and unremarkable article on July 21, 1990, in the *New York Times* had announced Judy Chicago's donation of *The Dinner Party* to the UDC in a ceremony that took place the day prior. Quoting the chair of the UDC Board of Trustees, Nira Hardon Long, the newspaper reported that the university was delighted at the donation, valued at $2 million, as a crucial inauguration for the campus's new multicultural arts center. "This will serve as the beginning of the university as a multicultural center for the expression of creative ideas for dealing with human dignity, freedom and equality."[6] The new facility would add a feminist component to the university's significant holdings of African American art.[7] As soon as Chicago arrived in Washington for the gift ceremony, she initiated a meeting with African American artists Sam Gilliam and Lou Stovall, hoping that the new multicultural arts center would bring overdue attention to their work.[8] Through the Flower (TTF) also enlisted Greg Edwards, an African American painter from California, to solicit works from major black West Coast artists, a group unrepresented in the UDC's collections.[9] Chicago's alliance building with black artists around the proposed multicultural center extended her practice of using the media to draw attention to the status of artists on the margins of the art world.[10]

The UDC board approved $80,000 to move, clean, and install *The Dinner Party* and to raise $1.2 million to remodel and build a new entrance for the aged and deteriorated Carnegie Library.[11] A city bond had already been approved for the renovations, insuring that all building funds would come from outside of the university's operating budget.[12] Fund-raising was underway to repay the university for the pledged $80,000, which included sponsorship of each of the thirty-nine plates by different groups and individuals; at $5,000 each, this alone could generate twice the amount extended by the university. Further, a single donor had pledged $225,000 on the condition of the acceptance of *The Dinner Party*, representing the largest single donation in the university's history.[13] Mervyn Dymally, a Democrat from Washington, DC, and enthusiast for the multicultural arts center, introduced legislation that matched every dollar the university raised with five from the federal government.[14] According to Dymally's formula, the day the multicultural center opened to the public, the university endowment would accrue nearly $3.2 million.[15] Foreshadowing imminent controversies, however, the *New York Times* reporter noted that, "when asked today if the Board had any hesitations about accepting *The Dinner Table* [*sic*] because of its sexual content, Ms. Long said the matter never came up for discussion."[16]

It was only a matter of time before the question of "sexual content" came up. In the meantime, the parties laid out the terms of the gift which included suitable measures "to protect a major work of 20th century art." Foremost, the terms established a permanent endowment for the maintenance, security, and curatorial staffing of *The Dinner Party*. Since the university had no provisions for creating a permanent endowment, the contract between Chicago and the UDC spelled out the breakdown and use of funds. Of the projected income from visitors to *The Dinner Party*, 25 percent would be allocated for the permanent endowment, 5–10 percent to TTF for administrative costs, and 10–15 percent to the artist. This would constitute the most money the artist ever earned from *The Dinner Party*. During the tour, Chicago had received 50 percent of the income generated from the audiotape she wrote and narrated, as well as a small percentage of other "ancillary materials" produced by TTF; she earned nothing from community or museum shows. Given the financial constraints of the cash-strapped university, Chicago agreed to waive her honoraria for any related speaking engagements and promotional events.[17] These arrangements translated into the university receiving approximately 65 percent of admission fees and 50 percent of the audio guide fees, and 20 percent of all fees going to replenish the endowment, essentially making *The Dinner Party* exhibit self-financing.[18]

On July 18, grumblings about the gift appeared in the *Washington Times*, a politically conservative daily founded in 1982 by Unification Church founder Sun Myung Moon. The article, written by African American journalist Jonetta Rose Barras, launched what would become a newspaper barrage of misinformation. A front-page article framed the renovation costs as part of an acquisition fee to purchase *The Dinner Party*, something the fiscally challenged university could ill afford. Further, the paper reported that *The Dinner Party* had been "banned in several art galleries around the country because it depicts women's genitalia on plates and has been criticized by some critics as obscene."[19]

The false claim that *The Dinner Party* had been "banned" was quickly followed by other untruths, particularly that Chicago wanted an endowed chair or special professorship at the UDC and that she personally stood to earn 25 percent of all revenues. The newspaper laid blame squarely on the board, the members of which gave approval without "seeing a photograph of the actual art," implying that, had the board seen images, they too would have instantly recognized the art as obscene. Board member Joseph Webb disagreed, saying that he was shown a photograph but did not see the plates as body parts, only art. "As a poet, I have no problem with the art," he pointedly commented.[20] Most damaging, the article linked unpaid staff salaries and cutbacks in student programs like football and continuing education classes to *The Dinner Party*. An unnamed source in the UDC president's office railed against spending money on art during a budget crunch: "It's ridiculous for them to spend that kind of money on art, when people aren't getting paid and programs are being cut. Plus this kind of art is not what the university should be getting."[21]

The following day, July 19, 1990, the paper ran another front-page piece by Barras that added two new salient elements. First, the paper addressed the thorny issue of home rule for the Distinct of Columbia and its dependence on the Congress to approve its budget in a patronizing manner, describing members of Congress as having "sharply rebuked the D.C. Council" for its approval of funds to exhibit "a dramatic piece of sexual sculpture," calling the decision "mismanagement" and "questioning the 'sanity' of officials," the paper reported.[22] Second, the article raised the increasingly contentious issue of government funding for the arts. Representative Dana Rohrabacher, a California Republican and leader in the congressional fight against federally funded obscene art, questioned "the values and taste" of UDC officials. "If they can spend their money on weird sexual art, I don't know why they expect we'll give them serious consideration."[23] The article also quoted Representative Stan Parris, a Virginia Republican and ally of conservative Republican senator Jesse Helms of North Carolina, as casting aspersions on the city's "poor" fiscal planning.[24] "That money for UDC for something that is clearly pornographic just goes into the deficit of the District and raises again the lack of fiscal responsibility."[25] The drumbeat of damning reportage continued. An editorial the following day in the *Washington Times* deepened the implied sexual scandal of the art: "Miss Chicago's sculpture actually depicts a table set with dinner plates serving up the vaginas—yes, Virginia, vaginas—of famous women of history." The editor sarcastically said that the only person familiar with the work in this editor's orbit was one of the "visual aid counselors at the dirty bookstore" and, according to him, "It's a dyke's-eye view of some of the tough broads of the past."[26]

With this, the genre was set: describe *The Dinner Party* in incendiary language—as obscene and pornographic; denounce the use of federal funds to support it as morally corrupting; misconstrue the costs and then denounce the university's board of trustees as fiscally challenged. The campaign generated enough smoke to obscure the rational choices of the UDC to invest in its DC campus and of the city council to defend local rule. A week later, on July 26, 1990, these narrative tactics went live on C-SPAN when the US House of Representatives debated for eighty-seven minutes the UDC budget as part of a larger DC appropriations bill.

The debate centered on an amendment offered by Representative Parris to subtract $1.6 million from the UDC budget request. A number of congressmen rose to give testimony justifying slashing the funds from the budget. Robert Dornan, Republican from California, could barely contain his disdain for the art, referring to *The Dinner Party* as "disgusting" twice during his three-minute speech. He also held up a copy of the *Washington Times* and read from it. "This thing is a nightmare. This is not art, it's pornography, 3-D ceramic pornography." Another California Republican, Dana Rohrabacher, added the scandal of waste. "The word is waste, absolute waste to show this weird sexual art that is an affront to the values of our people." Pennsylvania Republican Robert Walker called the UDC administration irresponsible for not paying their professors so they could buy art.[27]

As the melodrama over imperiled morality played on the floor of the

US House, it was hard to miss the simultaneous racial drama unfolding. Conservatives in the debate, all white men, squared off against home-rule supporters, all black. No women testified. Three supporters of home rule rose in turn to refute the amendment proposing to slash money from the UDC budget. While their arguments centered on home rule for the District of Columbia, they also defended the university's judgment, its fiscal competency, and its taste in art. California Democrat Ron Dellums offered the most eloquent argument. The debate about obscenity "was sound and fury signifying nothing." He continued, sounding themes more common in a gender studies seminar than the US House of Representatives: "What is pornographic are military weapons that look like phallic symbols capable of doing nothing but to destroy human life. You want to talk about pornography? Deadly art? Mr. Chairman, I find war immoral, I find poverty immoral."

Representative Bill Green of New York found it offensive that Congress assigned itself the obligation to determine what art Americans could see. He and Walter Fauntroy, a nonvoting member of Congress from the District of Columbia, reminded those gathered that the district had won home rule in 1973 and that the Congress had no business intervening in a matter that was rightly under the authority of the district.[28] Only Pat Williams, Democrat from Montana, made the case that *The Dinner Party* promised to bring money to the university based on the evidence of its successful tour and its place in "virtually every modern art book."[29] The debate was lopsided. Potential allies, including Massachusetts Democrat Barney Frank and Colorado Democrat Pat Schroeder, had no idea the vote on the Paris amendment was happening.[30] By the end of the debate, a majority of representatives supported the amendment to cut $1.6 million from the UDC budget request, and the district's budget moved to the Senate for approval.[31] Representative Williams dryly noted that "This sounds to me like a dry run for the National Endowment for the Arts [NEA] debate," which was scheduled to begin in September.[32]

The late summer debate built on a previous controversy over "obscene" art that unfolded in the nation's capital the previous summer. A retrospective of Robert Mapplethorpe's photographs, many of which explored homoeroticism and displays of male nudity, had been scheduled for the Corcoran Gallery of Art in the summer of 1989. The show had been partially financed with a grant of $30,000 from the NEA.[33] As with *The Dinner Party* NEA grant in 1978, the monies were for the display of the art, not for its production. The exhibition was abruptly canceled for fear of negative repercussions, especially its potential impact on the increasingly politicized process of NEA appropriations. Director Christina Orr-Cahall, eager to keep the Corcoran in the good graces of Congress, explained, "Our institution has always remained outside of the political arena, maintaining a position of neutrality on all such issues. In a city with such a great Federal presence, this has been essential."[34] Her justification left the DC arts and gay and lesbian communities and their allies incensed. Two weeks later, a crowd of seven hundred gathered outside the gallery to protest the cancellation of Mapplethorpe's show.[35] Representatives from the National Association of Artists, the Coalition of Washington Artists, the Washington Center of Photography, and the DC Arts Center participated in defense of the obligation of publicly subsidized institutions to bring "an aesthetic dialogue and a diversity of views to the public."[36] It was an embattled position to argue after nearly ten years of open government hostility to government funding for any art deemed hostile to Christianity, the family, and children, started by Ronald Reagan in 1980 when he proposed cutting all government funding for the arts.[37] The Perfect Moment exhibition subsequently opened for three weeks at the Washington Project for the Arts, where forty thousand viewers saw it.[38] The Mapplethorpe controversy continued when the show opened in Cincinnati in the fall of 1989 and resulted in the director of the Cincinnati Contemporary Art Center being indicted for promoting obscenity and child pornography.[39]

Indeed, 1989 proved to be a banner year for censorship supporters.[40] As the Perfect Moment generated press and national handwringing over the role of art and the state of free speech, conservatives went after Andres Serrano's work, particularly his photograph *Piss Christ*, which depicted a crucifix submerged in the artist's urine.[41] With the help of the *Washington Times*, the Reverend Donald Wildmon galvanized members of his fundamentalist organization, the American Family Association, to flood their congressional representatives' mailboxes with letters expressing their displeasure over the NEA's support of Serrano.[42] Republican senators Jessie Helms and Alfonse D'Amato (New York) organized thirty-six senators to sign a letter expressing their outrage to the NEA for funding "obscene" art. In the House, 107 members chimed in with their own petition. Conservative political leaders Pat Robertson and Patrick Buchanan used the Christian Broadcast Network and the *Washington Times* respectively to lambast the NEA. California representative Rohrabacher urged Congress to cut the agency's entire budget.[43] In that 1989 fall session, Congress ushered in a series of legislative acts that restructured federal funding to the arts, including a prohibition of funding for projects that "promote, disseminate or produce" materials considered obscene. These included "depictions of sadomasochism, homoeroticism, the sexual exploitation of children, of individuals engaged in sex acts and which, taken as a whole, do not have serious literary, artistic, political, or scientific value."[44] The NEA defended its mission, reminding anyone who would listen that it was forbidden from interfering with the artistic choices of its grantees.[45]

Six months later, in the summer of 1990, *The Dinner Party* became ensnared in the controversy. The Christian Television network and *700 Club* picked up the UDC story, urging listeners to keep the pressure on the Congress to block any funds that would aid the university's display of *The Dinner Party*. Conservative African American religious leaders jumped into the fray, calling the piece blasphemous and devilish.[46] Resisting pressure to infringe on DC home rule, a Senate subcommittee voted in July to restore the $1.6 million deduction from the UDC budget proposed by the Parris Amendment, on the grounds that it missed its intended mark. "The committee believes the Parris Amendment penalizes students and faculty for [a] decision taken by the board of trustees and misplaces the intended message," the *Dallas Morning News* reported, after noting that the entire Texas delegation had voted "overwhelmingly" to cut the UDC budget.[47] Rumor had it that Republican senator Phil Graham of Texas was willing "to champion" the Parris Amendment on the Senate floor, if it came to that, and Helms had the issue in his crosshairs.[48] Republicans were not the only critics. *Art in America* reported that Democratic senator Robert Byrd of West Virginia viewed the funds devoted to *The Dinner Party* as calling into question the "adequate stewardship of university resources."[49] Given the political climate in Washington toward both obscenity and government funding for the arts, it appeared to some observers that senators were looking for a cover for their support of the NEA, and backing the Parris Amendment would provide them just that. According to Lucy Lippard, who closely followed the debate, it appeared a deal had been struck "to let *The Dinner Party* go down the drain and save the NEA."[50]

As the Senate considered whether to debate the UDC budget, the *Washington Times* kept up a stream of critical coverage that linked university cutbacks to *The Dinner Party*. In fact, the "environment of instability" at the university—inability to meet scheduled pay raises for faculty, not paying summer faculty, cost overruns in the athletic program, decrepit physical plant—had been caused by falling enrollments and a revolving door of the president's office.[51] However, the paper's campaign against *The Dinner Party* succeeded. The paper reported in late summer that several faculty members, administrators, and students circulated a petition opposing the school's "acquisition" of *The Dinner Party*.[52] The petition announced that the signers "strenuously object on moral, ethical, aesthetic and constitutional grounds to the public display of 'The Dinner Party' at the university."[53] On August 24, the UDC faculty senate voted to decline the gift.[54]

Initially, the timing of the controversy—late summer, when both artists and politicians alike tend to leave the city—worked against Chicago. The link provided by *The Dinner Party* between local DC and national politics and between art and politics in the age of conservative rule only briefly catapulted the UDC budget into the national spotlight. In a rare instance of national television coverage, the *ABC Evening News* aired part of the House debate as another front in the ongoing culture wars.[55] In an editorial for the *Washington Post*, the UDC Board of Trustees chair, Nira Hardon Long, confirmed the seriousness of the stakes. "Our critics strike at the heart of basic human liberties in their assault on freedom of expression, academic freedom, and the autonomy of the people of the District of Columbia."[56] That said, facts of the situation could not be disputed: few supporters rose up to defend Chicago or *The Dinner Party* as the Congress debated the merits of feminist art.

Chicago and her husband, Donald Woodman, intensified their efforts to countervail the distorted coverage. Between them, they sent fourteen faxes to various journalists between July 17 and August 9 and fifty-one in September alone.[57] Chicago mobilized her supporters: TTF board member Mary Ross Taylor, feminist art collector Elizabeth Sackler, Chicago's Doubleday editor Loretta Barrett, former *Dinner Party* volunteer Audrey Cowan, Cleveland community show organizer Mickie Stern, and former project manager Diane Gelon, who requested the contact information for feminist author Naomi Wolf before catching the first flight to Santa Fe; all received regular updates.[58] Chicago directly contacted columnist Ellen Goodman and journalists at the *Los Angeles Times*, *Ms.* magazine, *Art in America*, *Der Spiegel*, the *Albuquerque Tribune*, and CBS News to get her side of the story out.[59] Others targeted politicians. Gelon, once at the offices of TTF, faxed names of representatives and senators on key committees to supporters so they could contact them directly.[60] Mary Ross Taylor closely tracked the issue through the Senate, particularly through the staffs of Texas senators Phil Graham and Sam Nunn, and functioned as the liaison for Chicago insiders in Washington from her home in Houston.[61] Taylor sent hundreds of packets of materials about the popularity of *The Dinner Party* along with letters of support to political supporters. Their collective efforts began to pay off. On July 27, the Hollywood Women's Political Committee, the largest women's fund-raising group for liberal candidates, wrote a letter urging defeat of the Parris Amendment to committee chairmen in hopes of turning the political tide.[62] People for the American Way, a progressive advocacy group founded in 1981 by television producer Norman Lear as a counter to televangelists Pat Robertson and Jerry Falwell, and the National Women's Political Caucus contacted senators in support of the UDC multicultural center.

By September, and with congressional NEA debates looming, the story finally garnered more sustained national media coverage. The *Washington Post* quoted the artist as saying that "The fierceness of the assault on 'The Dinner Party' is a reflection of the fierceness of white male reaction when their values are challenged."[63] *Ms.* magazine covered the story. "People must understand the symbolic nature of this assault. Women's right to expression is at stake here." It quoted Chicago as wryly noting that if any legislator wanted to move against artwork with sexual imagery they ought look "next door—at the Washington Monument."[64] The *Dallas Morning News* quoted Taylor hitting the same note: "Disinformation is the term we used in the Orwellian times to characterize lies."[65] UDC trustee Pat Mathis drew an analogy to fascism: "What is happening is a metaphor for a much more disturbing dynamic that is going on in the culture . . . one of the first things Hitler started to do was to sanitize the culture."[66]

Even with less incendiary reportage appearing, Chicago remained dismayed at the way conservatives' language describing *The Dinner Party* as obscene or potentially untoward repeatedly appeared in papers of record, particularly the *New York Times*. First the artist and then her lawyer sent memos warning the paper that they mischaracterized Chicago and her art. Taking issue at the characterization of her plates as "female genitalia," Chicago fired off, "I am not a medical illustrator and I would like you to cease misrepresenting my work." This was an imposition of "inappropriate, clinical terminology on my abstract, organic, aesthetic—not anatomical—forms." She concluded that, "It is shocking to me that the *New York Times* employs authoritatively the language of the right wing anti-arts faction in America." In a personal letter to journalist Michael Kaufman, Chicago explained that "It is very upsetting to me that the *New York Times*, despite all my efforts to 'tell the truth,' keeps presenting *The Dinner Party* in a way that denigrates the art, misrepresents the content, and belittles me. . . . It is contemptible and frustrating that the *Times* keeps suggesting that *The Dinner Party* is nothing but a 'bunch of cunts' on plates."[67] Fall classes resumed at the UDC, and students added their voices to the overheated atmosphere surrounding Chicago's proposed gift. On September 27, 1990, approximately two hundred students calling themselves Kiamsha! ("Wake up!" in Swahili) occupied two UDC administrative buildings in protest against the administration's allotting of its meager resources.[68] According to the *Washington Post*, students viewed *The Dinner Party* as the proverbial last straw, the latest in a "string of problems" in the running of the university. They submitted a list of twenty demands, including capital improvements, an "Afrocentric curriculum," better housing, more classes, and the resignation of the entire board, the majority of whom had been appointed by the discredited former mayor, Marion Barry.[69]

Within days, students from nearby university and college campuses arrived to offer their support. Twenty-four students from Howard University came to share their experiences from their campus takeover in 1989, joining supporters from American, Morgan State, Bowie State, Hampton, and George Washington Universities. The students respectfully declined a visit from the Reverend Al Sharpton, viewing his arrival as an unhelpful distraction.[70] The school remained shut down for over a week.[71] Photographs in the newspapers showed groups of young black men (no women) protesting outside campus buildings.[72] As the protest and media coverage continued, more and more UDC students viewed *The Dinner Party* as something being thrust upon them that they did not want. Chicago requested a meeting with the protesters, but the trustees refused, fearing it might inflame more controversy.[73]

Ironies abounded. First, the artist had long heard criticism over her lack of multicultural representation in *The Dinner Party*. While there was little to do to rectify that specific charge, Chicago nevertheless viewed the plights of women and of minority artists as related. Nonwhite, nonmale artists faced obstacles the art world still minimized. Yet her efforts to gift her major work to the black and underfunded UDC imploded. The predominantly black student body did not want art, they wanted more classes; the predominantly black DC representatives defended not *The Dinner Party* per se but their right to autonomy and control over their city's institutions; the city's black feminists remained silent, wanting neither to defend the icon of white feminism nor break from support for UDC students. The next day, Chicago withdrew her gift in a show of support for the protesting students.[74] In her October 2 press release, Chicago explained that "The gift of *The Dinner Party* was offered in support of the university and its programs. The current debate at UDC makes it obvious that the meaning of *The Dinner Party* is being distorted; it is a work of art aimed at promoting empowerment and a monument to those who have struggled for freedom. . . . We withdraw the gift in support of the students' right to determine their own destiny."[75] Representative Stan Parris also issued a statement and called for a restoration of $1.6 million into the DC budget: "My effort was never aimed at reducing funds to be used for education but to bring attention to just how far out of line the priorities of the board of trustees had become."[76]

What demanded attention, however, was not the actions taken by the UDC board members to enhance their institution, but the newly emboldened assaults on the arts by conservatives in the wake of the Mapplethorpe and Serrano incidents. Yet few feminists defended the artist or the art or denounced the orchestrated witch hunt launched in the name of fighting obscenity. Only Lucy Lippard came out in print in support of Chicago and of the multicultural arts center that might have brought new attention to the linked projects of feminism and multiculturalism. Writing in *Art in America*, Lippard explained the lost opportunity: "The proposed center at UDC could have inspired not only exhibitions and art-world attention but also a much needed historical analysis of the connections between feminism and the civil rights movement, on which it was modeled in the '60s."[77] She sadly noted the debilitating lack of alliance between progressive black and feminist artists and art supporters to defend the UDC and freedom of artistic expression.

While Lippard addressed the tensions between multiculturalism and feminism, between support for an art center and support for a predominantly black university in an overwhelmingly black city to set its own course, "Annforfreedom," the pseudonym of a DC feminist, offered an analysis of what the UDC scandal meant for the women's movement. She devoted the entire winter issue of her newsletter, the *Wise Woman*, to the UDC debacle. "Can you name 999 women important in human history? Well, then, how about 39? No? You are not alone. Most Americans cannot do so. The House of Representatives has been trying to make certain that this ignorance continues, and in the process, trying to suppress a classic feminist art project." She described the weak defense for *The Dinner Party* as part of the terrible bind in which the antipornography feminists found themselves: "In 1990, when anti-pornography issues had split feminists for nearly a decade, and caused some feminists to advocate an alliance with right wing Christians, the words 'pornography' and 'obscene' were enough to attract allies for the speaker, no matter how atrocious the lie." It was no accident, she wrote, that, "Men who oppose women's rights used the cover of anti-pornography stances to assault feminist art." Annforfreedom called on her feminist readers to take action. "The use of anti-pornography and anti-obscenity rhetoric must not be allowed to mask attacks on feminism, gay rights, and other movements attempting to increase human rights in society."[78] Feminist sociologist Carole S. Vance, writing in *Art in America* in 1989, did not defend *The Dinner Party* by name but articulated many feminists' deep apprehension about the conservative "war on culture." "We know that diversity in images and expression in the public sector nurtures and sustains diversity in private life," she wrote. "People deprived of images become increasingly vulnerable to attacks on their private expressions of nonconformity, which are inevitable once sources of public solidarity and resistance have been eliminated."[79]

The events that unfolded around the UDC gift, particularly its place in the debate over censorship and government funding for the arts in the 1980s, constituted an unusual feminist dilemma. The dilemma hung on two horns. On one side hung the unwillingness of many feminists to defend *The Dinner Party* as art, much less as important feminist art. In the words of *The New Art Examiner*, the art world had deemed it "a socio-historically important piece of kitsch [and] it had moved on to other things."[80] In other words, too many feminists doubted the piece's effectiveness as an ambassador for feminism and so did not defend it in print as art when conservatives attacked it as obscene. On the other side hung the legacy of the feminist sex wars over pornography. Battles over strategies for limiting sexually explicit imagery in the public spaces, the implications of a giant pornographic industry, and the ongoing problem of sexual violence against women had broken apart coalitions of feminist activists. Coupled with the high-stakes battles waged by conservatives in Washington around obscenity, homosexuality, feminism, and other "threats" to family values, liberal and left-leaning activists had little inclination to defend Chicago's vulva images as freedom of expression.[81] The attack on *The Dinner Party*, sandwiched between the Corcoran cancellation of the Mapplethorpe retrospective in the summer of 1989 and the trial and subsequent acquittal of the Cincinnati Contemporary Art Center director in the fall of 1990, confirmed the vulnerability of feminists and sexual minorities to the machinery of state censorship.[82] The campaign to discredit *The Dinner Party* as an obscene display of women's bodies eerily enacted the very outcome that anti-antipornography supporters had warned against in the feminist sex wars of the early 1980s: attempts to censor images under the banner of obscenity (and its implied victimization of some unspecified person) could and most likely would be used against images generated by feminists, queers, and others deemed nonnormative.

The impact of the scorned UDC gift radiated outward. Anticipating an even more bruising full congressional debate over arts funding later in the fall, the National Council on the Arts, an advisory group to the NEA, voted overwhelmingly to push back against an activist Congress determined to strip funding for any art it deemed obscene. The *New York Times* reported in days after Chicago withdrew her gift that, "after an emotional debate," the National Council on the Arts voted nineteen to two to ask the endowment's chair, John E. Frohnmayer, to "stop requiring recipients of endowment grants to agree in writing to comply with a Congressional directive banning the use of Federal money for work that might be deemed obscene or blasphemous."[83] Despite such stands, Washington retained a chilly atmosphere for art. TTF renewed its efforts to find a home for *The Dinner Party*, with supporters in Los Angeles, Santa Fe, Cleveland, and Boston exploring options for permanent housing in their cities.[84] In the meantime, *The Dinner Party* stayed crated in a facility in Northern California for the foreseeable future.[85] As it turned out, the UDC controversy, painful as it was, also seeded new possibilities.

The Feminist Art Movement, Redux

Sexual/textual politics.

In the wake of the 1990 UDC disaster and concerned with the climate of hostility toward government funding of the arts, Henry Hopkins, former director of the San Francisco Museum of Modern Art and now director of the Armand Hammer Museum of Art in Los Angeles, and senior curator Elizabeth Shepherd proposed showing *The Dinner Party* to "attempt a reevaluation of the piece and the issues that it raises."[86] It would take six years to pull off, but when *Sexual Politics: Judy Chicago's "Dinner Party" in Feminist Art History* opened in Los Angeles in 1996, it caused a stir.

The Dinner Party had not been on display in the US since 1982. Much had changed in the feminist art movement in the ensuing years, particularly in terms of conceptualizing art made by women and its relationship to feminist practice. Feminist theorists secured new homes for themselves across the academy, particularly in women's studies programs and art history departments, and from these vantage points, created new approaches to the study of culture and cultural production.[87] Yet while feminist theory gained new prestige in the academy in the 1980s, women artists still struggled to have their work shown, remaining underrepresented in the ranks of curators, in the number of solo shows they commanded, and in museum collections. No group dramatized this paradox more than the infamous Guerrilla Girls, who in the mid-1980s began to splash New York City art haunts with fact-filled, eye-catching posters documenting the lack of statistical success of women artists, like this one, written in girlish cursive in 1986:

> Dearest Art Collector,
> It has come to our attention that your collection, like most, does not contain enough art by women. We know that you feel terrible about this and will rectify the situation immediately.
> All our love,
> Guerrilla Girls[88]

Or this, under an image of a dollar bill divided, in 1985: "Women earn 2/3 of what men do; women artists earn 1/3 of what men artists do."[89] Known for their anonymous hit-and-run tactics, the group exposed the difficulty of changing the institutional art world.[90] Between 1973 and 1987, the Whitney Biennial of Contemporary Art, the event that inspired the feminist art activism on the East Coast in the early 1970s, gave unintended evidence for the unchanging status of women and minority artists through these groups' poor representation in its own shows.[91] The Guerrilla Girls hammered away broadly, not only at the Whitney. A reclining naked woman with a guerrilla mask posed the question in 1989: "Do women have to be naked to get into the Met. Museum?" The answer, after a quick "weenie count," a resounding yes: "less than 5% of the artists in the Modern Art sections are women, but 85% of the nudes are female."[92]

The connection between images of women as nudes and the status of women artists had been debated since the beginning of the feminist art movement. But in the 1980s, the relationship between sexual objectification of women and women's status came under new scrutiny, driven by developments in feminist activism and theory. The antipornography movement successfully politicized the issue of obscenity at the same time that anti-essentialist feminist theorists sought new avenues to sever the historic connection between women and their bodies. As ever, feminist art criticism hewed closely to trends in the broader feminist movement.

Recall that in 1971 Linda Nochlin sent waves through the art historical world when she asked the question, "Why Have There Been No Great Women Artists?"[93] Her answer: in the absence of institutional support, with significant restrictions on training women and conflicting attitudes toward women's professional work, few women artists achieved "greatness" as conventionally defined. That women artists had made significant work at all was a testimony to individual women's resilience in the face of pervasive and collectively experienced discrimination. Great women artists would be recognized as "great" only when the parameters of "greatness" were not set exclusively by and for men. This answer, stressing social and institutional obstacles as well as outstanding individual women harmonized perfectly with the early 1970s feminist interest in opening up institutions, crafting laws to end discrimination on the account of sex, and to provide equal opportunity to all citizens, notable and ordinary alike.

Ten years later, in 1981, two British feminist art historians turned Nochlin's question on its head in a signature gesture that announced that a new moment in feminist art history had begun.[94] Their critique built on the insights and intervention of feminists who came before them while also adding new theoretical imperatives that shifted the target of feminist engagement. Rozsika Parker and Griselda Pollock acknowledged that women had both been excluded from enjoying institutional support and been written out of history. But, they cautioned, "To see women's history only as a progressive struggle against great odds is to fall into the trap of unwittingly reasserting the established male standards as the appropriate norm." They argued that, "If women's history is simply judged against the norms of male history, women are once again set apart, outside the historical processes of which both men and women are indissolubly part. Such an approach fails to convey the specific ways that women have made art under different constraints at different periods, affected as much by factors of class as by their sex."[95]

Shaking the foundation of a unified female identity that had provided 1970s feminism with a base on which to build a movement, postmodernist feminists like Parker and Pollock hoped to create space for a different narrative of liberation. Rather than producing a history of women artists, they proposed to "analyze the relations between women, art and ideology" toward creating a theoretical framework for understanding the meaning of sexual difference itself. In a critical reorientation, their new direction shifted the ground for feminist intervention from the sociological to the psychoanalytic, from materiality (access) to subjectivity (ideology).[96] They explained that "ideology is not a conscious process, its effects are manifest but it works unconsciously, reproducing the values and systems of belief of the dominant group it serves."[97] To root out the ideology of femininity then was to dismantle, or deconstruct, the very classifications of art history itself.

Revisiting terrain covered by Miriam Schapiro and Chicago in the early 1970s, Parker and Pollock explained that ideology (not merely social discrimination) was "made manifest" in distinctions—distinctions between art made in studios and crafts made at home, between public viewing of art and domestic use of craft, between the professional artist and the woman who dabbled. These terms functioned as hierarchies of power (not only tangible outcomes of discrimination) that no simple revaluation of craft or inclusion of literal women into the category of "great artist" would alter. Stressing language and ideology rather than access to cultural and material resources, Parker and Pollock challenged feminists like Chicago with their use of women's history (singularly defined around any vagina-bearing bodies) as a strategy of empowerment. Such a history kept the categories (greatness, whiteness, privilege) intact even as it changed the subject from men to women. For instance, embroidery may well be considered one of women's richest contributions to culture, but "simply to glorify its history and to defend its value as a cultural product, leads us into the sentimental trap" where embroidery becomes "synonymous with femininity." To elevate embroidery was to insist on its inclusion in a system that denigrated the terms, spaces, and forms associated with femininity and thus by association literal women. Symbolizing femininity was an equally dangerous enterprise. According to Parker and Pollock, body art, "cunt art," could never accomplish its intended goal of reclaiming the female body for re-signification, since "Such images are dangerously open to misunderstanding. They do not alter radically the traditional identification of women with their biology nor challenge the association of women with nature. In some ways they merely perpetuate the exclusively sexual identity of women, not only as body but explicitly as cunt."[98]

This anti-essentialist orientation indeed marked a new direction for the feminist art movement.[99] Nochlin's call for tangible opportunities for literal women artists in 1971 was based on a view of women's agency and opportunity as a resource. In 1981, Parker and Pollock joined a linguistic turn that invested language as the terrain of both power and feminist battle. "Women's sense of self, their subjectivity, is not to be understood as a matter of social conditioning, for it is determined by the structures of the unconscious," they wrote. It was no longer enough to make "alternative" images of women. "In a patriarchal culture, femininity is not an alternative to masculinity but its negative . . . within the present organization of sexual difference which underpins patriarchal culture, there is no possibility of simply conjuring up and asserting a positive and alternative set of meanings for women. The work to be done is that of deconstruction."[100]

In the words of an art critic writing in the early 1980s, feminist postmodern aesthetic theory was no longer focused on "what representations say about women," but on the investigation of "what representation *does* to women."[101] Parker and Pollock rebuked Chicago specifically. Her efforts to "validate female experience" through accessible images, they argued, naively overlooked the fact that images are made meaningful through the viewer, "the gaze" in film critic Laura Mulvey's 1975 conception.[102] Building on Mulvey, Parker and Pollock explained that Chicago's vulva images "are easily retrieved and co-opted by a male culture because they do not rupture radically meanings and connotations of woman in art as body, as sexual, as nature, as object for male possession."[103]

Parker and Pollock's concern that the female body not be rendered into an object for male consumption was one they shared with many feminists, particularly activists in the antipornography movement. Feminist activism around the dilemma of images—specifically images of female sexuality in the service of male pleasure—had been building since the mid-1970s and, by the early 1980s, had reached a critical point.[104] Feminist artists had been early activists in the campaign against rape and sexual violence against women, producing a rich circuitry between art and politics in the early 1970s, particularly in Southern California.[105] But deep anxiety over censorship and its potential to backfire against feminist and queer sexual expression collided with equally felt outrage against the use of images of women's bodies by pornographers and their customers as the movement intensified.[106] In the 1980s, many academic feminist theorists, including art historians like Parker and Pollock, embraced the linguistic turn as a productive counterweight to the oppressive literalness of the feminist sex wars waging around them. Rather than engaging in what kind of images extended the feminist project (cunt art: good or bad for women?), they examined the production of gender—symbolically, linguistically, ideologically–as a strategy of cultural engagement. The postmodern target: to snip the discursive threads that held dominant narratives together, even if those threads (women constitute a group based on their shared bodies, for instance) had once been heralded as feminist. In different ways then, anti-essentialist feminist theory and the divisiveness of the antipornography movement each played a part in pushing "1970s feminism" into the past, casting it and its naive yet infectious investment in collectivity and sisterhood as bygone "history."[107]

The drift toward viewing the 1970s as a failed form of feminism animated much art critical theory in the 1980s, driven by the linguistic turn across the humanities and good old fashion backlash, a combination feminist art theorist Amelia Jones deemed a "strategic oblivion."[108] Jones first raised concerns about a so-called gender-neutral ("post-feminist") postmodern theoretical landscape in a 1990 article in *M/E/A/N/I/N/G*, a journal published by former Chicago student Mira Schor and Susan Bee that ran from 1985 to 1995.[109] In this piece, Jones identified the uncomfortable tendency of art critics to attribute the impact of feminism on the art world to the larger critique of language and ideology as structures of power, as if the postmodern critique of the mainstream enabled "feminism to become more itself." Such critics, she wrote, "promote the reduction and erasure of feminism" when they simply fold its analysis of the mainstream and the commodification of the female body into the larger postmodern project. Such absorption of feminism denied a generation of feminists' efforts to mobilize an effective answer to women's cultural and art marginalization and implied that "women should feel honored" to be considered a part of the humanist project. However, as she noted, feminists' inclusion came not "as subjects capable of producing their own counter-discourses to it, but as passive objects of its generous ('genderless') embrace." "Through the preceding argument, I have examined the insidious project currently at work to dis-arm feminists, coaxing us into sympathy with the broad postmodernist project by flattery, then extinguishing our tracks behind us. While we offered a 'new subjectivism,' this gesture obliterates our sex and anti-sexism by so generously/genderlessly including us as part of the 'universalist' subject of the art of the 1980s."[110]

Restoring "our tracks behind us," Jones provided a path back to the 1970s feminist art movement without dismissing it (as others did) as failed. She coupled concern with not having feminist "tracks" erased by postmodernism with her commitment to see gender at play, embedded and ideological at once. When in 1990, Hopkins invited Jones to curate a special conference and exhibit devoted to *The Dinner Party*, she agreed only if she could broaden the focus to include a reappraisal of its status within a broader context of feminist art from the 1960s to the 1990s.[111]

On April 24, 1996, *The Dinner Party* returned to display, the first US showing since 1983 and the first ever in LA, the city where it had been made.[112] A series of lectures, symposia, and events placed *The Dinner Party* in art historical and contemporary contexts; tellingly, no one addressed the most recent NEA and UDC controversies, opting instead to explicate feminist art on historically narrow and self-contained terms. In both academic and popular formats, Jones explained her hopes that the show could "reopen now-reified debates about feminist practice" and the "almost automatic dismissal of *The Dinner Party* by modernists, postmodernists and many feminists alike."[113] In a preopening interview, Jones spoke with the *LA Times*. "I'm hoping from the bottom of my heart that people will walk into the show and understand that this is not just a celebration of the 'Dinner Party.' It's certainly respectful toward that piece as far as it's held this position, but it's also a very careful—and I hope somewhat explosive—reopening of our understanding of the last 30 years."[114] Jones proposed to reopen debates in two ways. First to build a "broad visual history" that would highlight the breadth of the 1970s feminist art movement by including the work of other feminists dealing with similar themes, thus making *The Dinner Party* less exceptional; the second to examine the linguistic turn in the 1980s and 1990s and what it might have cost women artists.[115] In other words, Jones proposed to ask how postmodernism served feminism.

Jones created a rich historical context for *The Dinner Party* by showing it with over a hundred objects in total, including works from a number of Chicago's former students from the Feminist Art Program such as Suzanne Lacy, Karen LeCocq, Aviva Rahmani, Mira Schor, and Faith Wilding, as well as other well-known feminist artists such as Cindy Sherman, Betye Sarr, and Lauren Lesko.[116] This context ideally helped viewers to rethink elements of *The Dinner Party* commonly understood as problematic emblems of 1970s art by placing it alongside art from the 1980s and 1990s, reorienting viewers to think thematically, not chronologically. For example, in a subsection titled "Female Imagery: The Politics of Cunt Art," Jones juxtaposed the work of radical feminist artist Tee A. Corinne from the 1970s with the 1990s "lipstick" lesbian Millie Wilson to consider the implications of cunt art for lesbians and the diversity of feminist approaches to the body. Similarly, Jones included works from artists of color throughout to highlight the complications of any feminist "universalism."[117] At the same time, she did not surrender her view that a group of artists who shared common concerns existed. While Judy Chicago could not speak for the feminist art movement, neither should the feminist art movement silence Chicago. Jones explained that the exhibit "begins from the assumption that, like any cultural project, *The Dinner Party* did not spring spontaneously from the mind of one isolated 'genius.'" At the same time, it was not her intention to add to the "general opprobrium" in which the piece has been held by many 1980s poststructuralists, "who see it as paradigmatic of a naïve and putatively 'essentialist' arm of 1970s feminist art." "Rather, I hope here to look at the piece seriously and with respect for its conflicted but important position—whether as adulated icon of feminist utopianism or despised exemplar of essentialism (the unifying presentation of women's experience as 'essential' or biologically determined)—within the history of feminist art."[118]

However, some elements of this historical context proved hard to secure. Five prominent feminist artists from Chicago's generation—Mary Beth Edelson, Joyce Kozloff, Miriam Schapiro, Joan Snyder, and Nancy Spero, all based in New York—asked that their work not be included in the show.[119] They had little faith that a conference devoted to rethinking the place of *The Dinner Party* in feminist art history could sufficiently deflate its overblown centrality and the "heroization" of Chicago.[120] After all, in the words of one critic, Judy Chicago herself had become "the visual arts version of Helen Reddy," an attack that again used *The Dinner Party*'s popularity to discredit it as art.[121] Jones later reported that she tried to change Shapiro's mind, explaining that, "by refusing to have her work exhibited she was leaving the impression that Judy thought all this up by herself."[122] Chicago's former ally and friend from the CalArt's Feminist Art Program refused to change her mind. In the same spirit, Spero sent the museum and Jones "vitriolic" letters of protest.[123] In the exhibit catalog, Jones wrote that the protest by Chicago's peers surprised her: "I had no idea that this exhibition, in spite of my efforts to work within a historical and theoretical (rather than aesthetic or monographic) framework, would prove as controversial as the piece itself."[124] Jones told a reporter that she viewed the artists' refusal to participate as "self-defeating, because its viewing art history and the art world in this personal way."[125] Personal politics, indeed. Maybe the seventies weren't dead yet.

The second strategy that Jones employed involved reflecting on what the 1980s disavowed in feminist art practice. According to Jones, Parker and Pollock (via Mulvey) shared with *New York Times* critic Hilton Kramer a fear of pleasure and identification, of an image's seductive hold on a viewer.[126] The pleasure that viewers took in Chicago's images in *The Dinner Party*—the symbols that required no expert decoding to understand, its luscious colors, varied textures, and shimmering surfaces—skipped over the critical distance that both modernist and postmodernist critics upheld as fundamental to viewing art. In other words, the pleasure audiences took in seeing, as measured by its popularity or kitsch, ought no longer to be held against *The Dinner Party*. Chicago's aim to "activate the spectator," Jones suggested, took place through identification, not "distanciation."[127] She explained to the *LA Times* in 1996 that, "Looking back to the '80s, we can now see that the 'male gaze' rhetoric—the idea of getting away from representing the female body at all, to completely erase the possibility of men engaging pleasurably in representations of the female body—became a very prescriptive kind of dialogue. But one can also look at the incredible diversity within feminism, which now I would say is largely characterized precisely through its multiplicity. It never was a singular discourse, but even less now than ever."[128] With this, Jones attempted to bridge elite and popular reception, embracing the postmodern erasure of high and low art to bring on a more appreciative gaze to *The Dinner Party* specifically and 1970s feminist art more generally. Along the way she implied that seventies feminism had laid key artistic cornerstones, not ancillary offshoots, of postmodernism.[129]

The show ran for nearly four months and brought in a significant number of visitors—55,000 in total. Despite the crowds, *LA Times* art critic Christopher Knight gave it a scathing review in May and named it the "Outstandingly Bad Museum Show of 1996" in December.[130] The full review began by adopting the framework set out by Jones and stressing that recent feminism has "never been monolithic." Despite that, he announced it was "a fiasco. And not only because it uses a failed work of art as its fulcrum." The critic went after Jones as well as Chicago, clearly offended by the efforts to recontextualize *The Dinner Party*. In typical *Dinner Party* fashion, it got personal: "With a curator who is an ideologist, theory is privileged over practice. Art is thus misused, its efficacy undermined by curatorial trivialization. You want to run screaming from the room." Chicago's "notorious sculpture" that famously began a tour in 1979 that endured "nearly universal Bronx cheers from art critics and feminists alike" has been "foolishly trotted out at the UCLA/Armand Hammer Museum of Art as the catalyst for a look at feminist issues from the last quarter-century."[131] *Art in America* joined in, pointedly noting that *Sexual Politics* reactivated the atmosphere of hostility from mainstream critics and engulfed the exhibit in "an often mean-spirited buzz of disapproval" that was only exacerbated by widespread complaints about Chicago's careerism and renewed charges that she had exploited her volunteers. These old bugaboos threatened to overshadow Jones' important attempt to revision 1970s feminism through 1990s gender theory: *Sexual Politics* demonstrated that "essentialist imagery from the body" cannot easily be separated from "the experience of femininity as a kind of masquerade."[132]

Letters to the editor talked back to Knight's review. A UCLA art history professor called out the critic's ad hominem attack on Jones and his obvious dislike of *The Dinner Party*: "You don't need to be any kind of feminist to be aware that the real target of Knight's umbrage is one section of the show, Judy Chicago's 'Dinner Party' of 1974–79, made in Los Angeles but never before shown here. . . . The sheer flood of invective remains puzzling: Whether one 'likes' Chicago's work or not, its reconstitution here, in the context of the first substantive exhibition to chronicle the central role played by Los Angeles in the birth and growth of the American feminist art movement, is an important event."[133] And popular, he added.

A feminist writing in the *Women's Art Journal* noted that the absence of Chicago's feminist precursors Lee Bontecou and Louise Bourgeois had the unfortunate effect of generating another chapter in "Judyolatry" and once again suggested Chicago as the "ultimate source" of feminist art.[134] The spatial layout of the galleries lent credence to the charge. Audiences viewed *The Dinner Party* in its own darkened "reverential" space and the survey of feminist art in separate galleries, giving visitors the sense they had seen two shows.[135] Despite the problematic layout, the *New Art Examiner* declared the show a success, remarking that *The Dinner Party* "has stood the test of time much better than anyone could have imagined." The "sexual/textual politics" of the 1996 exhibit demonstrated to the reviewer the particularly gendered nature of the never-ending "fuss" about *The Dinner Party*—"a fuss that most likely would not have occurred if Chicago were a man."[136] Much in the art world and in feminism had changed since the 1983 showing of *The Dinner Party*, but the 1996 show proved in no uncertain terms that at least one element remained constant through it all: its controversy.

Yet forces inexorably changing the meaning of feminism in the 1980s and 1990s created the possibility for a new viewing of *The Dinner Party* to emerge. At the same time feminist activism (antipornography), feminist theory (anti-essentialism) and feminist art (postmodernism) converged in the 1980s to push 1970s feminism into "history," the new availability of feminist-themed popular culture offered a different context for understanding the meaning of *The Dinner Party*. This context harmonized with Chicago's celebration of women's culture, heritage, and unique resilience. Popular feminist-themed cultural products in the 1980s and 1990s spread the message of feminist transformation, woman by woman, without the consumer needing to take back the night, support the ERA, or give up high heels. Popular expressions of feminism in the 1980s and 1990s lay the groundwork for celebrating a new "postfeminist" era, one that rested on the belief that sexism (like 1970s feminism) was now the stuff of "history" and celebrated rather than deconstructed sexual difference.

Popular Feminism in a Postfeminist Age

The story of your vagina is the story of your life.

The chilling atmosphere of the culture wars and postmodern gender theory combined to push *The Dinner Party* into the dustbin of history, a place that eventually proved to be not such a bad place to relaunch its reputation. Yet as senators and feminists rolled their eyes at *The Dinner Party*'s representation of women in the 1980s and 1990s for very different reasons, an unexpected alternative context sprang up that enabled a new viewing of *The Dinner Party*'s feminism: the growing marketplace of feminist-themed culture that appeared in the wake of the women's liberation movement. The popularity of these texts testified to the growth of new audiences in the 1980s that used their dollars to consume feminist-themed movies, novels, and books. Focusing on the years between the last exhibit of *The Dinner Party* tour in the US in 1983 and the 1996 *Sexual Politics* exhibition makes visible the growth of this commercial market that both opened the doors of feminism to a wider public and provided an alternative (nonart historical) framework for viewing *The Dinner Party*. The story of marketplace popular feminism in the 1980s and 1990s also sheds light on the crucial role feminist-themed culture played in transforming a once-oppositional and deeply challenging political movement into a consumer-friendly belief in the value of women's difference.

As *The Dinner Party* opened for its final community show at the Fox Theatre in Atlanta, a bumper crop of feminist-themed culture appeared. Three examples from 1982—a novel, a study of women's morality, and a Hollywood film—demonstrate a popular feminism that celebrated women's difference even as it called for an end of gender-based discrimination. These three examples underscore the accessibility of feminist essentialism, Chicago-style.

Alice Walker's novel *The Color Purple* became the most acclaimed and discussed example of popular feminism of the 1980s.[137] The novel did for 1980s multicultural feminism what Erica Jong's *Fear of Flying* did for white 1970s feminism, putting into readers' hands a compelling narrative of a woman's coming into feminist or, in this case, womanist awakening.[138] Walker moved her main character, Celie, through a series of pleasures and dangers that brought her to a full-bodied awakening of her authentic self. Set in the 1930s, Walker structured the novel as a series of letters Celie writes to God as she struggles with painful experiences of abuse from friends and enemies alike. Raped by her stepfather as a girl, she had two children by him in quick succession, both of whom he took from her. The stepfather arranges for Celie to be married to an older man—Mr. Johnson, or "Mister"—who introduces her to his girlfriend, Shug, an attractive, sexually fluid blues singer. Celie's beloved sister, Nellie, escapes a similar fate—marriage to an abusive husband—by running off. Over a number of years and plot twists, Shug and Celie become episodic lovers and Shug tells Celie that Mister has been hiding letters from her. Celie finds the letters, discovers her sister Nellie has been living with African missionaries who, unbeknownst to them, have been raising Celie's two children whom they adopted years prior. Nellie, the two children and Celie reunite. Mister discovers a new appreciation for women as he ages and renounces violence toward them. Celie opens her own business sewing generously sized pants for women and, as the novel closes, lives in a nonmonogamous family devoted to each member's well-being.

Walker's novel explored the bonds of sisterhood, literal and metaphorical, among African American women whose shared circumstances leave them with few allies beyond themselves. Bonds here mean shared pain and suffering as well as shared pleasures. The bonds of love that tie the collective of women together—Celie, Nellie, Shug, and friends Sofia and Squeak—are historical, cultural, and emotional. Walker's support for lesbianism and bi-curious women challenged a reluctance shared by many Americans to represent same-sex acts as positive. At the same time, her highlighting of spiritual renewal in the face of systematic hardship celebrated the resiliency and protective gender conservatism of black America. In calling out sexism, homophobia, and sexual violence working in tandem with racism and racial pride, Walker's novel acted as a tutorial in multicultural feminist theory. *The Color Purple* earned accolades immediately, winning the American Book Award and the Pulitzer Prize for Fiction in 1983 and becoming standard reading in women's studies classes across the country. Steven Spielberg made the best-selling novel into a major Hollywood film in 1985, which, with its vivid portrayal of domestic abuse, triggered what some commentators called the most heated debate over the image of black people in the media "since the films *The Birth of a Nation* (1915) and *Gone with the Wind* (1939)."[139] The film cast, which included Oprah Winfrey, Danny Glover, and Whoopi Goldberg, all but guaranteed *The Color Purple*'s popularity and widespread distribution.[140]

Walker's novel became part of a new wave of canonical women's studies readings able to cross over the porous boundary between academics and activism, demonstrating the ongoing relevance of women's studies scholarship to the broader community of female readers. In doing so, *The Color Purple* joined a growing number of crossover texts that spoke to specialist and generalist alike. Carol Gilligan's *In a Different Voice* became another example of a crossover text that landed on community reading lists as well as university syllabuses. Published in 1982 by the staid Harvard University Press, the book examined the gender biases that structured the major theories of moral reasoning, concluding that women indeed spoke "in a different voice."[141] Gilligan argued that no matter the origin of the difference between men and women (psychological or biological), women forged their own path to moral developmental based on their own distinctive moral reasoning. Psychologists have long dismissed women's moral calculus as weaker or "less developed" than men's because women held people, not principles, as the highest priority of any moral system. This difference, Gilligan argued, reflected a set of values culled from women's social situation and history and as such ought to be held in as much regard as the values of established (male) authority.[142]

Facing critics who denounced her views as essentialist, Gilligan articulated the stakes for women if their "difference" continued to be lost in theories about men's superiority: "My critics take the ideas of self and morality for granted as these ideas have been defined in the patriarchal or male dominated tradition." In contrast, she tells the story of women who "constitute these ideas differently and hence tell a different story about human experience." "My critics say that this story seems 'intuitively' right to many women but is at odds with the findings of psychological research. This is precisely the point I am making and exactly the difference I was exploring: the dissonance between psychological theory and women's experience."[143] *In a Different Voice* became a bestseller, doing for moral development what Kate Millett's *Sexual Politics* did to modernist literary criticism in 1970. Translated into sixteen languages, *In a Different Voice* has sold nearly three-quarters of a million copies since its publication in 1982.[144] In 1996, *Time* magazine listed Gilligan among the twenty-five most influential Americans.

As Walker and Gilligan spread the good word about celebrating equality based on difference, the Hollywood film *Tootsie* underscored the availability of difference to everyone, male or female. Opening in theaters in December 1982, the film starred Dustin Hoffman and Jessica Lange, directed by Sydney Pollack.[145] Hoffman portrayed out-of-work actor Michael Dorsey, whose mercurial temper and arrogance made him the pariah of the New York theater world. Desperate for work, Michael auditioned for a female role in disguise as a woman and landed a job at a soap opera. His female self—Dorothy—was matronly, fastidious, and assertive; yet at the same time she engages in frank back talk to men and, still more shocking, refuses to tolerate the sexual overtures of a lecherous costar (more from homophobic fear than feminist righteousness). Through many ridiculous plot twists, Michael has a feminist awakening as a result of living life as an embodied woman. Not only does being an attractive woman take time and money, he discovers that men do not listen to women, even in soap operas, the most female of genres. Dorothy sets off a feminist revolution on and off set as her character grows more assertive and devoted fans call for more. Michael tells his love interest that he learned to be a better man by performing his deepest self as a woman. Judith Butler, move over. *Tootsie* was the second highest grossing film of 1982, second only to *E.T.*, and continues as one of the highest grossing comedies of all time. In 1998, the Library of Congress placed *Tootsie* on the National Film Registry.

When taken together, *The Color Purple*, *In a Different Voice*, and *Tootsie* had important similarities despite their significant differences. Most broadly, the overarching message of each celebrated women's unique experiences and cultures of resistance (based on friendship and family) while also noting the specific obstacles women faced from the fact of their status as women (poverty, racism, homophobia, sexism). Each shared a utopian glimpse of a world changed by the practice of identification between women and sense of gender solidarity based on that perceived commonality, even when the woman is a guy. Placed in this context, *The Dinner Party*, centered as it was on women's difference as a source of both empowerment and discrimination, harmonized with other popular texts that celebrated women in the early 1980s. A woman in 1982 might read *The Color Purple* or *In a Different Voice*, screen *Tootsie*, and view *The Dinner Party* as expressions of her feminist sympathies. In this way, a woman's consumer dollars could connect her with the ideas of feminism and made her cultural consumption a way to participate not in feminist political activism but a temporary, text-based feminist community.

The idea of feminism as a set of values or cultural experiences that one could have without participating in a social protest movement first appeared in feminist discussions about "backlash," a term that described a set of attacks against the gains of the women's movement. Providing a trademark name to the age, Susan Faludi's *Backlash* (1991) laid out the impact on feminist activism of a decade-long attack on women's accomplishments, autonomy, and choices through psychological fearmongering about single women and biological clocks by the national media.[146] Likewise, in *The Beauty Myth* (1991), Naomi Wolf connected unattainable standards of female beauty to women's growing political and economic gains, a self-imposed (yet socially orchestrated) hobbling of women at the moment they were poised to achieve meaningful equality.[147] In the tradition of Simone de Beauvoir's *The Second Sex* (1949), Betty Friedan's *The Feminine Mystique* (1963), and Germaine Greer's *The Female Eunuch* (1970), Faludi and Wolf produced tomes that were intended to rouse a distracted feminist nation back to action.[148]

Well-connected opponents met Faludi and Wolf on the battlefield of public opinion, further eroding simple notions of feminist solidarity. Katie Roiphe, in a popular 1993 diatribe against antipornography feminism, spelled out the connection between "sex, fear, and feminism."[149] Roiphe, daughter of feminist and novelist Anne Roiphe, and her surprising hit *The Morning After: Sex, Fear, and Feminism*, became synonymous with anti-feminist feminism—a style of engagement that attacked feminism as extreme and unbalanced in the name of saving its multiple accomplishments. For Roiphe, this meant reeling in feminist activism around sexual violence and sexual danger to reclaim sophomoric nights of drinking and sex from campus killjoys and Take Back the Night marches. She was only one in a series of professional feminists who turned on feminism in the 1990s, which most notably included Camille Paglia (*Sexual Personae*, 1990) and Christina Hoff Sommers (*Who Stole Feminism?*, 1994).[150] Roiphe, Paglia, and Sommers especially singled out women's studies programs and professors for teaching women to identify as victims.

Yet the narrative possibilities of popular feminism could be seen even in an age of backlash. During the 1990s, feminist-themed culture continued to thrive and sell. While *The Dinner Party* went on display on the West Coast at the Armand Hammer Museum in 1996, on the East Coast, audiences could go see Eve Ensler in her one-woman play, *The Vagina Monologues*, in New York's Broadway West Side Theatre (1994–99) or read Candice Bushnell's *New York Observer* column called "Sex and the City" (1994–96). Bushnell published the columns as a set of joined short stories in 1997, and the following year sold them to HBO, which made them into a cable serial with the same title.[151] *The Vagina Monologues* and *Sex and the City* became multimedia blockbusters of the late twentieth century, driven to financial heights by female consumers who embraced both with striking enthusiasm and loyalty. At the same time, *The Vagina Monologues* and *Sex and the City* suffered from the memory loss historically associated with antifeminist backlash: Ensler's play offered no feminist genealogy of itself, no sense that any woman had uttered the word *cunt* in a performance before she did. Her focus on vaginas, it would seem, fell on her like a vision. Likewise, Bushnell, and then HBO producer-writer Darrell Starr, built the story of four New York City friends on a history of sisterhood repressed so hard it simply disappeared, like memories of bad sex or child birth. The operating assumption of *Sex and the City* was that these women had no particular interest in how they won the freedom to live like men, but only that they lived as largely as did men, sexually and economically. They needed no history since their liberation as well-to-do white Americans was always already secured. Both *The Vagina Monologues* and *Sex in the City* contributed to the sense of 1970s feminism's historic accomplishments and its redundancy in contemporary bicoastal America.

The Vagina Monologues opened in 1994 and ran until 1999 before going on tour, steadily gaining a viewership as word of mouth spread the news that a play that uttered the word *vagina* 128 times left audiences giddy. After each performance, women lined up to speak with the actress to share their stories of violence and abuse and to offer their thanks.[152] Ensler described the ways the play connected her to other women in a 2000 interview: "One of the reasons I do this is that every night women leave that theater changed. I've had so many women come up to me after the show and say, 'I am so happy to have a vagina. I did not feel this way when I came into the theater.'"[153] Ensler's vagina talk clearly struck a cord.

Based on two hundred interviews with friends and friends of friends, Ensler's play highlighted women's experiences of embodiment and sexual difference, the stuff of early 1970s feminist culture, art, and activism—sex, love, rape, menstruation, mutilation, masturbation, birth, and orgasm. The vagina occupied the rhetorical center of the production because it occupied the center of women's identity, according to the playwright. "The story of your vagina is the story of your life, and women want to talk about their lives."[154] And talk they did. In "My Angry Vagina," a woman railed against the cold speculum, the "cold duck lips they shove inside you" during gynecological exams. This speculum was no tool of feminist empowerment as it had been in the early 1970s, when women's health activists ran seminars to encourage women to look at all parts of their bodies. Here it was part of a medical-industrial complex that alienated women from their bodies. "Why the scary paper dress that scratches your tits and crunches when you lie down so you feel like a wad of paper someone threw away? Why the rubber gloves? Why the flashlight all up there like Nancy Drew working against gravity, why the Nazi steel stirrups . . . my vagina's angry about those visits." Women's alienation from their bodies, or their vaginas, was the problem that might have once had no name but, thanks to Ensler, now had more names and stories than one could have ever imagined. For example, in "The Flood," an older Jewish woman explained the extent of her disassociation with her body when she announced that she hadn't "been down there since 1953." The play also sought to heal women's bodily dissociation from rape, incest, and war crimes. In "My Vagina Was My Village," a Bosnian woman described multiple brutal rapes that left her so cut off from her body as to be homeless. "I live someplace else now."[155]

To rehabilitate the vagina as beloved, *The Vagina Monologues* initiated a series of absurd questions to link identity back to the female body. "If your vagina got dressed, what would it wear?" Answers ranged from "a pink boa" to "an evening gown" and "a slicker"; interestingly, no vaginas suggested a burka or snood. At another point, vaginas are asked to speak. "If your vagina could talk, what would it say, in two words?" Hear them roar: "Slow down," "No, over there," "don't stop," "too hard," and "lick me."[156] Inside every empowered woman is an assertive vagina.

Given that Ensler's play offered no glance back to the history of vaginas or of feminist foremothers as *The Dinner Party* had, *The Vagina Monologues* spoke only of the endless present. Yet, even in this endless present, the ghost of the past nevertheless could be seen, if only in the shadows. One term of historicity used in *The Vagina Monologues* was the idea of "political correctness." This term and its naughty twin "political incorrectness" mark sites of Ensler's postfeminist push-back at the rules and strictures of 1970s feminism. In "Because He Liked to Look at It," a woman describes her complicated relationship to her vagina and to feminism's recent past: "I know the story. Vaginas are beautiful. Our self-hatred is only the internalized repression and hatred of the patriarchal culture. It isn't real. Pussys unite. I know all of it. Like, if we'd grown up in a culture where we were taught that fat thighs were beautiful, we'd all be pounding down milkshakes and cookies . . . but we didn't grow up in that culture. I hated my thighs and my vagina even more."

Similarly, in a monologue that brought Ensler much feminist criticism, "The Little Coochi Snorcher That Could," a thirteen-year-old girl (in later productions, aged to sixteen) described her sexual awakening with a twenty-four-year-old female neighbor. The sex they shared was pleasurable and for the young girl, transformative: "She tells me to always know how to give myself pleasure so I'll never need to rely on a man. In the morning I am worried that I've become a butch because I am so in love with her. She laughs but I never see her again. I realized later she was my surprising, unexpected, politically incorrect salvation."[157] The frank depiction of sex between a minor and an adult, pleasurable or not, angered some viewers who saw it as tacit support for pedophilia. It appeared that Ensler excused the violation because the adult was a lesbian and thus set up an indefensible double standard of behavior.[158] However, by the standard established by the monologue, this woman vetoed political correctness to partake in nonnormative "politically incorrect" pleasure. Pleasurable sex trumped feminist hangups about danger and coercion.

The characters of the long-running and enormously popular HBO series, *Sex and the City* (1998–2004) also viewed pleasurable sex as the ultimate trump card, the holy grail of women's lives, and also offered a push-back against 1970s feminism. The show, which won seven Emmys and eight Golden Globes during its six-year run, was best known for the frank talk among four friends about sex with their numerous male partners. Yet, in the spirit of a long-ago but not-quite-forgotten feminist sisterhood, the show established early on that the relationships among the women were more lasting and trustworthy than those with boyfriends. These beloved friends offered an emotional alternative to the compromising world of boyfriends and potential husbands. This feminist message could be easily gleaned, nestled as it was deep inside a show that rendered women's hard-won struggle for workplace equity and fair pay, rights to birth control and abortion, matters of such little relevance as to barely warrant a passing comment. Ditto its own absolute dependence on the Equal Credit Opportunity Act of 1974, which gave women the right to open their own lines of credit, including consumer credit cards.

Sexism and the feminist response it called forth had disappeared, relics of the past to be stepped over in four-inch heels. In episodes with titles like "Politically Erect" (season 3), "My Motherboard, Myself" (season 5), and "A Woman's Right to Shoes" (season 6), the series frankly played with its buried ancestry in 1970s feminism. The care the writers took to never let the hint of feminism frankly manifest itself was impressive, particularly whenever careerism proved difficult, allies at work hard to find, or the sex went bad.[159]

Much of feminist-themed culture in the 1990s tried to hide its seventies feminist heritage, seeing it as a set of "politically correct" strictures against pleasure. Nevertheless, feminist-themed culture in the 1990s continued to introduce ideals of women's equality while reveling in the difference sexual difference made in women's lives. Cast as a positive difference, not something to be dismantled, popular feminism in the 1990s recognized women's difference from men as a source of pleasure and fun as much as of vulnerability and pain. It showed, quite entertainingly at times, that sexual difference had survived feminist challenges to it. In this way, feminist-themed culture participated in making 1970s feminism into "history," showing readers and viewers that women could be equal without losing their difference. Ironically, or fortuitously, depending on where you sat, popular culture helped ready the way for a new audience for *The Dinner Party* and a new appreciation for what it symbolized. By making 1970s feminism into history, popular postfeminism took its founding insights into its DNA and made the celebration of women's difference appealing and affirming. When *The Dinner Party* next went on display in Brooklyn in 2002, it would do so proudly as history.

In Search of Permanence

The girls . . . are very happy to have a home.

The 1996 *Sexual Politics* exhibit at the Armand Hammer Museum renewed Chicago supporters' commitment to find *The Dinner Party* a permanent home. The conference had brought new attention to the historical importance of the piece and to its uncertain future. Despite efforts to secure a place for the work since 1989, nothing had been accomplished, and *The Dinner Party* remained in storage in New Mexico. By the fall of 1996, the process of finding a permanent exhibit space seemed chronically ineffective.

In the early 1990s, the TTF board raised funds and looked for institutions with which to partner, while also surveying possible sites for a stand-alone gallery. They cast a wide net, including the National Museum of Women in the Arts in Washington, DC, to situate it as part of a fine arts tradition, Seneca Falls, New York, to underscore its significance in women's history, and Santa Fe, the home of the artist.[160] The Cleveland community group, including Mickey Stein and Marcia Levine, renamed themselves *The Dinner Party* Site Project and looked for potential sites in the Midwest.[161] The American Association of University Women (AAUW) made finding "a home" for the piece their organization's priority in 1989, hoping their location in higher education would help the search for an institutional partner. Caroline Joyce from Illinois spearheaded a letter-writing campaign among AAUW members to raise funds. Hundreds of letters of support came from AAUW women in Wisconsin, Illinois, Florida, Maryland, New Mexico, and California to the offices of TTF.[162] TTF board members, including Pat Mathis from the UDC and Elizabeth Sackler, feminist from New York and TTF board member since 1989, also reached out to colleges and universities, hoping to find a receptive institution. When Mathis's efforts at the UDC blew up, Sackler offered to match funds with those of TTF to purchase land in Santa Fe.[163]

Sackler grew impatient with the slow process and in 1998, began to dream on a larger scale, envisioning a Museum for Feminist Art in which *The Dinner Party* would be a part.[164] The ambitious vision of an institutional location for feminist art provided a crucial step in Sackler's thinking. She became a board member at the Brooklyn Museum in 2000 and joined its collections committee in 2001. In 2002, Sackler acted. She not only agreed to donate *The Dinner Party* to the museum, but her name and considerable funds to create a new gallery devoted to feminist art.[165] To make it possible, the museum launched a $63 million capital campaign to rebuild its front entrance and to convert the 8,300-square-foot storage area into the Elizabeth A. Sackler Center for Feminist Art.[166] This time, no controversy erupted. In covering the opening the *New York Times* interviewed Brooklyn Museum director Arnold L. Lehman. "Twenty years ago, there were an enormous number of people who couldn't say the word 'vagina,' Mr. Lehman says, admitting that he, too, 'would have had a problem.'" But times changed, thanks in part to theater pieces like *The Vagina Monologues*. Now *The Dinner Party* "is the definitive work of feminist art."[167]

To celebrate the gift, the museum displayed *The Dinner Party* in 2002 in its cavernous first floor. Historicity, not controversy, marked the occasion. Roberta Smith in the *New York Times* christened it "almost as much a part of American culture as Norman Rockwell, Walt Disney, W.P.A. murals and the AIDS quilt." This exemplar of "*Our Body, Ourselves* phase" of 1970s feminist activism, she wrote, keeps getting better with age. "'The Dinner Party' outlines what might be called the second greatest story ever told." That story, she noted, "is simply this: the persistence of women in their struggle to achieve an equal chance to determine their own destinies and to be acknowledged for their full contribution to the survival and thriving of the human race as a whole. That survival and thriving is, of course, the No. 1 greatest story."[168]

When the permanent display of *The Dinner Party* opened in 2007 in the new gallery, it did so again as "history," as one of the elders of the feminist art movement. It opened along with an important new show, Global Feminisms, an exhibit of international feminist art since 1990.[169] The museum first directed visitors to *The Dinner Party*, moving them through the reverential sanctuary of the past before walking into the varied and diverse present of Global Feminisms. Remarkably, and not coincidentally, two weeks later the Museum of Contemporary Art in Los Angeles opened WACK! Art and the Feminist Revolution.[170] The canonization of 1970s feminist art had officially begun. *The Dinner Party*, the Helen Reddy of visual feminism, *The Woman's Room* of the museum world, the Walt Disney of the feminist art movement, had secured an honored place in it. No longer only deemed obscene, no longer an embarrassment of essentialism and unexamined racism, *The Dinner Party* arrived in Brooklyn as a monument to a movement that mattered.

For those critics still unwilling to view it as art, the only proper place for *The Dinner Party* was as "history." A reviewer in the *Women's Art Journal* noted that, "Now permanently ensconced at the Brooklyn Museum of Art,

[*The Dinner Party*] occupies an ironic position as a problematic work of 1970s feminist art. There is a certain paradox in the fact that Chicago's signature piece has found a final resting place in a major museum as an artifact of history."[171] Another stressed that *The Dinner Party* was most effective as a teaching device, a useful way to introduce students to the past, with all its pitfalls and optimism: "Its importance is due—at least in part—to the fact that it encapsulates so many of the concerns that were central to the new feminist art history and the burgeoning feminist art movement of the 1970s. . . . Faced with the task of introducing students to the notion of feminist art, still a contested subject in today's self-consciously 'post-feminist' cultural climate, one has only to show a slide of *The Dinner Party* and unpack its various aspects to instigate heated debate."[172]

Whether it was artifact or art, for Chicago, the meaning of *The Dinner Party* on permanent display was easy to grasp. It was less about history as a kind of mothballed irrelevancy and more about the broadest sense of it as a cultural record. For Chicago, "home" and history had always been the same. If some critics preferred to view *The Dinner Party* as a relic from the past, as "history," as a way of keeping it at a safe distance or as a way to manage their dislike of it, Chicago did not. She held history—women's inclusion into its grand narratives—as the ultimate goal, the ultimate home. The *New York Times* reported Chicago as saying that "The girls . . . are very happy to have a home."[173]

Taken literally, "the girls" Chicago referred to were the women of the plates. But "the girls" also represented a group much larger than the seated guests. While it surely included the 39 women seated at the table and 999 commemorated on the floor, it also included women represented through the runners, whose contribution to embroidery and to domestic arts shaped the practice of needlework; it included the names of the women in the Heritage Panels that comprised Chicago's version of world women's history in 1979; it included the named workers in the Acknowledgment Panels whose weekly practice of volunteering made *The Dinner Party* possible; it included the women whose sustained efforts resulted in the unconventional community tour of *The Dinner Party* and the women who helped find it a new "home" in Brooklyn. All these "girls"—Chicago and the women of *The Dinner Party*—found a home and a place in history.

EPILOGUE

A Prehistory of Postfeminism

IN THE SUMMER OF 1989, Judith Green from La Crosse, Wisconsin, wrote to Through the Flower describing how she first came to know about *The Dinner Party*. Her letter, like many others sent to the artist, testified to the circuitry of community and media through which *The Dinner Party* reached viewers, the well-worn paths between word of mouth, newspaper, and feminist reviews, consumer products, and audiences that had made the piece into one of the most famous feminist art blockbusters of all time.

When visiting Houston in the spring of 1980, Green convinced a friend to drive her to the Clear Lake City campus of the University of Houston because she had read an article in the paper about Chicago and the "associates carrying out a project about women, their history, and their art." Her friend, a "conservative," Green explains, was nevertheless "enthralled as we walked slowly around the exhibit." Green's letter records the ways that objects she bought spread the impact of *The Dinner Party*: "That day I bought a poster of the display and planned to see the piece again if I could. Subsequently, I found the book about the work's creation with color plates of each place setting. Sometimes I use that in the literature courses I teach at the University of Wisconsin and I have also lent the book to colleagues; some have bought their own copies and look forward themselves to being able to see this cooperatively created art work which is both more than craft and more than the sum of its parts." Posters and books allowed Green to take home pieces of her experience. She talked about it to family and students. When *The Dinner Party* opened in Chicago at another community venue, she told her students and took her husband to see it. "Both of us hope that *The Dinner Party* will have a home for permanent display because we both would like to see it several more times ourselves and we would like to tell our colleagues, friends and students to go and visualize this invaluable commemoration and chronology of women's creativity and culture."[1]

Green's letter hits upon many of the themes I've highlighted in my treatment of *The Dinner Party*, specifically my interest in the intersection of culture, popular culture, and populist tastes in the dissemination of feminist ideas. I started this project with the hope of restoring the role of audience interest and popular taste in the success of *The Dinner Party*, an element that the art institutional world tended to hold in low regard at best or, at worst, to see as a flaw of *The Dinner Party*. The case was not hard to make. Continually criticized and rejected by the art world, regularly dismissed by professional feminists (commentators whose feminist views constituted their expertise and thus their salaries), the public held steadfastly to their interest in seeing *The Dinner Party*, voted for it with their feet and wallets. In 1977, some read about it and went west (or south if they were already in California) to work in Chicago's Santa Monica studio; between 1979 and 1982, they organized groups to display it or bought tickets to view it in unconventional venues in Houston, Boston, Chicago, Cleveland, and Atlanta. They rented the artist's audio tour and purchased her books and memoirs, posters of her art, bumper stickers adorned with *The Dinner Party* logo, BBQ and box lunches, and tickets to concerts and lectures. From the mid-1970s to the mid-1990s they mailed in money to help make it, help tour it, and help secure for it a permanent viewing place. Thousands of women like Green were undeterred (or possibly incited) by the critics to go see it. Over a million people viewed *The Dinner Party* before the Brooklyn Museum became its permanent home.

The persistent popularity of *The Dinner Party* has made me think long and hard about what I understand about US feminism. The more I read about the production and reception of *The Dinner Party*, the more I have been struck by the seeming ability of the piece (and even the idea of the piece) to invoke a sense of identification among and between women, even if that identification was temporary, fleeting, or immediately held suspect. Its persistent appeal has raised questions for me about what, if anything, about the message of *The Dinner Party* drew viewers to it. I also wanted to know what about the piece made it hard for me to resist it. I have learned to put the ways I participated in (and at times secretly enjoyed) re-creating gender in a box with an instructional label: "Warning: Deconstruction required." Over the course of my research, I have learned that *The Dinner*

Party had—and has—an uncanny ability to pull viewers into its imagined category of "woman" if only for a few minutes or, for some, permanently; in the tradition of great cultural texts, it "works on"—engages, interpellates, moves—viewers on multiple levels simultaneously, including on the level of emotion. This ability to pull viewers in has happened repeatedly over many years and many venues, and continues to do so. I can't tell you the number of women who tell me they associate seeing *The Dinner Party* with tears—either her own or someone else's. *The Dinner Party*'s emotional appeal is, of course, the basis for its popular appeal and, ironically, a source of its feminist accomplishment.

The Dinner Party's popularity, the story of this book, underscores one undeniable fact that many have overlooked: the brilliance of *The Dinner Party* lies in its ornate, visually elaborate, riotously colorful, and simple emotional force. Its representation of women and its view of history speaks "straight to the heart," requires no decoding or interpretive framework to understand, demands no action be taken to prove allegiance. The experience—based on implied identification between "like selves" separated by time and culture—is the point, makes up its feminist message, and becomes the basis of its emotional power. As I have traced the debates that followed *The Dinner Party* over time (between 1975 and 2007), I've come to appreciate that while one might dislike the messenger, the message, and the imagery, or disapprove of the feminist artist, its feminist message, and its place in feminist art history, even dislike how it was made, how it is discussed, and how it never seems to go away, one still has to recognize that *The Dinner Party* communicates to audiences in a way that few pieces of art ever do.

The sheer popularity of *The Dinner Party* offers me, as a historian of 1970s feminism, a glimpse at an audience not often part of our written records: nonactivists. By *nonactivists* I mean people who did not necessarily bring to their viewing experience any familiarity with the ideas of feminism except what they had gotten from popular and media cultures. They might have heard about feminism, as I have suggested, from reading *The Color Purple*, *Ms.* magazine, or *Our Bodies, Ourselves*, or from watching *Tootsie* or *Right Out of History*, or seeing a Guerilla Girl poster on a street corner. They might have heard about the controversial artist and *The Dinner Party* from reading *Mother Jones*, the *Cleveland Plain Dealer* or *Chicago Tribune*, not from *Artforum* or *Art in America*. This made the hundreds of letters sent to the artist and the hundreds of comments left in the community guest books, the hundreds of small checks sent to the artist, the thousands of community tickets and amount of *Dinner Party*–related products sold valuable sources for me; these were much-needed populist correctives to the abundant fare of published records, printed media, and elite or specialized voices, many of whom dismissed *The Dinner Party* as bad art or bad feminism. These sources have offered me a way to trace one expression of popular interest in feminist-themed culture and possibly popular interest in feminism. Looking closely at the circulation of *The Dinner Party* has helped me see that much of what sustained an interest in feminism in the years when activism declined (or lost its appeal) was an appreciation of women's difference (however one defined that). In popular culture, feminism—simplified to the radical proposition of women's essential equality—had become associated with women's enjoyment of being women. *The Dinner Party*'s emotional appeal works so broadly because it bases its vision of women on their experience of sexual difference, of being women and girls in their families and societies. Women's experience of difference as represented in *The Dinner Party* both limits and enlivens them, gives women vantage points to see family and domestic life as the stuff of great art, and provides them with an unappreciated yet powerful alternative basis for political, religious, and scientific authority. One does not have to believe everything Chicago believes to feel the pull of her vision.

I have had a hard time accepting the ways that *The Dinner Party* worked on me. Returning to that box with the instructions for a minute, my training as a professional feminist in the 1980s was absolutely premised on upholding certain distinctions as unquestionable. First, that "women" and "men" were fictions that rested on the complicit involvement of biology, culture, and politics for their saliency. Second, that "experience" was a manipulated outcome of unconscious and embedded systems of authority and could never be invoked without great caution. Lastly, that cultural feminism—the emphasis in 1970s feminism on alternative institution building and women's unique if problematic real life difference—was ineffective as an agent of social change, wrong in its emphasis on women and not on gender, and not at all a promising approach for (then) young scholars like myself to take.[2] Imagine my surprise when I too cried in front of *The Dinner Party* in 2007 as my adolescent son and two nephews shrieked in horror at the vagina plates and swore off feminist art for all time. I had read about *The Dinner Party* for years but had assumed it was a unicorn. Let's just say I hold my training as a postmodern gender historian a little differently as a result of my encounter with *The Dinner Party*. I can now see the ways that sexual difference is a fertile ground for popular engagement with feminism and just possibly the only starting point for a lively understanding of what the next women's revolution might entail.

I hope that my cultural history of the feminist debates surrounding the production and reception of *The Dinner Party* provides a new angle to histories of feminism after 1970. Our accounts of second-wave feminism have demonstrated the varieties of political engagement that fall under its banner, from labor women to civil rights women, liberal Democratic and Republican women, hippy and countercultural women, to antiwar, anti-imperialism women.[3] These histories share an important focus on political activism. But sometime after the 1970s, the broad social movement aspect of the second wave began to de-escalate, and by the mid 1980s, with the feminist sex wars and the conservative takeover of the antipornography movement, feminist activism itself dispersed into a multitude of forms, formats, and directions; whatever centrifugal force had been holding the "movement" together, however loosely, broke and flung expressions of feminism across the social and cultural universe.

Given this, how can historians of feminism address their topic outside of a social protest or a social movement model? One suggestion I have explored here is to historicize the multiple ways that feminism from 1970 onward was never only a social protest movement but always involved culture, consumption, and an investment in individual therapeutics or personal change. By *therapeutics* I mean the use of feminist ideas to remake, rearrange, embellish, or repair an individual's sense of herself, with or without the help of a commodity. Early second-wave feminists identified the arena of "psychology and the self" as the proper and only place for a feminist "revolution." Socialist feminists might have targeted economic structures, but radical feminists targeted social roles, subjectivity, and the meaning making inside your head. This attention to personal feelings and to personal transformation as a road to feminist revolution made the ideas potent, engaging, and unmanageable. It made feminist insight not only about political action (collective) but also about personal change (individual). Targeting feelings and psychology made feminist ideas impressively versatile in application and breathtakingly vulnerable to co-optation. They quickly adhered to products, perhaps most famously in the "You've come a long way, baby," campaign from cigarette maker Virginia Slims. This simple and familiar phrase ("you've come a long way") embedded the product in a story of "you" traveling from point A (free of cigarettes and five pounds heavier) to a better point B (addicted and slim). Yes, Virginia, feminist ideas lived and thrived in a variety of settings, including the consumer market after 1970.

Interestingly, these traits—culture, consumption, and investment in individual therapeutics—are the very aspects attributed to "postfeminism," a form of feminism assumed to bear little resemblance to its implied precursor.[4] By postfeminism I mean a broad cultural discourse that paints the following rosy picture: sometime in the mid-1970s, America did away with sexism and other formal gender obstacles; by the 1980s a new era dawned when women attained full equality thanks to new laws, new agencies, and new protections. Blessedly, the humorless feminist hordes were told to stand down. Susan Faludi offers a contrasting characterization to this new age by calling it a "backlash" against feminism.[5] She demonstrates a sustained misinformation campaign in the popular media that painted a picture of US women as being overwhelmingly single or tragically infertile, in sum, a group made desperately unhappy by their equality and big careers. Backlash, or the rise of antifeminist media, worked in tandem with the growing conservatism after 1980 to set the stage for postfeminism in the 1990s, a style of gender pride that supported women's right to pole dance and vote.[6] Call it "enlightened sexism" as Susan Douglas does or a semipeaceful settlement between feminism and antifeminism on the terrain of popular culture, as I have elsewhere.[7] Whatever name you give it, postfeminism is based on the assumption that gender equality already exists. It does not presume all women's troubles are over or that all of women's problems come from the fact (or fictions) of gender, only that equality exists as a resource—something to call upon. It is a view chock-full of exceptions, problems, ambivalences, and falsehoods. Yet it would appear that the belief in women's equality is alive and well, despite evidence to the contrary.

What we couldn't see in the 1980s but can today is that in postfeminist eras (1920s, 1990s), culture (broadly defined) is not a sideshow to the main stage of politics, since the "post" actually marks the decline of political activism. Rather, in postfeminist eras, culture broadly and popular culture specifically carries the task of sustaining feminist insights, albeit in altered forms. In the absence of a focused movement or a temporary consensus around formal political goals (be it suffrage, ERA, or abortion access), culture moves to the forefront of feminist engagement as the main circuitry between ideas and people. Culture becomes a basis for feminist communities of all kinds—temporary, local, mass-mediated, time-bound, through texts and literal spaces. Through culture makers like Judy Chicago and the objects they produce, historians can trace threads of 1970s feminist insight as those insights become woven into the cultural fabric of US society (movies, television, literature, art), just as one may trace the feminist political movement as it disperses into institutions, nongovernmental organizations, and various governmental agencies. The ongoing life of feminist ideas in cultural and pop cultural arenas and through cultural products constitutes an important afterlife (even second life) of the social movement. Through them one can see the infectious agents of feminist thought continue to spread, person by person, audience by audience. I would go so far as to suggest that these cultural threads after 1970 helped to turn feminism from an oppositional social movement into a social value, so widely held and so commonplace that it no longer seems to require a political movement. These cultural threads constituted the bittersweet, compromised success of second-wave feminism.

Yet, as we know, social values (like women's equality) are not the same as social movements (like feminism). Social values harmonize with other dominant values and thus lose their challenge to "the way things are." Feminism as a movement for gender equality and in support of efforts to end discrimination against people "on account of sex" cannot sustain itself just through cultural products with their individualized targets of change. Feminism as a movement requires oppositional thinking. In this way, popular postfeminism marks a decline in the public's interest in a social movement that challenges gender roles, challenges the organization of the family or of heterosexual sex. Postfeminism undeniably constitutes a threat or dangerous "alternative" to (distraction from) feminist political activism.

At the same time, postfeminism also has the DNA of 1970s feminism in it, and along with it, a potential for social challenge at its heart. Seventies feminism and the postfeminist 1990s share common themes, specifically when one looks at culture. Ironically, postfeminism fundamentally relies on (and then disavows) the narratives and tropes of seventies feminism to establish its view of the world. It acknowledges sexual difference as an ongoing reality, it acknowledges women's difference as biologically and socially created, and it enjoys much of that difference. Postfeminism carries the 1970s feminist values of identification between women ("we are a group"), recognition (and misrecognition) of commonality ("we are sisters!" as well as "are we sisters?"), the importance of self-transformation and self-authoring (woman as authenticating subject), of "women's cultures" of resistance ("together we can get by"). At the same time, by disavowing its heritage in a social protest movement, postfeminism can't reckon with ongoing sex discrimination, sexual violence, and nitty-gritty economic details like pay differentials because to do so would invoke the specter of the humorless, unattractive, and abrasive (and potentially queer or man-hating) seventies feminist and her angry, activist sisters. There's no emotional appeal in that anymore.

However, we can think like feminists even in a postfeminist age by recognizing the infectious germ of feminist ideas as they move out, forward, and through time, place, and medium. The texts that preserve and circulate feminist ideas might disappoint us with their obvious comfort with "how things are," with market values and national pride. But if we don't read as feminists in search of women's resiliency and pride, we run the risk of not seeing how much feminism—as a cultural resource—continues to do for women, one encounter at a time.

Notes

INTRODUCTION

1. Susan Hill, interview with author, July 2011.

2. See Gail Levin, *Becoming Judy Chicago: A Biography of the Artist* (New York: Harmony Books, 2007); Laura Meyer, "A Studio of Their Own: The Legacy of the Fresno Feminist Experiment," in Laura Meyer, ed., with essays by Laura Meyer and Faith Wilding, *A Studio of Their Own: The Legacy of the Fresno Feminist Experiment*, (Fresno: Press at the California State University, Fresno, 2009); Edward Lucie-Smith, *Judy Chicago: An American Vision* (New York: Watson-Guptill Publications, 2000).

3. Judy Chicago, *Through the Flower: My Struggle as a Woman Artist* (New York: Penguin, 1975), 55.

4. Lisa Gail Collins and Margo Natalie Crawford, eds., *New Thoughts on the Black Arts Movement* (New Brunswick, N.J.: Rutgers University, 2006); Scott Kurashige, *The Shifting Grounds of Race: Black and Japanese Americans in the Making of Multicultural Los Angeles* (Princeton, N.J.: Princeton University Press, 2010); Laura Pulido, *Black, Brown, Yellow, and Left: Radical Activism in Los Angeles* (Berkeley: University of California Press, 2006).

5. This compressed biography is based on Levin, *Becoming Judy Chicago*, and Judy Chicago, *Through the Flower*.

6. Michael Kammen, *Visual Shock: A History of Art Controversies in American Culture* (New York: Vintage Press, 2006), 181.

7. Ibid., 183.

8. Susan Sontag, "Against Interpretation," in *Against Interpretation and Other Essays* (New York: Basic Books, 1966), 268; Lucy Lippard, *A Different War: Vietnam in Art* (Bellingham, Wash.: Whatcom Museum of History and Art, and Seattle, Wash.: Real Comet Press, 1990).

9. Levin, *Becoming Judy Chicago*, 117.

10. Michael Kammen, *Visual Shock: A History of Art Controversies in American Culture* (New York: Vintage Press, 2006), 181.

11. Kellie Jones, "Black West, Thoughts on Art in Los Angeles," in Lisa Gail Collins and Margo Natalie Crawford, eds., *New Thoughts on the Black Arts Movement* (New Brunswick, N.J.: Rutgers University, 2006), 43–74.

12. Vivien Green Fryd, "Suzanne Lacy's *Three Weeks in May*: Feminist Activist Per-

formance Art as "Expanded Public Pedagogy," *NWSA* Journal 19, no. 1 (spring 2007): 23–38.

13. Gallery 32 and Its Circle, organized by Carolyn Peter, director and curator of the Laband Art Gallery, and Damon Willick, assistant professor of modern and contemporary art history, Loyola Marymount University, 2008.

14. "A Date with Judy: Dialogue with Judy Chicago, Suzanne Lacy and Faith Wilding," unpublished article for *Images and Issues*, 1980—letter dated December 26, 1980, 6.

15. Ibid., 4.

16. Lisa Gail Collins, "The Art of Transformation: Parallels in the Black Arts and Feminist Art Movements," in Lisa Gail Collins and Margo Natalie Crawford, eds., *New Thoughts on the Black Arts Movement* (New Brunswick, N.J.: Rutgers University, 2006), 273–96.

17. My approach to the consumer market is informed by Elizabeth Chin, *Purchasing Power: Black Kids and American Consumer Culture* (Minneapolis: University of Minnesota Press, 2001); Thomas Frank, *The Conquest of Cool: Business Culture, Counterculture, and the Rise of Hip Consumerism* (Chicago: University of Chicago Press, 1997); Marilyn Halter, *Shopping for Identity: The Marketing of Ethnicity* (New York: Schocken Books 2000); John Seabrook, *Nobrow: The Culture of Marketing, the Marketing of Culture* (New York: Vintage Press, 2000).

18. Feminist engagement with popular culture is extensive. Here are a few that have informed my approach: Kim Akass and Janet McCabe, eds., *Reading "The L Word"* (London: I. B. Tauris, 2006); Alice Echols, *Hot Stuff: Disco and the Remaking of American Culture* (New York: Norton, 2010); Barbara Ehrenreich, Elizabeth Hess, Gloria Jacobs, *Remaking Love: The Feminization of Sex* (Garden City, N.J.: Anchor Press, 1987); Sarah Gamble, ed., *Feminism and Postfeminism* (New York: Routledge, 1998); Laura Grindstaff, *The Money Shot: Trash, Class and the Making of TV Talk Shows* (Chicago: University of Chicago Press, 2002); Molly Haskell, *From Reverence to Rape: The Treatment of Women in the Movies* (Chicago: University of Chicago Press, 3rd ed., 1987); Astrid Henry, *Not My Mother's Sister: Generational Conflict and Third-Wave Feminism* (Bloomington: Indiana University Press, 2004); Mandy Merck, Naomi Segal, Elizabeth Wright, *Coming Out of Feminism?* (London: Blackwell Press 1998); Susan Jeffords, *The Remasculinization of America: Gender and the Vietnam War* (Bloomington: Indiana University, 1989); Merri Lisa Johnson, ed., *Third Wave Feminism and Television: Jane Puts It in a Box* (London: I. B. Tauris, 2007); Tania Modleski, *Feminism without Women: Culture and Criticism in a "Postfeminist" Age* (New York: Routledge, 1991); Janice Radway, *A Feeling for Books: The Book of the Month Club, Literary Taste, and Middle-Class Desire* (Chapel Hill, N.C.: Duke University Press, 1997); Beretta E. Smith-Shomade: *Shaded Lives: African-American Women and Television* (New Brunswick, N.J.: Rutgers University Press, 2002); Sasha Torres, *Black, White and in Color: Television and Black Civil Rights* (Princeton N.J.: Princeton University Press, 2003).

19. Susan Douglas, *Where the Girls Are: Growing Up Female with the Mass Media* (New York: Times Books, 1994), 7.

20. Ibid., and Bonnie Dow, *Prime-Time Feminism: Television, Media Culture, and the Women's Movement since 1970* (Philadelphia: University of Pennsylvania Press, 1996).

21. Amy Erdman Farrell, *Yours in Sisterhood: "Ms." Magazine and the Promise of Popular Feminism* (Chapel Hill: University of North Carolina Press, 1998), 5.

22. Lisa Marie Hogeland, *Feminism and Its Fictions: The Consciousness-Raising Novel and the Women's Liberation Movement* (Philadelphia: University of Pennsylvania Press,

1998); Farrell, *Yours in Sisterhood*; Douglas, *Where the Girls Are*; Dow, *Prime-Time Feminism*.

23. Anita Diamant, *Boston Phoenix*, December 1979.

24. Catharine MacKinnon, *Feminism Unmodified: Discourses on Life and Law* (Cambridge, Mass.: Harvard University Press, 1987).

25. Verta Taylor and Leila Rupp, "Women's Culture and Lesbian Feminist Activism: A Reconsideration of Cultural Feminism," *Signs* 19, no. 1 (autumn 1993): 32–61.

26. Lisa Duggan and Nan Hunter, *Sex Wars: Sexual Dissent and Political Culture* (New York: Routledge, 1995); Jane Gerhard, *Desiring Revolution: Second-Wave Feminism and the Rewriting of American Sexual Thought, 1920–1982* (New York: Columbia University Press, 2001).

27. Alice Echols, "The Taming of the Id: Feminist Sexual Politics, 1968–83," in Carole S. Vance, ed., *Pleasure and Danger: Exploring Female Sexuality* (London: Pandora, 1984), 51.

28. Lisa Duggan, "Censorship in the Name of Feminism" (1984), in Lisa Duggan and Nan Hunter, *Sex Wars: Sexual Dissent and Political Culture* (New York: Routledge, 1995); Ann Snitnow, Christine Stansell, and Sharon Thompson, *Powers of Desire* (New York: Monthly Review Press, 1983); Carole S. Vance, ed., *Pleasure and Danger: Exploring Female Sexuality* (London: Pandora, 1984).

29. Taylor and Rupp, "Women's Culture and Lesbian Feminist Activism," 32.

30. Ellen Willis, "Radical Feminism and Feminist Radicalism," *Social Text* 9/10 (spring–summer 1984): 91–118, 92.

31. Alice Echols, *Daring to Be Bad: Radical Feminism in America, 1967–1975* (Minneapolis: University of Minnesota Press, 1990).

32. See Flora Davis, *Moving the Mountain: The Women's Movement in America since 1960* (New York: Touchstone Books, 1991); and Farrell, *Yours in Sisterhood*.

33. Varda Burstyn, ed., *Women against Censorship* (Vancouver: Douglas & McIntyre, 1985); Lynn S. Chancer, *Reconcilable Difference: Confronting Beauty, Pornography, and the Future of Feminism* (Berkeley: University of California Press, 1998); Gerhard, *Desiring Revolution*.

34. These are impressive contributions, which include Benita Roth, *Separate Roads to Feminism: Black, Chicana, and White Feminist Movements in America's Second Wave* (New York: Cambridge University Press, 2003); Kimberly Springer, *Living for the Revolution: Black Feminist Organizations, 1968–1980* (Durham, N.C.: Duke University Press, 2005); and Winnie Brines, *The Trouble between Us: An Uneasy History of Black and White Women in the Feminist Movement* (New York: Oxford University Press, 2007).

35. Nancy Cott, *The Grounding of Modern Feminism* (New Haven, Conn.: Yale University Press, 1987) and Mari Jo Buhle, *Feminism and Its Discontents* (Cambridge, Mass.: Harvard University Press, 2000).

36. For example, Anne Enke uses space rather than labels to define and trace feminism. See *Finding the Movement: Sexuality, Contested Space, and Feminist Activism* (Chapel Hill, N.C.: Duke University Press, 2007); Wendy Kline focuses on targets of feminist activism in *Bodies of Knowledge: Sexuality, Reproduction, and Women's Health in the Second Wave* (Chicago: University of Chicago Press, 2010).

37. Eve Ensler, *The Vagina Monologues* (New York: Villard, 2001). See Christine M. Cooper, "Worrying about Vaginas: Feminism and Eve Ensler's *The Vagina Monologues*," *Signs: Journal of Women in Culture and Society* 32, no. 3 (2007): 727–58.

38. Hilary McLeod to Judy Chicago, April 26, 1982, Judy Chicago Papers, Arthur and

Elizabeth Schlesinger Library on the History of Women in America, Radcliffe Institute for Advanced Study, Harvard University (hereafter JCP), carton 25, file 2. Emphasis in original.

39. Diane Gelon, interview with author, January 30, 2010.

40. Susan Brownmiller, *In Our Time: A Memoir of a Revolution* (New York: Dell, 1999); Karla Jay, *Tales of the Lavender Menace: A Memoir of Liberation* (New York: Basic Books, 1999); Terry Wolverton, *Insurgent Muse: Life and Art at the Woman's Building* (San Francisco: City Lights, 2002); Echols, *Daring to Be Bad.*

CHAPTER ONE. Making Feminist Artists

1. Gail Levin, *Becoming Judy Chicago: A Biography of the Artist* (New York: Harmony Books, 2007), 136.

2. Interview with the author, July 11, 2010.

3. "Judy Chicago and Lloyd Hamrol Interview Each Other," *Criteria: A Review of the Arts* 1, no. 2 (November 1974): 9. Quoted in Levin, *Becoming Judy Chicago*, 137.

4. Laura Pulido, *Black, Brown, Yellow and Left: Radical Activism in Los Angeles* (Berkeley: University of California Press, 2006).

5. Faith Wilding, "Gestations in a Studio of Our Own: The Feminist Art Program in Fresno, California, 1970–1971," in Laura Meyer, ed., *A Studio of Their Own: The Legacy of the Fresno Feminist Experiment* (Fresno: Press at the California State University, Fresno, 2009), 79–102, 80–81.

6. Lillian Faderman, "Joyce Aiken: Thirty Years of Feminist Art and Pedagogy in Fresno," in Jill Fields, ed., *Entering the Picture: Judy Chicago, The Fresno Feminist Art Program and the Collective Visions of Women Artists* (New York: Routledge, 2012), 145–57, 146.

7. Quoted in Judith Dancoff, "Judy Chicago Interview," *Everywoman* 2, no. 7, issue 18 (May 1971): 4.

8. Priscilla English, "An Interview with Two Artists from *Womanhouse*," *New Woman* (April/May 1972): 36–43, 37, Judy Chicago Papers, Arthur and Elizabeth Schlesinger Library on the History of Women in America, Radcliffe Institute for Advanced Study, Harvard University (hereafter JCP), carton 11, file 37.

9. Ibid., 38.

10. Jack Glenn Gallery ad, *Artforum* 9, no. 2 (October 1970): 20.

11. Jack Glenn Gallery ad, *Artforum* 9, no. 4 (December 1970): 36.

12. Levin, *Becoming Judy Chicago*, 139.

13. Quoted in William Wilson, "Judy Chicago Exhibition at Cal State Fullerton Gallery," *Los Angeles Times*, November 2, 1970, 4.

14. Women's Ad Hoc Committee/Women Artists in Revolution/WSABAL, "To the Viewing Public for the 1970 Whitney Annual Exhibition," in Hilary Robinson, ed., *Feminism-Art-Theory: An Anthology 1968–2000* (Malden, Mass.: Blackwell Publishers, 2001), 56–57, 56. See chapter 2.

15. Rozsika Parker and Griselda Pollock, *Old Mistresses: Women, Art and Ideology* (New York: Pantheon Books, 1981), 6.

16. Joanna Gardner-Huggett, "The Women Artists' Cooperative Space as a Site for Social Change: Artemisia Gallery, Chicago (1973–1970)," in Fields, ed., *Entering the Picture*, 174.

17. Ibid.

18. Los Angeles Council of Women Artists, 1976. Reprinted in Faith Wilding, *By Our Own Hands: The Women Artist's Movement, Southern California, 1970–1976* (Santa Monica: Double X, 1977), 21.

19. Valerie Smith, "Abundant Evidence: Black Women Artists of the 1960s and 1970s," in Fields, ed., *Entering the Picture*, 119–31, 123.

20. L. Ryan Musgrave, "Liberal Feminism, from Law to Art: The Impact of Feminist Jurisprudence on Feminist Aesthetics," in "Women, Art, and Aesthetics," special issue, *Hypatia* 18, no. 4 (autumn 2003): 214–35, 225.

21. Kimberly Springer, *Living for the Revolution: Black Feminist Organizations, 1968–1980* (Durham, N.C.: Duke University Press, 2005).

22. Kellie Jones, "Black West, Thoughts on Art in Los Angeles," in Lisa Gail Collins and Margo Natalie Crawford, eds., *New Thoughts on the Black Arts Movement* (New Brunswick, N.J.: Rutgers University Press, 2006), 43–74.

23. Thailia Gouma-Peterson and Patricia Mathews, "The Feminist Critique of Art History," *Art Bulletin* 69, no. 3 (1987): 326–57, 329, 327.

24. Cristin C. Rom, "One View: The Feminist Art Journal," *Women's Art Journal* 2, no. 2 (autumn 1981–winter 1982): 19–24, 19.

25. Women's Ad Hoc Committee/Women Artists in Revolution/WSABAL, "To the Viewing Public for the 1970 Whitney Annual Exhibition" (1970), reprinted in Hilary Robins, ed., *Feminism-Art-Theory: An Anthology, 1968–2000* (Malden, Mass.: Blackwell, 2001), 56–57, 56. Emphasis in original.

26. Mary D. Garrard, "Feminist Politics: Networks and Organizations" in Norma Broude and Mary Garrad, eds., *The Power of Feminist Art: The American Movement of the 1970s, History and Impact* (New York: Harry N. Abrams, 1994), 88–103, 90–91.

27. Linda Nochlin, "Why Have There Been No Great Women Artists?," *Artforum* 1971, reprinted in *Women, Art, and Power and Other Essays* (New York: Harper & Row, 1988), 145–75; Rom, "One View," 19–20.

28. Gouma-Peterson and Mathews, "Feminist Critique of Art History," 329; editorial, *Feminist Art Journal* (April 1972): 2.

29. The Museum of Philadelphia Civic Center followed up in the spring of 1974 with another show of work of 81 contemporary women artists, chosen by five female curators, "Women's Work: American Art 1974." Gloria Orenstein, "Review Essay: Art History," *Signs* 1, no. 2 (winter 1975): 505–25, 518.

30. "The Los Angeles County Museum of Art," Los Angeles Council of Women Artists, 1976. Reprinted in Wilding, *By Our Own Hands*, 21.

31. Wilding, *By Our Own Hands*, 1.

32. Ibid., 18.

33. Lise Vogel, "Fine Arts and Feminism: The Awakening Consciousness," *Feminist Studies* 2 (1974): 3–37.

34. English, "Interview with Two Artists from *Womanhouse*," 38.

35. Nancy Youdelman, "Reflections on the Feminist Art Class at FSU, Fresno 1970–71," unpublished, 2008. Quoted in Wilding, "Gestations in a Studio of Our Own," 85.

36. *Art Journal* 31, no. 3 (fall 1971): 48, JCP, carton 11, file 38.

37. Chris Rush to Faith Wilding, email July 7, 2008. Quoted in Wilding, "Gestations in a Studio of Our Own," 85.

38. Judy Chicago, *Through the Flower: My Struggle as a Woman Artist* (New York: Penguin, 1975), 74.

39. English, "Interview with Two Artists from *Womanhouse*," 38.

40. Chicago, *Through the Flower*, 74.

41. Wilding, "Gestations in a Studio of Our Own," 81.

42. Laura Meyer with Faith Wilding, "Collaboration and Conflict in the Fresno Feminist Art Program," in Fields, ed., *Entering the Picture*, 45–63, 48.

43. Wilding, "Gestations in a Studio of Our Own," 82; Annelise Orleck, *Storming Caesar's Palace: How Black Mothers Fought Their Own War on Poverty* (Boston: Beacon Press, 2005); Linda Gordon, *Pitied but Not Entitled: Single Mothers and the History of Welfare* (New York: Free Press, 1994).

44. Moira Roth, "Interview with Suzanne Lacy," from oral history interview with Suzanne Lacy, March 16 and 24 and September 27, 1990, Archives of American Art, Smithsonian Institution. Reprinted in Fields, ed., *Entering the Picture*, 78–86, 79.

45. Wilding, "Gestations in a Studio of Our Own," 82–83.

46. Ibid., 84, 86.

47. Laura Meyer, "A Studio of Their Own: The Legacy of the Fresno Feminist Experiment" in Meyer, ed., *Studio of Their Own*, 3–34, 6.

48. Wilding, *By Our Own Hands*, 9.

49. Meyer, "Studio of Their Own," 15.

50. Winifred Breines, *The Trouble between Us: An Uneasy History of White and Black Women in the Feminist Movement* (New York: Oxford University Press, 2006).

51. Roth, "Interview with Suzanne Lacy," 80.

52. Meyer, "Studio of Their Own," 7.

53. Chicago, *Through the Flower*, 73.

54. Nancy Youdelman and Karen LeCocq, "Reflections on the First Feminist Art Program," in Fields, ed., *Entering the Picture*, 64–77, 65.

55. Meyer, "Studio of Their Own," 16.

56. Chicago, *Through the Flower*, 83.

57. Wilding, *By Our Own Hands*, 11.

58. Estelle Freedman, "Separatism as Strategy: Female Institution Building and American Feminism, 1870–1930," *Feminist Studies* 5, no. 3 (fall 1979): 512–29.

59. Wilding, *By Our Own Hands*, 11.

60. Chicago, *Through the Flower*, 74.

61. Wilding, *By Our Own Hands*, 12.

62. Judy Chicago, "Establishing a Feminist Art Program," unpublished, JCP, carton 11, file 17. This became an installation titled *I Tried Everything* (1972) by Suzanne Lacy, Dori Atlantis, Jan Lester, and Nancy Youdelman after they transferred to CalArts. Meyers, *Studio of Their Own*, figures 35–38.

63. Chicago, "Establishing a Feminist Art Program."

64. Meyer with Wilding, "Collaboration and Conflict in the Fresno Feminist Art Program," 59.

65. Wilding, *By Our Own Hands*, 13.

66. The literature on the transformation of college classrooms by the anti Vietnam War movement and the counterculture is vast. See Robert Cohen and Reginald Zelnik, eds., *The Free Speech Movement: Reflections on Berkeley in the 1960s* (Berkeley: University of California Press, 2002); Todd Gitlin, *The Sixties: Years of Hope, Days of Rage* (New York: Bantam, 1993); Gretchen Lemke-Santangelo, *Daughters of Aquarius: Women of the Counterculture* (Lawrence: University of Kansas Press, 2009); Ruth Rosen, *The World Split Open: How the Women's Movement Changed America* (New York: Penguin 2001).

67. Chicago, "Establishing a Feminist Art Program."

68. Chicago, *Through the Flower*, 78.

69. Levin, *Becoming Judy Chicago*, 148.

70. Karen LeCocq, *The Easiest Thing to Remember: My Life as an Artist, a Feminist, and a Manic Depressive* (Bloomington, Ind.: 1st Books Library, 2002), 54.

71. LeCocq, *Easiest Thing to Remember*, 55–56, 57–58 (emphasis in original), 62.

72. LeCocq quoted in Meyer, "Studio of Their Own," 16.

73. Judy Chicago, "Consciousness-Raising," unpublished, JCP, carton 11, file 17.

74. Vanalyne Green to Faith Wilding, email August 8, 2008. Quoted in Wilding, "Gestations in a Studio of Our Own," 86.

75. Meyer, "Studio of Their Own," 16.

76. Levin, *Becoming Judy Chicago*, 148.

77. Ibid., 149.

78. Chicago, *Through the Flower*, 80.

79. Chicago, *Through the Flower*, 84–85, 87, 85.

80. Kathy Davis, *The Making of Our Bodies, Ourselves: How Feminism Travels Across Borders* (Durham, N.C.: Duke University Press, 2007); Wendy Kline, *Bodies of Knowledge: Sexuality, Reproduction, and Women's Health in the Second Wave* (Chicago: University of Chicago Press, 2010).

81. Wilding, "Gestations in a Studio of Our Own," 96.

82. LeCocq, *Easiest Thing to Remember*, 61.

83. Youdelman and LeCocq, "Reflections on the First Feminist Art Program," 65.

84. Ulrike Müller, "Re-Tracing the Feminist Art Program," at http://www.encore.at/retracing/index2.html. Accessed on July 19, 2010.

85. Meyer, *Studio of Their Own*, n.p., figures 6–9.

86. Ibid., figure 37.

87. Ibid., figure 25.

88. Ibid., figure 26.

89. Ibid., figures 19, 20, 21.

90. Isabel Welsh and Judy Chicago, "My Menstrual Life," December 1971, unpublished, JCP, carton 11, file 38.

91. Meyer, "Studio of Their Own," 12.

92. Judith Dancoff, director, *Judy Chicago and the California Girls* (film), 1971/2008, www.judychicagoandthecaliforniagirls.com.

93. Wilding, "Gestations in a Studio of Our Own," 97.

94. Shulamith Firestone, *The Dialectic of Sex: The Case for Feminist Revolution* (New York: Morrow, 1970).

95. Wilding, "Gestations in a Studio of Our Own," 96.

96. *Art Journal* 31, no. 3 (fall 1971): 48, 48, and 49.

97. Chicago, *Through the Flower*, 82–83. Emphasis in original.

98. Judy Chicago and Miriam Schapiro, "The Liberation of the Female Artist," undated, JCP, carton 6, file 1.

99. Judy Chicago to Admissions, California Institute of Arts, letter March 27, 1971, JCP carton 11, file 17. Emphasis in original.

100. Chicago, *Through the Flower*, 89, 90, 90.

101. Ibid., 90.

102. Wilding, *By Our Own Hands*, 14.

103. Meyer, "Studio of Their Own," 18–19.

104. Suzanne Lacy Oral History oral history interview with Suzanne Lacy, March 16 and 24 and September 27, 1990, Archives of American Art, Smithsonian Institution.

105. Ann Kalmbach to Judy Chicago, letter July 14, 1972, JCP, carton 11, file 17.

106. Joy Merrill to Judy Chicago, letter Jan. 4, 1972, JCP, carton 11, file 17.

107. Miriam Schapiro, "The Education of Women as Artists: Project *Womanhouse*," *Art Journal* 31, no. 3 (spring 1972): 268–70, 268.

108. Judy Chicago, *Through the Flower*, 104.

109. Wilding, *By Our Own Hands*, 25.

110. Chicago, *Through the Flower*, 194.

111. Coined by Mira Schor in "Miss Elizabeth Bennett Goes to Feminist Boot Camp," in *A Decade of Negative Thinking: Essays on Art, Politics, and Daily Life* (Durham, N.C.: Duke University Press, 2009), 75–87.

112. Schapiro, "Education of Women as Artists," 268.

113. For the importance of showing signs of labor in art, see Laura Meyer, "From Finish Fetish to Feminism: Judy Chicago's *Dinner Party* in California Art History," in Amelia Jones, ed., *Sexual Politics: Judy Chicago's "Dinner Party" in Feminist Art History* (Berkeley: University of California Press, 1996), 46–81.

114. LeCocq, *Easiest Thing to Remember*, 72.

115. Mira Schor to Mrs. Moss, letter November 7, 1971. Reprinted as "Miss Elizabeth Bennett Goes to Feminist Boot Camp," in Schor, *Decade of Negative Thinking*, 75–87, 79.

116. LeCocq, *Easiest Thing to Remember*, 73.

117. Schor to Moss.

118. Chicago, *Through the Flower*, 108, 109.

119. See, for example, Mari Jo Buhle, *Feminism and Its Discontents: A Century of Struggle with Psychoanalysis* (Cambridge, Mass.: Harvard University Press, 1998); Nancy Cott, *The Grounding of Modern Feminism* (New Haven, Conn.: Yale University Press, 1987); Christine Stansell, *The Feminist Promise: 1792 to the Present* (New York: Random House, 2010).

120. Jo Freeman, "The Tyranny of Structurelessess" (1970), reprinted in Rosalyn Baxandall and Linda Gordon, eds., *Dear Sister: Dispatches from the Women's Liberation Movement* (New York: Basic Books, 2000), 73–75.

121. Chicago, *Through the Flower*, 108–9, 108.

122. Schapiro, "Education of Women as Artists," 268.

123. Chicago, *Through the Flower*, 110–11.

CHAPTER TWO. Making Feminist Art

1. Site-specific art was first described in 1975 by Peter Frank in "Site Sculpture," *Art News*, October 1975. See also Lucy Lippard, "Art Outdoors, In and Out of the Public Domain," *Studio International*, March–April 1977.

2. L. Ryan Musgrave, "Liberal Feminism, from Law to Art: The Impact of Feminist Jurisprudence on Feminist Aesthetics," in "Women, Art, and Aesthetics," special issue, *Hypatia* 18, no. 4 (autumn 2003): 214–35, 226.

3. Betty Friedan, *The Feminine Mystique* (New York: Dell, 1963); Judy Syfers, "I Want a Wife," *Ms.* magazine 1 (spring 1971); Pat Mainardi, "The Politics of Housework," in Robin Morgan, ed., *Sisterhood Is Powerful* (New York: Vintage Press, 1970), 501–9.

4. For histories of Cold War–era family life, see Elaine Tyler May, *Homeward Bound:*

American Families in the Cold War (New York: Basic Books, 1988); Ruth Feldstein, *Motherhood in Black and White: Race and Sex in American Liberalism* (Ithaca, N.Y.: Cornell University Press, 2000); Jessica Weiss, *To Have and To Hold: Marriage, the Baby Boom and Social Change* (Chicago: University of Chicago Press, 2000). On feminism and motherhood, see Lauri Umansky, *Motherhood Reconceived: Feminism and the Legacies of the Sixties* (New York: New York University Press, 1996).

5. Winifred Breines, *The Trouble between Us: An Uneasy History of White and Black Women in the Feminist Movement* (New York: Oxford University Press, 2006); Gloria Hull, Patricia Bell Scott, and Barbara Smith, eds., *But Some of Us Are Brave: All the Women Are White, All the Blacks Are Men: Black Women's Studies* (New York: Feminist Press, 1993); Cherrí Moraga and Gloria Anzaldúa, eds., *This Bridge Called My Back: Writings by Radical Women of Color* (New York: Kitchen Table Press, 1983); Benita Roth, *Separate Roads to Feminism: Black, Chicana, and White Feminist Movements in America's Second Wave* (New York: Cambridge University Press 2003); Kimberly Springer, *Living for the Revolution: Black Feminist Organization, 1968–1980* (Durham, N.C.: Duke University Press, 2005).

6. This is based on my readings of published records by and about CalArts FAP students.

7. Robbin Schiff, *Nightmare Bathroom*, *Womanhouse* catalog, http://womanhouse.refugia.net/. Accessed on August 3, 2010.

8. *Womanhouse* catalog, http://womanhouse.refugia.net/. Accessed on August 3, 2010.

9. Arlene Raven, "*Womanhouse*," in Norma Broude and Mary D. Garrad, eds., *The Power of Feminist Art: The American Movement of the 1970s, History and Impact* (New York: Harry N. Abrams, 1994), 48–65, 48.

10. Ibid., 52.

11. Miriam Schapiro, "The Education of Women as Artists: Project *Womanhouse*," *Art Journal* 31, no. 3 (spring 1972): 268–70, Judy Chicago Papers, Arthur and Elizabeth Schlesinger Library on the History of Women in America, Radcliffe Institute for Advanced Study, Harvard University (hereafter JCP), carton 11, file 38.

12. Vicki Hodgetts, *Eggs to Breasts*, *Womanhouse* catalog, http://womanhouse.refugia.net/. Accessed on August 4, 2010.

13. Schapiro, "Education of Women as Artist," 269.

14. Susan Frazier, *Aprons in Kitchen*, *Womanhouse* catalog, http://womanhouse.refugia.net/. Accessed on August 4, 2010. Ellipses in original.

15. Beth Bachenheimer, Sherry Brody, Karen LeCocq, Robin Mitchell, Miriam Schapiro, and Faith Wilding, *Dining Room*, *Womanhouse* catalog, http://womanhouse.refugia.net/. Accessed on August 4, 2010. Ellipses in original.

16. Ibid. 55, 57.

17. Camille Grey, *Lipstick Bathroom*, *Womanhouse* catalog, http://womanhouse.refugia.net/. Accessed on August 4, 2010.

18. Beth Bachenheimer, *Shoe Closet*, *Womanhouse* catalog, http://womanhouse.refugia.net/. Accessed on August 4, 2010.

19. Sandy Orgel, *Linen Closet*, *Womanhouse* catalog, http://womanhouse.refugia.net/. Accessed on August 4, 2010.

20. Jan Lester, *Personal Space*, *Womanhouse* catalog, http://womanhouse.refugia.net/. Accessed on August 4, 2010.

21. Karen LeCocq and Nancy Youdelman, "Leah's Room from Collette's *Cheri*," *Womanhouse Catalog*, http://womanhouse.refugia.net/. Accessed on August 4, 2010.

22. Christine Rush, *Necco Wafers*, *Womanhouse* catalog, http://womanhouse.refugia.net/. Accessed on August 4, 2010.

23. Schapiro, "Education of Women as Artists," 269.

24. Oral history interview with Suzanne Lacy, March 16 and 24 and September 27, 1990, Archives of American Art, Smithsonian Institution.

25. Judy Chicago, *Through the Flower: My Struggle as a Woman Artist* (New York: Penguin, 1975), 127.

26. Cheri Gaulke, "Acting Like Women: Performance Art of the Woman's Building" (1980), in Lynda Frye Burnham and Steve Durland, eds., *Citizen Artists: Twenty Years of Art in the Public Arena: An Anthology from* High Performance *Magazine, 1978–1998*, http://www.communityarts.net/ca/index.php. Accessed on January 17, 2008.

27. For accounts of contemporary feminism, see Susan Douglas, *Enlightened Sexism: The Seductive Message that Feminism's Work Is Done* (New York: Times Books, 2010); Ariel Levy, *Female Chauvinist Pigs: Women and the Rise of Raunch Culture* (New York: Free Press, 2006); Jessica Valenti, *Full Frontal Feminism: A Young Woman's Guide to Why Feminism Matters* (Seattle, Wash.: Seal Press, 2007).

28. Judy Chicago, "Cunt and Cock" (1970), reprinted in Chicago, *Through the Flower*, 208–13.

29. Chicago, *Through the Flower*, 213, 131.

30. Raven, "*Womanhouse*," 58.

31. Ibid., 58.

32. Faith Wilding, "Waiting" (1971), reprinted in Chicago, *Through the Flower*, 213–17.

33. Chicago, *Through the Flower*, 118, 118–19.

34. *The Birth Trilogy*, Performance section, *Womanhouse* catalogue, http://womanhouse.refugia.net/. Accessed on August 9, 2010.

35. See Louise Newman, *White Women's Rights: The Racial Origins of American Feminism* (New York: Oxford University 1999); Barbara Reeves-Ellington, ed., *Competing Kingdoms: Women, Mission, Nation and the American Protestant Empire, 1812–1960* (Durham, N.C.: Duke University Press, 2010).

36. Chicago, *Through the Flower*, 120.

37. Raven, "*Womanhouse*," 61.

38. Alexis Krasilovsky, "Report on the West Coast Women's Art Conference," privately published, February 1972. Quoted in Wilding, *By Our Own Hands*, 31.

39. Wilding, *By Our Own Hands*, 31.

40. Glueck quoted in Gail Levin, *Becoming Judy Chicago: A Biography of the Artist* (New York: Harmony Books, 2007), 198.

41. Wilding, *By Our Own Hands*, 31.

42. Levin reports that 180 women attended the conference, and Wilding, 150. See Levin, *Becoming Judy Chicago*, 198; Wilding, *By Our Own Hands*, 31.

43. Chicago, *Through the Flower*, 121, 124.

44. Sandra Burton, "Bad Dream House," in "The American Woman," special issue, *Time* magazine (20 March 1972), 77.

45. William Wilson, "Lair of Female Creativity," *Los Angeles Times*, February 21, 1972, JCP, carton 11, file 37.

46. Betty Liddick, "Emergence of the Feminist Artist," *Los Angeles Times View*, January 17, 1972, 1, 6, JCP, carton 11, file 37.

47. *Everywoman*, March 1972.

48. Anaïs Nin, introduction to Chicago, *Through the Flower*, xii.

49. Karen LeCocq, *The Easiest Thing to Remember: My Life as an Artist, a Feminist, and a Manic Depressive* (Bloomington, Ind.: 1st Books Library, 2002), 77.

50. Gloria Steinem, foreword to Eve Ensler, *The Vagina Monologues* (New York: Villard, 1998), xiv.

51. Lucy Lippard, "Household Images in Art," *Ms.* magazine 1, no. 9 (March 1973): 22.

52. Liddick, "Emergence of the Feminist Artist," 6.

53. Marilyn Wachman, "Warning: 533 N. Mariposa Ave., May Be Hazardous to the Ego of Male Chauvinist Pigs," *California Apparel News*, February 11, 1972, 10, JCP, carton 11, file 27.

54. Schapiro, "Education of Women as Artists," 270.

55. "*Womanhouse* Opens," *LA Free Press*, February 4 1972, JCP, carton 11, file 37.

56. Levin, *Becoming Judy Chicago*, 198.

57. Lynne Littman, directed by Parke Perine, aired on KCET in February 1972; Johanna Demetrakas, *Womanhouse* (1972), color video (New York: Women Make Movies, 1996 Conversion).

58. Chicago, personal journal, quoted in Levin, *Becoming Judy Chicago*, 199.

59. Mira Schor, "Miss Elizabeth Bennett Goes to Feminist Boot Camp," in *A Decade of Negative Thinking: Essays on Art, Politics, and Daily Life* (Durham, N.C.: Duke University Press, 2009), 75–87, 83.

60. Sandra Sider, "Womanhouse: Cradle of Feminist Art," Art Spaces Archive Projects, http://as-ap.org/sider/resources.cfm. Accessed on August 12, 2010.

61. LeCocq, *Easiest Thing to Remember*, 78.

62. Ulrike Müller, "Re-Tracing the Feminist Art Program," http://www.encore.at/retracing/index2.html. Accessed on August 1, 2010.

63. These evaluations can be found in ibid.

64. Ibid.

65. Wilding, *By Our Own Hands*, 28.

66. Schor, "Miss Elizabeth Bennett Goes to Feminist Boot Camp," 75–87, 81, 82, 83.

67. Ida Foreman, Sandra Cocker, Karen LeCocq, Faith Wilding, Robin Mitchell, Mira Schor, Rena Small, and Shawnee Wollenmann are among the women who continued to make or teach art. See Müller, "Re-Tracing the Feminist Art Program."

68. Karen LeCocq to Judy Chicago, letter February 3, 1973, JCP, carton 11, file 19.

69. Müller, "Re-Tracing the Feminist Art Program."

70. Levin, *Becoming Judy Chicago*, 195.

71. Müller, "Re-Tracing the Feminist Art Program."

72. Wilding, *By Our Own Hands*, 14.

73. Raven, "*Womanhouse*," 50.

74. Levin, *Becoming Judy Chicago*, 221.

75. Interview with the author, July 11, 2010.

76. Thailia Gouma-Peterson and Patricia Mathews, "The Feminist Critique of Art History," *Art Bulletin* 69, no. 3 (1987): 326–57, 332.

77. Musgrave, "Liberal Feminism, from Law to Art," 227.

78. Gouma-Peterson and Mathews, "Feminist Critique of Art History."

79. Jacqueline Skiles, "The Status of Women in the Arts Worldwide," in Cindy Lyle, Sylvia Moore, and Cynthia Navaretta, eds., *Women Artists of the World* (New York: Midmarch, 1984), 69–76.

80. "Situation Report," *Time* magazine, March 20, 1972.

81. Mary D. Garrard, "Feminist Politics: Networks and Organizations," in Norma

Broude and Mary D. Garrard, eds., *The Power of Feminist Art: The American Movement of the 1970s, History and Impact* (New York: H. N. Abrams, 1994), 88–101, 93; Eleanor Dickinson, "The History of the Women's Caucus for Art," in Kathy A. Halamka and Karen Frostig, eds., *Blaze: Discourse on Art, Women and Feminism* (London: Cambridge Scholars Press, 2007).

82. Levin, *Becoming Judy Chicago*, 202.

83. *Womanspace Journal* 1, no. 1 (February/March 1973): 8–9.

84. Wilding, *By Our Own Hands*, 49–50.

85. Ibid., 51, 52.

86. Ibid., 54.

87. Chicago to Cindy Nemser, letter November 1972, quoted in Levin, *Becoming Judy Chicago*, 224.

88. Brochure quoted in ibid., 231.

89. Levin, *Becoming Judy Chicago*, 231.

90. Laura Meyer, "The Woman's Building and Los Angeles's Leading Role in the Feminist Art Movement," in Sondra Hale and Terry Wolverton, eds., *From Site to Vision: The Women's Building in Contemporary Culture* (ebook, 2007), 71–102, 77. http://womans building.org/fromsitetovision/pdfs/Meyer.pdf. Accessed on August 16, 2010.

91. Suzanne Lacy, "The L.A. Woman's Building," *Art in America* 62, no. 3 (May–June 1974). Reprinted in Suzanne Lacy, *The Pink Glass Swan: Selected Feminist Essays on Art* (New York: Norton, 1995),84–88, 86.

92. Lacy, "L.A. Woman's Building," 85.

93. Judy Chicago, personal journal, December 1973. Quoted in Levin, *Becoming Judy Chicago*, 242.

94. Meyers, "Women's Building and Los Angeles's Leading Role in the Feminist Art Movement," 72–73.

95. Nancy Marmer, *Art News* (summer 1973), quoted in Lacy, "L.A. Woman's Building," 86.

96. Lacy, "L.A. Women's Building," 86. Terry Wolverton, *Insurgent Muse: Life and Art at the Woman's Building* (San Francisco: City Lights Book, 2002).

97. Personal interview, Ann Isolde, Los Angeles, January 2010; personal interview, Juliet Myers, Santa Fe, June 2009; personal interview, Jan DuBois, Santa Fe, June 2009. These three *Dinner Party* volunteers were among those who heard about the Woman's Building and Chicago's involvement with it.

98. Meyer, "Women's Building and Los Angeles's Leading Role in the Feminist Art Movement," 77.

99. Cheri Gaulke, interview by Michelle Moravec, Woman's Building Oral History Project, 6 August 1992, Los Angeles, Calif. Quoted in Meyer, "Women's Building and Los Angeles's Leading Role in the Feminist Art Movement," 81.

100. Personal interview, Isolde.

101. Gouma-Peterson and Mathews, "Feminist Critique of Art History," 335.

102. Judy Chicago, personal journal, December 1974. Quoted in Levin, *Becoming Judy Chicago*, 263.

103. Skiles, "Status of Women in the Arts Worldwide," 335.

104. Personal interview, Judy Chicago, June 2009.

CHAPTER THREE. The Studio as a Feminist Space

1. Judy Chicago Papers, Arthur and Elizabeth Schlesinger Library on the History of Women in America, Radcliffe Institute for Advanced Study, Harvard University (hereafter JCP), carton 15, file 14. A substantial bibliography of the emergent field used by Chicago for her research included titles that would become canonical, such as Lois Banner, "Writing Women's History," *Journal of Interdisciplinary History* (1971); Gerda Learner, *Black Women in White America* (New York: Vintage, 1972); Bernice Carroll, *Liberating Women's History: Theoretical and Critical Essays in Women's History* (Urbana: University of Illinois Press, 1976); Claudia Koonz and Renate Bridenthal, *Becoming Visible: Women in European History* (Boston: Houghton Mifflin, 1977). See JCP, carton 15, file 15.

2. Anne M. Valk, "Living a Feminist Lifestyle: The Intersection of Theory and Action in a Lesbian Feminist Collective," *Feminist Studies* 28, no. 2 (summer 2002), 303–32.

3. Suzanne Staggenborg, "Beyond Culture versus Politics: A Case Study of a Local Women's Movement," *Gender and Society* 15, no. 4 (August 2001), 507–30.

4. On the promise and perils of cultural feminism, see Linda Alcott, "Cultural Feminism verse Post-Structuralism: The Identity Crisis in Feminist Theory," *Signs* 13, no. 3 (spring 1988): 405–36; Alice Echols, *Daring to Be Bad: Radical Feminism in America, 1967–1975* (Minneapolis: University of Minnesota Press, 1989); Jane Gerhard, *Desiring Revolution: Second-Wave Feminism and the Rewriting of American Sexual Thought, 1920–1983* (New York: Columbia University Press, 2001); Staggenborg, "Beyond Culture versus Politics"; Verta Taylor and Leila Rupp, "Women's Culture and Lesbian Feminist Activism: A Reconsideration of Cultural Feminism," *Signs* 19, no. 1 (autumn 1993): 32–61.

5. Gail Levin, *Becoming Judy Chicago: A Biography of the Artist* (New York: Harmony Books, 2007), 215.

6. Edward Lucie-Smith, *Judy Chicago: An American Vision* (New York: Watson-Guptill Publications, 2000), 22, 29; Judy Chicago, *Through the Flower: My Struggle as a Woman Artist* (New York: Penguin, 1975), 36, 58.

7. See *Multi-Colored Atmosphere* (1970) and *Smoke Goddess V* (1972).

8. Judy Chicago, *"The Dinner Party": A Symbol of Our Heritage* (Garden City, N.Y.: Doubleday/Anchor Books, 1979), 8, 11, 11.

9. With the advent of mass production, china painting became a "hobbyist" technique in the US." Laura Meyer, "From Finish Fetish to Feminism: Judy Chicago's *Dinner Party* in California Art History," in Amelia Jones, ed., *Sexual Politics: Judy Chicago's "Dinner Party" in Feminist Art History* (Berkeley: University of California Press, 1996), 46–81, 61.

10. Shirley Kassman Rickert, "Thoughts on Feminist Art," *Strait* 2, no. 8 (February 7–21, 1973): 17. Quoted in Levin, *Becoming Judy Chicago*, 220.

11. The group included Arlene Raven, Miriam Schapiro, Faith Wilding, and Lucy Lippard, among others.

12. Gloria Orenstein, "Review Essay: Art History," *Signs* 1, no. 2 (winter 1975): 505–25; Cindy Nemser, "The Women Artists' Movement," *Feminist Art Journal* 2, no. 4 (winter 1973–74): 4–6.

13. Judy Chicago, "Woman as Artist," *Everywoman* 2, no. 7 (1972): 24–25.

14. Judy Chicago and Dextra Frankel, "Foreword to Catalogue," in *Twenty-one Artists Visible Invisible* (Los Angeles: Long Beach Museum of Art, 1972). Orenstein, "Review Essay," 517–18.

15. Marjorie Kramer, "Some Thoughts on Feminist Art," *Women and Art* 1 (1971): 3.

16. Pat Mainardi, "A Feminine Sensibility?" *Feminist Art Journal* 1, no. 1 (1972): 25.

17. Judith Stein, "For a Truly Feminist Art," *Big News* 1, no. 9 (1972): 3. Emphasis in original.

18. Orenstein, "Review Essay," 520.

19. See Chicago, *"Dinner Party"* (1979), entry January 20, 1977, 34.

20. Chicago, *"Dinner Party"* (1979), 25, 26, 27.

21. Ibid., 27.

22. In brief, the process involved jiggering, carving, glazing, firing, and china painting to produce a single plate. Chicago, personal journal, September 10, 1976. Reprinted in Chicago, *"Dinner Party"* (1979), 34.

23. Levin, *Becoming Judy Chicago*, 278.

24. Chicago, *"Dinner Party"* (1979), 27. See entry Sunday, May 9, 1976, for the evolving list of helpers, 30.

25. Diane Gelon, interview with the author, January 30, 2010. By the beginning of 1976, Chicago had in place a core staff who took on more and more of the management of the project, including Judye Keyes, Kathleen Schneider, Rachel Seaman, and Robyn Hill.

26. Chicago, *"Dinner Party"* (1979), 35.

27. Chicago applied for numerous grants, from Exxon, Virginia Slims, and Helene Rubenstein as well as the National Endowment for the Arts, Ford Foundation and the Guggenheim. See JCP, carton 16, files 1–16.

28. Worker Statements, Diane Gelon, JCP, carton 19, file 3.

29. Ibid.

30. Ibid.

31. Ibid.

32. Ibid., confirmed by correspondence with author, July 28, 2011.

33. The women are listed as having donated between $25 and $300, JCP, carton 15, file 44.

34. Donor lists, JCP, carton 19, file 22.

35. Worker Statements, Diane Gelon, JCP, carton 19, file 3.

36. Levin, *Becoming Judy Chicago*, 288.

37. Ann Isolde, March 2, 1977, personal diary, in possession of Ann Isolde.

38. Chicago, *"Dinner Party"* (1979), 36–37.

39. Flyer 1978, JCP, carton 15, file 12.

40. The San Francisco Textile Workshop contracted with Chicago to train eight women who paid for the education themselves ($125 per person) and four women for whom the studio paid the tuition fees. Diane Gelon, interview with author, June 2010.

41. Susan Hill, interview with author, January 12, 2010.

42. *The Dinner Party Survival Manual, 1977*, JCP, carton 18, file 14.

43. Susan Hill, "Needleworkers' Information Index," 12, JCP, carton 16, file 34, listed $75 for a two-month segment. Flyers from 1978 list $175 as the cost, JCP, carton 15, file 12.

44. Bonita Boulio, letter 1978, JCP, carton 18, file 22.

45. Audrey Wallace, letter 1978, JCP, carton 18, file 22.

46. Cherie Fraine, letter 1978, JCP, carton 18, file 22.

47. Anita Johnson, letter 1978, JCP, carton 18, file 22.

48. *Dinner Party Survival Manual, 1977.*

49. Jan Marie DuBois, interview with author, July 2, 2009.

50. Of the thirty-five women who filled out forms, twelve listed word of mouth;

six, notices seen in the Women's Building; and six, information from someone already working at the studio. Of the six women who arrived after reading about the project, most listed an art-related publication, such as *Art in America*. Dinner Party Worker information forms, 1977, JCP, carton 18, file 31.

51. Six men worked on *The Dinner Party* and are shown in the Acknowledgment Panels, http://www.brooklynmuseum.org/eascfa/dinner_party/acknowledgement_panels/index.php. Accessed August 7, 2012.

52. Hill, interview with author.

53. Laura Pulido, *Black, Brown, Yellow and Left: Radical Activism in Los Angeles* (Berkeley: University of California Press, 2006).

54. Carolyn Taylor-Olson, Dinner Party Worker information forms, 1977, JCP, carton 18, file 32.

55. Dinner Party Worker information forms, JCP, carton 18, files 31–37.

56. Dinner Party Worker information forms 1976, JCP, carton 18, file 33.

57. Ibid., file 34.

58. Ibid.

59. Ibid., file 31.

60. Ibid., file 33.

61. Ibid., file 31.

62. Ibid.

63. Ibid., file 32.

64. Ibid.

65. Ibid., file 34.

66. Interview with author, July 2, 2009.

67. Ibid.

68. Levin, *Becoming Judy Chicago*, 292.

69. Untitled clipping from the *Plain Dealer*, May 25, 1978, 7, JCP, carton 16, file 7.

70. Waronker and Pruce worked on the woven banners. Untitled clipping from the *Plain Dealer*, May 25, 1978, 7, JCP, carton 16, file 7.

71. Jeanne Van Atta, "Lo and Behold, I Can Do It!," in *What She Wants*, April 1978, clipping, JCP, carton 16, file 7.

72. Barbara Isenberg, "Invitation to a Women-Only Dinner," *LA Times*, April 6, 1978.

73. Untitled clipping from the *Plain Dealer*, May 25, 1978, 7, JCP, carton 16, file 7; "Lo and Behold, I Can Do It!"; Levin, *Becoming Judy Chicago*, 291.

74. Judy Chicago, with Susan Hill, *Embroidering Our Heritage: "The Dinner Party" Needlework* (Garden City, N.Y.: Anchor Books, 1980), 144.

75. Susan Hill to author, email July 14, 2009.

76. Diane Gelon's diary, JCP, carton 81, file 3.

77. Ibid.

78. For a fuller account of 1970s feminists' examination of heterosexuality, see Gerhard, *Desiring Revolution*.

79. Jan Marie DuBois, for example, describes herself as a radical lesbian separatist in these years, and mapped the entire West Coast feminist art scene through networks of lovers and former lovers. Interview with author, July 2, 2009.

80. Gelon reports that Dorothy remained married in Cleveland, dying of cancer in the 1990s. Gelon to author, email July 14, 2009.

81. Shannon Hogen, interview with author, January 13, 2010.

82. Chicago, *"Dinner Party"* (1979) 221.

83. Hogen, interview with author.

84. Ann Isolde, interview with author, January 13, 2010.

85. Founders' statement, *Elbows and Tea Leaves: Front Range Women in the Visual Arts (1974–2000)*, 25th anniversary exhibition catalog (Boulder, Colo.: Boulder Museum of Contemporary Art, 2000), 5. The 1974 founding members of Front Range included Micaela Amato, Sally Elliott, Jaci Fischer, Fran Metzger, and Helen Redman.

86. Isolde, interview with author.

87. Hill, interview with author.

88. Histories on feminist groups and collectives include the documentary film on the feminist art group Heresies, *The Heretics* (2009); Kathy Davis, *The Making of "Our Bodies, Ourselves": How Feminism Travels Across Borders* (Chapel Hill, N.C.: Duke University Press, 2007); Wendy Klein, "The Making of *Our Bodies, Ourselves*," in Stephanie Gilmore, ed., *Feminist Coalitions: Historical Perspectives on Second-Wave Feminism in the United States* (Urbana: University of Illinois Press, 2008), 63–84; Anne Enke on alternative feminist institution-making in the Midwest, *Finding the Movement: Sexuality, Contested Space, and Feminist Activism* (Chapel Hill, N.C.: Duke University Press, 2007); Duchess Harris on the Combahee River Collective, "All of Whom I Am in the Same Place," *Womanist* 2, no. 1 (fall 1999): 9–17, 20–21; Anne Valk, on the Furies, in "Living a Feminist Lifestyle: The Intersection of Theory and Action in a Lesbian Feminist Collective," *Feminist Studies* 28, no 2 (summer 2002): 303–32. Personal accounts include Susan Brownmiller, *In Our Time: A Memoir of a Revolution* (New York: Dial 2000); Karla Jay, *Tales of the Lavender Menace: A Memoir of Liberation* (New York: Basic Books, 2000); Roxanne Dunbar-Ortz, *Outlaw Woman: A Memoir of the War Years, 1960–1975* (San Francisco: City Lights, 2001); Terry Wolverton, *Insurgent Muses: Life and Art at the Woman's Building* (San Francisco: City Lights, 2002).

89. Workshop correspondence, 1977–1978, JCP, carton 18, file 28.

90. Ibid.

91. Hill, "Needleworkers' Information Index," 11, no date.

92. Worker Statements, L. A. Olson, JCP, carton 19, file 3.

93. Worker Statements, Dorothy Goodwill, JCP, carton 19, file 3.

94. No name recorded, letter, JCP, carton 18, file 28.

95. Worker Statement, Anne Marie Pois, JCP, carton 19, file 3.

96. Terry Blecher, "Woman/Artist/Educator," thesis, Goddard Graduate Program, 9, JCP, carton 18, file 27.

97. Ibid., 12.

98. Ellen Herman, *The Romance of American Psychology: Political Culture in the Age of Experts* (Berkeley: University of California Press, 1995); Gretchen Lemke-Santagelo, *Daughters of Aquarius: Women of the Sixties Counterculture* (Lawrence: University of Kansas Press, 2009); and Lauri Umansky, *Motherhood Reconceived: Feminism and the Legacies of the Sixties* (New York: New York University Press, 1996).

99. Blecher, "Woman/Artist/Educator," 17.

100. Ibid., 90–91.

101. Adrienne Weiss, in "The First Dinner Party Studio Sketch Book," volume started in October 1976, JCP, 94f, 1V.

102. Unsigned journal entry, October 19, 1976, in "First Dinner Party Studio Sketch Book."

103. DP worker statements 1978, JCP, carton 19, file 3.

104. Worker Statements, Marti Rotchford, JCP, carton 19, file 3.

105. Unsigned and undated journal entry in "First Dinner Party Studio Sketch Book."

106. Blecher, "Woman/Artist/Educator," 94.

107. The critical comments were entered between March and August 1977 in "First Dinner Party Studio Sketch Book."

108. Worker Statements, Thelma Brenner, JCP, carton 19, file 3.

109. Unsigned, undated journal entry in "First Dinner Party Studio Sketch Book."

110. Hill, "Needleworkers' Information Index."

111. Fay Evans, November 7, 1976, in "First Dinner Party Studio Sketch Book."

112. Robyn Hill to JC, letter March 18, 1977, JCP, carton 18, file 20.

113. JC to Robyn Hill, letter March 24, 1977, JCP, carton 18, file 20.

114. Chicago, *"Dinner Party"* (1979), 29, 32, 32, 40.

115. Ibid., 34, 35, 35, 42.

116. Ibid., 31, 35, 36.

117. For an analysis of the place of psychology in second-wave feminism, see Mari Jo Buhle, *Feminism and Its Discontents: A Century of Struggle with Psychoanalysis* (Cambridge, Mass.: Harvard University Press, 2000); Jane Gerhard, *Desiring Revolution*; Ellen Herman, *Romance of American Psychology*.

118. On the role of cultural production and consumption in lesbian communities in the 1970s, see Heather Murray, "Free for All Lesbians: Lesbian Cultural Production and Consumption in the United States in the 1970s," *Journal of the History of Sexuality* 15, no. 2 (May 2007): 251–75; and Wolverton, *Insurgent Muses*.

CHAPTER FOUR. Joining Forces

1. Early feminist writings that offered feminist theory as history, by no means exhaustive, include Kathleen Barry, *Female Sexual Slavery* (Englewood Cliffs, N.J.: Prentice Hall, 1979); Susan Brownmiller, *Against Our Will: Men, Women, and Rape* (New York: Simon and Shuster, 1975); Phyllis Chesler, *Women and Madness* (London: Allen Lane, 1974) and *About Men* (New York: Bantam Books, 1979); Mary Daly, *Beyond God the Father: Toward a Philosophy of Women's Liberation* (Boston: Beacon Press, 1973) and *Gyn/Ecology: The Metaphysics of Radical Feminism* (Boston: Beacon Press, 1978); Barbara Ehrenreich with Deirdre English, *Witches, Midwives and Nurses: A History of Women Healers* (New York: Feminist Press at CUNY, 1972) and *For Her Own Good: Two Centuries of the Experts' Advice to Women* (Garden City, N.Y.: Anchor, 1978); Susan Griffin, *Women and Nature: The Roaring Inside Her* (New York: Harper and Row, 1978); Adrienne Rich, *Of Woman Born: Motherhood as Experience and Institution* (New York: Norton, 1976).

2. Winifred Breines, *The Trouble between Us: The Uneasy History of White and Black Women in the Feminist Movement* (New York: Oxford University Press, 2006); Flora Davis, *Moving the Mountain: The Women's Movement in America since 1960* (New York: Simon and Shuster, 1991); Susan Douglas, *Where the Girls Are: Growing Up Female with the Mass Media* (New York: Random House, 1994) and *Enlightened Sexism* (New York: Times Books, 2010); Sara Evans, *Tidal Wave: How Women Changed America at Century's End* (New York: Free Press, 2003); Ruth Feldstein, *Motherhood in Black and White: Race and Sex in American Liberalism, 1930–1965* (Ithaca, N.Y.: Cornell University Press, 2000); Alice Kessler-Harris, *In Pursuit of Equity: Women, Men, and the Quest for Economic Citizenship in Twentieth-Century America* (New York: Oxford University Press, 2001); Nancy MacLean, *Freedom Is Not Enough: The Opening of the American Workplace*

(Cambridge, Mass.: Harvard University Press, 2008); Elaine May, *Homeward Bound: American Families in the Cold War Era* (New York: Basic Books, 1988); Benita Roth, *Separate Roads to Feminism: Black, Chicana, and White Feminist Movements in America's Second Wave* (New York: Cambridge University Press, 2003); Christine Stansell, *The Feminist Promise: 1792 to the Present* (New York: Random House, 2010); "The Future of Feminism," *CQ Researcher* 16, no. 14 (April 14, 2006): 313–36.

3. See the collection of essays on the historiography of US feminism in Nancy Hewitt, ed., *No Permanent Waves: Recasting Histories of U.S. Feminism* (New Brunswick, N.J.: Rutgers University Press, 2010).

4. For an analysis of "women's culture" in 1970s feminism, see Verta Taylor and Leila Rupp, "Women's Culture and Lesbian Feminist Activism: A Reconsideration of Cultural Feminism," *Signs* 19, no. 1 (autumn 1993): 32–61. Groundbreaking applications of "women's culture" in the mid- to late 1970s include Carol Smith Rosenberg, "The Female World of Love and Ritual: Relations between Women in the 19th Century," *Signs* 1, no. 1 (1975): 1–29; Adrienne Rich, *Of Woman Born: Motherhood as Experience and Institution* (New York: Norton, 1976); and Nancy Chodorow, *The Reproduction of Mothering: Psychoanalysis and the Sociology of Gender* (Berkeley: University of California Press, 1978).

5. Susan Hill, interview with author, January 11, 2010.

6. Quoted by Hill, interview with author.

7. Hill interview with author.

8. Susan Hill, "Needleworkers' Information Index," 14, Judy Chicago Papers, Arthur and Elizabeth Schlesinger Library on the History of Women in America, Radcliffe Institute for Advanced Study, Harvard University (hereafter JCP), carton 16, file 34.

9. Judy Chicago with Susan Hill, *Embroidering Our Heritage: "The Dinner Party" Needlework* (Garden City, N.J.: Anchor Books, 1980), 11. Susan Hill, interview with author, July 22, 2011.

10. Gail Levin, *Becoming Judy Chicago: A Biography of the Artist* (New York: Harmony Books, 2007), 278.

11. Hill, "Needleworkers' Information Index," 15.

12. Hill interview with author, January 11, 2010.

13. Judy Chicago, *"The Dinner Party": A Symbol of Our Heritage* (Garden City, N.Y.: Anchor Books, 1979), 30.

14. Chicago with Hill, *Embroidering Our Heritage*, 14.

15. Ibid., 15.

16. Ibid., 15.

17. Hill interview with author, January 11, 2010.

18. Chicago, *"Dinner Party"* (1979), 220.

19. Stretching the linen was a very difficult and time-consuming process. See Chicago with Hill, *Embroidering Our Heritage*, 16.

20. Susan Hill, "Guidelines for Needleworkers," no date, JCP, carton 16, file 23.

21. Judy Chicago, interview with author, June 30, 2009.

22. Traditional frames stretch smaller portions of the cloth being worked, allowing the rest of the piece to drape around the frame.

23. Chicago with Hill, *Embroidering Our Heritage*, 16.

24. Chicago interview with author.

25. Hill, "Needleworkers' Information Index," 18.

26. Chicago, interview with author.

27. Hill, "Needleworkers' Information Index," 19.
28. Ibid., 15.
29. Ibid., 16.
30. Chicago with Hill, *Embroidering Our Heritage*, 281–281.
31. Hill, interview with author, July 22, 2011.
32. Chicago with Hill, *Embroidering Our Heritage*, 51.
33. Hill, "Needleworkers' Information Index," 16.
34. Hill interview with author, July 22, 2011.
35. Chicago with Hill, *Embroidering Our Heritage*, 20.
36. Diane Gelon, speaking in Johanna Demetrakas, *Right Out of History* (video, Phoenic Learning Group, 1980).
37. See chapter 3 for a breakdown of volunteers' work experiences.
38. Hill interview with author, January 11, 2010.
39. Worker statements, 1978, JCP, carton 19, file 3.
40. Worker Statements, Susan Hill, JCP, carton 19, file 3.
41. Amazon Runner, JCP, carton 17, file 23.
42. Ibid.
43. Ibid.
44. Worker Statements, Kathleen Schneider, JCP, carton 19, file 3.
45. Worker Statements, Susan Hill, JCP, carton 19, file 3.
46. "The First Dinner Party Studio Sketch Book," October 22, 1976, JCP, 94f, IV.
47. Worker Statements, Susan Hill, JCP, carton 19, file 3.
48. Schneider quoted in Chicago with Hill, *Embroidering Our Heritage*, 36.
49. "First Dinner Party Studio Sketch Book."
50. Chicago with Hill, *Embroidering Our Heritage*, 40–42.
51. Stevie Martin in "Dinner Party Creation, Sophia," JCP, carton 17, file 21.
52. Karen Valentine quoted in "First Dinner Party Studio Sketch Book," November 1, 1976.
53. Worker Statements, Susan Hill, JCP, carton 19, file 3.
54. Chicago with Hill, *Embroidering Our Heritage*, 153, 177, 84.
55. Mary Daly was a favorite at the studio. See Mary Daly, *The Church and the Second Sex* (Boston: Beacon Press, 1968), *Beyond God the Father*, and *Gyn/Ecology*. See also Andrea Dworkin, *Woman Hating* (New York: Plume, 1974) and *Our Blood: Prophesies and Discourses on Sexual Politics* (New York: Pergee, 1976). See also excerpts of Chicago's journal, particularly March 17, 1975, in Chicago, *"Dinner Party"* (1979), 25.
56. Dorothy Polin, "Mary Wollstonecraft Runner," JCP, carton 17, file 23.
57. Adrienne Weiss, "Mary Wollstonecraft Runner," JCP, carton 17, file 23.
58. Chicago with Hill, *Embroidering Our Heritage*, 212.
59. Weiss quoted in "Mary Wollstonecraft Runner."
60. Chicago with Hill, *Embroidering Our Heritage*, 217.
61. Ibid., 212.
62. Worker Statements, Susan Hill, JCP, carton 19, file 3.
63. Levin, *Becoming Judy Chicago*, 292.
64. Terry Blecher, "Woman/Artist/Educator," thesis, Goddard Graduate Program, 81, JCP, carton 18, file 27.
65. Hill interview with author, January 11, 2010.
66. For example, see Zillah Eisenstein, ed., *Capitalist Patriarchy and the Case for Socialist Feminism* (New York: Monthly Review Press, 1978) and *The Radical Future of*

Liberal Feminism (New York: Longman, 1981); Juliet Mitchell, *Women's Estate* (London: Penguin, 1971); and Anne Oakley and Juliet Mitchell, eds., *The Rights and Wrongs of Women* (London: Penguin, 1976). See also Laura Lee Downs, *Writing Gender History* (London: Oxford University Press, 2004.)

67. Chicago, *"Dinner Party"* (1979), 12, 56.

68. Amy E. Butler, *Two Paths to Equality: Alice Paul and Ethel M. Smith in the ERA Debate, 1921–1929* (Albany: State University of New York Press, 2002); Nancy Cott, *The Grounding of Modern Feminism* (New Haven, Conn.: Yale University Press, 1989); Ellen DuBois, *Feminism and Suffrage: The Emergence of an Independent Women's Movement in America, 1848–1869* (Ithaca, N.Y.: Cornell University Press, 1978): Sally McMillen, *Seneca Falls and the Origins of the Women's Rights Movement* (New York: Oxford University Press, 2009). Chicago donated *The Dinner Party* library to the University of New Mexico–Valencia campus. It has its own section called the *Through the Flower Library by and about Women* and currently has over 2,100 volumes.

69. Diane Gelon to author, email September 21, 2010.

70. Diane Gelon to author, email October 17, 2010.

71. Ann Isolde, personal diary, October 8, 1976. In possession of Ann Isolde.

72. Ann Isolde, interview with author, January 13, 2010.

73. Researchers included Katie Amend, Ruth Askey, Diane Gelon, Ann Isolde, Laure McKinnon, Juliet Myers, Anne Marie Pois, and Karen Schmidt.

74. Group interview with *Dinner Party* workers, with author, January 12, 2010.

75. Chicago, *"Dinner Party"* (1979), 237.

76. Group interview with author.

77. Katie Amend quoted in Chicago, *"Dinner Party"* (1979), 236.

78. Chicago, *"Dinner Party"* (1979), 98. Isolde, unfortunately, tossed out these file boxes sometime around 2000. Isolde, interview with author, January 12, 2010.

79. Juliet Myers quoted in Chicago, *"Dinner Party"* (1979), 237.

80. Group interview with author.

81. Chicago, *"Dinner Party"* (1979), 98.

82. Ibid., 98. Emphasis in original.

83. Chicago, *"Dinner Party"* (1979): Ajysyt, 99; Catherine Deshayes, 148; Maria del Refugio Garica, 171; Joan of Arc, 148; Isabel Pinochet, 172; Ida B. Wells, 183.

84. Chicago, *"Dinner Party"* (1979), 116–17, 194–96.

85. Ibid., 181–83.

86. Isolde, personal diary, June 19, 1978.

87. Ann Isolde, personal diary, June 19, 1978. In possession of Ann Isolde.

88. Katie Amend, interview with author, January 12, 2010.

89. Quoted in Chicago, *"Dinner Party"* (1979), 238.

90. For a close-up of the Heritage Panels, see http://www.brooklynmuseum.org/eascfa/dinner_party/heritage_panels/index.php. Accessed on August 9, 2012.

91. China Boutique and Judy Chicago, letter agreement November 10, 1976, JCP, carton 15, file 13.

92. Helene Simich, Martie Rotchford, Shannon Hogan, Sandra Marvel, and Louise Simpson staffed the graphics team. See Chicago with Hill, *Embroidering Our Heritage*, 283.

93. Shannon Hogan, interview with author, January 13, 2010.

94. Shannon Hogan quoted in Chicago, *"Dinner Party"* (1979), 239.

95. Ken Gilliam, group interview with author, January 12, 2010. For images, see http://

www.brooklynmuseum.org/eascfa/dinner_party/heritage_floor/making.php. Accessed on August 9, 2012.

96. Ann Isolde quoted in Chicago, *"Dinner Party"* (1979), 238.

97. Architecture notes, March 1977, JCP, carton 15, file 13.

98. Group interview with author.

99. Ken Gilliam, interview with author, January 12, 2010; Chicago, *"Dinner Party"* (1979), 16.

100. Chicago, *"Dinner Party"* (1979), 242, 221, 224.

101. Each of the twelve legs of the tables cost $65 for a total of $780. Aluminum supports to reinforce the tables cost $690. "Architecture for DP," JCP, carton 15, file 13.

102. Isolde, personal diary, September 25, 1978.

103. Chicago, *"Dinner Party"* (1979), 13, 245–55. Sentences run like a banner over the top of every page in the book.

104. Group interview with author.

105. Ann Isolde quoted in Chicago, *"Dinner Party"* (1979), 19, 236.

106. Gilliam interview with author.

107. Chicago, *"Dinner Party"* (1979), 21, 22.

108. Lisa Tickner, "The Body Politic: Female Sexuality and Women Artists since 1970," in Rozsika Parker and Griselda Pollock, eds., *Framing Feminism: Art and the Women's Movement 1970–1985* (New York: Pandora Press, 1987), 263–76.

109. Anne-Marie Sauzeau-Boetti, "Negative Capability as Practice in Women's Art," *Studio International* 191, no. 979 (1976): 24–25.

110. Linda Alcott explicates this dilemma in "Cultural Feminism verse Post-Structuralism: The Identity Crisis in Feminist Theory," *Signs* 13, no. 3 (spring 1988): 405–36. Alice Echols most famously denounces the idea of women's culture in "The New Feminism of Yin and Yang," in Ann Snitow, Christine Stansell and Sharon Thompson, eds., *Powers of Desire: The Politics of Sexuality* (New York: Monthly Review Press, 1983), 439–59, and "The Taming of the Id: Feminist Sexual Politics, 1968–83," in Carole S. Vance, ed., *Pleasure and Danger: Exploring Female Sexuality* (Boston: Routledge and Kegan Paul, 1984), 50–72. For examples of this ongoing debate in the arts, see Parker and Pollock, *Framing Feminism*; and Hilary Robinson, *Feminism-Art-Theory: An Anthology 1968–2000* (Malden, Mass.: Blackwell Publishers, 2001).

111. Chicago, *"Dinner Party"* (1979), 94–96.

112. Hill interview with author, January 11, 2010.

113. Leonard Skuro quoted in Chicago, *"Dinner Party"* (1979), 223.

114. Ibid., 38.

115. Ibid., 225.

116. Hill interview with author, January 11, 2010.

117. Isolde interview with author, January 13, 2010.

118. Chicago, *"Dinner Party"* (1979), 227.

119. Judye Keyes quoted in ibid., 226.

120. Sharon Kagan quoted in Chicago, *"Dinner Party"* (1979), 227.

121. Chicago, *"Dinner Party"* (1979), 49.

122. Carole Drennan, Susan Larson, and Lucille Graham, "After *The Dinner Party*: A Reading List," no date, in possession of Mary Ross Taylor.

123. Chicago interview with author, January 11, 2011.

124. Chicago quoted in Jan Butterfield, "Guess Who's Coming to Dinner?," *Mother Jones* 4, no. 1 (January 1979): 20–28. Emphasis in original.

125. Judy Chicago interview with author, January 11, 2011.

126. Untitled document, 1976, JCP, carton 14, file 34. Emphasis in original.

127. Diane Gelon, interview with author, January 11, 2011.

128. Judy Chicago, proposal for "Revelations of the Goddess," no date, JCP, carton 14, file 11.

129. Coletta Reid to Sheila de Brentville, letter August 8, 1976, JCP, carton 14, file 11.

130. Chicago, "Revelations of the Goddess," draft 1, 1976, 1–2, 18–19, JCP, carton 14, file 12.

131. Chicago interview with author, January 11, 2011.

132. Chicago, *"Dinner Party"* (1979), 240.

133. Diane Gelon, NEA grant proposal, 1978, JCP, carton 18, file 12.

134. Chicago, *"Dinner Party"* (1979), 243.

135. Chicago, interview with author, January 11, 2011.

136. Gelon, NEA grant proposal, 1978.

137. Correspondence, San Francisco tapestry workshop, JCP, carton 18, file 12.

138. Correspondence, San Francisco tapestry workshop, JCP, carton 16, file 7.

139. Quoted at http://www.brooklynmuseum.org/eascfa/dinner_party/entry_banners/index.php. Accessed August 9, 2012.

140. Group interview with author.

CHAPTER FIVE. Going Public

1. "Dinner Party Ledger, 1974–1979." In possession of Judy Chicago as of August 31, 2011.

2. Judy Chicago to author, email August 31, 2011.

3. "Dinner Party Ledger."

4. Ibid.

5. Judy Chicago to author.

6. Diane Gelon to author, emails October 15, 2010.

7. Ibid.

8. Ibid.

9. Winifred Wandersee, *On the Move: American Women in the 1970s* (Boston: Twayne Publishers, 1988), 188.

10. Diane Gelon, personal diary, IWY, Houston, November 1977, Judy Chicago Papers, Arthur and Elizabeth Schlesinger Library on the History of Women in America, Radcliffe Institute for Advanced Study, Harvard University (hereafter JCP), carton 81, file 5.

11. Ibid.

12. Diane Gelon, interview with author, January 30, 2010.

13. Bess Abell to Diane Gelon, letter April 27, 1978. In possession of Diane Gelon.

14. "Fundraising, 1977–1978" folder, JCP, carton 16, file 17.

15. Gelon interview with author, and travel log 1978–1979, possession of Diane Gelon.

16. Gelon travel log.

17. Gelon interview with author.

18. Gelon, personal diary, April 20, 1978.

19. Gelon, interview with author, and date book.

20. Fund-raising letter to National Women's Political Caucus, August 10, 1978, JCP, carton 15, file 27.

21. Gelon, personal diary, November 19, 1979. Emphasis in original.

22. "Fundraising, 1977–1978" folder, JCP, carton 15, file 41.

23. Susan Brownmiller, *In Our Time: Memoir of a Revolution* (New York: Random House, 1999).

24. "Book Controversy" folder, JCP, carton 12, file 4.

25. Angela Cox, February 7, 1979, JCP, carton 12, file 4.

26. Loretta Barrett, February 9, 1979, JCP, carton 12, file 4.

27. *Publishers Weekly* 217, no. 24 (June 20, 1980), clipping, JCP, carton 12, file 28.

28. Gelon interview with author.

29. "Fundraising 1977–1978" folder, JCP, carton 15, file 41.

30. Ibid.

31. Carolyn Bronstein, *Battling Pornography: The American Feminist Anti-Pornography Movement, 1976–1986* (New York: Cambridge University Press, 2011), 93–97.

32. "Grants, 1977" folder, JCP, carton 16, file 17.

33. Gelon interview with author.

34. "Grants, August 1977" folder.

35. Phyllis Lichenstein to Judy Chicago, letter November 18, 1978, "Fundraising" folder, JCP, carton 15, file 42.

36. "Fundraising" folder.

37. *The Dinner Party* correspondence, JCP, carton 15, file 43.

38. "Fundraising" folder.

39. *Dinner Party* correspondence.

40. F. Maloff to Judy Chicago, letter December 12, 1978, "Fundraising" folder.

41. Kathy Hyatt to Judy Chicago, letter February 1, 1979, *Dinner Party* correspondence.

42. Stephanie Spencer to Henry Hopkins, letter 13 April 1978, JCP, carton 15, file 29.

43. *Dinner Party* correspondence 1979, JCP, carton 15, file 31.

44. The count is based on files in JCP, carton 15.

45. To Christina Orr, letter July 29, 1977, *Dinner Party* correspondence, JCP, carton 15, file 34.

46. Susan Hill to author, email July 15, 2009.

47. Susan Hill, millennium runners, JCP, carton 85, file 4.

48. Hill email to author.

49. International Dinner Party, JCP, carton 15, file 26.

50. Gail Levin, *Becoming Judy Chicago: A Biography of the Artist* (New York: Harmony Books, 2007), 306.

51. Moira Roth, "Suzanne Lacy's Dinner Parties," *Art in America*, April 1980, 126.

52. Suzanne Lacy to author, email February 9, 2011.

53. San Francisco opening, JCP, carton 22, file 47.

54. Program for "A Celebration of Women's Heritage," JCP, carton 83, file 22. Levin, *Becoming Judy Chicago*, 306.

55. San Francisco opening.

56. JCP, carton 15, file 30.

57. "San Francisco Museum of Modern Art 75th Anniversary: Henry Hopkins," conducted by Lisa Rubens and Richard Cándida Smith, 2006, Regional Oral History Office, the Bancroft Library, University of California, Berkeley; (c) San Francisco Museum of Modern Art, 2008.

58. Jean A. Rosenfeld to Judy Chicago, letter July 2, 1979, JCP, carton 10, file 1.

59. Jane C. Whitehead to Judy Chicago, letter August 4, 1979, JCP, carton 10, file 1.

60. Marsha G. Harris to Judy Chicago, letter July 31, 1979, JCP, carton 10, file 1.

61. Mark Stevens, "Guess Who's Coming to Dinner?," *Newsweek*, April 2, 1979, 92.

62. Henry Hopkins quoted in Mildred Hamilton, "'The Dinner Party' Left without a Second Sitting," *San Francisco Sunday Examiner and Chronicle*, July 1, 1979, 6.

63. Judy Chicago with Susan Hill, *Embroidering Our Heritage: "The Dinner Party" Needlework* (Garden City, N.J.: Anchor Books, 1980), 265.

64. To see *The Dinner Party* and listen to Chicago's tour, see http://www.brooklyn museum.org/eascfa/dinner_party/home.php. Accessed on August 4, 2012. Posted by the Brooklyn Museum's Elizabeth A. Sackler Center for Feminist Art.

65. Judy Chicago, *"Dinner Party": From Creation to Preservation* (London: Merrell, 2007), 62.

66. Chicago, *"Dinner Party"* (1979), 69.

67. Chicago with Hill, *Embroidering Our Heritage*, 80–81, 85.

68. Chicago, *"Dinner Party"* (2007), 69

69. Judy Chicago with Susan Hill, *Embroidering Our Heritage*, 84.

70. Judy Chicago for the Brooklyn Museum Cell Phone Gallery Guide, Hypatia, 4085.

71. Ibid.

72. Chicago with Hill, *Embroidering Our Heritage*, 275.

73. Ibid., 126–28.

74. Ibid., 144.

75. Judy Chicago for the Brooklyn Museum Cell Phone Gallery Guide, Christine de Pisan, 4130.

76. Ibid.

77. Judy Chicago for the Brooklyn Museum Cell Phone Gallery Guide, Anna van Schurman, 4150.

78. Chicago with Hill, *Embroidering Our Heritage*, 272.

79. Ibid., 194.

80. Judy Chicago for the Brooklyn Museum Cell Phone Gallery Guide, Anne Hutchinson, 4155.

81. Chicago, *"Dinner Party"* (2007), 84.

82. Chicago with Hill, *Embroidering Our Heritage*, 205.

83. Ibid., 204–6.

84. Judy Chicago for the Brooklyn Museum Cell Phone Gallery Guide, Mary Wollstonecraft, 4170.

85. Chicago, *"Dinner Party"* (2007), 88.

86. Judy Chicago for the Brooklyn Museum Cell Phone Gallery Guide, Ethel Smyth, 4195.

87. Chicago, *"Dinner Party"* (2007), 92.

88. Judy Chicago for the Brooklyn Museum Cell Phone Gallery Guide, Susan B. Anthony, 4180.

89. Chicago, *"Dinner Party"* (2007), 89.

90. Judy Chicago for the Brooklyn Museum Cell Phone Gallery Guide, Margaret Sanger, 4200.

91. Chicago, *"Dinner Party"* (2007), 93.

92. Judy Chicago for the Brooklyn Museum Cell Phone Gallery Guide, Natalie Barney, 4205.

93. Judy Chicago for the Brooklyn Museum Cell Phone Gallery Guide, Virginia Woolf, 4210.

94. Chicago, *"Dinner Party"* (2007), 96.

95. Susan Hill to author, email July 8, 2011.

96. Marilynn Woodsea, "The Dinner Party," *Womanspirit* 23 (March 1980): 50.

97. Lucy Lippard, "Dinner Party a Four-Star Treat: A Feminist Counterpart of the Sistine Chapel," *Seven Days*, April 27, 1979, 27–29, 27.

CHAPTER SIX. The Tour That Very Nearly Wasn't

1. Judy Chicago, interview with author, January 20, 2011.

2. Diane Gelon to Bill Woodward, letter June 15, 1979, Judy Chicago Papers, Arthur and Elizabeth Schlesinger Library on the History of Women in America, Radcliffe Institute for Advanced Study, Harvard University (hereafter JCP), carton 15, file 30.

3. Diane Gelon to National Gallery of Canada in Ottawa, letter June 21, 1979, JCP, carton 15, file 30.

4. Bruce Chambers to Diane Gelon, letter June 7, 1979, JCP, carton 15, file 30.

5. Gelon's letter reported the exchange: "As there is no precedent or practice at the Gallery for permitting persons or institutions outside the Gallery and its staff to exercise any control over Gallery programming your revision is unacceptable. The Gallery therefore regrets that it will have to cancel the exhibition." Diane Gelon to Bill Woodward, letter June 15, 1979, JCP, carton 15, file 30.

6. Rawsay Lawless to Diane Gelon, letter August 7, 1979, JCP, carton 22, file 43.

7. Mary Ross Taylor, interview with author, November 16, 2010.

8. Bruce Chambers to Diane Gelon, letter June 7, 1979, JCP, carton 15, file 30.

9. Diane Gelon, personal diary, November 12, 1978, JCP, carton 81, file 5.

10. Nancy Lane Fleming, "The Dinner Party," *Houston Breakthrough*, June 1979, 12–14.

11. Mildred Hamilton, "The Dinner Party Left without a Second Sitting," *San Francisco Sunday Examiner and Chronicle*, July 1, 1979, 6, JCP, carton 22, file 15.

12. Carolyn Bronstein, *Battling Pornography: The American Feminist Anti-Pornography Movement, 1976–1986* (New York: Cambridge University Press, 2011); Steven C. Dubin, *Arresting Images: Impolitic Art and Uncivil Actions* (New York: Routledge, 1992).

13. Budget, 1979, JCP, carton 15, file 26.

14. The plates were valued between $5,000 and $8,000 apiece; the runners varied from $8,000 to $15,000; the three millennium runners at $10,000 each; the banners $5,000; the tiles for the Heritage Floor $36,000; the six Heritage Panels $14,000; and photo documentation panels $22,500, totaling over $700,000 in value. Insurance information, JCP, carton 21, files 6 and 7.

15. Susan Rennie and Arlene Raven, "The Dinner Party: An Interview with Judy Chicago," *Chrysalis* 4 (January 1978): 89–101, 91, 92.

16. Clipping file, 1979, JCP, carton 22, file 51.

17. Michelle Celarier, "No 'Feminist Political Statements' for Seattle Art Museum," *Seattle Sun*, September 26, 1979, 9, 11, JCP, carton 22, file 15.

18. Letters to the editor, *Seattle Sun*, September 23, 1979, JCP, carton 22, file 15.

19. Letters to the editor, *Seattle Sun*, September 28, 1979, JCP, carton 22, file 15.

20. Regina Hackett, "Feminist Artist's Blast at Seattle," clipping dated February 1980, JCP, carton 22, file 15.

21. Martha Brown, Karen Hagberg, and Maxine Sobel to Bruce Chambers, letter June 26, 1979, Museum correspondence, JCP, carton 15, file 30.

22. Alexandra Speyer to Judy Chicago, letter, no date, JCP, carton 22, file 43.

23. Roger Trietly to Diane Gelon, letter July 5, 1979, JCP, carton 15, file 30.

24. Museum correspondence 1979, JCP, carton 15, file 30.

25. Johanna Demetrakas, director, *Right Out of History* (film), 2008, Phoenix Learning Group.

26. Judy Chicago, interview with author, January 11, 2011.

27. Diane Gelon, interview with author, January 30, 2010; Fleming, "Dinner Party," 14.

28. Before the San Francisco opening, Gelon had contacted and been turned down by the Baltimore Museum of Art, the Institute of Contemporary Art in Boston, Cornell University, the University of Texas at Austin, the New Orleans Museum of Art, the Walker Art Center in Minneapolis, and the Corcoran Gallery of Art in Washington, DC, among other venues. Museum Correspondence, 1976–1978, JCP, carton 15, file 33.

29. Lloyd Herman to Judy Chicago, letter May 11, 1976, Rejection letters, 1975–1977, JCP, carton 15, file 33.

30. Mrs. J. De Memil to Judy Chicago, letter, Rejection letters, 1975–1977, JCP, carton 15, file 33.

31. Anita Diamant, untitled interview with Judy Chicago, *Boston Phoenix*, December 19, 1979. JCP, carton 15, file 26.

32. Gelon interview with author.

33. Suzanne Burger, "Interview with Diane Gelon," *Sister Source: A Midwest Lesbian/Feminist Newspaper* 1, no. 1 (August 1, 1981): 1, 7, 7.

34. Judy Chicago and Diane Gelon, joint interview with author, January 11, 2011.

35. Ross Taylor interview.

36. Kristi Rangel-King, "Hubbard Shares Africa Passion," *Houston Chronicle*, February 28, 2002, 3.

37. Nathan Fain, "'Dinner' Is Ready," *Houston City Magazine*, March 1980, 33.

38. Ross Taylor interview with author.

39. Fian, "'Dinner Is Ready." Michel Ennis, "The Woman Who Came to Dinner," *Texas Monthly*, May 1980, 154–62, 156.

40. Ennis, "Woman Who Came to Dinner," 154.

41. Ross Taylor interview with author; Fain, "'Dinner' Is Ready"; Gail Levin, *Becoming Judy Chicago: A Biography of the Artist* (New York: Harmony Books, 2007), 320.

42. Mary Ross Taylor to author, email January 5, 2011.

43. Contributions to *The Dinner Party* Exhibition, Houston 1980, in possession of Mary Ross Taylor.

44. Ross Taylor to author.

45. "Prof Gets First Tiles on Heritage Floor," *University of Houston at Clear Lake City Newsletter* 6, no. 1 (spring 1980): 5.

46. Mary Moore quoted in "Professors Sponsor Plates for 'Dinner Party,' *UHCLIDIAN* 5, no. 6 (December 4, 1979): 8.

47. *Galveston Daily News*, April 13, 1980, 2-B.

48. Mary Ross Taylor, interview with author, January 13, 2011.

49. Annie Alexander, "The Dinner Party Opens as UHCL Presents Gigantic Exhibit," *Exchange News*, March 3, 1980, 1–2, 4.

50. First Unitarian Church newsletter (Houston, Tex.), April 1980. In possession of Mary Ross Taylor.

51. Ross Taylor interview, January 13, 2011.

52. Carole Drennan, Susan Larson, and Lucille Graham, "After *The Dinner Party*: A Reading List," JCP, carton 15, file 30.

53. The Women's Forum, Memorial Drive Presbyterian Church; St. Joan's International Alliance, Houston Chapter Catholic Feminist Organization; the Women's Group, First Unitarian Church; and the Bookstore are listed as sponsors. Drennan, Larson, and Graham, "After The Dinner Party: A Reading List," JCP, carton 15, file 30.

54. Among the events that Calvin Cannon brought to the UHCL were the US premiere of German composer Karlheinz Stockhausen's *Sirius* (1978), the premiere of Robert Wilson's play, *I Was Sitting on My Patio. This Guy Appeared. I Thought I Was Hallucinating* (1978), and conceptual artist Mel Chin's monumental waterwheel, *Keeping Still* (1979). Gretchen Mieszkowski, *Houston Dinner Party Thirty Year Anniversary Catalogue*, March 2011, in the author's collection.

55. Calvin Cannon quoted in Carolyn Truedell Morgan, "Controversial 'Dinner Party' Opens March 8," *UHCLIDIAN*, Feb. 26, 1980. Cited in Jonathan W. Zophy, *Building a University: A History of the University of Houston-Clear Lake 1974 to Present* (Houston: Seascape, 2005), 112, n35.

56. Mimi Crossley, "The Women Who Came to Dinner," *Houston Post*, November 27, 1979, 15A.

57. Mimi Crossley, "The Men in the Kitchen of 'The Dinner Party,'" *Houston Post*, March 25, 1980, B1.

58. Ibid., B4.

59. Mildred Hamilton, "Judy Chicago's 'Dinner Party' to Open in Houston," *San Francisco Examiner*, September 13, 1979, 36.

60. *Houston Arts: A Newsletter of the Cultural Arts Council of Houston* 3, no. 1 (winter 1980): 6–7.

61. Ross Taylor to author.

62. Ennis, "Woman Who Came to Dinner," 160.

63. Ibid., 156, 154.

64. Ibid., 160.

65. Ibid., 154.

66. Ross Taylor to author.

67. Ennis, "Woman Who Came to Dinner," 157, 159.

68. Donna Tennant, "A Monumental Work of Art," *Houston Chronicle*, March 9, 1980, 14, 31; Ennis, "Woman Who Came to Dinner," 162,

69. Office of the Chancellor, University of Houston at Clear Lake City, memo October 16, 1980. In possession of Mary Ross Taylor.

70. Mieszkowski, *Houston Dinner Party Thirty Year Anniversary Catalogue*.

71. BWAA fundraising, no date, JCP, carton 19, file 16.

72. Mickey Stern, interview with author, March 3, 2011.

73. Judy Chicago, interview with author, September 17, 2011.

74. Levin, *Becoming Judy Chicago*, 326.

75. The International Quilting Bee, Through the Flower, http://throughtheflower.org. Accessed August 15, 2012.

76. Cynthia Dettelbach, "Editor's Thoughts: *The Dinner Party*," *Cleveland Plain Dealer*, April 5, 1981, JCP, carton 19, file 29.

77. Helen Brush to Judy Chicago, form, no date, Documentation, International Quilting Bee, Through the Flower, Belen, New Mexico.

78. Amaralin Glorioso to Judy Chicago, form, no date, Whittier School, room 11, Berkeley Calif., Documentation, International Quilting Bee, Through the Flower.

79. On Constance Premnath Dass: Amrita Dass to Judy Chicago, April 1980, Documentation, International Quilting Bee, Through the Flower. On women during the Yom Kippur War: Miriam Sharon, *Women Sand Tent City, Sinai Desert, 1980*, Documentation, International Quilting Bee, Through the Flower. On human right activists in South Africa: Peter Dawson to Judy Chicago, August 24, 1984, Documentation, International Quilting Bee, Through the Flower.

80. The Names Project AIDS Memorial Quilt began in 1987, though it was inspired by the murder of Harvey Milk in 1978.

81. Joan Mister to Diane Gelon, letter September 3, 1979, JCP, carton 20, file 10.

82. NEH grant application, Washington Women's Art Center, JCP, carton 20, file 10.

83. Through the Flower Northwest to Judy Chicago, letter February 1980, JCP, carton 21, file 18.21.18.

84. Judy Chicago to Through the Flower, photocopied letter June 16, 1980, filed with Letter to Judy Chicago from Through the Flower Northwest, February 1980, JCP, carton 21, file 18.21.18.

85. Levin, *Becoming Judy Chicago*, 322.

86. Ibid. Ross Taylor to author.

87. BWAA fund-raising, no date, JCP, carton 19, file 16.

88. April Hankins to author, email February 24, 2011.

89. Christine Temin, "'Dinner Party' Coming to Boston," *Boston Globe*, June 22, 1980, JCP, carton 19, file 16.

90. Christine Termin, "Boston Center for the Arts Still Building, Still Struggling," *Boston Globe*, October 4, 1981, 1.

91. Levin, *Becoming Judy Chicago*, 322.

92. Temin, "'Dinner Party' Coming to Boston."

93. Hankins to author.

94. BWAA fund-raising.

95. Invitation to the Great Hall, JCP, carton 19, file 16.

96. Loretta Barret to Don Best, memo June 12, 1980, JCP, carton 19, file 16.

97. *The Dinner Party Catalogue*, Boston, July 4, 1980. JCP, carton 19, file 16.

98. Boston Correspondence, JCP, carton 19, file 16.

99. Hélène Cixous, *The Laugh of the Medusa*, published in 1976 (reprint, New York: Oxford University 2007), originally published as *Le rire de la Méduse* (1976); Luce Irigaray, *Speculum of the Other Woman*, published in 1985 (Ithaca, N.Y.: Cornell University Press), originally published as *Speculum de l'autre femme* (1974), and *This Sex Which Is Not One* (*Ce sexe qui n'en est pas un*, 1977) and *When Our Lips Speak Together* (1977), published in 1985 (Ithaca, N.Y.: Cornell University Press).

100. Gloria T. Hull, Patricia Bell Scott, and Barbara Smith, eds., *All the Women Are White, All the Blacks Are Men, But Some of Us Are Brave: Black Women's Studies* (New York: Feminist Press, 1992); Duchess Harris, "All of Whom I Am in the Same Place," *Womanist* 2, no. 1 (fall 1999): 9–17, 20–21; Benita Roth, *Separate Roads to Feminism: Black, Chicana, and White Feminist Movements in America's Second Wave* (New York: Cambridge University Press, 2003); Kimberly Springer, *Living for the Revolution: Black Feminist Organizations 1968–1980* (Chapel Hill, N.C.: Duke University Press, 2005).

101. Brooklyn correspondence, JCP, carton 19, file 23.

102. Hankins to author.

103. Stern interview.

104. Levin, *Becoming Judy Chicago*, 326.

105. Stern interview.

106. Gloria Steinem coined the "click!" moment to refer to a sudden experience of feminist awareness. Amy Erdman Farrell, *Yours in Sisterhood: "Ms." Magazine and the Promise of Popular Feminism* (Chapel Hill: University of North Carolina Press, 1998), 152.

107. Marcia Levine, interview with author, February 28, 2011.

108. Ibid.

109. Dorothy Goodwill, "Introduction," *Judy Chicago, Cleveland, Ohio, May 10–August 9, 1981*, catalog, JCP, carton 2, file 10.

110. Goodwill, "Introduction."

111. Dettelbach, "Editor's Thoughts."

112. Stern interview.

113. Levine interview.

114. Dorothy Shinn, "Dinner Party Turns into a Costly Affair," *Akron Beacon Journal*, March 25, 1981, JCP, carton 19, file 29.

115. Institute for Futures Studies and Research, University of Akron, no date, JCP carton 19, file 30.

116. Shinn, "Dinner Party Turns into a Costly Affair."

117. "Breakfast with Judy Chicago Is an Emotional Experience," *Akron Beacon Journal*, April 19, 1981, JCP, carton 19, file 29.

118. "The Dinner Party Exhibition—Comparative Budgets," in possession of Diane Gelon.

119. Cynthia Dettelbach, "Dialogue, Controversy Served at Dinner Party," *Cleveland Jewish News*, May 8, 1981, 31.

120. "Breakfast with Judy Chicago Is an Emotional Experience."

121. Marcia Levine interview.

122. Ann Marie Lipinski, "Controversial 'Dinner Party' Planned for Chicago Exhibit," *Chicago Tribune*, June 23, 1981, A6.

123. Ann Marie Lipinski, "Chicago Cancels Its Invitation to the Dinner Party," *Chicago Tribune*, July 30, 1980, 11.

124. Ibid.

125. *The Dinner Party Catalogue, Chicago, September 1981.* JCP, carton 19, file 28.

126. Lipinski, "Chicago Cancels Its Invitation to the Dinner Party."

127. *Dinner Party Catalogue, Chicago, September 1981.*

128. Ann Marie Lipinski, "An Invitation to 'The Dinner Party,'" *Chicago Tribune*, September 6, 1981, JCP, carton 19, file 28.

129. Burger, interview with Diane Gelon, 7, JCP, carton 19, file 28.

130. Lipinski, "Invitation to 'The Dinner Party.'"

131. Ibid.

132. Ibid.

133. Ibid.

134. Nancy Cott, "An Experiment of Women, 1893," *New York Times*, July 19, 1981, A9.

135. Chicago correspondence, JCP, carton 19, file 28.

136. South Loop Planning Board, undated press release, JCP, carton 2, file 11.

137. Ibid.

138. Ibid.

139. Sarah Craig, "'Dinner Party' Financing Stirs Controversy," *Gay Life*, November 20, 1981, 7, JCP, carton 2, file 12.

140. Judy Chicago, *Beyond the Flower: The Autobiography of a Feminist Artist* (New York: Viking, 1996), and *"The Dinner Party": From Creation to Preservation* (New York: Merrell, 2007).

CHAPTER SEVEN. Debating Feminist Art

1. Gail Levin, *Becoming Judy Chicago: A Biography of the Artist* (New York: Harmony Books, 2007), 316.

2. Grace Glueck, "Art People," *New York Times*, January 2, 1981, C18.

3. Nan Robertson, "4,500 Guests, Most of them Women, Answer the Dinner Party Invitation," *New York Times*, October 18, 1980, 52.

4. Vance Muse, "Pitfalls Amid the Rewards of 'Audio Tours," *New York Times*, June 3, 1981, C18.

5. Glueck, "Art People."

6. Robertson, "4,500 Guests, Most of them Women, Answer the Dinner Party Invitation."

7. Michael Botwinick, 1994 letter for Permanent Housing Fundraising packets, Judy Chicago Papers, Arthur and Elizabeth Schlesinger Library on the History of Women in America, Radcliffe Institute for Advanced Study, Harvard University (hereafter JCP), carton 21, file 28.

8. Hilton Kramer, "Bad Taste," *New York Times*, October 17, 1980.

9. Susan Crean, "The Dinner Party: Indigestion for the Establishment," *Broadside*, 8.

10. Quoted in ibid.

11. Jan Butterfield, "Guess Who's Coming to Dinner?," *Mother Jones* 4, no. 1 (January 1979): 20–28, 20.

12. Blair, "The Womanly Art of Judy Chicago," *Mademoiselle*, January 1981, 99–101, 151–53, 153. Emphasis in original.

13. Michael Ennis, "The Woman Who Came to Dinner," *Texas Monthly*, May 1980, 154–62, 155.

14. Arthur Asa Berger, *Chronicle of Higher Education*, no date, clipping, JCP, carton 22, file 42.

15. Ibid.

16. Unsigned editorial, *Boston Globe*, August 28, 1981, clipping, JCP, carton 22, file 42.

17. Virginia M. Allen, "Judy Chicago and the Myth of Matriarchy," *New Boston Review*, September/October 1979, 12–13, 12.

18. Kramer, "Bad Taste."

19. Dick Feager, "About Butterflies or Something Else," Cleveland newspaper clipping, JCP, carton 19, file 30.

20. Lawrence Alloway, "Art," *Nation*, November 15, 1980, 524.

21. Art Jahnke, "Oh Waiter, What's This Butterfly Doing in My Soup?," *Real Paper* (Boston), July 1980.

22. Robert Hughes. "An Obsessive Feminist Pantheon: Judy Chicago's Dinner Party Turns History into Agitprop," *Time* magazine, December 15, 1980, 63–64.

23. John Richardson, *New York Review*, 18–20, 20, clipping, JCP, carton 22, file 42.

24. Judy Chicago quoted in Anita Diamant, *Boston Phoenix*, December 1979.

25. Anita Diamant to Judy Chicago, letter December 18, 1979, JCP, carton 15, file 26.

26. Chicago quoted in Diamant, *Boston Phoenix*, December 1979. Emphasis in original.

27. April Kingsley, "The I-Hate-to-Cook 'Dinner Party,'" *Ms.* magazine, June 1979, 30–31.

28. John Perreault, "No Reservations," *SoHo News*, October 22, 1980, 19.

29. Laura Holland, "It's Art! It's Feminism! It's 'The Dinner Party'!!!" *Valley Advocate* 3, no. 49 (July 23, 1980): 18–19.

30. Hal Fisher, *Artforum*, summer 1979, 76.

31. Hughes, "An Obsessive Feminist Pantheon"; Fisher, *Artforum*; Jahnke, "Oh Waiter, What's This Butterfly Doing in My Soup?"; Robert Taylor quoted in Diane Gelon, "The Critic's Voice: Who Speaks for Us?," *Sojourner*, October 1980, 5; Kay Larson, "Dinner Belles," *Village Voice*, October 22–28, 1980, 77; Dorothy Shinn, "The Gospel According to Judy Chicago," *Beacon: The Sunday Magazine of the Akron Beacon*, July 5, 1981, 4 (quoted in Levin, *Becoming Judy Chicago*, 327); Mark Stevens, "Guess Who's Coming to Dinner?," *Newsweek*, April 2, 1979, 92; Kramer, "Bad Taste."

32. Nanette Morin, *Current*, July 17–23, 1980, 3.

33. Kay Larson, "Dinner Belles," *Village Voice*, October 22–28, 1980, 77.

34. Blair, "Womanly Art of Judy Chicago," 100.

35. Allan Artner, "'Newsworthy' Art Events: Too Often, Not Worth the Fuss," *Chicago Tribune*, September 20, 1981, E77.

36. Amei Wallach, "Unconventional 'Dinner Party,'" *Newsday*, October 26, 1980.

37. Marta Hallowell, "Chicago Comes to Brooklyn," *New York*, October 20, 1980, 50–55, 50.

38. Richardson, *New York Review*, 18–20, 18.

39. Wallach, "Unconventional 'Dinner Party.'"

40. Lawrence Alloway, "Art," *Nation*, November 15, 1980, 524.

41. Hallowell, "Chicago Comes to Brooklyn," 52.

42. Kathleen Driscoll-Knoll, Living/Forum, Living Pages, *Boston Globe*, August 17, 1980.

43. Perreault, "No Reservations."

44. Suzanne Muchnic, "An Intellectual Famine at Judy Chicago's Feast," *Los Angeles Times*, April 15, 1979, J3.

45. Carrie Rickey, "Judy Chicago: *The Dinner Party*," *Artforum*, January 1981, 72–73.

46. *Boston Globe* critic quoted in Gelon, "Critic's Voice."

47. Allan Artner, "Inanity Outweighs the Controversy of 'Dinner Party,'" *Chicago Tribune*, September 14, 1981, B8.

48. Michael Kammen, *Visual Shock: A History of Art Controversies in American Culture* (New York: Vintage, 2006), 317–20.

49. Amy Erdman Ferrell, *Yours in Sisterhood: "Ms." Magazine and the Promise of Popular Feminism* (Chapel Hill, N.C.: Duke University Press, 1998).

50. Judy Chicago, interview with author, January 25, 2011.

51. Carolyn Bronstein, *Battling Pornography: The American Feminist Anti-Pornography Movement, 1976–1986* (New York: Cambridge University Press, 2011).

52. Susan Rennie and Arlene Raven, "*The Dinner Party*: An Interview with Judy Chicago," *Chrysalis* 4 (January 1978): 89–101, 98.

53. Holland, "It's Art!"

54. Alice Walker, "One Child of One's Own," *Ms.* magazine, summer 1979, reprinted as "One Child of One's Own: A Meaningful Digression within the Work(s)—An Ex-

cerpt," in Gloria Hull, Patricia Bell Scott, and Barbara Smith, eds., *All the Women Are White, All the Blacks Are Men, But Some of Us Are Brave* (New York: Feminist Press, 1982), 37–44, 43.

55. Diane Ketcham, "On the Table: Joyous Celebration," *Village Voice*, June 11, 1979, 47–49, 48.

56. Crean, "Dinner Party."

57. "The Dinner Party," *Sojourner*, December 1980, 32.

58. Lauren Rabinovitz, "Issues of Feminist Aesthetics: Judy Chicago and Joyce Wieland," *Woman's Art Journal* 1, no. 2 (1980): 38–41, 40.

59. Rennie and Raven, "*The Dinner Party*," 93.

60. Ibid., 94, 96, 94.

61. Susan Minnicks, "Whose Dinner Party Is It, Anyway?," *Sojourner*, October 1980, clipping, JCP, carton 2, file 8.

62. Sue Diehl, "'The Dinner Party,' San Francisco Museum of Modern Art, March 17–June 17, 1979," *Frontiers: A Journal of Women's Studies* 4, no. 2 (summer 1979): 74–75, 75.

63. Ellen Willis, *Village Voice*, November 5–11, 1980, 32.

64. Marilynn Woodsea, "*The Dinner Party*," *Womanspirit* 23 (March 1980): 50.

65. Lolette Kuby, "The Hoodwinking of the Women's Movement: Judy Chicago's *Dinner Party*," *Frontiers* 6, no. 3 (autumn 1981): 127–29, 128.

66. Anne Marie Pois, "A Reply to Kuby's Review," *Frontiers* 6, no. 3, (autumn 1981): 129–30.

67. Eunice Lipton, "Ain't Misbehavin': At Chicago's *Dinner Party*," *Cleveland Beacon* 1, no. 5 (June 1981): 4–7, 6.

68. Ibid., 6.

69. "Recapturing Our History: An Interview with Dorothy Goodwill and Jeanne Van Atta," *Cleveland Beacon* 1, no. 5, (June 1981): 4–7, 4, 7, 5, 6.

70. Lucy Lippard, "Judy Chicago's *Dinner Party*," *Art in America*, April 1980, 115–25, 119, 115, 117, 125.

71. Hilary Robinson, "Reframing Women," *Circa* 72 (1995): 18–23. Reprinted in Hilary Robinson, ed., *Feminism-Art-Theory: An Anthology, 1968–2000* (Oxford: Blackwell, 2001), 534–39, 536.

72. Judy Grosfield to Judy Chicago, letter July 20, 1980, JCP, carton 25, file 1.

73. Mary Ann Sestili to Judy Chicago, letter May 11, 1980, and Amy Drinker to Judy Chicago, letter August 14, 1980, JCP, carton 25, file 1.

74. Donna Anthony to Judy Chicago, undated letter, JCP, carton 25, file 1.

75. Marianne Van Fossen to Judy Chicago, letter January 18, 1981; Joan Riegel to Judy Chicago, letter October 5, 1981; Desmond Gaffney to Judy Chicago, January 15, 1981, all in JCP, carton 25, file 1. Laurie White to Judy Chicago, letter June 10, 1982, JCP, carton 25, file 3; Christina Hurst to Judy Chicago, letter 6 January 1981, JCP, carton 25, file 1; Hilary McLeod to Judy Chicago, letter April 26, 1982, JCP, carton 25, file 3.

76. Cheryl Dyer to Judy Chicago, letter January 6, 1981, JCP, carton 25, file 1; Barb Nef to Judy Chicago, letter April 29, 1981, JCP, carton 10, file 3.

77. Liz Adelinau to Judy Chicago, letter January 1981, JCP, carton 25, file 1.

78. Pamela Joy Roper to Judy Chicago, undated letter, JCP, carton 25, file 8.

79. Kathleen Martin to Judy Chicago, letter January 11, 1980, JCP, carton 10, file 2.

80. Dorothy Grant to Judy Chicago, letter March 17, 1982, JCP, carton 25, file 2.

81. Camille Corpo to Judy Chicago, undated letter, JCP, carton 25, file 3.

82. Kathleen Martin to Judy Chicago, letter January 11, 1980, JCP, carton 10, file 2.

83. Jennifer Stabler to Judy Chicago, undated letter, answered November 21, 1980, JCP, carton 10, file 2.

84. Liz Adelinau to Judy Chicago, letter January 1981, JCP, carton 25, file 1.

85. Unsigned letter to Judy Chicago, letter October 18, 1980, JCP, carton 24, file 32.

86. Kathleen Martin to Judy Chicago, letter January 11, 1980, JCP, carton 10, file 2.

87. Lauri Poklop to Judy Chicago, letter August 19, 1980, JCP, carton 24, file 32.

88. D. Harris to Judy Chicago, letter September 15, 1981, JCP, carton 10, file 3.

89. Margaret Loewen Reimer to Judy Chicago, letter June 2, 1982, JCP, carton 25, file 3.

90. Cleveland comment book, May through August 1981. In possession of Ann Mackin.

91. William Wing to Judy Chicago, letter October 21, 1980, JCP, carton 10, file 2.

92. Shirley Bradley, RN, to Judy Chicago, letter March 26, 1980, JCP, carton 24, file 32.

93. Letter September 2, 1980, JCP, carton 24, file 32.

94. Patricia Smith to Judy Chicago, letter July 14, 1980, JCP, carton 24, file 32.

95. Boston comment book, 1980, JCP, carton 19, file 18.

96. Cleveland comment book, May through August 1981. In possession of Ann Mackin.

97. Ibid.

98. Boston comment book.

99. Ibid.

100. Cleveland comment book.

101. Boston comment book.

102. Ibid.

103. Cleveland comment book.

104. Ibid.

105. Boston comment book.

106. Cleveland comment book.

107. Ibid.

108. Ibid.

109. Boston comment book.

110. Ibid.

111. Ann Mackin, "Values in Voices: Judy Chicago's *The Dinner Party*, Cleveland Exhibit, May 10–August 9, 1981, The Audiences Speak," MA thesis, Ursuline College, 2006, 39.

112. Cleveland comment book.

113. Ibid.

114. Cleveland comment book.

115. Boston comment book.

116. Cleveland comment book.

CHAPTER EIGHT. From Controversy to Canonization

1. Judy Chicago, "*The Dinner Party*": *From Creation to Preservation* (New York: Merrell, 2007), 276–77.

2. Through the Flower to the University of the District of Columbia, undated memo, Judy Chicago Papers, Arthur and Elizabeth Schlesinger Library on the History of Women in America, Radcliffe Institute for Advanced Study, Harvard University (hereafter JCP), carton 22, file 22.

3. Ibid.

4. Judy Chicago, personal journal, December 11, 1975, reprinted in Judy Chicago, *"The Dinner Party: A Symbol of Our Heritage* (New York: Doubleday/Anchor, 1979), 29.

5. Judy Chicago, "The Struggle for Preservation," conclusion in Chicago, *"Dinner Party"* (2007), 269–88, 281; Lucy Lippard, "Uninvited Guests: How Washington Lost 'The Dinner Party,'" *Art in America* 79 (December 1991): 39–49, 39.

6. Barbara Gamarekian, "A Feminist Artwork for University Library," *New York Times*, July 21, 1990.

7. Chicago, "Struggle for Preservation," 281.

8. Lippard, "Uninvited Guests," 47.

9. Ibid., 41.

10. For example, W.E.B.—West-East Bag—attempted to bring lesser-known female artists to the attention of art critics by presenting them with more well known artists, like Chicago.

11. This figure—$1.2 million, was consistently inflated to $1.6 million, an error first made by journalist Jonetta Rose Barras ("UDC's $1.6 Million 'Dinner': Feminist Artwork Causes Some Indigestion," *Washington Times*, July 18, 1990, 1, 7) and then spread throughout the reportage. See Lippard, "Uninvited Guests," 41.

12. Alice Thorson, "Hungry Conservatives Crash the Dinner Party," *New Art Examiner* 18 (October 1990): 56.

13. Lippard, "Uninvited Guests," 41.

14. Ibid.

15. Ibid.

16. Barbara Gamarekian, "A Feminist Artwork for University Library," *New York Times*, July 21, 1990.

17. Elsye Grinstein, president, TTF, "Terms of the Gift," JCP, carton 22, file 15.

18. Ibid.

19. Barras, "UDC's $1.6 Million 'Dinner,'" 1.

20. Joseph Webb quoted in ibid., 7.

21. Barras, "UDC's $1.6 Million 'Dinner,'" 7.

22. Jonetta Rose Barras, "D.C. Council's 'Sanity' Questioned as Hill Learns of 'Dinner Party,'" *Washington Times*, July 19, 1990, 1 and 6, 1.

23. Ibid., 1.

24. Lippard, "Uninvited Guests," 43.

25. Barras, "D.C. Council's 'Sanity' Questioned as Hill Learns of 'Dinner Party,'" 6.

26. Wesley Pruden, "A Big Dinner Bell, But No Groceries," *Washington Times*, July 20, 1990.

27. C-SPAN, July 26, 1990. Video, in possession of Through the Flower.

28. Ibid.

29. Ibid.

30. Lippard, "Uninvited Guests," 43.

31. John Smith, "Congress Shoots an Arrow into UDC's Art," *Washington Times*, July 27, 1990, 1 and 6, 1.

32. Ibid.

33. Barbara Gamarekian, "Corcoran, to Foil Dispute, Drops Mapplethorpe Show," *New York Times*, June 14, 1989.

34. Ibid.

35. Richard Meyer, "The Jessie Helms Theory of Art," *October* 104 (spring 2003): 131–48, 137.

36. Barbara Gamarekian, "Crowd at Corcoran Protests Mapplethorpe Cancellation," *New York Times*, July 1, 1989.

37. Margaret Quigley, "The Mapplethorpe Censorship Controversy," *Public Eye*, http://www.publiceye.org/theocrat/Mapplethorpe_Chrono.html. Accessed on April 26, 2011.

38. Peggy Phelan, "Serrano, Mapplethorpe, the NEA, and You: 'Money Talks, October 1989,'" *TDR* 34, no. 1 (spring 1990): 4–15, 7.

39. Robin Cembalest, "Who Does It Shock? Why Does It Shock?" *Art News*, March 1992, 32–33; Robin Cembalest, "The Obscenity Trial: How They Voted to Acquit," *Art News*, December 1990, 136–41; Rochelle Gurstein, "High Art or Hard-Core? Misjudging Mapplethorpe: The Art Scene and the Obscene," Current Debate, *Tikkun* (November–December 1991), 70–80; Judy Light, "Jury Acquits Museum in Landmark Art Trial," *Dancemagazine* (December 1990), 12–13; Jayne Merkel, "Art on Trial," *Art in America* (December 1990), 41–46.

40. Robert Storr, "Art, Censorship, and the First Amendment: This Is Not a Test," *Art Journal* 50, no. 3 (autumn 1991): 12–28.

41. Michael Kammen, *Visual Shock: A History of Art Controversies in American Culture* (New York: Vintage, 2006), 277–80.

42. Phelan, "Serrano, Mapplethorpe, the NEA, and You," 5.

43. Ibid., 6.

44. Meyer, "Jessie Helms Theory of Art," 137; Quigley, "Mapplethorpe Censorship Controversy."

45. Quigley, "Mapplethorpe Censorship Controversy."

46. Lippard, "Uninvited Guests," 45.

47. Ellen Sweets, "The Chicago Story," *Dallas Morning News*, September 16, 1990, C1 and 10, C10.

48. Ibid., C10. On Jesse Helms, see Correspondence, UDC controversy, in possession of Mary Ross Taylor.

49. "Indigestion from 'Dinner Party'?," *Art in America*, September 1990.

50. Lippard, "Uninvited Guests," 41.

51. Jonetta Rose Barras, "Financial Inquiries Crash 'The Dinner Party' at UDC," *Washington Times*, July 20, 1990, 1 and 6, 6.

52. Ibid., 6.

53. Ibid., 6.

54. "Controversial Artwork Gift May Squeeze Books Out of Library," *American Libraries*, October 1990, clipping, JCP, carton 22, file 20.

55. Smith, "Congress Shoots an Arrow into UDC's Art," 1.

56. Nira Hardon Long, "'The Dinner Party': A Matter of Basic Human Liberties," *Washington Post*, August 9, 1990.

57. UDC correspondence, JCP, carton 22, files 17 and 19.

58. Ibid., files 19 and 20.

59. Ibid., file 20.

60. Ibid., file 21.

61. Mary Ross Taylor to the Honorable Debra Danburg, undated fax, in possession of Mary Ross Taylor. Taylor to author, email April 8, 2011.

62. UDC correspondence, JCP, carton 22, file 23; Lippard, "Uninvited Guests," 45.

63. Judy Mann, "Art and Sexual Power," *Washington Post*, September 12, 1990, D3.

64. Mary Suh, "Guess Who's *Not* Coming to Dinner?," *Ms.* magazine, September/October 1990, 87.

65. Mary Ross Taylor quoted in Sweets, "Chicago Story," C10.

66. Pat Mathis quoted in ibid., C10.

67. UDC correspondence, JCP, carton 22, file 13.

68. Keith Harrison and Gabriel Escobar, "UDC Students Take Over Two Buildings," *Washington Post*, September 27, 1990, 1.

69. Ibid.

70. Ibid.

71. Jonetta Rose Barras and Michael Cromwell, "UDC Staff, Protesters Seem to Be at Impasse," *Washington Times*, October 1, 1990.

72. See "University Won't Host Dinner Party," *Art News*, December 1990, 60–61, for the most extraneous racialization of the controversy; others include the *Washington Times*, September 27, October 1, and October 3, 1990.

73. Lippard, "Uninvited Guests," 47.

74. Carlos Sanchez and Ruben Castaneda, "Chairman Negotiating Resignation; Gift of 'The Dinner Party' Revoked," *Washington Post*, October 3, 1990, D1 and D4, D1.

75. Judy Chicago, announcement October 2, 1990, JCP, carton 22, file 15.

76. Sanchez and Castaneda, "Chairman Negotiating Resignation," D1.

77. Lippard, "Uninvited Guests," 49.

78. Annforfreedom, "The Attacks on Judy Chicago and *The Dinner Party*," *Wise Woman* 11, no. 2 (1990–1991): 2–7, quotes on 1, 5, 2, and 7, JCP, carton 22, file 36.

79. Carole S. Vance, "The War on Culture," *Art in America* 77, no. 9 (September 1989): 39–44.

80. Thorson, "Hungry Conservatives Crash the Dinner Party."

81. For accounts of family values in the 1980s, see Donald Critchlow, *Phyllis Schlafly and Grassroots Conservatism: A Woman's Crusade* (Princeton, N.J.: Princeton University Press, 2007); Janice Irvine, *Talk about Sex: The Battles over Sexual Education in the United States* (Berkeley: University of California Press, 2004); Rebecca Klatch, *Women and the New Right* (Philadelphia: Temple University Press, 1988); Catherine Rymph, *Republican Women: Feminism and Conservatism from Suffrage through the Rise of the New Right* (Chapel Hill: University of North Carolina Press, 2006).

82. Vance, "War on Culture."

83. William Honan, "Fronnmayer Is Asked to End Written Pledge," *New York Times*, August 4, 1990.

84. Chicago, "Struggle for Preservation," 283.

85. Richard Mahler, "The Battle of Chicago," *Los Angeles Times*, October 12, 1990, F1–2.

86. Henry Hopkins, foreword in Amelia Jones, ed., *Sexual Politics: Judy Chicago's "Dinner Party" in Feminist Art History* (Berkeley: University of California Press, 1996), 10.

87. Diane Elam and Robyn Wiegman, eds., *Feminism Beside Itself* (New York: Routledge, 1995); Florence Howe, ed., *The Politics of Women's Studies: Testimony from Thirty Founding Mothers* (New York: Feminist Press, 2000); Patrice McDermott, *Politics and Scholarship: Feminist Academic Journals and the Production of Knowledge* (Chicago: University of Illinois Press, 1994).

88. Guerilla Girls quoted in Josephine Withers, "The Guerrilla Girls," *Feminist Studies* 14, no. 2 (summer 1988): 284–300, 285.

89. Guerrilla Girls webpage, http://www.guerrillagirls.com/posters/twothirds2.shtml. Accessed April 25, 2011.

90. Michael Kammen, *Visual Shock: A History of Art Controversies in American Culture* (New York: Vintage, 2006), 325.

91. Withers, "Guerrilla Girls," 287.

92. Guerrilla Girls webpage, http://www.guerrillagirls.com/posters/getnaked.shtml. Accessed April 25, 2011.

93. Linda Nochlin, "Why Have There Been No Great Women Artists?" in V. Gornick and B. Moran, eds., *Women in Sexist Society* (New York: Basic Books, 1971).

94. Norma Broude and Mary Garrad, *Power of Feminist Art* (New York: Harry Abrams, 1996); Helena Reckitt, ed., and Peggy Phelan, collaborator, *Art and Feminism* (London: Phaidon Press, 2001).

95. Rozsika Parker and Griselda Pollock, *Old Mistresses: Women, Art and Ideology* (New York: Pantheon Books, 1981), xviii–xix; Rozsika Parker and Griselda Pollock, "Critical Stereotypes: The Essential Feminine or How Essential Is Femininity?" (1981) reprinted in Reckitt, *Art and Feminism*, 230–31.

96. Craig Owens, "The Discourse of Others: Feminists and Postmodernism," in Hal Foster, ed., *The Anti-Aesthetic: Essays on Postmodern Culture* (Seattle, Wash.: Bay Press, 1983), 57–82.

97. Parker and Pollock, *Old Mistresses*, 80.

98. Ibid., 65, 127.

99. Thalia Gouma-Peterson and Patricia Mathews, "The Feminist Critique of Art History," *Art Bulletin*, September 1, 1987.

100. Parker and Pollock, *Old Mistresses*, 132.

101. Owens, "Discourse of Others," 81.

102. Laura Mulvey, "Visual Pleasure and Narrative Cinema," *Screen* 16, no. 3 (autumn 1975): 6–18.

103. Parker and Pollock, *Old Mistresses*, 130.

104. Lisa Duggan and Nan Hunter, *Sex Wars: Sexual Dissent and Political Culture* (New York: Routledge, 1996); Jane Gerhard, *Desiring Revolution: Second-Wave Feminism and the Rewriting of American Sexual Thought, 1920–1982* (New York: New York University Press, 2001).

105. Vivien Green, "Suzanne Lacy's *Three Weeks in May*: Feminist Activist Performance Art as 'Expanded Public Pedagogy,'" *NWSA Journal* 19, no. 1 (spring 2007): 23–33.

106. Carolyn Bronstein, *Battling Pornography: The American Feminist Anti-Pornography Movement, 1976–1986* (New York: Cambridge University Press, 2011); Susan Brownmiller, *In Our Time: Memoir of a Revolution* (New York: Random House, 1999).

107. Julie Springer made a similar connection in her double review of Amelia Jones's edited volume, *Sexual Politics*, and Judy Chicago's *Beyond the Flower*, in *Women's Art Journal* 20, no. 1 (spring–summer 1999): 52–54, 52.

108. John Toews, "Intellectual History after the Linguistic Turn: The Autonomy of Meaning and the Irreducibility of Experience," *American Historical Review* 92, number 4 (1987): 879–904; Susan Faludi, *Backlash: The Undeclared War against American Women* (New York: Anchor Books, 1992); Amelia Jones, "Strategic Oblivion: 1970s Feminist Art in 1980s Art History," in *Memory and Oblivion: Proceedings of the XXIXth International*

Congress of the History of Art, held in Amsterdam, September 1–7, 1996 (Amsterdam: Klewer Academic Publishers, 1999), 1043–48.

109. Amelia Jones, "'Post-Feminism': A Remasculinization of Culture?" *M/E/A/N/I/N/G* 7 (1990): 29–40. Page numbers are for the reprint in Hilary Robinson, ed., *Feminism-Art-Theory* (Malden, Mass.: Blackwell, 2001), 496–506; Amelia Jones, "Feminism, Incorporated: Reading 'Post-Feminism' in an Anti-Feminist Age," *Afterimage* (December 1992), 10–15.

110. Jones, "'Post-Feminism,'" 500, 504.

111. Springer, review, 52.

112. Hopkins, foreword, 10. *The Dinner Party* remained on display in LA until August 18, 1996.

113. Amelia Jones, "Sexual Politics: Feminist Strategies, Feminist Conflicts, Feminist Histories," in Jones, *Sexual Politics*, 22–38, 37.

114. Suzanne Muchnic, "Push-Pull of Feminist Art," *Los Angeles Times*, April 21, 1996.

115. On the resurgence of interest in 1970s "essentialist" art in the 1990s, see Emily Apter, "Questions of Feminism: Essentialism's Period," *October* 71 (winter 1995): 8–9.

116. Springer, review, 53; Gail Levin, *Becoming Judy Chicago: A Biography of the Artist* (New York: Harmony Books, 2007), 386.

117. Jennie Klein, "Sexual/Textual Politics: The Battle over the Art of the 70s," *New Art Examiner* 24 (1996): 26–31, 30.

118. Jones, "Sexual Politics," 24.

119. Ibid., 25.

120. Springer, review, 52.

121. Unattributed quote in Courtney Bailey, "Feminist Art and (Post)Modern Anxieties," *Genders* 32 (2000): 1–42, 35.

122. Amelia Jones quoted in Levin, *Becoming Judy Chicago*, 386.

123. Amelia Jones quoted in ibid., 386.

124. Jones, "Sexual Politics," 24.

125. Amelia Jones quoted in Levin, *Becoming Judy Chicago*, 386.

126. Jones, "Strategic Oblivion," 1045.

127. Ibid., 1045.

128. Muchnic, "Push-Pull of Feminist Art."

129. To see a fuller development of this argument, see Judith K. Brodsky and Ferris Olin, "Stepping Out of the Beaten Path: Reassessing the Feminist Art Movement," *Signs* 33, no. 2 (winter 2008): 329–42.

130. Christopher Knight, Art in Review, 1996, *Los Angeles Times*, December 29, 1996.

131. Christopher Knight, "More Famine than Feast: Focusing on the Flawed 'Dinner Party' Undermines 'Sexual Politics,'" *Los Angeles Times*, May 2, 1996.

132. David Joselit, "Exhibiting Gender," *Art in America* 85 (January 1997): 37–39, 37.

133. Donald Preziosi, Counterpunch, *Los Angeles Times*, May 13, 1996.

134. Springer, review, 52.

135. Ibid.

136. Klein, "Sexual/Textual Politics," 30.

137. Alice Walker, *The Color Purple* (New York: Pocket Press, 1982) and *The Same River Twice: Honoring The Difficult* (New York: Scribner, 1996); for the debates it spawned among African American feminist critics, see Trudier Harris, "On *The Color Purple*: Stereotypes, and Silence," *Black American Literature Forum* 18, no. 4 (winter 1984): 155–61.

138. Erica Jong, *Fear of Flying* (New York: Penguin 1972). For 1970s feminist fiction,

see Gerhard, *Desiring Revolution*; Lisa Marie Hogeland, *Feminism and its Fictions: The Consciousness-Raising Novel and the Women's Liberation Movement* (Philadelphia: University of Pennsylvania Press, 1998).

139. Jacqueline Bobo, "*The Color Purple*: Black Women as Cultural Readers," in Jacqueline Bobo, Cynthia Hudley, and Claudine Michel, eds., *The Black Studies Reader* (New York: Routledge, 2004), 177–92, 179.

140. Dollar figure at Internet Movie Database, http://www.imdb.com/title/tt0088939/business. Accessed May 5, 2011.

141. Carol Gilligan, *In a Different Voice: Psychological Theory and Women's Development* (Cambridge, Mass.: Harvard University Press, 1982).

142. Cressida J. Heyes, "Anti-Essentialism in Practice: Carol Gilligan and Feminist Philosophy," in "Third Wave Feminisms," special issue, *Hypatia* 12, no. 3 (summer 1997): 142–63.

143. "Reply by Carol Gilligan," *Signs* 11, no. 2 (winter 1986): 324–33, 325.

144. Harvard University Press, http://www.hup.harvard.edu/catalog.php?isbn=9780674445444. Accessed on May 2, 2011.

145. *Tootsie*, directed by Sydney Pollack, distributed by Columbia Pictures, December 17, 1982.

146. Faludi, *Backlash*.

147. Naomi Wolf, *The Beauty Myth: How Images of Beauty Are Used against Women* (New York: Doubleday, 1991).

148. Simone de Beauvoir, *The Second Sex* (New York: Vintage, 1953); Betty Friedan, *The Feminine Mystique* (New York: Pocket Books, 1963); Germaine Greer, *The Female Eunuch* (New York: Harper, 1970).

149. Katie Roiphe, *The Morning After: Sex, Fear, and Feminism on Campus* (Boston, Mass.: Little, Brown, 1993).

150. Camille Paglia, *Sexual Personae: Art and Decadence from Nefertiti to Emily Dickenson* (New Haven, Conn.: Yale University Press, 1990); Christina Hoff Sommers, *Who Stole Feminism? How Women Have Betrayed Women* (New York: Simon and Schuster, 1994).

151. Candice Bushnell, *Sex and the City* (New York: Grand Central Publishing, 1997).

152. See Christine Cooper, "Worrying about Vaginas: Feminism and Eve Ensler's 'The Vagina Monologues,'" *Signs* 32, no. 3 (2007): 727–58; Kim Hall, "Queerness, Disability, and 'The Vagina Monologues,'" *Hypatia* 20, no. 1 (winter 2005): 99–119.

153. Eve Ensler, interview, Women.com (2000), http://www.randomhouse.com/features/ensler/vm/qna.html. Accessed on May 3, 2011.

154. Ibid.

155. Eve Ensler, *The Vagina Monologues* (New York: Villard, 2001), 71, 25, 63.

156. Ibid., 15–17, 19–21.

157. Ibid., 53–54, 82.

158. Rachel Kranz, "Going Public: 'The Vagina Monologues,'" *Women's Review of Books* 17, no. 10/11 (July 2000): 26–27.

159. For other commentary on the series, see Susan Douglas, *Enlightened Sexism: The Seductive Message that Feminism's Work Is Done* (New York: Times Books, 2010), 170–175; Pamela Butler and Jigna Desai, "Manolos, Marriage, and Mantras: Chick Lit-Criticism and Transnational Feminism," *Meridians* 8, no. 2 (2008): 1–31.

160. Levin, *Becoming Judy Chicago*, 371.

161. Marcia Levin, interview with author, February 28, 2011.

162. Permanent Housing, 1988–1990, JCP, carton 22, files 11–14.

163. Levin, *Becoming Judy Chicago*, 376.

164. Ibid., 392.

165. Ibid., 394.

166. Carol Vogel, "A Brooklyn Home for Feminist Art," *New York Times*, December 5, 2003.

167. M. G. Lord, "The Table Is Set, at Last, in a Home," *New York Times*, September 8, 2002.

168. Roberta Smith, "For a Paean to Heroic Women, a Place at History's Table," *New York Times*, September 20, 2001.

169. Robin Pogrebin, "Ms. Chicago, Party for 39? Your Table's Ready in Brooklyn," *New York Times*, February 1, 2007; Josephine Withers, "All Representation Is Political: Feminist Art Past and Present," *Feminist Studies* 34, no. 3 (fall 2008): 456–75.

170. Holland Cotter, "Feminist Art Finally Takes Center Stage," *New York Times*, January 29, 2007.

171. Cassandra Langer, "Woman's Art, Inc.," *Women's Art Journal* 25, no. 1 (spring–summer 2004): 61–64, 61.

172. Jo Dahn, "Dining in, Dining Out," *Ceramic Review* (2007), 24–26, 26.

173. Pogrebin, "Ms. Chicago, Party for 39?"

EPILOGUE. A Prehistory of Postfeminism

1. Dr. Judith Green to TTF, letter July 10, 1989, Judy Chicago America, Radcliffe Institute for Adva Papers, Arthur and Elizabeth Schlesinger Library on the History of Women in nced Study, Harvard University, carton 22, file 26.

2. For example, see Judith Butler, *Gender Trouble: Feminism and the Subversion of Identity* (New York: Routledge 1990); Diana Fuss, *Essentially Speaking: Feminism, Nature, and Difference* (New York: Routledge, 1989); Joan Scott, *Gender and the Politics of History* (New York: Columbia University Press, 1999); Alice Echols, *Daring to Be Bad: Radical Feminism in America, 1968–1975* (Minneapolis: University of Minnesota Press, 1988).

3. See, for example, Winifred Breines, *The Trouble between Us: An Uneasy History of Black and White Women in the Feminist Movement* (Oxford: Oxford University Press, 2006); Dorothy Sue Cobble, *The Other Women's Movement: Workplace Justice and Social Rights in Modern America* (Princeton, N.J.: Princeton University Press, 2004); Anne Enke, *Finding the Movement: Sexuality, Contested Space, and Feminist Activism* (Chapel Hill, N.C.: Duke University Press, 2007); Sara Evans, *Personal Politics: The Roots of Women's Liberation in the Civil Rights Movement and the New Left* (New York: Vintage, 1979) and *Tidal Wave: How Women Changed America at Century's End* (New York: Free Press, 2003); Ruth Rosen, *The World Split Open: How the Modern Women's Movement Changed America* (New York: Penguin, 2006); Benita Roth, *Separate Roads to Feminism: Black, Chicana, and White Feminist Movements in America's Second Wave* (New York: Cambridge University Press, 2004); Kimberly Springer, *Living for the Revolution: Black Feminist Organizations, 1968–1980* (Chapel Hill, N.C.: Duke University Press, 2005).

4. Ann Brooks, *Postfeminisms: Feminism, Cultural Theory and Cultural Forms* (New York: Routledge 1997); Angela McRobbie, *The Aftermath of Feminism* (London: Sage, 2009); Yvonne Tasker and Diane Negra, *Interrogating Post-feminism* (Durham, N.C.: Duke University Press, 2007).

5. Susan Faludi, *Backlash: The Undeclared War against American Women* (New York: Crown Publishers, 1981).

6. Susan Douglas, *Enlightened Sexism: The Seductive Message that Feminism's Work is Done* (New York: Times Books, 2010); Ariel Levy, *Female Chauvinist Pigs: Women and the Rise of Raunch Culture* (New York: Free Press, 2005); Deborah Siegel, *Sisterhood Interrupted: From Radical Women to Grrrls Gone Wild* (New York: Palgrave Macmillan, 2007).

7. Douglas, *Enlightened Sexism*; Jane Gerhard, "*Sex and the City*: Carrie Bradshaw's Queer Postfeminism," *Feminist Media Studies* 5, no. 1 (March 2005): 23–36, 41.

Index

Abell, Bess, 154, 155
Ad Hoc Women Artist's Group, 24
Akers, Pat, 118
Akron Beacon Journal, 204
Amend, Katie, 130, 132–33
Appelt, Evelyn, 133
Artforum, 22, 23, 211, 220, 222, 285
Art in America, 1, 23, 72, 164, 211; on congressional culture war, 255, 256, 259, 260, 270; on *The Dinner Party*, 224, 232, 285
Atkinson, Ti-Grace, 29, 37, 49
Atlantis, Dori, 36, 37, 65

Barrett, Loretta, 156, 157, 256
Biggs, Marjorie, 114, 168, 171
Black Arts Movement, 9–10, 23–25
Blecher, Terry, 100–103, 126
Boston Center for the Arts (BCA), 200
Boston Globe, 200, 201, 211, 217, 221, 222
Boston Phoenix, 187, 201, 219
Boude, Susan, 37
Brody, Sheri, 50
Brooklyn Museum, 24, 213; *The Dinner Party*, 1981, 168, 211–14, 246; *The Dinner Party*, permanent display 2002–2007), 246, 280–82, 284

CalArts, 38, 39, 41–46, 48–50, 52, 61, 65–67, 126. *See also* feminist art programs
Cannon, Calvin, 189, 190–93
central core imagery, 137–41, 165–67, 170–75, 217–19
Chicago, Judy, 6–8, 210, 280–82; accusation of exploitation of *The Dinner Party* workers, 18, 227–28; *The Birth Project* (1980–1985), 210; *The Dinner Party*, art, 111–16, 134, 137–42; *The Dinner Party* studio, 76–80, 84–87, 105–8, 125–26; feminist art movement, 65–75, 81–84; feminist art programs, 26–47; *Great Ladies* (painting, 1974), 73, 81; "The Heavenly Banquet" (manuscript), 144–46; The Holocaust Project (1985–1993, with Donald Woodman), 210; *Let It All Hang Out* (painting, 1973), 81; *Powerplay* (painting, 1982–1987), 210; *Red Flag* (photolithograph, 1971), 53; *Reincarnation Triptych* (painting, 1973); *Through the Flower* (memoir), 112, 128, 165, 189, 215, 235–36; Through the Flower (nonprofit), 160, 183, 193, 194, 195, 200, 205, 234, 249, 283; *Through the Flower* (painting, 1973), 81; *Womanhouse* (art installation), 53, 55, 57–60
Chicago Tribune, 206, 211, 214, 221, 223, 285
Chrysalis, 92, 185, 212, 225, 227
Cleveland Plain Dealer, 1, 204, 211, 285
Color Purple, The (Walker) 248, 272–74, 275

consciousness raising: in *The Dinner Party* studio, 77, 88–89, 94–105; in the feminist art movement, 61, 64, 73; in feminist art programs, 30–34, 41–47, 51–52, 57–68
cunt art, 37–40, 67, 217, 245, 264–86

de Bretteville, Sheila, 25, 41, 71–72, 232
Dellums, Ron, 253
Demetrakas, Johanna, 65, 132, 187; *Right Out of History*, 119, 190, 194, 203, 285
Dinner Party, The: acknowledgment panels, 2, 228; in Atlanta, 194, 199, 246; in Boston, 194, 199–202; in Chicago, 194, 199, 205–9; in Cleveland, 194, 199, 202–5; essentialism in, 17, 77, 137–42, 148, 234, 281; feminist coverage, 224–34; financial history, 149–65; guests, 169–71, 176, 201, 220; heritage floor, 126–37; heritage panels, 133; in Houston, 188–94, 199; millennium triangles, 163, 168–69, 171, 172; non-museum tour), 180–211; plates, 137–42; press coverage, 213–23; public response, 234–44; religious staging, 131, 142–47, 220–24, 231; runners, 111–26; studio process, 97–105, 116–37; workers, 87–97
DuBois, Jan Marie, 170

Ensler, Eve, *The Vagina Monologues*, 15–16, 247, 276–78
essentialism, feminist critique of, 224–26, 229, 247, 268–71

Faludi, Susan, 275, 288
female aesthetic, 74, 80–84, 224–25, 232, 24
feminism: abortion activism, 4, 110, 156, 288; antipornography, 4, 225, 229, 259–63, 265–71, 287; cultural, 3, 10, 13–16, 78, 107, 286; in *The Dinner Party* studio, 124, 141, 142, 192, 209, 234, 283–90; Equal Rights Amendment (ERA), 4, 5, 192, 230, 288; essentialism, 13, 38, 202, 224; goddess worship, 104, 142–44; popular, 248, 271–79, 283–90; postfeminism, 6, 279, 288–90; postmodernism, 263, 266, 267–69; separatism, 5, 13, 30, 63, 68, 232; sex wars 14, 145, 260, 265, 287; women of color, 111, 202; women's culture, 117–26, 129, 132, 148
Feminist Art Journal, 24, 82
feminist art movement: 1970s, 8–10, 23–26, 67–74; 1980s, 261–71, 281
feminist art programs, 18, 68, 73, 74, 98, 200; at CalArts, 41–46, 48–50, 52, 61, 65–67, 126; at Fresno State College, 26–38, 40
Feminist Studio Workshop (FSW), 69, 71–74, 126, 137, 227
Firestone, Shulamith, 37, 49
Ford Foundation, 154, 155, 158, 197
Fraine, Cherie, 120–21
Frankel, Dextra, 22, 82
Fresno State College, 26–38, 40. *See also* feminist art programs
Friedan, Betty, 49, 113, 153, 172, 203, 275

Gelon, Diane: art history research, 86, 128, 151–52, 164; on Chicago, 105, 128; feminist networking, 150–58; fundraising for *The Dinner Party*, 86–88, 146, 150–56, 159; on the studio, 18, 95, 98, 103, 106, 119, 135, 146
Gilliam, Ken, 88, 117, 134, 135–37, 139, 153, 168
Gilligan, Carol, 273–74
Goodwill, Dorothy, 93–96, 100, 203–5, 230–32
government funding for art, debates concerning, 252–53, 255–61, 270
Green, Vanalyne, 33, 34, 37
Guerrilla Girls, 262

Halpern, Miriam, 79
Hankins, April, 200, 201, 206
Harper, Paula, 41, 42
Hill, Robyn, 86, 104
Hill, Susan, 85–88, 91, 94, 97, 100–101, 106; *Embroidering Our Past*, 177; managing the loft, 112–26, 135, 140, 227; SFMOMA, 163
Hirshhorn Museum, 154, 197
Hogan, Shannon, 95, 96, 133–34

Hopkins, Henry, 87, 158, 160–66, 178–79, 182, 185; in Houston, 191–92; Sexual Politics exhibition, 261, 267

International Dinner Party (1979), 163–64
International Quilting Bee (1980), 196
International Year of the Woman Conference, 151–52, 189
Ireland, Elaine, 102, 118, 168, 171
Iskin, Ruth, 73, 151, 152, 164
Isolde, Ann, 96, 86–88, 116, 128–31, 134–37; banners, 146; FSW, 73; Heritage Floor, 128–29, 131–32, 134, 137; Hispanic women's meeting, 135–36

Jewish Feminist Organization, 152
Jones, Amelia, 266–70, 276

Kagan, Sharon, 140
Keyes, Judye, 86, 139–40, 163
Krause, Pearl, 114

Lacy, Suzanne, 10, 27–28, 33, 41, 55, 72, 163–64, 267
LeCocq, Karen, 33–36, 43–44, 52–56, 63–66, 267
Lester, Jan, 33, 54, 57, 61, 66
Levine, Marcia, 203–5, 256, 280
Lippard, Lucy, 24, 61, 63, 74, 98; Congressional funding, 255, 259; and *The Dinner Party*, 164, 177, 178, 224, 232–33

Mademoiselle, 1, 215, 221
Malcolm, Ellen, 154
Mapplethorpe, Robert, 253–54
Mathis, Pat, 248, 257, 280
Memorial Art Gallery, University of Rochester, 161, 182–87
Mother Jones, 1, 143, 215, 285
Ms. magazine, 12, 113, 285; and *The Dinner Party* tour, 186, 237; funding for *The Dinner Party*, 86, 155, 213; and NEA debates, 257; reviews of *The Dinner Party*, 211, 220, 224, 226, 242, 256
multiculturalism, 160, 212, 224, 225, 234, 240, 259
Myers, Juliet, 92–93, 130

National Black Feminist Organization (NBFO), 24
National Endowment for the Arts (NEA), 86, 146, 157–59, 253–57, 261, 267
National Endowment for the Humanities (NEH), 89, 154, 198, 201
National Women's Political Caucus (NWPC), 154, 213, 257
New York Review, 218, 222
New York Times: on *The Dinner Party*, 207, 211, 213, 214, 221, 228; on the permanent display, 281, 282; on the University of the District of Columbia gift, 249, 250, 257, 258, 261; on *Womanhouse*, 61, 64
Nochlin, Linda, 24, 65, 69, 128, 263, 264

Parker, Rozsika, 263–65, 269
Parris, Stan, 252, 253, 259
Parris Amendment, 252–53, 255, 257, 259
performance art, 9, 32, 43, 50, 55–56
Pollock, Griselda, 263–65, 269
postfeminism, 6, 279, 288–90
postmodernism, 263, 266, 267–69

Raven, Arlene, 71, 72, 152, 164; on *Womanhouse* 50, 53, 58, 60, 66
Right Out of History, directed by Johanna Demetrakas, 119, 190, 194, 203, 285
Ringgold, Faith, 23–24
Rohrabacher, Dana, 251, 252, 254
Roiphe, Katie, 275, 276
Rotchford, Marti, 102, 133
Rush, Chris, 26, 50, 54

Saar, Betye, 24
Sackler, Elizabeth, 256, 280, 281
San Francisco Museum of Modern Art (SFMOMA), 158, 159, 161, 166, 182
San Francisco Tapestry Workshop (SFTW), 89, 146
Schapiro, Miriam, 34, 38–39, 69, 74, 79; and CalArts, 41–47; and the feminist art movement, 74, 76, 81, 82, 137, 264, 268; *Womanhouse*, 50, 51, 52, 54, 61, 64–67, 70
Schmidt, Karen, 86
Schneider, Kathleen, 86, 121–23, 173
Schor, Mira, 44, 65, 66, 266, 267

Seattle Art Museum, 161, 183, 185, 234; cancellation, 182–86
Seattle Sun, 186
Serrano, Andres, 254
Sex and the City, 276, 278–79
Sexual Politics Conference, UCLA (1996), 247, 261, 267–70, 280
sex wars 14, 145, 260, 265, 287
Simich, Helene, 88
Skuro, Leonard, 85, 88, 135, 139–40
Sojourner, 212, 224, 226, 227
Stegall, Lael, 154, 197, 213
Steinem, Gloria, 63, 153, 155
Stern, Mickey, 203–5, 256

Taylor, Mary Ross, 188, 256–57
Texas Monthly, 193, 216
Through the Flower (Chicago; memoir), as inspiration, 112, 128, 165, 189, 215, 235–36
Through the Flower (nonprofit), 160, 183, 195, 200, 249; letters, 193, 194, 205, 234, 283
Through the Flower (painting, 1973), 81
Through the Flower Northwest, 198–99

University of Houston at Clear Lake (UHCC), 189, 190, 193–95
University of the District of Columbia (UDC) controversy, 248–61

Vagina Monologues, The (Ensler), 15–16, 247, 276–78
Valentine, Karen, 86, 118, 123
Village Voice, 221, 224, 226, 228
von Briesen, Constance, 118, 168

Walker, Alice: *The Color Purple*, 248, 272–74; on *The Dinner Party*, 226, 229, 232, 233, 241, 242
Warhol, Andy, 8, 193
Washington Post, 256, 257, 258
Washington Women's Art Center (WWAC), 154, 197–98
Weiss, Adrienne, 102, 124–25, 168
West Coast Conference of Women Artists, 61
West Coast feminist art movement, 2, 18, 24, 25, 40
West-East Bag (WEB), 61, 63, 72
Wilding, Faith: and CalArts, 42; and cunt art, 35–38, 137; and the feminist art movement, 10, 40, 66, 267; and feminist art programs, 27, 28, 30, 33; and *Womanhouse*, 57–59, 52, 65
Williams, Brooke, 14
Willis, Ellen, 14, 224, 228–29
Wolf, Naomi, 256, 275
Wollenman, Shawnee, 34, 54
Womanhouse, 49–55; impact on Chicago, 79–80, 97, 106–7, 112; performance art at, 55–61; in the press, 61–65; students, 42–47, 65–69
Woman's Building, Los Angeles, 69, 72–75, 78, 97, 126, 227
Womanspace, 69, 70, 71, 72
Womanspirit, 177, 212, 229
Women Artists in Revolution (WAR), 23
Women in the Arts (WIA), 24
Women, Students, and Artists for Black Art Liberation (WSABAL), 23
Woodman, Donald, 210, 211, 256, 257, 259
Woodsea, Marilyn, 177, 178, 229

Youdelman, Nancy, 26, 30, 34, 36, 54, 66

Zurilgen, Cheryl, 31, 34

SINCE 1970: HISTORIES OF CONTEMPORARY AMERICA

Jimmy Carter, the Politics of Family, and the Rise of the Religious Right
by J. Brooks Flippen

Rumor, Repression, and Racial Politics: How the Harassment of Black Elected Officials Shaped Post–Civil Rights America
by George Derek Musgrove

Doing Recent History: On Privacy, Copyright, Video Games, Institutional Review Boards, Activist Scholarship, and History That Talks Back
edited by Claire Bond Potter and Renee C. Romano

"The Dinner Party": Judy Chicago and the Power of Popular Feminism, 1970–2007
by Jane F. Gerhard